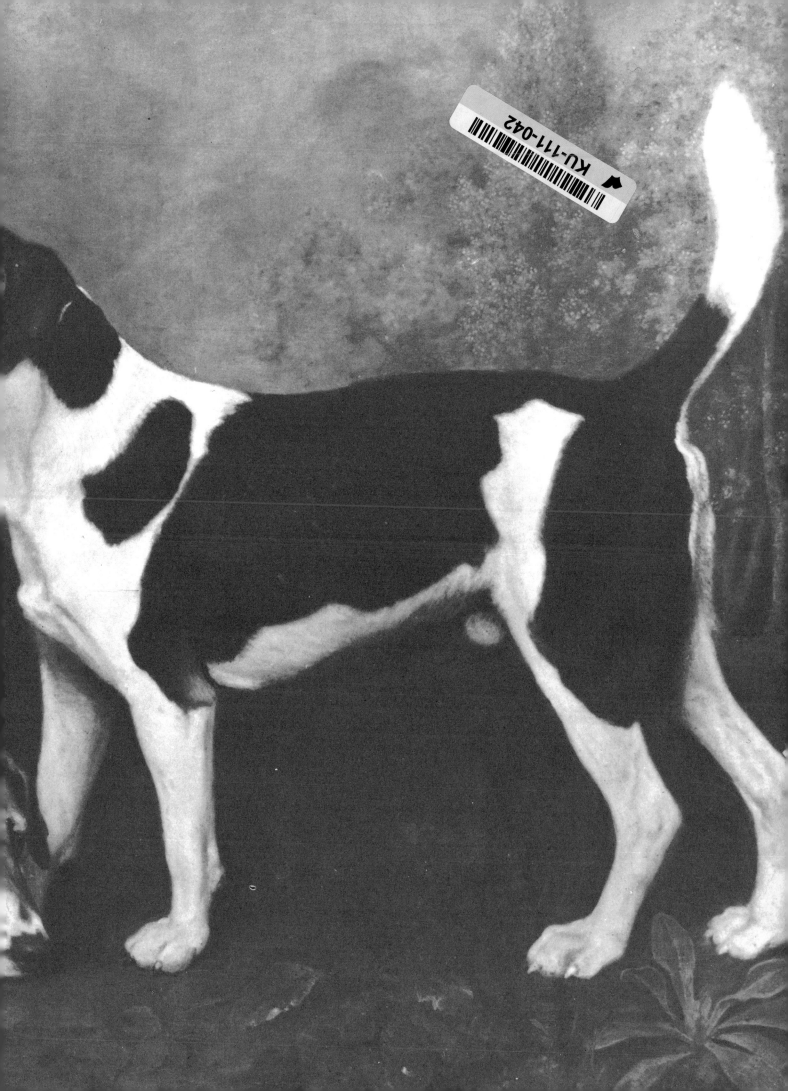

# All about
# Dogs

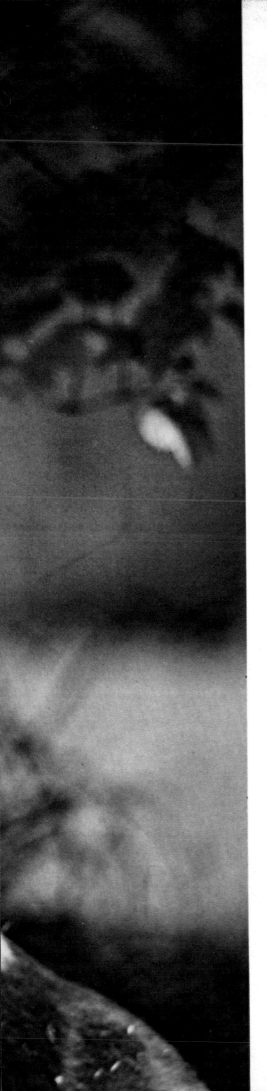

# All about
# Dogs

## Foreword by
## Barbara Woodhouse

ORBIS PUBLISHING·LONDON

**ACKNOWLEDGMENTS**

*All the photographs in this book are Orbis Copyright with the exception of the following:*

S. C. Bisserot: 53, 120 – Camera Press Ltd: 188 – Anne Cumbers: 15T&B, 47, 71, 76/77, 93, 94CL, 108, 111B, 114, 124, 185, 190B, 197, 198/199, 201, 223, 231, 240 – Joseph Elwell: 139 – Mary Evans Picture Library: 5, 46, 81, 107, 137, 169, 219 – Fotostampa Embrione: 82, 83, 203B – J. Mead: 54/55 – S. Prato: 142, 199, 239, 203T – Anne Roslin-Williams: 56, 73, 74, 87, 92, 94TL, 94/95, 95B, 110, 111T, 119T, 122, 127B, 130CT, 153, 176T – Sally Anne Thompson: Cover, 10/11, 12TL, 12TR, 12BL, 13T&B, 14, 20/21, 24/25, 27B, 36, 40, 52, 53TL, 58/59, 61, 68, 70, 80, 86, 88, 90, 97, 98, 99, 101, 102/103, 105, 106, 112/113, 115, 125, 126, 131, 146, 162, 164B, 165, 167, 173, 174, 177, 181, 191, 193, 200, 207B, 208/209, 213B, 216, 220, 234 – John Wallace: 16, 26B, 27T, 29, 33T, 39, 147, 195 – Diana Wyllie: 28T.

Endpapers: detail from Hound and Bitch in a Landscape by Stubbs, courtesy of The Tate Gallery, London.

Printed in Italy by IGDA, Officine Grafiche, Novara.   ISBN 0 85613 033 8

# Foreword

Many thousands of years ago, dogs were the companions of men, hunting their food and even fighting the wild beasts which threatened them. Man recognized that here was a loyal, loving animal which cost little to own and which would give lasting affection until it could no longer raise its head or wag its tail. Then it would be replaced by another dog which would carry on this tradition.

Dogs are misunderstood in many households: people often do not realize the extent of their faithfulness, intelligence and character, which will develop if they are educated, fed, loved, and given the chance to become 'one of the family'. But it is not only in uncaring homes that dogs are badly treated: there are many over-sentimental owners who buy a dog to replace a child and treat it as such, with little idea that a dog is not a human being.

Dogs have instincts which humans do not possess; for example, our noses give us none of the information that dogs' noses give them, and half the fun of a walk for a dog is the scents it picks up. If a dog never goes beyond the streets of a big town, it is not really enjoying life to the full. This is not to say that one should not keep a dog in a big town; dogs should live where they are wanted, loved, and treated with the respect they deserve. And they are considered worthy of this respect all over the world, bringing companionship and love into the lives of millions of people, young and old.

Dogs of every shape and size, both pedigree and mongrel, exist in the world today, and all have a contribution to make to the life of mankind. This new dog encyclopedia *All About Dogs* will make a wonderful addition to the library of anyone who loves and admires dogs. Perhaps even a few dog haters who cannot resist looking at the pictures and reading the fascinating text will find something in it to change their minds. But if this book has anything to do with it, your dog will be loved and cared for as dogs should be, and you will have a feast of good reading and a wealth of beautiful colour pictures which will give this book an honoured place on the bookshelves of all devotees of man's best friend.

*Barbara Woodhouse*

# Contents

CHAPTER I
CARE AND MANAGEMENT
Which is the right dog for you?                                    10
Selecting and rearing a puppy                                      14
Mongrels                                                           17
The feeding and grooming of dogs                                   20
Your dog in health and sickness                                    25
Obedience training for your dog                                    29
Psychology of the dog                                              32
Mating and gestation in dogs                                       36
Dog breeding for profit                                            39
Preparing your dog for the Show                                    43

CHAPTER II
HOUND GROUP
Afghans, Salukis and Borzois                                       47
The American Foxhound                                              51
The Basset Hound                                                   52
Beagles, Harriers and Foxhounds                                    54
Bloodhounds                                                        58
Coonhounds                                                         61
Dachshunds: Long-Haired, Smooth-Haired, Wire-Haired, Miniature
    Long-Haired, Miniature Short-Haired, Miniature Wire-Haired     62
Elkhound and Finnish Spitz                                         65
Irish Wolfhound and Deerhound                                      68
Rhodesian Ridgeback and Basenji                                    70
Unusual Hound breeds: Otterhounds, Swedish Foxhounds,
    Portuguese Warren Hound, Swiss Laufhound (Jura)                73
Whippets and Greyhounds                                            76

CHAPTER III
GUNDOG GROUP
Continental Gun Dogs: Small Muster lander, Pointing Wirehaired Griffon,
    Vizsla, Italian Spinone                                        82
Pointers: German Shorthairs, Weimaraners and Pointers             84
Retrievers: Chesapeake Bay, Curly-Coated, Flat-Coated,
    Golden, Labrador                                               88
Setters: English, Gordon, Irish, (Red)                            91
Spaniels: Clumber, Field, Sussex, Irish and American Water        95
Spaniels: Cocker                                                   98
Spaniels: Welsh and English Springer and Brittany                 103

## CHAPTER IV
## TERRIER GROUP

Airedale, Irish, Welsh and Lakeland Terriers                            108
Bull Terrier                                                           112
Cairn, West Highland White and Australian Terriers                     117
Dandie Dinmont and Glen of Imaal Terriers                              120
The Fox Terrier                                                        122
Four Terriers: Kerry Blue, Bedlington, Scottish, Soft-coated Wheater   125
Two working Terriers: Jack Russell and Patterdale                      128
Manchester and Border Terriers                                         130
Norwich and Norfolk Terriers                                           132
Skye and Sealyham Terriers                                             134

## CHAPTER V
## UTILITY GROUP

Akita, Keeshond and Iceland dog                                        138
Boston Terrier                                                         141
Dogs of the Bulldog breed: French and English                         144
Chow Chow                                                              147
Dalmatians                                                             150
Three lesser known breeds: Leonberger, Schipperke, Canaan dog          153
Three miniature breeds from Tibet: Tibetan Spaniel, Tibetan Terrier,
  Lhasa Apso                                                           156
Two unusual Terriers: Mexican Hairless, Shih Tzu                       159
Poodles: Standard, Miniature and Toy                                   163
Schnauzers: Giant, Standard and Miniature                             166

## CHAPTER VI
## WORKING GROUP

Alsatians                                                              170
Boxers                                                                 173
Briard                                                                 177
Continental Sheepdogs: Maremma, Groenendael, Tervuren                  180
Collies: Rough, Smooth, Bearded                                        184
Corgis: Pembroke, Cardigan                                             188
Dobermann                                                              191
Great Dane                                                             194
Three working breeds from Hungary: Kuvasz, Puli, Komonder              197
Mastiffs: Bullmastiff, Tibetan Mastiff,                                200
          Neapolitan Mastiff                                           203
Old English Sheepdog                                                   204
Four Spitz breeds: Samoyed, Norwegian Buhund, Malamute, Siberian Husky 206
Mountain dogs: St. Bernard, Bernese, Pyrenean                          208
Four working dogs: Rottweiler, Newfoundland, Bouvier des Flandres,
  Anatolian                                                            212
Shetland Sheepdog                                                      216

## CHAPTER VII
## TOY GROUP

Chihuahua                                                              220
English Toy, Japanese Chin, Maltese and Silky Terrier                  223
Continental toy breeds: Italian Greyhound, Pomeranian, Papillon,
  Miniature Pinscher, Griffon Bruxellois, Petit Brabançon              226
King Charles Spaniels                                                  230
Pekingese                                                              233
Pug                                                                    236
Yorkshire Terrier                                                      239

# Chapter I
# Care and Management

# Which is the right dog for you?

CHOOSING a dog to join the household can be something of a gamble. But the hazards can be much reduced if the prospective owner bears certain points in mind.

One thing that greatly influences the choice is the breed of dog the individual has owned in the past, and the experiences that have produced a liking or disliking for that breed. If the former dog was a mongrel, then such considerations do not count because the inheritance which produced that mongrel may never reappear again. That is why it is always best to buy a pedigree dog if you can afford it. At least with a pedigree dog you know roughly what size it will be, and you can find out about the way it is likely to behave from others of the same breed that you have seen or heard about. With a mongrel this is not possible.

It is not advisable to visit a Lost Dogs Home, so filled with sentiment that you take home the first dog with appealing eyes that begs to be adopted. Although there are thousands of strays that do make ideal pets, there are many more thousands that do not. You have no method of knowing whether these strays are dirty in the house, whether or not they were born wanderers only coming home to bed and food, or whether they enjoy biting the postman. They may detest men or perhaps women. Worse still, they may have been infected already with some disease that will result in the new owner incurring big veterinary surgeon's bills at the very outset.

Admiration for a particular breed of dog is one thing, ownership is another. Many admire the Old English Sheepdog whose appeal is well known to advertisers. If they knew how much grooming and bathing the dog needs to keep it so beautiful they would not wish to own one unless they had plenty of time and skill to carry out this beauty treatment. However, this particular breed is ideal for a big house and is easy to train. Other large dogs like the Pyrenean Mountain dog, whose temperament is not always as calm as it looks, or the Great Dane, have been known to dash playfully behind people or to bump into them, knocking them to the floor. These breeds are not for timid or nervous

*There are over 285 breeds of dog to choose from, so take your time before making a final decision.*

people, nor for very small people, but there are exceptions.

It is important to know why you are buying the dog. Is it as a companion for the children or a status symbol? Is it to be another much-loved member of the family which will be given nearly all the same privileges as the family, and as far as possible, be included in any plans that the family make? If the latter, then the family car should be large enough to take the dog whenever possible, since dogs do not like being left at home. It also means that one member of the family must take it for exercise and accept responsibility for buying and preparing the right food. Above all, one person must be responsible for that dog's initial training, although all members of the household should know the right commands to use.

Exercise is not a great problem if the dog lives at all times with its owner in the house. If it is a much-loved and loving dog it will usually follow its owner wherever he goes. Accompanying the owner on a shopping expedition might entail walking two or three miles, so if this dog is also getting one good walk of about a mile, and about fifteen minutes' free run on its own, it will get all the exercise it needs for bodily health. People who say large dogs should not live in flats or towns may be mistaken. In most towns there are public open spaces which are safer than some parts of the country. For in the country there is often the danger of broken glass left by careless picnickers, sharp stumps of trees, insecticides which are a danger to the dog's eyes and health, and—in some places— liquid sewage spread on fields, which may give the dog a most unwelcome smell!

The money available to maintain a dog will influence choice. Big dogs like St. Bernards cannot be fed on a small weekly budget. Any big dog must have one-and-a-half to two pounds of meat a day and up to a pound of biscuits, plus vitamins, minerals and trace elements. Extra milk will have to be bought when your dog is a puppy, and really good lean meat or really good tinned food. The dog will need inoculations, its nails cutting, and its teeth cleaning at regular intervals. It is wise to take out insurance against third party risks, and possibly against veterinary expenses. You should also take into consideration the cost of boarding the dog when you and your family go on holiday and have to leave your pets behind.

12

*A Pekingese (top left); a Border Terrier (centre left); a Great Dane (above); and a Dalmatian (left)*

All these things cost more for a large dog than for a small one, except perhaps for the insurance cover which rarely stipulates the size of the dog, (although certain breeds may be barred). So don't choose a very large dog if it means having to starve yourself to feed it.

One breed I would not recommend to flat dwellers is the Afghan Hound. These dogs really do need room and plenty of exercise; they are very difficult to train to return to their owners on command and they have a habit of looking far away into the distance and paying not the slightest attention to what their owner wants. Only with much kind but firm training are Afghans safe to be set free in a park with any hope of getting them to return to the owner when ordered to do so. In spite of this, the breed is becoming more and more popular in both America and the UK, regardless of its suitability for the owner or for the owner's environment.

If you live in a town, a very suitable medium-sized dog is the Golden Retriever. This dog does not seem to mind the lack of sporting facilities. Dalmatians, Weimaraners and Labradors are also very good-natured and easy to keep.

Dobermanns, or Dobermann Pinschers, are medium sized dogs which are smart and alert in appearance, need the minimum of attention to keep their shining coats in condition, and are very intelligent. German Shepherd Dogs, known as Alsatians in Britain, are also clever dogs which are intensely loyal and which can be trained to perform any duty. It is a breed which has achieved top place in the Kennel Club registrations of Britain and America. When choosing a puppy, avoid any which show signs of nervousness. However, this applies to any breed.

Of the smaller size of dog for town dwellers, the breeds to choose are Cavalier King Charles Spaniels and King Charles Spaniels. Many people don't know the difference between the two, but some breeders will freeze you with a glassy stare if you confuse the two. So make certain which breed you want before approaching the breeder of a Cavalier or a King Charles. These small dogs need very little exercise to be happy, although they enjoy walks. They have a placid nature, are good with children, and are easy to train. On the other hand the breed needs a lot of brushing, washing and combing to keep its coat presentable and in a hygienic condition. This should be considered before choosing this breed. A busy person may prefer a dog like a Bedlington which, once trimmed, remains neat without much trouble.

*The Afghan Hound (above) and the St. Bernard (left) are both large dogs which need regular grooming and exercise*

Beagles are pack dogs quite unsuitable for town dwellers. Even country dwellers should think twice before buying a Beagle. This breed likes running after scents rather than being with its owner. It is so attractive when a puppy that many families have bought one, only to realise that it is not the home-loving dog they had hoped for.

Small dogs like English Toy Terriers, Manchester Terriers, Poodles, Pekingese and Whippets are all suitable for town dwellers, provided there are public open spaces to let them run in.

There are over 285 breeds of dog to choose from, so take your time before choosing. Remember that the dog you select will be with you for the next twelve years or so. It is not fair to any dog to be turned out of your home to be sold, given away, or destroyed, just because you made a mistake when you bought it. Read all about the breed you are thinking of buying. Do not go out in a hurry and buy the first dog you see. For once bought, the dog is yours and you are his, and for as long as your pet lives, it is your sole responsibility. This is the ideal and cannot always be achieved, but you must strive towards it at all times.

# Selecting and rearing a puppy

CHOOSING a puppy is an important event in any dog owner's life. For if he selects the wrong puppy and has a sick dog on his hands, or one with a disagreeable temperament or one that is malformed in any way, he may have trouble for the rest of the puppy's life.

Having decided on the breed, you will have to look for the right breeder and the right litter from which to choose a puppy. If you do not know anyone who has puppies to sell, you can always consult the sales columns of dog magazines or you could ask the Kennel Club to put you in touch with a breeder of repute. Never buy a puppy from a street market.

You must make up your mind whether you want the dog as a pet, or whether later on you would like to show it or breed from it. If you wish to do either of the latter you will need to choose very carefully. Study the breed standards that are set out by the Kennel Club so that you are familiar with the requirements laid down. If you intend breeding, be sure to buy a sound puppy, insofar as it is

*Right: most puppies thrive on a mixed diet of milk, baby cereal, lean meat, brown bread, coley fish and dog meal. Below: all these puppies are bold and inquisitive. Avoid choosing a timid puppy that hides shyly in a corner. Left: a Great Dane puppy*

possible to judge a puppy at about eight weeks old. Never be tempted to buy the runt of a litter.

Then shall it be a dog or a bitch? If a future litter is considered, the choice must be a bitch. Apart from that, a bitch is usually more amenable to training, more demonstrative to its owner, but will come into season twice a year when she will have to be protected from dogs if unwanted puppies are to be avoided. If effective supervision is doubtful, the removal of the ovaries (spaying) will prevent any possibility of a litter. A dog is just as affectionate and loyal although perhaps more independent. It is just a matter of personal preference.

Arrange for the puppy to be inoculated at about the age of 12 weeks against distemper, leptospirosis and hepatitis. comes to greet you should certainly be considered. Look at its eye; if it is wide open and bright that is the one to choose. A sad dull eye indicates a puppy that will not thrive. Look at the coat and condition. At eight weeks the puppy should be reasonably plump, with a coat that is supple and shiny. The skin should lift in folds without causing any pain to the puppy.

Before you take the puppy back you should prepare for its welcome and comfort in the home. Have an indoor kennel made into which it can be put to rest, away from children or another dog. Rest is essential for small puppies; they sleep three-quarters of the day. It is easier to house-train a puppy with an indoor kennel, taking it out straight from the kennel to where it is allowed to relieve itself, so that it never gets a chance to soil the floor. Also, when you leave the house you know it is safe in its kennel. Eventually the top and door of the kennel can be removed, leaving the sides and floor as a permanent bed if yours is a small dog.

It is important to teach other members of the household—particularly children— to leave the puppy in peace when it is in its bed or indoor kennel. Never let children maul a puppy, for this makes the animal bad-tempered if it is tired. Many puppies become aggressive if hauled out of their sleeping quarters and over-tired puppies don't flourish.

The majority of puppies thrive on milk and some baby cereal, scraped lean beef, coley fish, and brown bread or dog meal. Five meals a day are necessary at first; eventually they can be reduced to one or two a day. From the condition of the puppy and its motions it is possible to judge whether the dog is being fed correctly. Over-feeding causes an excessive number of motions in a day; this often results in the puppy being dirty in the house, a condition it cannot help.

Leave water for it, and a marrow bone with the marrow taken out, remembering

to use the centre of the marrow bone only, never the ends, as puppies become unwell or very constipated if they eat the gristle at the end of the bone. The marrow is too fat for them and can cause diarrhoea and acidosis.

Begin house training immediately the puppy comes to your home. You will have to take the dog out of the house at least every two hours. It is advisable that the puppy from the very start of its life with you should relieve itself outside the house. This is one reason why it is advisable to buy a puppy in late spring or summer, for in winter it is very cold for owner and puppy to go outside at six a.m. for the first week or two. This is very necessary, for no puppy can last from the previous night to later than six a.m., even at three months old. If possible, put cat litter or turf at the end of the indoor kennel, for the puppy will soil on that if it has to. Puppies will not soil their bedding if litter or grass is available.

Start obedience training in a small way the day the puppy comes to you. Do not take it to bed with you when it shrieks. Put its kennel near a radiator or in a really warm place. A puppy shrieks because it is cold; a warm puppy settles down easily. Naturally at first it misses its companions and the warmth of the other puppies. A meat meal last thing at night to give a full stomach, a cosy thick blanket to sleep on in a draught-free warm place—these things produce a quiet, sleeping puppy. You will have to learn to tolerate the dog's shrieking for two or three days if you are to win this battle of wills.

Encourage the puppy to come to you when called. A tit-bit often helps in the first instance, but this must not develop into a habit or the puppy will only come when given something. Remember that all animals love praise. Give your dog plenty of toys to play with, but avoid woolly bears with eyes that fall out to reveal big pins at the other end. A ball, a

*Rest is essential for a puppy; it sleeps for three-quarters of the day. At the kennels it has probably been left undisturbed, but when it has been sold and goes to a new home it is likely that it will be played with too much. Never let children maul a young puppy*

rubber bone and a safe rag doll are good playthings.

Arrange for the puppy to be inoculated at about the age of 12 weeks against distemper, leptospirosis and hepatitis. It takes the puppy a month after the injections to develop sufficient immunity for it to be allowed to meet other dogs, so you should not take it for walks before this period has elapsed. There should be no ill effect from these inoculations, but if the puppy becomes unwell, consult the vet immediately.

Put a cat collar on a toy dog, and a small leather one on a bigger animal, on the day it comes to your home. Make sure it is neither too loose nor too tight. Pay no attention to the scratching and biting that goes on in its efforts to rid itself of the collar—it will become accustomed to wearing it in a very short time. The use of a harness should be avoided as it is not as effective in controlling the dog, especially a large one, later on. The puppy can first be put on a lead for a few minutes daily at about nine weeks old, and should walk well on the lead by about three months. Do everything in small stints. If you are not used to training a puppy, read a book about it so that you start on the right lines from the very beginning.

A puppy is very like a small baby: it needs good food at regular intervals, warmth, play, security and kindness combined with firmness in training, and a certain amount of privacy and peace to sleep without being disturbed.

The hard work involved in making a puppy into a member of the family will be amply rewarded by the fun and companionship your pet will provide.

# Mongrels

A mongrel is the result of a mating between two dogs without a pedigree, or from a pedigree dog mated to a non-pedigree dog, or from dogs of two different breeds each with a pedigree. The term 'cross-bred' is usually confined to the cross of two different breeds, although it can also be applied to the result of a mating between a pedigree dog and a mongrel. In some countries the breeding between two related breeds of dog is recognized by the official Kennel Club (although not in Britain), the resulting puppies being called 'interbreds'.

Although no definite numbers are known, it is certain that the number of mongrels in the world far exceeds the number of pure-bred pedigree dogs. In Britain it is estimated that there are over three million, in the USA over thirty million, while throughout the world there are over one hundred and fifty million.

A pedigree dog is one that has a recorded genealogy registered with the official dog organization of the country in which the dog lives, such as the Kennel Club in Britain and the American Kennel Club. To develop a breed to the point

*Over three million of the dogs in Britain are mongrels, while in the USA the figure is as high as thirty million*

where it becomes a recognized pedigree dog, it is necessary for the dogs to breed true for at least five generations and then for the controlling body to accept this. In some cases a breed may not apply for recognition and remains officially mongrel. Thus the working collie often seen with sheep is a breed, but not a 'recognized' one, and the same applies to the Jack Russell Terrier. Dogs of these breeds have pedigrees and selective breeding occurs to improve the stock and yet they are, strictly speaking mongrels.

A pedigree dog is occasionally bred with another breed to improve its character, strength or conformation. Thus at one time the Deerhound was crossed with the Greyhound, and the resulting puppies, although officially mongrels, bred with Deerhounds until they bred true as Deerhounds. The result, after a number of generations, was improved stock.

If you wish to own a pet dog, then consider cost, temperament, health and intelligence. The cost of a mongrel is usually low. If it is possible to see the dog's parents, so much the better. The temperament of mongrels is usually very good. It is advisable to enquire whether a dog is good with children; this will usually help you come to a decision.

The mongrel, or its ancestor, was the original dog. All the breeds that we know today have developed from selective breeding of dogs without a pedigree. The mongrel does not conform to any Standard, has no fixed shape, size or colour, but it has also the blessing that, because selective breeding over many generations has not occurred, it rarely suffers from any of the hereditary defects that are sometimes seen in pedigree dogs. The mongrel had at one time to live by its wits. Some selection must have occurred here, as the fittest and most intelligent had the best chance of survival. Therefore, in many cases, the mongrel is highly i telligent. As with any intelligent dog (or child for that matter) it is not sufficient to provide good food and plenty of exercise. Mental stimulus is also needed. When young, play and 'toys' are sufficient but, from 6 months of age, training at a training school, with the owner taking part, is an advantage. This training is useful as it makes the dog more obedient, but its main purpose is to enable the dog to develop mental maturity. This is the same as for the child who needs to attend school in order to learn and to develop mental stability for future adulthood.

The owner of a mongrel puppy is at a disadvantage when compared with the owner of a pedigree pup in that he or she cannot be certain how the puppy will develop physically. As mongrels do not breed true, it is impossible to forecast its shape, size, coat and colour.

The mongrel does present one great problem to society. Whereas the pedigree dog is usually bred with care and thought, the mongrel is sometimes allowed to breed in an unlimited fashion. Puppies are given away to homes where they are not truly wanted. It is the mongrel that so often finds its way to homes for stray dogs, not the pedigree dog. In the USA approximately 1,500 dogs are born every hour, compared with the human birth rate of only 415 per hour. So great is the problem that an American research worker has suggested a number of partial solutions: there should be greater encouragement for the sterilization of dogs, an increase in the cost of a dog licence and stricter enforcement of the licensing laws. Dogs in towns should only be allowed out if on a lead, and a tax should be levied on dog foods to provide income to study methods of controlling the canine population. Most of all, owners must become more responsible.

A sense of proportion must, however, be maintained. We need our pets and the mongrel is one of these. It is the most popular of dogs, if numbers are an indication of popularity. It is an ideal pet provided it is cared for in the right way. But the mongrel should only be allowed to breed if it is certain that good homes can be found for all the puppies produced. The mongrel has a place in our world; it deserves the same care, attention and affection, and good training as any pedigree dog. It seems that the only reason why the mongrel is sometimes held in disrepute is human prejudice. People like long written pedigrees although these, in themselves, have little meaning. The mongrel is a dog, no more, no less. As a pet it is as good, or bad, as it is made.

*Mongrels make ideal pets; they are good with children, are not faddish about food and usually enjoy good health*

# The feeding and grooming of dogs

THE dog is basically a carnivore, that is, an animal designed by nature to live on meat, and it is fitted for this purpose with a strong set of teeth which have sharp points to make tearing and ripping easier. Compare such teeth, for example, with those of cattle (which are herbivores or vegetarians), whose teeth are ridged and suitable for grinding.

In the wild, members of the dog family such as the wolf, the coyote, the fox, the jackal and the hunting dog, depend on hunting prey for survival. But the dog has long been a domesticated creature and has gradually come to adapt itself to the human way of life. Consequently, although it still requires a diet rich in protein (if necessary including fish as well as meat) in order to remain fit and well, this can be, and usually is, supplemented by cereals in a variety of appetizing forms.

The question of feeding is a highly controversial one among experts in dog management. Basically the argument centres on the comparative merits and disadvantages of fresh and artificially preserved foods. Although there is a wide selection of fresh, frozen, dried and tinned foods sold specifically for dogs, many owners still prefer to feed their animals only on raw or cooked meat obtained directly from a butcher or slaughter-yard. In spite of the claims advanced by some petfood manufacturers, it has not been established that tinned or dried foods are more nutritious than fresh meals, although in most cases the former are certainly more convenient to handle.

Since there is so much dispute and discussion about feeding animals, it would be unwise to lay down any hard and fast rules concerning diets for dogs. There are, nevertheless, tested procedures which experienced breeders have been using very successfully for many decades, and it is important for dog owners to be familiar with the sound and basic principles underlying these methods.

Puppies require more food, per body weight, than do adult dogs, and they thrive best when fed four times daily. When fully grown, one main meal per day will be quite sufficient to keep the dog healthy. At first puppies normally feed from the dam, suckling milk within half an hour or so of being born. A bitch in good health will have enough milk to nourish her litter, provided she is not required to rear an excessively large number of whelps. The ideal number will depend on her condition and, of course, on her breed.

A bitch of the larger variety of gundog, for instance a Setter or a Retriever, is capable of producing as many as 12 puppies, but the rearing of such a large litter is best left to the experienced dog owner and the expert breeder. A beginner should not hesitate to ask the advice of the local veterinary surgeon. Some healthy bitches can cope with up to 12 pups, but it all depends on the individual animal. On the other hand, it might be advisable to agree to the vet putting some of the puppies painlessly to sleep, keeping a maximum of six. It is much better to have half-a-dozen sturdy, well-boned puppies that with luck will find a ready sale, than a dozen undersized, slightly built little creatures that are likely to spend far too much time at the vet's being treated for disorders brought about by lack of proper rearing and nourishment.

The brood bitch needs lavish feeding if she is to do justice to a litter of any size. This means fresh meat, milk and wholemeal dog biscuits, together with such supplements as bonemeal and seaweed powder, or calcium and minerals in other forms. After the fourth week, the amount of meat given should be increased.

About two-and-a-half to three-and-a-half weeks after the puppies are born – the precise period depends on the size of the litter and the condition of the dam – it becomes necessary to commence supplementary feeding for the litter. The puppies should be offered tiny portions of scraped raw beef. Only fresh, good quality shin beef or stewing steak is suitable. It should be prepared as follows: the meat is left in one large piece and not cut into chunks. Place it on a board and with a fairly sharp knife scrape the surface, producing a mushy paste which is highly digestible.

A very small portion of this paste is pushed into the puppy's mouth; the little creature rapidly becomes accustomed to the taste and begins eating greedily. This feeding is done individually. Only one or two mouthfuls are offered the first day, the quantity being gradually increased until each puppy consumes a spoonful at a meal, such meals being given at least twice a day. At the same time the puppies can be encouraged to lap milk or a milk food once or twice daily.

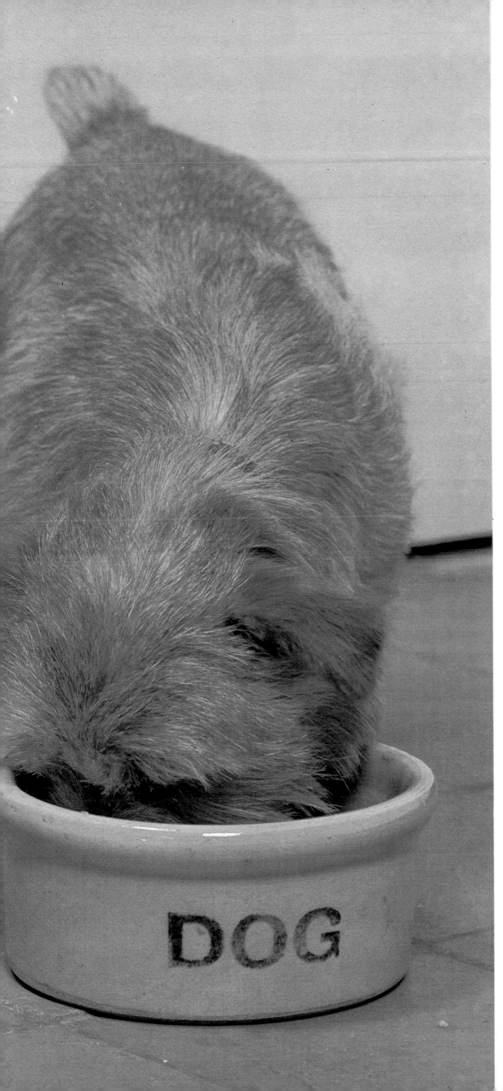

The breeder must be guided by the puppies' appetites. A well-fed puppy looks plump and well-rounded but in no way blown-out or distended. Once artificial feeding begins, the mother's milk gradually decreases, though she usually produces sufficient to nourish her puppies during the night hours. Eventually the bitch is taken away from the puppies for increasingly long intervals, and by the time the puppies reach the age of six-and-a-half to eight weeks, they should be independent of the bitch's milk. From six weeks onwards puppies require four meals daily. These are a breakfast and a supper of milk in one form or another, plus two intermediate meals of minced or chopped meat (preferably raw or only lightly cooked) mixed with puppy-grade biscuit meal soaked to a crumbly, moist consistency with broth.

Food is best fed at room temperature, or with the chill taken off it, but not really hot. It should never be offered straight from a refrigerator. Food should be given without additional moisture as sloppy foods are unsuitable for dogs of any age.

By the time a puppy is four or five months old it will probably become uninterested in one of its meals, a sign that this may be dropped and the day's rations divided into three. There are exceptions. A greedy dog has been known to eat until it makes itself ill. But as a rule two meals daily will be sufficient for the average puppy and finally no breakfast will be needed. One large solid dinner of meat and biscuits then becomes the rule. The times of day are not important; what is essential is regularity. Obviously when a young animal is being fed four times daily it is wise to space out the meals as evenly as possible. The adult dog can fed at midday or in the evening, whichever is more convenient.

Anybody buying a puppy should ask the breeder for a diet chart and endeavour to follow this for the first few weeks. Slight variations are unlikely to do harm but it can be very upsetting for a small puppy to change its environment and to find itself eating completely different foods as well. Once a puppy suffers an upset stomach it may take a long time for it to recover, and a setback of this nature can inhibit normal growth and development.

It is occasionally difficult for a new owner to follow another person's instructions to the letter. For instance, certain foods are hard to obtain in some areas, and this is particularly the case with dogs bred in one country and exported to another. In most cases similar types of food can be purchased. Deep freezing has helped to solve this problem for many, but it is important to see that any foods stored in this manner are well

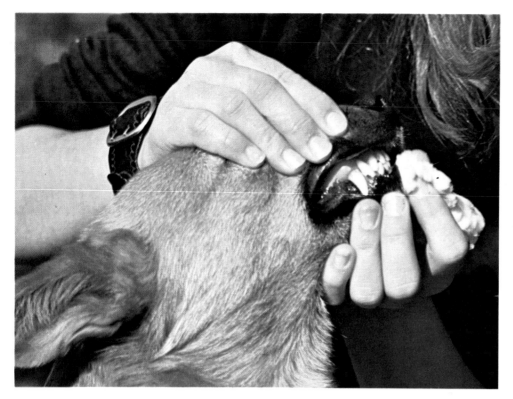

*Your dog's dental health is very important; remove tartar by using canine toothpaste. Right: stripping removes dead fur and gives a better effect than clipping*

defrosted before given as food. Severe stomach troubles may follow the consumption of chilled meat or semi-frozen biscuit meal.

Some dogs have a liking for fish, and while this offers a welcome variation, it is not advisable to feed them on nothing else. The preparation of fish needs great care since it must either be carefully filleted or boiled in a pressure cooker until the bones are soft. Fish bones can choke a dog and are very dangerous. The same remarks apply to rabbit meat. Rabbit was once a popular food for dogs but in these days it is sufficiently scarce to be rated a luxury. Dogs relish well-cooked rabbit, but remember that the brittle bones are a hazard and may even prove lethal.

Small dogs are often fed on chicken, which they love but, as with fish and rabbit, all bones must be very carefully removed. Some commercial kennels have experimented by procuring large quantities of chicken heads and necks from factories and boiling these to pulp. The resultant mess appears palatable but the principal objection lies in the difficulty of ensuring that the heads do not contain the implanted hormones sometimes used to fatten birds for the table. Widespread sterility among breeding stock has been the outcome of such dietary experiments in some kennels.

Bullock's tripes and sheep's paunches are one form of fresh meat that, when obtained direct from a slaughterer, are

eagerly devoured. Dogs thrive on them in spite of the fact that at least one nutritional expert states that they lack essential nutrients. Sheep's paunches bought from the slaughterer are dark green in colour, smelly and unpleasant to handle since they are usually filled with half-digested vegetation and must be laboriously washed under running water. Some kennel owners feed bullock's tripes raw, either minced or cut into pieces. Others prefer to boil it and feed it cooked. Tripe sold in butcher's shops for human consumption has been bleached and is not suitable for dogs.

Other offal obtainable for pets are those parts known as throttles, melts (spleen) and lights (lungs). These can usually be bought from slaughterhouses but not from butchers selling meat for human consumption. These can be a standby if nothing else is available at the time but are not recommended for regular use in the dog kitchen. Most dogs love cooked liver and small scraps of it can be found in many a pocket at dog shows when it is necessary to keep a dog alert in the ring for the judge's inspection. As a titbit, liver has no equal, but it has a laxative effect and is therefore not suitable for main meals. A small portion of liver, mixed with other foods, is always appreciated, however, and can be most helpful in persuading a finicky feeder to enjoy its meals.

A bone should be given at least once a week in addition to the normal diet. Bones are an excellent method of keeping a dog's teeth clean and free from tartar. Large marrow bones are the most suitable. Chocolates and sweets of any kind should

not be given. All sugars are extremely fattening and also very bad for the dog's teeth. Feeding the dog at the table and giving it scraps between meals are practices strongly to be deplored.

The dog should always have access to a supply of fresh water. Milk can be given to puppies and breeding bitches. No more than a small saucerful should be given each day since it can have a laxative effect on some dogs and be the cause of excessive fatness in others.

The quality of a dog's coat is governed by the state of its health and this is entirely determined by the manner in which the animal is fed and exercised. In other words, good grooming starts from within and no amount of hard work with brush and comb can produce the right effect if

the dog is not thoroughly healthy and in good condition at all times.

A thin, ribby animal should always be tested for worms by a veterinarian and, if necessary, treated. At the same time, the dog must be built up by careful feeding. As much fresh food as it will eat, together with any tonics or supplements suggested by the vet, should result in an improved condition.

Regular exercise plays a major part in a dog's life. A road walk on a lead, together with free frolic in a park or meadow, should be a daily pleasure for both dog and owner. The amount of exercise required depends on the size and build of the dog, and its age.

Small Toy dogs, like their bigger relations, enjoy a romp and a game, but can be satisfied with short, brisk walks. Large active dogs really need a walk of several miles daily, though it must be remembered that when exercised loose, the dog covers three or four times as much ground as its two-legged companion would over the same area.

Racing greyhounds are trained by long, slow-paced walks on hard roads, a minimum of six miles per day on a leash being routine, together with occasional 'pipe-openers' in the form of brisk gallops on tracks or in open country. Exterior care for greyhounds and, indeed, for all breeds with similar short, smooth hair, consists of brushing with a short-bristled brush, followed by massage with both hands. A final finish with a soft, clean chamois leather, or piece of velvet, puts the polish

on the coat and makes it smooth.

Long-haired breeds require careful and very regular combing. The choice of comb is important, since one with the teeth set too close will tear out the hair. Steel combs are best and are obtainable from pet shops and from stalls at dog shows (where the widest selection is always to be had). Advice can usually be sought as to the best type to use on any particular variety of coat.

For most long-coated dogs, daily brushing and twice-weekly combing can usually be depended upon to keep the dog properly groomed. The grooming must be thorough. Novice owners often overlook the less obvious parts such as the thick hair beneath the armpits and close to the elbows, and the easily-matted hair

beneath the chest. The long hair underneath the tail and the featherings on the legs, forming 'trousers', are of great importance. Some breeds—notably Setters and Spaniels—need the hair between the toes kept short with scissors. Other breeds, Wire-haired Terriers and Poodles, for example, are likely to require professional trimming from time to time. The expert's task is made extremely difficult, however, if the dog has been neglected between visits and so it is the responsibility of the owner to groom it regularly.

Very young puppies of most breeds eventually grow heavy coats, although the process is slow. They do not need a great deal of grooming to begin with but, as it will be necessary for them to submit to prolonged brushing and combing and, perhaps, clipping, at some future time, it is advisable to accustom them to it when they are young. The way to do this is to put the puppy on a table and go over it with a brush. Be careful not to let the dog slip off the table or become frightened. It will soon come to enjoy its toilet and jump up, tail wagging, at the familiar sight of the grooming equipment.

It is best not to bath young puppies unless this is absolutely unavoidable. When a dog needs a bath, great care must be taken to see that it does not fall or frighten itself in the water. A rubber mat for it to stand on will give it confidence, and the water must be warm, but not at all hot. Short-haired dogs can be rubbed dry with clean towels; profusely coated dogs, such as the Old English Sheepdog and the Afghan Hound, are usually dried by gentle brushing in front of a heater, since towelling will tangle the coat.

Although the word 'grooming' is commonly applied to the use of a brush and a comb, the owner should extend it to include the care of eyes, ears, feet and teeth. Eyes may need bathing, while ears should be inspected from time to time and carefully cleaned with cotton wool. Take a lesson from a vet or an experienced dog owner before attempting to probe the inside of a dog's ears. Toenails may or may not require clipping, depending on the shape of the foot and the amount of running the dog does on hard surfaces. Scissors are not suitable; nail-clippers can be obtained which cut the nails neatly without splitting them. Care is needed to avoid cutting the quick and drawing blood. Teeth may need scaling by an expert, but the formation of tartar can be halted by regular brushing with a special canine toothpaste.

Always take care of grooming materials. The brushes and the chamois leathers or velvet pads should be kept spotlessly clean. See that the well-groomed dog has a clean bed to lie on. Always inspect the skin for parasites and deal promptly with any signs of fleas or lice. There are many powders and shampoos designed to combat these pests. Likewise, there are scores of widely advertised coat dressings, sprays and so on, some of which no doubt have their uses. But nothing takes the place of sensible feeding, ample exercise, scrupulously clean accommodation and regular brushing and combing, in keeping the dog looking its best and in prime condition.

*Below: ears should be inspected regularly and any wax removed with cotton wool*

# Your dog in health and sickness

*Dogs respond well to training, becoming bored with nothing to interest them*

WHEN you get your new puppy from the breeder, it is important to find out how the puppy was fed, how much was given and when. In other words obtain a diet sheet so that you can carry on in the same way. A puppy has a small stomach and needs a number of meals a day. As your pet grows the amount of food will have to be increased, although the number of meals each day can be gradually reduced. A puppy at eight weeks will need four or five meals a day; at four months it will need three meals daily and this can be reduced to two a day when it is six months old.

Bear in mind that every dog is an individual; consequently all rules regarding feeding must be adjusted to your dog. Some dogs tend to cut down the number of meals they eat even before they reach the ages mentioned above; others appear to be always hungry and to need more meals a day for a much longer time.

As a general guide remember it is difficult to overfeed a puppy provided it obtains enough exercise. Rub your fingers over its ribs; there should be a thin layer of fat over them. If you have difficulty in feeling these ribs it shows that your dog may be overweight. This test is a good one for an adult dog too.

Dogs like routine, so try to provide meals at the same time each day. It is a good idea to weigh a dog every three months, so that if its weight is gradually increasing over the years this can be noticed and stopped by slightly reducing the amount of food given, or by increasing the exercise.

It is not a good idea to allow your dog to exercise itself unaccompanied. The number of accidents caused by this practice is large and they often result in injury or death for the dog and the humans involved. A long walk every day is better than a short one five days a week and long hikes at the weekend. It is important not to allow your puppy to go where other dogs have been until you have had your pet inoculated against disease. The veterinary surgeon will do this for you.

As well as keeping a record of your dog's weight, it is also a good idea, if you own a bitch, to record when she comes into season and how long it lasts.

When a bitch is in season or 'on heat' she is particularly attractive to male dogs and is ready for mating. The record you keep might be helpful in saving the life of your bitch if she ever developed trouble in the uterus. In any case such a record is always useful, as you can work out when her next season is due. Bitches normally come into season every six months and this lasts for 21 days, but every bitch's season is slightly different. The important point to watch is that your bitch is regular to her own cycle. A healthy bitch does not stop her seasons when she becomes old.

Dogs need mental exercise. They are intelligent animals and are like children who become bored if they do not go to school and use their brains. They respond to mental stimuli. A puppy cannot learn very much at first. It is enough at the outset to start house training. This is usually easier in the summer than the winter, for pups are not always anxious to go out in cold wet weather.

Always praise for good behaviour and scold for bad mistakes. Never hit the pup or 'rub his nose in it'. It is pointless to scold a puppy for a mistake–urinating in the wrong place, for example–unless this can be done at the time the puddle is made. A puppy's memory is short and it will probably feel that you are being unreasonable if you chastise it for a puddle in the wrong place made some time ago, for this will have been forgotten. The great thing is perseverance: just keep on and on and praise good behaviour. You may feel you are fighting a losing battle, but you will win in the end.

When a puppy is six months old it is ready for 'school'. Although you can omit any training other than that which you can give yourself, it is advantageous to a dog to take it to a training class. There it learns obedience and so becomes easier to manage. More important, the training makes it use its brain; it learns to work things out, and this matures the dog mentally. It becomes a better dog and a better companion.

It is an old wives' tale that a bitch benefits by having a litter of puppies. It is often much better for the bitch not to have pups. But if you want her to breed, then make sure that you will be able to find homes for the litter before you start. As a guide, never breed from a bitch until her second season, or until she

*Above: a healthy puppy is covered with
a thin layer of fat without being
overweight, and should be playful.
Below: your pet will enjoy family outings.
Facing page: puppies need plenty of rest
and like the routine of regular meals*

is a year old. And if she has not had a
litter before, do not start breeding with
her after she is four years of age,
because whelping becomes more difficult
as the bitch gets older.

A bitch carries her puppies for
approximately 63 days (nine weeks).
Unfortunately there is no pregnancy test
available but between the twenty-third and
twenty-seventh day a vet can often feel the

puppies inside. After this time there is no
way of detecting them until the seventh
or eighth week. By then they can often
be seen moving when the bitch is lying
relaxed. It is sensible to tell your vet
that your bitch is expecting puppies and to
give him the date you think they are due
to appear.

Always have your vet's telephone
number ready in case you need to
consult him. Get in touch with him if your
bitch does not have puppies within two
days after the date or if she gets very
excitable. And you should contact him
during the actual birth if the bitch has
been straining for two hours and nothing
has happened; if she has had some

puppies and you think that there are
more but she has not produced any for
two hours; or if a puppy is halfway out
and has become stuck. Here you might
be able to help with a gentle pull backwards and downwards. First wrap the
part of the pup that is showing in a
clean cloth, hold it gently but firmly
enough to prevent it slipping, and ease the
puppy out. Let your bitch do the work;
when she strains hold the puppy so that
when she relaxes it does not return to its
former position. On the next contraction
do the same thing and the puppy should
soon appear.

This help is particularly important
when the pup is coming out backwards,
as it must be able to take its first
breath within a short period. *Never* force
the puppy out – if it cannot be eased out,
wait until expert help is available. And if
you are worried about anything that
appears to be abnormal, telephone the
vet immediately.

Breeding a litter is an exciting experience, full of interest, but sometimes a
bitch will escape when in season and all
too often the result is an unwanted litter.
It is not always realized that a bitch will
try to reach a dog when in that condition
and extra precautions should be taken to
keep her safe. She can be spayed (neutered),
it is true, but it seems a pity to do this
because she may well be desired to breed
again later.

As dogs age, they develop special
problems which should be considered.
Old dogs require more care and attention than youngsters. Although their spirit
is strong they should be exercised with
consideration and should not become

overtired. This particularly applies when the weather is very hot, wet or cold. They should be fed more frequently and a careful watch kept for signs of ill health, such as a cough, increased thirst or a change in the coat. The teeth may become covered with scale the ears dirty, the nails too long or the eyes changed in colour. Many conditions can be cured or checked if seen early enough. Delay, because you fear what the vet might say, can do more harm than good.

You can, of course, treat by yourself anything of which you know the cause and feel capable of curing, such as a sore on a leg or a tiny cut, but call the vet if recovery is not prompt. Naturally the more experienced with dogs you are, the more conditions you will feel capable of treating. You will be able to see fleas and deal with them but if you find the skin is showing signs of a rash when the fleas are gone, obtain expert help. Never treat by yourself anything that you do not recognize. If in doubt, always ask for the advice of an expert.

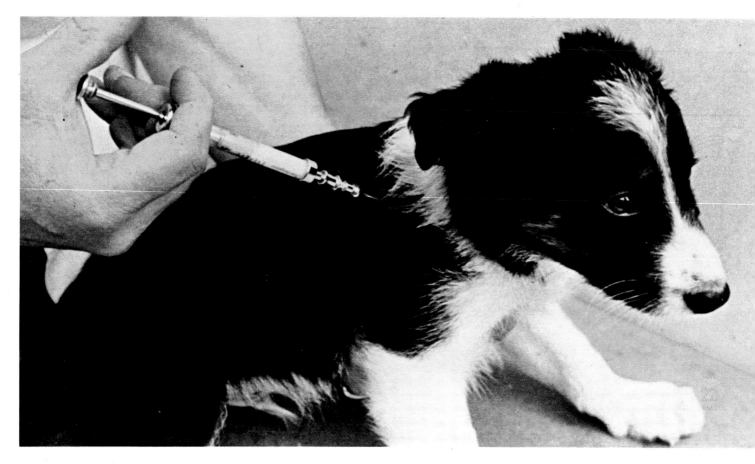

# Vaccinating your puppy

When you first obtain your puppy it is extremely important to make a visit to the veterinary surgeon a priority. He will recommend the dog to be vaccinated against four very serious canine diseases—hepatitis, distemper, leptospirosis and (in the USA) rabies. All these diseases are, in the majority of cases, fatal. Since prevention is always better than cure, vaccination is clearly the best possible course.

## CANINE HEPATITIS
CAUSE, SYMPTOMS AND TREATMENT:
Canine hepatitis is caused by an infectious virus which attacks mainly the liver and the gastro-intestinal tract, producing symptoms of listlessness, thirst, dehydration, diarrhoea, vomiting and loss of appetite. The temperature rises and there is great abdominal discomfort. Treatment should always be left to the veterinary surgeon who will hospitalize the dog immediately. Home treatment afterwards consists of giving the dog a bland diet and any medicines prescribed. Unfortunately, for some time after the dog is cured it can still transmit the disease.
PREVENTION:
Puppies are more susceptible to hepatitis than older dogs, but are very unlikely to contract it if they are inoculated at 10 to 12 weeks. A multiple vaccination provides immunity against hepatitis, distemper and leptospirosis, but boosters will be necessary throughout the dog's life.

## DISTEMPER
CAUSE, SYMPTOMS AND TREATMENT:
Distemper is a virus infection caused by contact with the infected urine or faeces of another dog. Symptoms may not be apparent for the first week after infection, and could be confused at first an upper respiratory ailment. There is listlessness, a running nose and eyes, a cough and loss of appetite. The dog will seem miserable and its temperature will be above normal. It may be sensitive to light and may even suffer from convulsions. The nervous system will be affected and cause twitching and champing of the jaws. The vet will prescribe antibiotics. However, the disease lowers the dog's resistance so much that it could develop a serious secondary infection such as meningitis.
PREVENTION:
A puppy nursing at its mother's milk receives her immunity (if she is immune). After weaning (at about four weeks) the vet will probably give it antiserum or globulin every two weeks, until it is able to respond to vaccination, at 10 to 12 weeks. The puppy is revaccinated six months after this, and then at yearly intervals, but your veterinary surgeon will decide exactly when and what type of immunization to use.

## LEPTOSPIROSIS
CAUSE, SYMPTOMS AND TREATMENT:
There are two strains of this disease, which is caused by bacteria transmitted through the urine of an infected dog or a rat. The bacteria, called spirochaetes, attack the dog's kidneys and liver, causing symptoms similar to those of hepatitis. The eyes and skin eventually turn yellowish, but at this stage the dog usually dies. The disease is transmissable to humans, and is often fatal.
PREVENTION:
Inoculation helps prevent this disease, and protects humans as well as the dog.

## RABIES
CAUSE, SYMPTOMS AND TREATMENT:
A disease of the nervous system, rabies is a virus carried in the saliva of an infected animal, and is nearly always transmitted by a bite. It inflames the brain, causing behavioural changes which could be either the 'dumb' or the 'furious' kind. In the dumb kind, the dog is listless and lethargic, its jaw hanging open uselessly and drooling saliva. In furious rabies, the dog is irritated by anything that moves and will attack and bite all who approach it. It is always fatal to both animals and man if not treated. Fortunately, rabies no longer exists in Britain, though it does occur in quarantine kennels.
PREVENTION:
Vaccination repeated yearly.

# Obedience training for your dog

On the way to a training session. First, the dog should be taken to open ground where there is no danger from traffic, and there allowed to get rid of its high spirits before settling down to 15 minutes of lesson time. Inset: the training about to begin

**HEEL**

With the dog on the left side hold the lead in the right hand. Give the command 'Heel' and move forward briskly. If the dog does not respond give him a jerk with the right hand and praise well with the left when he does respond. The lead should be long enough to hang slack from the collar down to the dog's knees and up to the handler's right hand. Never keep the lead tight nor attempt to pull the dog into position.

**SIT**

Stand on the dog's right facing him. Grasp the collar in the right hand and place the left on his rump. Give a firm command 'Sit' and simultaneously pull back with the right hand and push down with the left. Praise well at the slightest sign or response. Remember that if he sits for two seconds and you tell him to get up that is a step forward. If he sits for two hours and gets up when he feels like it that is a step back.

**DOWN**

Stand in the same position as above and make the dog sit. Place the left hand on his withers (top of the shoulder blades) and grasp his forelegs in the right hand. Give the command 'Down'. Push with the left hand and simultaneously pull his forelegs forward. With all training it is important to praise well when the dog responds, but in teaching the 'down' do not make too much fuss of the dog or he will immediately get up again.

THERE is no such thing as absolute obedience from a dog. In every dog's life comes a moment when the commands of the owner are ignored, not heard or forgotten. It is at that particular moment that extreme annoyance or even something akin to hatred enters the owner's heart—and that makes matters worse. For dogs pick up this emotion by telepathy and are frightened to come back to the owner, after having committed that sin of disobedience. This occurs especially with a sensitive and normally very obedient dog.

One of the biggest hazards the dog owner has to face when he first starts training his dog is amateur advice. There is always someone willing to tell him not to train his dog until it is six months old. This is incorrect. The right time to commence training is the very first day the dog joins the household.

Even before this the owner should thoroughly acquaint himself or herself with the right way to train a dog. All the necessary knowledge to get your dog to obey the many varied commands cannot be passed on in the space of an article. An outline can be given of the essentials, including the owner's general attitude towards his dog. The detailed commands are best learned by going and watching a reputable trainer at work, or by reading a good book on dog training. This is necessary because very few inexperienced dog owners have the right tone of voice in the beginning to train a dog to a high standard of obedience. Changes of tone of voice and the commands used are the most important things in training.

The person who yells at the dog may get obedience out of fear. The person who whispers may get the same obedience because the dog is attending, and is intrigued by the soft tones used, and is tuned into the owner's wishes and commands. Indeed, at times the owner need not give a command at all—even for an absolutely untrained dog—to do what is wanted, because the dog is interested in the person it is associating with, and so the merest signals are sufficient.

There are so many things that distract a dog, particularly in the country, that the owner must make sure that his commands take precedence over the interest of a smell or another dog. You must not play second fiddle to a smell! Now it is all very well to advocate this, but how does the ordinary dog owner achieve this ideal?

Training a dog is not all done by love and kisses. Sometimes the dog has to be punished for bad behaviour—such as attacking another dog, threatening to bite the handler or for not returning to its owner on call. If you tend to be over-sentimental it may be necessary for you to abandon the idea of training the dog yourself. Take the dog and yourself to a reputable dog training school.

Once the owner has learned how to give commands, how to give praise and is happy training his dog, it will respond. There are, of course, some dogs that are mentally unstable and therefore untrainable. For these, unfortunately, there is no cure to be found with proper handling. However, there are many nice dogs available that are eager to please, and this is the sort of dog

the prospective owner should look for.

When a puppy is 10 weeks old, training can begin. If you leave training too late, the dog may have learned many bad habits, and by then it is possible that you will have become discouraged by the worry and work brought on by a disobedient puppy. An atmosphere then exists which is detrimental to effective lessons in obedience.

The conditions under which the dog has to live are, of course, very important to its welfare. It must be able to get reasonable exercise in a safe place where initially it can get rid of its high spirits before settling down to 15 minutes of lesson time. If your routine makes it essential for you to be away from your home all day—and as a consequence of which your dog will be alone there—you should reconsider your decision to keep a dog, for it can amount to cruelty.

Your mental attitude, as the dog's owner, is also most important. You must remember to be calm and consistent. Do not pass on all the ups and downs of life to the dog in its training lessons as some highly-strung individuals are apt to do. Be consistent in praising the dog after it has obeyed your command. To praise the dog one day and the next day expect it to do everything without praise will not help its progress.

In order to train a dog to walk obediently on and off the lead, it is necessary in the training sessions to use a special kind of collar chain called a choke chain. There are two types on the market. One with small thin links—which looks like a watch-

 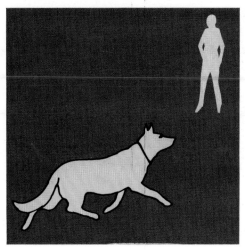 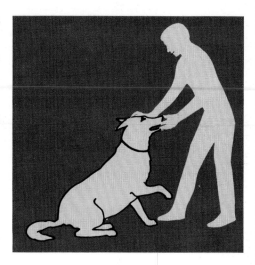

## STAY

When the dog has been taught to sit and lie down, put it in either position with its lead on. Tell the dog to 'Stay' and move in front of him holding the lead in one hand. Stand facing him for a few seconds, then return and praise him for staying. Once he has learnt to 'Stay' on the lead, remove it and gradually increase both the distance between you and the dog, and the time the dog will 'Stay'.

## COME

This is one of the first things a puppy should learn—indoors or in the garden. Don't wait until he sees another dog in the park and expect him to understand something he has never been taught. Call him by name in a friendly tone and see that he comes every time you call him. Most dogs that will not come when called have been taught this by owners who call the dog and then scold him for some 'crime' such as chasing a cat.

## DOS AND DON'TS

Do keep each lesson short so that neither you nor the dog become bored or bad-tempered with something which should be fun for you both. Always do the training yourself, as the dog's owner. Different voices will confuse your dog and no progress will be made at all. Don't punish a dog for not obeying a command, for he will come to associate the command with punishment. Do show affection when your dog does well.

chain—is quite useless for training the dog kindly. The right sort to use is the one with thick links. This gives more control and is less likely to do any damage to the dog's coat. The thin-linked chain can really hurt a dog when pulled, whereas the thick-linked chain, jerked in a downward direction can encourage a nervous dog, can correct a puller in a few minutes, and can help put the dog into the down position quickly and without struggling. A thin-linked chain on the other hand can cause resistance and even a bite for the handler.

An 18 inch length is suitable for a small dog and up to 10 inches longer than this for the bigger breeds. There is a right and wrong way of using the choke chain. First hold the chain by the two rings which are at each end. Lift the chain up by the right hand and drop it through the ring held in the left hand. The chain is then put on the dog so that it pulls upwards and automatically loosens when the pressure is relaxed.

The training session must be held daily to achieve success. Success only comes with repetition. But the lesson should not go on too long. The owner must want to train the dog; training should not be looked upon as a chore or a nuisance. The owner must be consistent in commands. He should not think it remarkable that the dog dislikes the next-door neighbour as much as he does—for dogs pick up thoughts. If you secretly enjoy the dog showing aggression, that dog will not easily stop doing so on command, for your voice will be saying one thing but your thoughts will be thinking the

opposite. The dog is always tuned to thoughts rather than words; you cannot deceive a dog.

When a dog repeatedly refuses to return to its owner it is because the owner is not very attractive to the dog. If the dog really and truly loved its owner it would not let the owner out of its sight, and if the owner disappeared the dog would look for him immediately. Running away from a dog that will not come to command is always better than chasing it.

You may have to enlist the help of friends to teach your dog to return to you. If they spread out in a field and have long leather leads in their hands, they can give the running-away dog a flick with the lead and tell it to 'Go to your mistress!' or 'Go to your master!' as the case may be. This unfriendly attack by strangers has a remarkably good effect on the dog and it usually learns that to return to its handler means getting affection, while running away may meet with wallops.

Unfortunately, few people will help in this way. The over-sentimental attitude may mean they would prefer to see a dog get lost or run over rather than give it one flick that might teach it what to do. Instant correction at the time is worth hours of training in a school or home.

It is difficult to achieve obedience if there are many people in the household. For there is likely to be someone who spoils the dog, or who oozes sympathy with a dog when it is defying its owner, or who actively sympathizes with the dog and tries to stop the handler making it do what he wants. Under these circumstances the

sensible dog owner has a poor chance of obtaining obedience.

Everyone in contact with a dog must be consistent in commands and behaviour to get the best out of the pet.

Some people think they can escape the work of training a dog themselves by sending it away to kennels to be trained for them. This is like buying a car before learning how to drive.

Occasionally a dog is a nervous type which clings to its owner. This is the dog that frets terribly when left by its owner, making it almost impossible for the owner to go anywhere without the dog.

The problem may arise of keeping a dog from howling or barking when left alone. The dog should be left alone, in spite of everything, for lengthening periods each week, training it to trust the owner. But it takes great firmness of purpose to resist the appeal in the eyes of such a dog.

Sending such a dog away to be trained would probably break its heart, or alternatively it might get so attached to the trainer that it could fret when returned to its rightful owner.

There is only one person who should train the dog and that is its owner. The rest of the family should try and learn how he or she does it, and if possible use the same tones of voice.

Obedience only comes with daily training, consistent training, loving but not over-sentimental training, and your ability to show appreciation, in a completely uninhibited manner, of what your dog learns. People who are introverts do not make good trainers.

# Psychology of the dog

AS a hunter, the dog possesses a large repertoire of predatory behaviour patterns, such as herding, tracking and retrieving, which are potentially of great value to man. Three important aspects of canine psychology determine the relative ease with which man can utilize these; first, the fact that the dog, being a highly social animal, will work for social reinforcement – praise from its handler – as a reward. Secondly, the diversity of modern dogs provides a wide range of personality types, each selectively bred to enhance a certain type of performance. Thirdly, the dog's great capacity to modify its behaviour through training enables us to develop and channel its abilities.

Dogs have a highly social nature. However, that does not mean that it is harmful to keep a single dog in the home. A pup that is reared in the company of humans will interact with them as social companions. Nevertheless, dogs can become distressed if forced to remain alone without canine or human company for any length of time.

Laboratory studies have shown that a new environment causes most distress to a pup of six to seven weeks old, and yet this is the age at which most are sold into new homes. Pups reared by their mother in a large field begin to venture onto new ground at about 12 weeks, and when tested in a new environment give very few distress calls at this age. However, it is not wise to leave the transition from litter to new home much later than this. Kennel-born pups intended for guide-dog training advance best if placed in homes by 13 weeks; those placed after this age never completely lose their timidity. Nine to ten weeks old seems a reasonable compromise.

Developmental studies have shown that early experience is very important in determining the social and general behaviour of the adult dog. If young animals are deprived of varied experience they remain timid and do not develop adequate behaviour in response to new situations.

Play is important for the development of behaviour and social relationships. With a single pup, the owner should supply the playful stimulation, but at the same time he should discourage hard biting and very rough play, as an adult dog would. This early training teaches a pup to regulate its behaviour and so to avoid eliciting aggressive responses from its companions.

Exercise is rewarding both for its beneficial effect on physical health and for the stimulation it provides. If allowed off the leash the dog will exercise itself and also seek contact with other dogs. Even a dog which has been fully socialized to humans will work to meet other dogs, and to investigate the odours left by them. There is no reason why contact between free-ranging dogs should be distressing for the owners, as serious fights are rare. Aggressive behaviour increases when the dog is restrained. Those who want to avoid aggressive encounters should let their dogs free wherever it is reasonably safe to do so, as the well-adjusted dog has many ways of appeasing dominant animals and of avoiding hostility if it arises.

Studies of the temperament, trainability and problem-solving behaviour of five different breeds has shown that, although the average performances of the breeds were different, each breed contained individuals whose performance was scattered throughout the entire range. Breeds certainly differ in their timidity towards

*Dog owners should not interfere with dogs' social encounters. A well-adjusted dog has ways of appeasing aggression in other dogs*

strangers, but there is little to suggest th
this is an inflexible quality which ca
never be overcome.

Another factor which influences pe
sonality is sex: males tend to be mo
aggressive and to be dominant ov
females of similar size. Age also affec
personality. Observation of Eskimo do
suggests that the juveniles do not defer
their territory until they reach sexu
maturity. They do not respond to t
borders of adjacent territories either, wi
the result that they are continually bei
chased by their neighbours. Similarl
suburban dogs as they mature, becon
more likely to drive strangers off the
property, and less likely to respor
submissively to an approach by an adu
dog.

Early experience has a far-reachir
influence on the development of person
lity. At one extreme, laboratory tests ha
shown that dogs raised in small isolatio
cages were slow at problem-solving. Th
also attended unselectively to eve
change in their environment, long aft
a normally reared dog would have ceas
to respond to repetitive stimulation. Do
reared under semi-restricted conditio
may also be timid with strange obje
and places, and in addition to behaviour
signs of distress, they may also sho
abnormal patterns of electrical activity
the brain. In addition, frightening expe
iences when the dog is young can produc
lasting problems.

All dogs show the ability to modi
their behaviour through training. Trai
ing for any task consists of establishin
an association between a certain signa
the desired act and a reinforcement, a
for example, a hand signal, an approac
by the dog, and a caress from the handle
Dogs are sensitive to signals from the
owners. Working sheep-dogs show this t
a high degree, constantly attending an
responding to visual and auditory signa
from their owners over great distance

The Russian physiologist, Pavlov,
famous for his investigations into associa
tive learning in dogs. He showed that th
association between the presentation c
food and a natural (or unconditionec
response such as salivation could b
extended. He extended this by always pr
senting the sound of a bell in conjunctio
with the food. The dog soon came t
associate these two stimuli and to saliva
at the sound of the bell even in the absenc
of food. Besides sounds, visual and tacti
stimuli can be used as conditioned stimul
Even time can become a conditione
stimulus: if it is fed every fifteen minute

*All dogs have the ability to modify their behaviour through training. This fact enables certain dogs to be trained for responsible work (above and left)*

a dog will soon begin to salivate at the end of the interval, even when the food is not presented.

The phenomenon is called 'classical conditioning'. Although it is of little use to the owner for training purposes because everyday conditions are not suitable, it has been useful in a number of laboratory studies for measuring the limits of the dog's powers of discrimination. For example, Pavlov conditioned his dogs to associate an oval shape, but not a circle, with food. Then he gradually made the oval shape more circular until he found the point at which the dogs could no longer tell it from a circle.

Psychologists have demonstrated a second type of associative process, 'operant conditioning', in which the animal comes to associate an act of its own with the arrival of a reward, such as the pressing of a bar to obtain food. This technique is used to study sensory discrimination, motivational state and performance at learning tasks, but dog-handlers can apply it to everything from the teaching of the simplest everyday command to the most complex sequences of actions.

Social reinforcement—praise by word or brief physical contact—is the foundation of all dog training. It is adequate reward for even the most difficult of tasks. Titbits are impractical and their use in training should be discouraged.

As training progresses, the ratio of correct responses to rewards given can be increased, so that the dog is rewarded less frequently. However, even the well-trained dog must be rewarded occasionally, and it should be remembered that, in addition to social contact, freedom is also rewarding to dogs, and a pup will be slow to come when called if its approach is always followed by restraint. This difficulty is easily avoided by calling him on some occasions for petting and play. Just as a friendly tone and caress are adequate as positive social reinforcers, so a growling tone and perhaps a brief shake by the scruff of the neck are adequate as negative reinforcers.

Several points emerge from laboratory studies of operant conditioning which all dog-handlers should bear in mind. For success, the dog must be in good condition. It must be on good terms with the trainer, and the training routine and situation should be carefully controlled to ensure that the dog is not distracted. The signal to which it is expected to learn to respond must be clear; words and hand movements should be brief, deliberate and clearly differentiated; and the signal must remain constant throughout training. A correct response must be followed immediately by a reward. Finally, the training session should end before the dog becomes fatigued.

*Dogs are highly sensitive to signals from their owners; this is important in the training of gun dogs*

It is wise for the owner to hold his training sessions after a period of relative restriction for the dog, and not after its main exercise period. In addition to rewarding desired responses, the owner can negatively reinforce (punish) undesired responses. In house training, for example, the pup should regularly be placed on the desired spot which can be a sheet of newspaper. Urination should be rewarded immediately, leading to an association between paper, urination and reward—positive reinforcement. At the same time, urination off the paper should be punished by the use of a disapproving tone—negative reinforcement.

Man can progress gradually and consistently towards the development of a subtle and delightful system of communication between himself and his dog. An exhilarating relationship can come into being which depends upon the dog's social nature and great responsiveness to training, as well as on the personality of the individual dog. A dog provides warmth, companionship and a sense of being needed. But, perhaps most important of all, there is the sheer pleasure of enjoying the dog's vitality and naturalness in play, and having fun because your dog is.

# Mating and gestation in dogs

THERE can only be one valid reason for breeding dogs and that is, in order to produce, or to try to produce, good specimens of a particular breed. This does not mean that breeding and selling pups in the hope of making a profit, or for the joy and interest of raising a litter, are in any way reprehensible reasons for doing so, providing that they are secondary to the main consideration, which must be to breed and rear creditable specimens of a breed.

Breeding dogs, then, is something more than merely increasing the canine population, of mating any bitch irrespective of her condition or quality to the most convenient dog of her breed. The need to consider the quality of the stock which a mating is likely to produce means that great demands are made on the breeder's knowledge, skill and experience. The challenge of these demands makes dog breeding an extremely absorbing occupation.

The first essential must obviously be a suitable bitch from which to breed. If you are thinking of breeding from a family pet, it is necessary to decide, honestly and dispassionately, whether or not she has the qualities required of any brood bitch. In all breeds the first consideration must be the bitch's temperament. She must be neither unduly nervous nor vicious, for either trait might be transmitted to and intensified in her offspring. She must be a mature bitch, having reached her second or third season, but not an old one. She must be in good physical condition, neither too thin nor too fat, for the strain of a pregnancy and of subsequently rearing a litter can be very demanding unless she is in good health.

If the bitch is of a breed which suffers from any hereditary defects, or if she has any defects which are at all likely to be inherited, careful consideration should be given to these before she is mated. It may be that the presence of such defects, in a bitch which is without any compensating qualities, suggests that she should not be used for breeding. Nevertheless, an otherwise outstandingly good bitch may carry some minor hereditary defect, which would be eradicated in her pups if she were mated to a good dog not carrying these defects.

In choosing a mate for the bitch, her pedigree and the faults and qualities of her ancestors should be carefully studied, and the choice of a dog should be based on the compatibility of his pedigree, and the faults and qualities which it contains. These too should be studied, in conjunction with those in the bitch's pedigree. A dog should not be chosen if the only reason is that he is convenient or cheap. The choice of dog requires a great deal of knowledge, both of the contents of the respective pedigrees and of the way in which various characteristics are inherited. A basic knowledge of the mechanics and laws of inheritance (genetics) is desirable but it is not possible here to cover adequately such a complex subject. There are several excellent books devoted to the genetics of the dog and these should be read by prospective breeders. The owner of the stud will also probably want to approve your bitch before allowing his dog to mate with her. He also is interested in getting the best possible pups, since his reputation depends on the quality of the dogs he breeds. A poor litter is bad publicity for his stud. Most stud owners require a copy of the bitch's registration papers, a photograph of the bitch, and a health certificate from the veterinary surgeon. If you own a large breed (such as a St. Bernard) the stud owner will probably want an X-ray, since it could have hip dysplasia, a hereditary defect; any dog suffering from this should not be bred.

A bitch should come into season (and so be ready for mating) at fairly regular intervals, varying from four to twelve months or even longer, depending on the breed and on the individual bitch. Breeds with a relatively short history of domestication tend to come into season less frequently. If a bitch is to be used for breeding, a careful record of the frequency and duration of her seasons should be kept so that her eventual visit to the stud dog can be planned well in advance.

The imminence of oestrus may be predicted by observing in her a tendency to urinate frequently, by an unaccustomed excitability and perhaps an unusual quarrelsomeness. The onset of oestrus is characterized by a swelling of the vulva, by the discharge of a blood-laden mucus and by the bitch becoming extremely attractive to and attracted by dogs. As the season progresses the discharge will become less discoloured, and at some point between the eighth and the fifteenth day she will be ready to be mated. This readiness may, in some breeds, last for several days. In others it may last no more than a few hours. During this time the bitch will accept and usually encourage the attentions of a dog and she must be mated during this short period.

The owner of the stud dog to be used must be warned well in advance of the likely date of the mating, so that he or she can make any necessary arrangements. It is customary to take the bitch to the dog. A fee, which will vary according to the reputation of the dog, will be paid to the dog's owner. It must be emphasised that the fee is for the dog's services and not for the ensuing pups. So it is in the interests of the bitch's owner to seek out an experienced dog with a good fertility record, and to take the bitch only when she is ready to be mated. If you send the bitch prematurely to the stud, she will have to be boarded by the stud owner until she is ready to be mated, and this will add to the cost. Many stud

*Left and below: pregnant bitches. The gestation period for a dog is about 63 days*

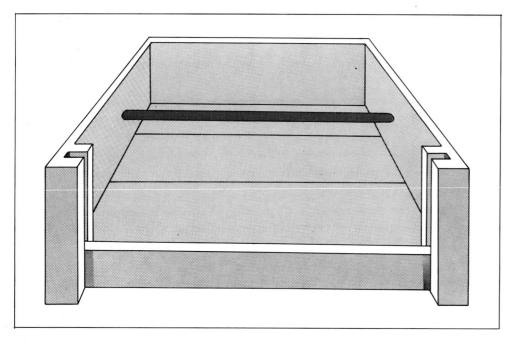

*Above: a whelping box. This should be sited in a warm place, and the bitch introduced to it well before the birth, so that she can adjust to her surroundings*

owners allow a repeated mating if the first is unsuccessful, but if this fails too, then the breeder has lost his money.

The act of mating itself may take only a few minutes, but with a maiden bitch (and particularly with a bitch which is unaccustomed to the company of other dogs) it may take several hours to accomplish. The bitch may resent the dog's attentions and may have to be held before a mating can be successfully accomplished. Such a situation makes demands on the skill and knowledge of those who assist at the mating, as well as on the experience and enthusiasm of the dog.

Once a mating has been achieved, the bitch should, as far as possible, be kept quietly in her accustomed surroundings for a few days. These first few days, when implantation of the fertilised ova takes place, have a considerable effect on the subsequent litter. The bitch can then resume her normal life. Exercise and food should follow the customary pattern for the first half of her pregnancy, which in normal circumstances will last for about 63 days. During the last month violent or strenuous exercise should be avoided. Nevertheless, it is important that the bitch takes some exercise in order to maintain the good physical condition which will enable her to withstand the strain of bearing and rearing her litter much better than a bitch which is out of condition. Bitches that are muscularly soft, or fat, are less likely to conceive than fit animals, and are far more likely to experience difficult births. During the latter part of the pregnancy the bitch's food should be given in smaller, more frequent meals. Pay attention to the nutritional quality of the food: better food rather than more food should be the aim. The basic nutritional requirements of the dog are fully discussed in other articles.

Every breeder looks for signs that the bitch, so carefully mated, has conceived. Such signs may not at first be very obvious. The vulva will cease to discharge but may remain slightly enlarged, and the bitch's appetite or temperament may become capricious. Later in the pregnancy the teats may become noticeably enlarged and, particularly if she is carrying a large litter, her abdomen will also become enlarged. A more positive early diagnosis can sometimes be made by skilled palpation, but this is not a technique which should be attempted by a novice under any circumstances.

When the bitch is thought to be about to give birth to her litter, the breeder will anxiously watch for signs that the birth is imminent. If no such signs are apparent by the sixty-fifth day the advice of a Veterinary surgeon should be sought, for such delays are potentially far more serious than an early birth. A day or two before whelping a bitch may show some reluctance to take exercise. She may seek out and, in her own way, prepare what she regards as a suitable place in which to have her pups. This may not always coincide with the breeder's choice. The bitch should have been introduced to suitable whelping quarters which are dry, warm and secure, well before she is due to whelp. This will give her time to become accustomed to her new surroundings, so that she will feel at ease there and will accept that this is where she is going to give birth.

For the majority of breeds, whelping is a perfectly normal process. For some, however, such as those which are exceptionally small or which have exaggerated physical features, it may often need skilled and, possibly, surgical assistance. Even for a strong and fit young bitch of a normal breed there exists the possibility of trouble, and any good breeder will be at hand to supervise the whole process unobtrusively, until the last puppy has been born and the whole litter is feeding vigorously from a contented bitch.

During the first stage of labour, the dilation, relaxation and lubrication of the birth passage takes place. This stage may take only a few hours or it may last a full day. Providing that the breeder is quite sure that the bitch is still in the first stages of labour, no undue alarm need be felt if it is prolonged; until this stage is complete the actual birth cannot proceed. The signs which accompany the first stage may not be obvious to the novice who may only become aware that the birth process has started when the bitch moves into the second stage.

During this second stage contractions will become increasingly obvious and more frequent, and the bitch will pant energetically. The contractions slowly force the puppies, one by one, down the birth passage until, if all goes well, the first is born. Its birth is closely followed by the arrival of the placenta. The bitch will proceed to clean the pup, to stimulate its breathing and circulation by licking it vigorously. She will gnaw through the umbilical cord unless her mouth, as it does in some breeds, prevents her from doing so, and she will eat the placenta. She should be allowed to do so, since the placenta contains a substance which stimulates the production of milk, and the whole process of cleaning her pups will stimulate her maternal instincts. This process will be repeated as each pup is born. The intervals between births may be no more than a few minutes, or up to a hour, and will tend to become longer as the bitch tires. Providing that the bitch is not straining fruitlessly, and that the contractions continue strongly and rhythmically, there is no cause for alarm. If the bitch's contractions cease or become feeble or irregular, or if they are to no avail and the bitch seems ill at ease, veterinary assistance should be sought without delay. The life of the remaining pups and possibly the bitch herself may depend on prompt action being taken under these circumstances.

When the bitch has had her litter and cleaned them all, and they are suckling vigorously in a clean, warm bed, she should be given a warm milky drink. The breeder can then relax for a short time, looking forward to the work and fun involved in rearing a litter of puppies, which can be one of the most satisfying experiences one can have.

# Dog breeding for profit

THIS article could possibly be entitled 'How to breed dogs without losing too much money', for it is necessary to dispel the illusion that fortunes can be made this way. It is true that from time to time headlines are made by spectacular sales of champions who nearly always go to buyers overseas – often for prices running into four figures. But for every outstanding animal of this description, the average breeder will have produced a quantity of specimens sold merely as pets and probably for sums that did not cover rearing costs. Furthermore, very high prices are paid only for show dogs that have proved themselves by their wins at shows, and taking dogs to a succession of shows around the country – campaigning show dogs as it is called – is very expensive, as well as requiring great determination and dedication.

*Puppies are most attractive at two months old and have great appeal*

Relatively few people set out to found a large kennel. The majority begin by buying a well-bred bitch of a favoured breed as a pet for the family. If they have been clever or fortunate in their choice, it is certain that at some time somebody knowledgeable will say 'That's a nice bitch you have there. You should take a litter of puppies from her.'

This starts a train of thought, leading to negotiations with a stud dog owner and finally to puppies under everybody's feet on the kitchen floor. This may spell doom to future dog-breeding plans or it may act as a spur to further endeavours.

There are many facets to dog breeding, not the least being the choice of breed, the time of year when the litter is ready for sale, the manner by which the puppies are fed and reared and the area in which the owner lives. Generally speaking, serious dog breeders – by which we mean those people who breed several, or many, litters every year as a regular course of events – are also exhibitors. They spend a great deal of money and a lot of time taking their adult stock to dog shows and they do not do this unless they have a measure of success and a share of the prizes as a reward. Since prizes at dog shows are negligible and rarely cover the expenses of entry fees and travel, the energy and outlay expended are for the honour and glory alone.

Once an exhibitor has a good name and is known to produce winning stock, he or she will receive enquiries for puppies for breeding and from buyers who want dogs for pets. It is such owners who will eventually decide to try breeding from the bitches they have bought and while there are good reasons why they may enjoy their experiment, there is no certainty that they will profit by it.

If they themselves are unknown in the world of dog showing, buyers are unlikely to beat a path to their doors. This is where timing and location are of importance when there are puppies ready for new homes. Generally speaking, many people begin to think about buying a dog at the turn of the year, when the worst of the winter is past and it seems to be an opportune time for bringing up and training a young animal.

A certain amount of trade takes place before Christmas but the average household, especially where small children are concerned, is disorganized at this time and it cannot be said that Christmas is the very best time to give a young puppy the attention it requires. The present-day trend is to accept this and to think about a pet when the rush of festivities dies down. The giant dog shows, such as the Westminster in the USA and Crufts in England, are heralded by a great deal of publicity. Consequently, just afterwards breeders

receive numerous enquiries for pedigree puppies from the public.

The demand for dogs continues throughout spring but as summer holidays draw near there is a marked falling off of enquiries. Few boarding kennels will accept dogs under six months of age and not everybody can take a puppy to an hotel or boarding house. Those people travelling abroad are certainly unable to do so. This means that a young dog can be an embarrassment unless there is a relative or friend who will undertake to care for it and can be trusted to do so.

Consequently, if they have not bought a new dog in the early part of the year, many families put off doing so until they return from holiday. This may be late August, September or October; breeders who offer litters for sale in early autumn often find no difficulty in placing stock with willing buyers. The trouble is that it is by no means possible to be sure of having puppies born at the right times.

Bitches come into season when nature decides and, although this happens normally at six-monthly intervals, even this is uncertain. The first season starts as a rule when the bitch is eight or nine months old. Some bitches come into season only once a year and many are quite irregular. It is this kind of hazard that makes dog breeding so unpredictable.

The unknown breeder whose brood

*Even a small litter of puppies becomes expensive to rear after a few weeks*

bitch has not been successfully exhibited at shows is not in a position to ask high prices for puppies – no matter how promising they may appear to be. The fact that the dam was expensive when purchased from a celebrated kennel does not mean that her own puppies will command a similar figure. In fact it would be wiser to ask less and so try to make sure of selling the litter before the cost of feeding the puppies becomes too great.

Present-day prices mean that even the litter of a small or medium-sized breed is quite an expensive proposition by the time the puppies are eight weeks old – the age at which they are normally ready for sale. Over this age, appetites increase and the young dogs grow at what may seem an alarming rate, while the food bills rapidly increase. Furthermore, the puppies leave the most attractive, chubby stage of development and often go through a gangling, teenage period when they are very much less attractive and so have a reduced customer-appeal.

However, if the breed is a popular one, if the puppies are well-reared, and if they are about two months of age at the right time of year, there is every chance that they can be sold at a profit. At the very least it may be that the cost will be recovered and the

---

lack of profit may be offset by the pleasure the litter has given the household.

If the first attempt at dog breeding has been reckoned successful, it may well be that another dog breeder has entered the Fancy. A second brood bitch will be acquired, another litter bred and disposed of (with perhaps the pick of the puppies retained with a view to the show ring) and the new breeder is up and away and into the frenetic, hectic world of showing dogs. It is a fascinating, demanding hobby that the clever ones turn into profit, while the majority are satisfied with the thrills and the achievements without counting the costs more often than is necessary.

The most successful breeders are those who start in this simple fashion. The less successful are the few who, with limited knowledge or experience, decide to plunge into dog breeding on a large scale. They buy a country property, erect expensive kennels and runs, buy a number of dogs and bitches and consider themselves in business. This is not the way to found a profitable kennel. There have been more than a few instances of hopeful individuals who have been into the dog game and out of it again in a very short space of time. Plunging into dog breeding on a large scale is almost certainly the quickest way there is to lose a lot of money.

In any event, a breeding kennel has to be established for a considerable length of time and needs to enjoy the success that comes from experience and good management before it can hope to become a profit-making concern. The size of the kennel is of paramount importance. A small kennel that can be conveniently run by the owner, with perhaps some help from other members of the family, starts off well by being freed from the burden of the heavy cost of outside labour. A slightly larger kennel cannot be well kept without the assistance of one or more kennelmaids or kennelmen and usually it is impossible for such an establishment to avoid losing money.

Once kennel help is required, the only hope of coming out on the right side financially is to enlarge it. Small kennels or very large kennels have a chance of becoming profitable enterprises but the likelihood of the medium-sized dog-breeding kennel making money is poor indeed. Apart from the overhead charges which include rates, electricity and running repairs, there are a number of items required by even quite small kennels: transport, advertising, veterinary attention, food, milk, medicines, grooming materials and attachments, crates, bedding, sawdust,

*The owner can run a small kennel with help from other members of the family but a larger kennel will need one or more kennelmaids to keep it going*

disinfectants, brooms, shovels, wheel-barrows, incinerators, collars, chains and leads.

These day-to-day requirements are additional to the capital expenditure involved in the building of kennels, strong wired runs and exercising paddocks. Kennel owners today have to think of sums which would have seemed prohibitive a few years ago. Costs should be carefully calculated before any ambitious project is begun.

As it is virtually impossible to separate successful dog-breeding from successful dog-showing, the costs of exhibiting must be considered. Travelling accounts for the largest part of the expense, for it includes the cost of overnight stays in hotels. Entry fees, meals and similar items also account for a considerable part of exhibiting expenses. The majority of exhibitors go to shows by car; a few travel by rail and many join together to hire a private coach. This last form of travel is perhaps the most economical and sometimes the most convenient. The high cost of hotel accommodation leads many people to invest in motor or trailer caravans which are also convenient. These are becoming very popular with exhibitors.

Because dog-breeding is expensive, many breeders enlarge the scope of operations by taking in dogs for boarding. A properly conducted boarding kennel is a profitable one and is often a great help in making a breeding kennel pay its way. Even so, the number of people who are involved either in dog-breeding or dog-boarding or both as their sole source of income must be small indeed. For many it is predominantly a hobby which may or may not produce an income. In such cases it is often the wife who runs the kennel, the husband following his own occupation and giving assistance as time allows.

When founding a kennel the old adage 'nothing but the best is good enough' is undoubtedly worth following. Poor specimens cost just as much to feed and keep as do champions. Unsuccessful breeders are often those who achieve nothing better than second best insofar as their livestock is concerned; then they wonder why others get to the top of the tree first.

Not everybody can afford to buy champion dogs and indeed the best show dogs are not often for sale. Wise breeders know that it is not easy to breed very outstanding animals of any species. They know, too, that others have been tempted by large financial gains to part with stock that, had it remained at home, would have gone on producing winners over the years – becoming a money-spinner of value far in excess of the sum for which it was sold.

The improvement of the breed should always be of paramount importance to a breeder, amateur or professional. It is of supreme importance to match the characteristics of the bitch to the stud dog chosen. The selection of a suitable mate is a process which demands considerable thought and a detailed examination both of the bitch's pedigree and those of the available dogs. The aim should be, as far as possible, to breed puppies which possess all the desirable characteristics of their breed and to breed out any faults. Thus a study of pedigrees is essential to the novice breeder. He also needs a measure of advice from knowledgeable people in the breed circle; fortunately such individuals are usually generous in this respect. If good bitches are mated to the best and most suitable stud dogs, and the progeny carefully and properly reared, one or two of the best animals may be retained and the kennel upgraded in this way. Puppies that have not been selected for retention by the breeder will be for sale and will play a part in recouping some of the original outlay. The youngsters that are kept will require sensible feeding and training. As they develop, small faults may become apparent or – in some cases – even major defects, so that it is necessary to discard them and to find homes for them as pets, for clearly they are not going to make the grade as show dogs.

It is the capacity to make such decisions that reveals the breeder's skill. Certain dog breeders are what is known as 'kennel blind'. This term is applied to people who can see no fault in their own stock. All their puppies are perfect to them. Consequently they do not discard the animals that are not good enough to breed from and so they never raise the standard of their stock. There are many people who fall into this category, who seem never to develop 'an eye for a dog', even after years of breeding. This is obviously a great handicap and can seriously affect the success of a kennel.

To be successful, the breeder must learn to evaluate the young stock in the kennel, retaining a puppy or puppies that seem to possess potential for breeding. Such a breeder also knows just when a young adult dog has reached its peak. Many a young dog has a spectacular career in the show ring. Inevitably the time arrives when, by virtue of its winnings or its age, the animal can only be entered in the higher classes. It then becomes apparent that it is not sufficiently outstanding to hold its own with the opposition. A decision has to be made to drop the youngster from the show team. If it is a female it may still be valuable for breeding. Its possibilities as a stud force are less, because the demand is for the progeny of the leading show dogs; although there are exceptions, in general this rule does hold.

*Building kennels, wired runs and exercising paddocks is an expensive business*

# Preparing your dog for the show

A considerable amount of care and expertise is necessary if the good points of a dog are to be displayed to a show judge to the best advantage. The dog must be trained to walk on a lead without pulling in any direction, and to stand still when required to do so. The judge will wish to inspect the teeth, so the prospective exhibit must learn to allow a stranger to look in its mouth, and to have a strange hand feeling shoulders, lifting feet to examine the pads, pressing the back and so forth. A dog that is to be prepared for the noisy, bustling atmosphere of a show should be exercised on a leash in towns and shops, and encouraged to accept the advances made by passers-by.

Different breeds usually require different kinds of coat care. For example, a smooth-haired breed, such as a Beagle or a Greyhound, needs careful brushing, but a comb is rarely used. Experts produce a handsome glossy sheen to the coat by finishing it off with a polishing cloth, using a soft, dry, clean chamois leather, a piece of velvet or an old silk scarf. Dachshunds also have short hair, but are sometimes inclined to develop bare patches, often on the large pendulous ears. The old-fashioned and usually effective remedy for this has always been coconut

oil, and there are other reliable preparations which can be prescribed by a veterinary surgeon. Smooth Fox Terriers have coats not unlike the breeds mentioned above but it is usual to trim the ears, neck and 'pants'. Breeds such as the Alsatian (German Shepherd Dog) and the Pembroke Welsh Corgi, to mention only two from a group, are characterized by fairly short coats, harder outer hairs and a thick woolly undercoat. These benefit from brushing and combing, and require no trimming or clipping. Like the very smooth-haired group, they are relatively easy for the novice exhibitor to prepare. The same cannot really be said for dogs of the type carrying long, soft, flowing featherings, such as the Afghan Hound, which is a truly magnificent sight in full coat and in show condition, but a sorry spectacle indeed when neglected. The Old English Sheepdog is another breed covered with long hair, but of a much

harsher texture than the coat of the Afghan. It is no less demanding, however, and requires regular attention at all times. The gundog breeds include the Labrador Retriever, which falls midway between the short-coated specimens and the dogs of Corgi type, and has a coat that is easily kept tidy. But all the Spaniels and Setters call for a certain amount of brushing and combing, and most receive some tidying-up before a show. The ear flaps, neck, pants, and feet in particular need to look neater than they would do if untrimmed.

Poodle puppies may be shown with a profuse body coat and with just the face and feet clipped down to the skin. This is called the Puppy Clip. The generally accepted and popular clip for adult show Poodles is known as the Lion Clip. A great deal of practice is necessary before a Poodle can be successfully clipped for show, but it is remarkable how many people learn to prepare their own stock and

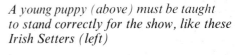
*A young puppy (above) must be taught to stand correctly for the show, like these Irish Setters (left)*

put them into the ring looking smart.

It is, however, a completely different matter where some of the Terrier breeds are concerned. All the wire-haired, harsh-coated Terriers require trimming, and the craft is difficult to learn, although there are a number of specialists who produce marvellous results on dogs they handle at shows. Some owner-breeders consider it an advantage to allow a professional to trim their exhibits. Cairn Terriers and their 'cousins', the West Highland Terriers, require considerably less trimming than, say, the Wire Fox Terrier, the Airedale, or the Welsh and Lakeland Terriers. These are all breeds that need much plucking and clipping before a show, and there is a right time and a wrong time to do this. The expert knows just when a dog's coat should be stripped right down so that it has the correct amount of time to grow to an ideal length before a show. A moderately good dog, expertly trimmed, can look impressive in the ring, but a good dog, shown in rough coat or badly stripped, can easily fail to catch the eye of the judge. The Border Terrier is a harsh-coated dog and probably one of the most simple, from a grooming angle, to keep. Skye Terriers are harsh-coated but not wire-haired, and must be well cared for if matting and tangles are to be avoided. One Irish breed–the Soft-Coated Wheaten Terrier–must not be trimmed at all. Its Standard of Points requires it to be shown as nature intended.

The Toy Group embraces a wide variety of coat. The Griffon comes in two types–the smooth and the rough–the latter with harsh, wiry hair that needs a certain amount of trimming. Pekingese, and Maltese Terriers (not included in the Terrier group in spite of the misleading name) have long, soft, profuse hair that needs careful brushing to maintain good condi-

*Regular grooming is essential, even for the smooth-coated Cardigan Corgi*

tion, without tearing out the feathering which so greatly enhances the overall appearance of the breeds. Pomeranians have stand-off coats in contrast to the 'dripping fringes' of the Peke and the Maltese. The Pom's ears are neatened round the edges and the hair immediately beneath the plumed tail is cut short round the anus.

The Yorkshire Terrier–another 'Terrier' classified as a Toy by the Kennel Club–presents different problems. It has ultra-fine, very straight, silky hair, and judges pay great attention to colour, quality and length of coat when appraising this breed. An exhibition Yorkshire Terrier needs a lot of conditioning and expert grooming if it is to look good. Most exhibitors tie up the hair in curl papers (usually referred to as 'crackers') and keep them that way for much of the time between shows, and particularly while the dogs are boxed and travelling.

Many breeds benefit from a bath before a show and for some it is essential. The wire-haired and harsh-coated dogs are never washed immediately before a show, however, since a hard coat is one of their most important characteristics, and immersion in water would make the hair

soft and woolly for days. White dogs are usually cleaned with specially prepared chalk, the powder being well brushed out before the dog goes into the ring. After a bath, the dog must be thoroughly dried and not allowed to catch cold. Keep it in a warm place for a few hours. Always dry the ears carefully, otherwise canker can result. While the dog is in the bath it is a good idea to examine its teeth and claws. Teeth may need scaling with a proper metal instrument, or brushing with one of the special toothpastes sold for dogs. Alternatively, ordinary toothpaste can be used.

Claws should not need cutting if the dog receives sufficient exercise on roads or concrete, and if the feet are round and tight. Dogs kept too much indoors, exercised mainly on grass, or whose feet are elongated, will need manicures at regular intervals. Scissors are unsuitable, and pro-

*These Beagles have been carefully groomed and trained for an outside show*

per nail clippers must be used. It is important to notice the 'quick' that grows inside each claw, for if cut too close, the dog suffers pain and the nail bleeds. The quicks inside light-coloured toe-nails are easily seen, but with black nails it is more complicated. If a dog has a mixture of pale and black nails, as sometimes happens, clip the light nails first and see how far down the quick extends. Then start clipping the dark nails, taking off a very small piece each time. Probably the dog will fidget uneasily and try to withdraw its foot as a sign that you are getting close to the tender spot. It is essential to have an assistant to hold the dog both for teeth-cleaning and nail-cutting.

The amount of grooming equipment which needs to be taken to the show varies. Some exhibitors can go to the show with no more than a comb in their pocket; others, who have long-haired dogs, have

to take a large amount of equipment. However, if adequate grooming has been done before the show, there should be little need for extensive treatment on arrival. Many owners of small Toy breeds, whose coats require a lot of attention, take a small folding table on which to stand the dog.

From all this it will be seen that it is important for a novice exhibitor to obtain expert advice before attempting to prepare any dog for the show ring. A visit to a show or two may help to give some idea of what is required, and after this the best course is to have a consultation with the breeder from whom the dog was bought. The breeder is the most suitable person to advise the owner whether or not the dog is good enough to show, and will either offer to trim it—if this is necessary—or suggest some other experienced person who can do it. The breeder can

also suggest adjusting the feeding to put on or take off weight.

In certain cases it may prove advisable to let a professional handler have the dog in good time before a show so that it can be properly trained, conditioned, prepared, and handled in the ring to advantage. Fees are charged for such services, but if the dog is a really good one it should be given the best opportunities to make a name for itself. Competition at dog shows is very keen, for in Britain more top class pedigree dogs are shown than anywhere else in the world. However good a dog may be, it has to be on form if it is to beat other good dogs in open competition. For the novice breeder time and effort are needed to learn all the do's and don'ts of showing.

# Chapter II
# Sporting Dogs
# Hound Group

# Afghans, Salukis and Borzois

THE supremely elegant and aristocratic Afghan Hound attracts attention wherever it goes, and is easily recognizable by its proud head carriage, regal action, flowing coat and 'trousers', and long silky top-knot on the head. Sometimes called the 'Monkey Dog' because of its facial appearance, it is one of the earliest of the Eastern greyhounds. The tribesmen hunters of Afghanistan have a traditional belief that it was the dog taken into Noah's Ark. Be that as it may, there can be no doubt that the breed is very ancient. Prehistoric rock carvings discovered in Afghanistan prove that these hounds, looking much as they do today, were kept as hunting dogs as long ago as 2,200 BC; and there is further evidence taking them back to even remoter times. A papyrus dated from between 4,000 and 3,000 BC mentions the breed as being of Egyptian origin, specifically from the Sinai Peninsula.

It is not known when the hounds were first introduced into Afghanistan. The traders who brought them must have travelled through Persia, but there is no mention of the routes that were taken. Once arrived in Afghanistan, however, they were found to be very adaptable to extremes of climate and were ideally suited to local conditions, fulfilling the need for a strong, speedy dog capable of hunting the wolf, wild ass, markhor, ibex and gazelle. In this exceptionally harsh

*The three breeds shown on this page, Afghans (above left), Salukis (left) and Borzois (below) are all gazehounds which hunt by sight rather than by scent*

*Although the Afghan (above) was bred as a hunter, it makes an excellent house dog*

and inhospitable land, which averages 6,000 feet above sea level and where the temperature is usually below zero for three months of the year, the dog grew a long coat for protection from the elements. Its body was gradually modified to suit its work in the rugged, mountainous country, becoming more short-coupled (shorter in the distance between front and back) than that of its greyhound cousins. It developed wide and high hipbones, and huge paws with dense featherings between the pads, providing a firm footing on rough terrain.

The Afghan is not as fast on the straight as the smooth Greyhound or the Saluki, but the unique structure of its hipbones enable it to turn with lightning speed, as well as imparting tremendous power when it leaps over obstacles, which occur when hunting on craggy mountain slopes. Neither is the high tail carriage a mere ornament, for it enables the hound to be distinguished in dense undergrowth.

Afghanistan must be given full credit for the development of this outstanding and handsome breed. The head is long, with a prominent occiput, the foreface having a slight stop and the jaws being very powerful. The skull is surmounted by a silky top-knot. For show purposes a black nose is preferred, but liver is acceptable in a light-coloured dog. The eyes are nearly triangular, preferably dark, although a golden eye is not a fault. The ears are set low, carried close to the head and covered with long, silky hair.

The neck should be strong, the forequarters long and sloping, well set back, and the forelegs should be straight and well boned. The back must be level and well muscled, falling away slightly to the rear. The chest is deep and should provide

plenty of lung and heart space. The hindquarters are powerful, well bent, and the stifles are well turned. The forefeet are very large in length and breadth, and covered with long, thick hair; the hind feet are less broad. The tail should not be too short, and must be set low with a ring at the end, and sparsely feathered. The coat can be of any colour but must not be trimmed or clipped.

The Afghan was first imported into Britain in 1907 and British breeders were responsible for introducing the hound to the countries of the Commonwealth, to Europe and, in 1926, to the United States. It now enjoys worldwide acclaim and ranks high in the popularity tables of the canine world. Although something of an individualist, the Afghan is quick to learn and eager to please, is extremely gentle and loving with children, and is altogether a loyal and interesting pet.

The breed is not usually responsive to a high measure of obedience training. For this reason it is not ideally suited to town life, with its traffic hazards. Nevertheless, although it is essentially a hunting breed, many owners find that it adapts well to urban conditions, provided, of course, that it is adequately exercised.

The unusual beauty of the Afghan must not be allowed to blind a prospective owner to its basic needs. It is extremely strong and fleet of foot and, being a large dog (26 to 29 inches at the shoulder), it must be given plenty of space, a great deal of exercise, and food commensurate to its size. It will eat up to 2 lb of meat and $\frac{1}{2}$ lb of biscuit meal a day. Furthermore, the heavy coat requires regular and dedicated grooming.

An even older Eastern hunting breed which can claim to be one of the most ancient of all domesticated dogs, is the Saluki or Gazelle Hound. This dog was portrayed on the tombs of Egyptian

Pharaohs some 5,000 years ago. Depicted complete with its heavily feathered, dropping ears and gracefully carried tail, the Saluki has remained unchanged throughout the centuries, and is one of the few breeds that has not been tailored to suit man.

Although the Saluki is probably older it has been established that the Smooth Greyhound type also existed in ancient Egypt. Taking the Saluki as the original type of hound, it can be assumed that the other varieties were the result of selective breeding—a procedure understood and adopted by the Egyptians and desert nomads, despite their obvious lack of knowledge about genetics.

The Bedouin Arabs must take the credit for preserving this fascinating breed. To them the Saluki is a prized possession, a nobleman among dogs, so highly treasured that it is permitted to enjoy the choicest titbits from the plate and the finest linen from the bed. The pedigrees of these cherished hounds are often recounted in song and in this way handed down from father to son. Beautifully written pedigrees have been discovered on parchment over a thousand years old.

The Saluki varies in type, depending on its country of origin, which may be anywhere within the enormous region extending from Arabia to the steppes of Siberia and from North Africa to India. The coat can either be smooth, without feathering on ears and tail, or longish and silky in texture, with abundant feathering on ears, tail and backs of legs. The feathered variety is the most common and by far the most popular.

The height of the Saluki varies greatly from 23 to 28 inches, bitches tending to be smaller than dogs. The head is long and narrow, but with a moderately wide skull between the ears. It possesses long stretching limbs, a muscular neck and sloping shoulders. The deep ribs and flexible loins, combined with racy hindquarters, show that the dog is fashioned for speed, rapid turning, running over rough terrain, and endurance. Elegant in outline, graceful in movement, the symmetry of this hound is very pleasing.

Colour, too, varies enormously. Fawns ranging from pale cream to red, are most common, being almost universal in Arabia. From Asia Minor and Syria come the black and tans, black and silvers and tricolours; additionally, fawns and varying shades of grey and fawn grizzles are common everywhere. Whatever the colour there is almost invariably a white tag to the tail. The shape of the Saluki is allied to that of an English Greyhound and, as one of the numerous Eastern greyhound breeds, comes under the classification of the 'gazehound' family—a hound that hunts primarily by sight, not by scent.

Although its graceful appearance may

suggest that it is well suited to adorn the drawing room of a comfortable town house, this is no place for the Saluki. It is by nature a hunter, with boundless energy that must be consumed. So it must have plenty of exercise–more than it can get in a town park. The Saluki was established in Britain long before its introduction to the USA, the American Kennel Club granting recognition in 1927.

The Saluki tends to be shy and rather wary of strangers, sometimes ignoring them with an air that borders on utter aloofness. But it thrives on human companionship and becomes extremely affectionate and loyal to its owner, as well as being good with children. It appreciates a certain amount of attention as reassur-

*The Saluki (above and below) is by nature a hunting dog and consequently needs plenty of exercise. Without this it can become destructive*

ance that it is an important member of the household. Scrupulously clean in habit, it is one of the few breeds that does not emit a doggy odour.

Although a hardy breed in natural surroundings, a Saluki does not enjoy being kennelled and should be given a large, draught-free bed or, better still, a favourite armchair. Feeding is simple, for 1 lb of meat, together with biscuit meal, is usually enough for its daily needs. The dog should be groomed regularly; teeth should be kept clean and toenails cut as necessary.

The average lifespan of a Saluki is 13 to 14 years. So remember, when choosing this breed, that your dog, complete with hunting instincts, will be with you for some considerable time.

Built on similar lines to the Greyhound, the Borzoi is much taller and more powerful. Its body formation gives clear indication of great speed, combined with strength and agility, but retains an elegance that is difficult to surpass in the canine world. Its long, silky coat, which may either be flat, wavy or rather curly, greatly enhances its appearance. Colours vary but are usually white, or white with fawn, brindle, red, blue, black or grey markings. It possesses a very long, lean head with a flat and narrow skull, giving an impression of a Roman nose when viewed in profile. Its small, thin ears are placed far back on the head. The deep chest is somewhat narrow and the back rather arched. It has powerful, well-muscled loins and lengthy thighs with low-set hocks to give the all-important propelling power to the back legs. A feature of this breed is the densely feathered

# Breed Standard: the Afghan Hound

**CHARACTERISTICS**
The Afghan Hound should be dignified and aloof with a certain keen fierceness.

**GENERAL APPEARANCE**
The gait should be smooth and springy with a style of high order. The whole appearance of the dog should give the impression of strength and dignity combining speed and power.

**EYES**
Should be dark for preference. Nearly triangular, slanting slightly upwards from the inner corner.

**EARS**
Set low and well back, carried close to the head. Covered with long silky hair.

**MOUTH**
Level, but scissors bite should not penalize.

**NECK**
Long, strong with proud carriage of the head.

**FOREQUARTERS**
Shoulders long and sloping, well set back, well muscled and strong without being loaded. Forelegs straight and well boned, straight with shoulder, elbows held in.

**BODY**
Back level, moderate length, well muscled, the back falling slightly away to the stern. Loin straight, broad and rather short.

**HINDQUARTERS**
Powerful, well-bent and well-turned stifles. Great length between hip and hock with a comparatively short distance between hock and foot.

**FEET**
Forefeet strong, very large in length and breadth, covered with long thick hair. Toes arched. Hind-feet long, covered with long thick hair.

**TAIL**
Not too short. Set on low with ring at the end. Raised when in action. Sparsely feathered.

**COAT**
Long and very fine texture on ribs, fore- and hind-quarters and flanks. From the shoulder backwards and along the saddle the hair should be short and close in mature dogs. Hair long from the forehead backward, with a distinct silky 'top-knot'. On the foreface the hair is short.

**COLOUR**
All colours are acceptable.

**WEIGHT AND SIZE**
Ideal height: Dogs 27 to 29 inches. Bitches 2 to 3 inches smaller.

**FAULTS**
Any appearance of coarseness; skull too wide and foreface too short; weak underjaw; large round or full eyes; neck should never be too short or thick; back too long or too short.

tail which is carried low when the dog is in motion, never erect above the back.

This handsome sporting dog is best kept in the country, with plenty of free exercise area. Like the Saluki and Afghan Hound, the Borzoi is a gazehound, hunting by vision. It must be taught to respect other domestic animals from an early age otherwise it may take to chasing sheep and other livestock. Although it loves to live as part of the family and makes a faithful and affectionate companion, it is equally at home in a draught-free kennel especially if there is another dog to keep it company. If it is the only dog in the household it seems to be happier indoors.

Considering its size, the Borzoi is not at all clumsy or over-boisterous once past puppyhood. It is excellent with children and most appreciative of human company. Although not as easily trained as say, a Collie, it can be taught obedience better than other gazehounds.

Regular grooming is necessary, with particular attention being paid to the heavy featherings. Teeth and nails also require periodic treatment. It should be noted that a Borzoi tends to shed its coat once a year, usually in the spring.

Feeding presents few problems, an adult dog requiring approximately 1½ to 2½ lb of meat each day, with other supplements as necessary. The life expectancy is, on average, 18 years.

Because of its size and hunting instincts careful thought must be given, prior to purchase, to the amount of exercise the hound requires. The prospective owner must be prepared to go out with the dog on cold, wet winter days as well as in the height of summer. This is the principal reason why a Borzoi is not a recommended town breed, particularly in a flat.

The graceful and elegant Borzoi is understandably considered by many to be the most beautiful member of the entire greyhound family. It too is of very ancient origin and was more recently kept by the Russian aristocracy for hunting wolves, hence its alternative name of Russian Wolfhound. Before the Revolution the breed was kept in packs for hunting, and the dogs were held in high esteem throughout Eastern Europe. Since that time, however, it appears that few large kennels have survived in the U.S.S.R. although the Borzoi has certainly not disappeared completely from its native land. There are evidently a number of modest scale breeders and many hounds are still exported to the West to improve existing stock. But in Britain, as in other countries of Western Europe, the Borzoi is kept purely as a companion or for show.

*The Borzoi owner must be prepared to give plenty of time to his pet; the breed needs companionship and a great deal of exercise*

# American Foxhounds

WHEN William the Conqueror invaded England he was accompanied by his big staghounds, each capable of pulling down a deer, which was the only quarry fit to be hunted by a king. If anyone had suggested to William that the time would come when his noble staghounds would be forced to give way to hounds trained to hunt the fox, he would be lucky to escape with his life and the loss of an ear or tongue.

Nonsense it may have been in those far off days but the fact remains that it was from the Norman staghounds that the English foxhound traces his descent, which means that the American Foxhound can also claim an equally aristocratic lineage.

The American Foxhound is lighter in build than its English cousin and although both have a common ancestry and have been inter-bred freely, there are distinct differences between the two, both physically and in the different hunting activities for which they are bred.

There can be little doubt that it was an Englishman named Robert Brook who, in 1650, sailed to America, then a Crown Colony, bringing with him his pack of hounds who are now recognized to have been the ancestors of the various strains now bred in the United States. There were further importations in 1742 while it is reported that George Washington initiated further imports several years later. There was also a gift of several French hounds from Lafayette and arrivals from Ireland gave further impetus to hound breeding. It is obvious that so many strains bred in different parts of the country led to great differences. This has now been partially corrected and a great deal of attention is being paid by Masters of Foxhounds to breeding a more standard type.

American Foxhounds are used in packs of about twenty or more to hunt the fox in the conventional manner while a single hound is used to trail a fox which is then shot. Trail hounds, also called drag hounds, are raced and hunted on a drag, speed being all important. There is also a great interest in field trials in which individual hounds compete. It is thus apparent that despite attempts to breed a standard type, it is necessary to encourage characteristics which will aid the dog to perform its duty in widely differing sports.

*The American Foxhound has a common ancestry with its English Cousin*

## Breed Standard: the American Foxhound

### GENERAL CHARACTERISTICS
A strong, graceful hound of substance but lighter in build than the English Foxhound. It is also leggier but it must be muscular, possess a good nose, stamina, as well as having a melodious E-sounding voice.

### HEAD AND SKULL
The skull should be fairly long, slightly domed at the occiput with a cranium that is both full and broad.

### EARS
Set on moderately low. They are long, reaching when drawn out nearly to the tip of the nose. Fine in texture, fairly broad, with an almost total absence of erectile power. Round at the tip. Sitting close to the head with the forward edge slightly turning in toward the cheek.

### EYES
Large, set well apart, soft and houndlike. Expression gentle and pleading; of a brown or hazel colour.

### NOSE
Fair length, straight and square cut with the top moderately defined.

### FEET
Straight with a fair amount of bone. Pasterns short and straight. Feet should be fox-like; pad full and hard. The toes should be well-arched with strong nails.

### BODY
Neck should rise free and light from the shoulders; strong yet not loaded and of medium length. The throat should be clean and free from folds of skin but a slight wrinkle below the angle of the jaw is allowable. Defects include a thick, short neck carried on a line with the top of the shoulders; throat showing dewlap and folds of skin ('throatiness'). The shoulders should be sloping, clean and muscular but not heavy. The chest should be deep; a girth of 28 inches in a 23 inch hound is considered good. The ribs should be well sprung with the back ribs extending well back.

### HINDQUARTERS
Hips and thighs should be strong and well muscled giving an abundance of propelling power. Stifles strong and well let down. The feet should be close and firm.

### TAIL
Set moderately high. Carried gaily but not turned forward over the back. Should have a slight curve with very slight brush.

### COAT
A close, hard, hound coat of medium length. A short thin coat, or of soft quality, is considered a defect.

### HEIGHT
Dogs should not be under 22 inches or more than 25 inches. Bitches should not be under 21 inches or over 24 inches at the withers.

# The Basset Hound

THE French have always preferred hunting with hounds of scent and it is to William the Conqueror that e owe the many varieties of hounds now red in Britain and the USA. The Norman knights hunted with large stag ounds many times the size of the low-ung Basset. Nevertheless, both owe their rigin to the hounds bred by St Hubert n the sixth century and carried on after is death by the monks of the abbey which e founded.

However, neither St Hubert nor the reeders of his day had any inkling of he science of genetics and many centuries vere to pass before such knowledge ecame of any practical help to livestock reeders. Even so, by trial and error, our orefathers achieved their objectives. In ome districts the terrain demanded a ound which could work its way through horn and scrub which would immobilize longer-legged hound. Observation vould have shown that the consistent nating of hounds smaller than usual vould eventually result in a small variety vhich would breed true. Some would have he perception to introduce a smaller reed to bring down size and then breed back to the type of hound they envisaged. In this way, hounds like the Basset must have been produced, although the modern type would bear little resemblance save size to their remote ancestors.

The first Bassets to come to Britain were in the form of a present sent to Lord Galway in 1866. The breed aroused immediate interest and a Basset Hound Club was formed in 1883, the Kennel Club sanctioning entries in the Stud Book in the same year. The breed was regarded as a show dog for many years and then, in 1884, several packs were formed to hunt hares. Few of these survived for long but one of the best was the Walhampton Basset Hounds hunt formed by Godfrey and Christopher Heseltine. This pack hunted the New Forest up to 1932 when the Mastership was taken over by Colonel E. F. S. Morrison and the name of the pack changed to the Westerby, under which name it still hunts today.

As a hunter, the Basset is very versatile. In Britain, the usual quarry is the hare but in the USA he is often used to hunt foxes, rabbits and pheasants, his low build enabling him to flush game from very thick cover. He has even been known to rival the Coonhound in treeing racoons and squirrels. With the exception of the bloodhound, the Basset has the keenest nose of all dogs and perseverance in hunting a line is a noted trait. It has been said that a Basset following scent until nightfall will sleep on the line and resume hunting with the first light. Easy to follow on foot, a Basset pack will give pleasure to anyone interested in studying the way in which hounds unravel an intricate line over every sort of terrain. The pleasure is enhanced when the hounds give voice—a lovely bell-like melody unsurpassed by any other breed.

However, it is not necessary to hunt to enjoy the companionship of this lovable breed and a single specimen will adapt to family life. It must be admitted that a Basset is a solemn looking character but this does not imply that he has a miserable nature. On the contrary, the Basset loves playing with people or other dogs, is perfectly safe with children, and naturally obedient—well, most times anyway, for there are times when his fine nose is investigating a puzzling scent that he appears to be deaf to his master's voice.

In appearance, the Basset Hound is short-legged and of great substance, showing quality and balance, and moving with a smooth, free action in which the forelegs reach well forward and the hind legs show powerful thrust. He must move true from front and rear and the toes must not be dragged. The Basset temperament is calm and unhurried, very loyal and not given to fawning upon strangers.

There is also a variety developed purely for hunting by Colonel Morrison, known as the Basset Hound (English). The Masters of the Basset Hounds Association met at Aldershot in 1959 and decided to admit these cross-bred hounds, via an Appendix, to the Stud Book. The English Bassets retain the true Basset characteristics of the original Bassets but differ in being straighter and longer in the leg and having shorter ears. They are also more lively and faster.

A similar hound to the Basset is the Griffon Basset Vendeen which originated in Vendée in France. There are three types, Briquet, Grand Basset and Petit Basset. Hard working, sound and sturdy, they show a great aptitude for hunting and have excellent noses in common with all Basset varieties. The coat is thick and wiry and there is a choice of colours, some being grey or grizzled, others having a combination of orange, black, grey, gold and tan with white. There are also tri-colours usually black, tan and white, or grey, tan and white.

*The sad, serious expression in the drooping eyes of the Basset Hound (apparent even in puppies) is an endearing characteristic*

## Breed Standard: the Basset Hound

### GENERAL CHARACTERISTICS
A short-legged hound of considerable substance, well balanced and full of quality. Action is most important. A smooth free action with forelegs reaching well forward and hind legs showing powerful thrust.

### HEAD AND SKULL
Domed, with some stop and the occipital bone prominent; of medium width at the brow and tapering slightly to the muzzle; the general appearance of the foreface is lean but not snipy. The skin of the head should be so loose as to wrinkle noticeably when drawn forward or when the head is lowered.

### NOSE
Entirely black, except in light-coloured hounds, when it may be brown or liver.

### EYES
Brown, but may shade to hazel in light-coloured hounds, neither prominent nor too deep set. The expression is calm and serious.

### EARS
Set on low but not excessively so and never above the line of the eye, very long and supple.

### MOUTH
The teeth level with a scissors bite, although if they meet edge to edge it is not a fault.

### NECK
Muscular and fairly long, with pronounced dewlap.

### FOREQUARTERS
Shoulder-blades well laid back and shoulders not heavy. Forelegs short, powerful and with great bone; elbows turned neither in nor out.

### BODY
The breast bone slightly prominent but the chest not narrow or unduly deep; the ribs well rounded and sprung and carried well back. The back rather broad, level and with withers and quarters of approximately the same height.

### HINDQUARTERS
Full of muscle and standing out well, giving an almost spherical effect from the rear.

### FEET
Massive, well knuckled-up and padded. Toes are neither pinched together nor splayed.

### TAIL
Well set on, rather long, strong at the base and tapering, with coarse hair underneath.

### COAT
Smooth, short and close, without being too fine.

### COLOUR
Generally black, white and tan or lemon and white.

### HEIGHT
Height 13 to 15 inches.
USA not exceeding 14 inches. Height over 15 inches disqualifies.

# Beagles, Harriers and Foxhounds

SIMILAR in type, conformation and colouring, these three old-established varieties of hound vary mainly in size. The Beagle is thought to be one of the oldest hounds of the chase. There is no doubt at all that man has, from time immemorial, kept hounds with pendant ears, such animals possessing the ability to hunt by scent in direct contrast to the greyhound type of dog (gazehound) which pursues its quarries by sight, relying very much on its speed, and does not have particularly good scenting ability. They are therefore put to different uses.

As far back as the reign of King Henry VII (1457–1509) we find references to little hounds actually called Beagles, but long before that there were Greek writers describing hounds that 'give tongue with a clanging howl'. Chaucer, in his immortal 'Canterbury Tales', when speaking of a lady dog lover, wrote 'Of smalle houndes hadde she, that she fedde . . . But sore wept she, if on of them were dedde.'

King James I was devoted to his dogs, some of which were Beagles, and King Charles II hunted a pack on Newmarket Heath. King George IV was so proud of

his Beagles that he had his portrait painted with them milling about him. And, of course, Queen Victoria and the Prince Consort kept many of this breed.

Beagles have varied in size for a long time, the 'pocket' Beagle standing not more than 10 inches at the shoulder, though such small hounds have never been really numerous. Many packs have hunted with hounds measuring 12 or 13

*The Foxhound (far left) is the largest of the three breeds. Left: the Beagle makes a good pet Below: a fox hunt*

inches, however, and those Masters whose country is rough and encompasses much ploughed land, dykes and ditches, prefer a larger hound measuring anything from 14 to 16 inches high. Beagles are hunted on foot, and consequently it is generally the smaller hounds that show the best sport. It is very hard work keeping up with a 15 inch or 16 inch hound.

Beagles are used to hunt hares, which tend to run in circles. Therefore those who enjoy watching hounds work have a better opportunity to do so with Beagles than many who follow Foxhounds.

*Harriers, which look similar to Foxhounds, are slightly smaller. They do not usually make very good house pets*

In appearance the Beagle is a fairly compact dog with legs of medium length. Strong bone, neat cat feet and well-let-down hocks are required, with straight front legs, a fairly long neck and a level back. The head is the Beagle's attraction, with a deep, square muzzle, brown, pleading eyes and long low-set leathers as the ears are called. What is referred to as a tail in other breeds is called a 'stern' in hunting jargon. The Beagle's stern is carried up, slightly sickle-shaped and never curved over the back, which is a very serious fault. The hair is short and smooth and glossy, and also very waterproof, an important point since hounds may be required to spend long hours hunting in all sorts of weather conditions.

In recent years the Beagle has achieved considerable popularity as a show dog and household companion. Its size, coat and pleasant disposition make the show Beagle a very suitable family dog providing it is sensibly managed and properly trained from puppyhood. Badly managed a Beagle can be wilful and headstrong as is often the case with pack hounds, but when well disciplined it makes a good pet. All hounds have a tendency to wander and only those owning well-fenced gardens should keep them. Beagles are very intelligent and quick to learn. They can be obstinate, but once they grasp what they have to do, they never forget.

The Beagle, although affectionate and attached to its family, will never show that constant desire for attention that some of the toy breeds display. The Beagle has its own ways of finding satisfaction; this is through its inquisitive and questing nature. So although it will enjoy being patted and told it is a 'good dog', your Beagle will retain an independence not found in the majority of breeds.

As a family pet the Beagle must be well controlled. It will take advantage of human weakness if it is given the chance. If allowed to do as it likes, on occasion it will trade on this and soon will be the master of the household. The trouble springs partly from the irresistible appeal of the Beagle puppy even when it is being a nuisance and chewing up the telephone directory or one of the best cushions. However amusing the situation may appear to be, it is unwise to show your amusement, for the puppy is intelligent enough to realize it has made you laugh and so has reduced your annoyance.

What, then, are the essentials in training a Beagle to be a family pet? Firm handling is essential from the very start however young the dog. Remember the old saying that there are no bad dogs–only bad owners. If, when fully grown, your Beagle is something of a nuisance, then you, as its owner, are to blame. Being house-trained is the first step. The puppy must learn that it is only allowed to relieve itself outside the house. The puppy must be put out of doors and not allowed to come in until it has relieved itself. This should be first thing in the morning, last thing at night, after a meal and when it wakes up from a sleep in the daytime.

This means that the owner, too, must go outside to supervise. So it is advisable to acquire your Beagle in the spring or summer, when going outside is not likely to be such an ordeal as it is in cold weather. Remember that you may be half an hour in the garden waiting for Nature to take its course.

Inside the house the puppy must never be allowed to roam about unsupervised. So when you are busy, your pet must be

# Breed Standard: the Beagle

## GENERAL APPEARANCE
The Beagle is a compactly built hound without any coarseness, and it should convey the impression of great stamina and activity.

## HEAD AND SKULL
The head should be of a fair length and powerful, but without being coarse. The skull is domed, moderately wide with an indication of peak. The stop should be well defined, the muzzle not snipy and the lips well flewed. The nose should be black and broad, and the nostrils should be well expanded.

## EYES
The eyes should be brown, dark hazel or hazel, with a mild expression, and they should not deep set or bulgy.

## EARS
The ears should be long, set on low and fine in texture. They should hang in a graceful fold close to the cheek.

## NECK
The neck of the Beagle should be moderately long and slightly arched, and the throat should show some dewlap.

## FOREQUARTERS
The shoulders should be clean and slightly sloping. The forelegs should be quite straight, of good substance and well rounded in bone.

## BODY
The body should be short between the couplings and well let down in the chest. The ribs should be fairly well sprung and well ribbed up. The loins should be powerful and should not be tucked up.

## HINDQUARTERS
The hindquarters of the Beagle should be very muscular about the thighs. The stifles and hocks should be well bent and the hocks should be well let down.

## FEET
The feet should be round, well knuckled up, and strongly padded.

## TAIL
The tail should be of moderate length, set on high, and carried gaily, but should never be curled over the back.

## COAT
For the Smooth variety, the coat should be smooth, very dense and not too fine or short and for the Rough variety, the coat should be very dense and wiry.

## COLOUR
Any recognized hound colour.

## SIZE
Desirable height is 13 to 16 inches. Maximum height in USA is 15 inches.

---

put somewhere where it can be left unwatched—in a pen in the garage, or the indoor lavatory or out-house. Line the floor with newspaper.

The Harrier is not unlike the Beagle in many respects, though in general it resembles the Foxhound even more closely, being rangier in build, longer in the head and usually has a longer neck. Foxhounds and Harriers have been interbred to some extent, hence the similar appearance. There are few pure Harriers left today.

In height the Harrier measures anything from 16 to 21 inches at the shoulder. The hunting characteristics of the Harrier differ from those of the Beagle or Foxhound, the latter being too fast to provide good sport since the poor hare has little chance of escape. With a slower pursuer the hare will wind, double back, circle, dive through hedgerows, and with every possible trick endeavour to elude the pack—and it often succeeds. It is fascinating to watch hounds on the scent, noses down, sterns waving and to hear their 'music' as they dash away. Then they may halt, puzzle out a line, running to and fro, not uttering a sound as they quarter the ground until suddenly one hound gets the scent, gives tongue with the peculiar deep-throated, bell-like tone and away goes the pack again with the followers panting along behind.

Harriers are sometimes hunted on foot and sometimes on horseback, even when hunting the hare. They have also been used for fox-hunting. They do not normally make good pets.

Foxhounds are the largest of the family, averaging 24 inches at the shoulder, with bitches an inch or two less. Apart from size they differ little from Harriers in structure. All the family share the accepted hound colours. A popular combination is tri-colour, which is a white background, marked with patches of black and tan, or tan, lemon and white. Lemon pied is also a popular colour. This is a white hound, marked with tan or pale yellowish patches or flecks. A hound whose white portions are 'freckled' with yellow or blue spots is known as 'mottled'.

Beagles, harriers or foxhounds maintained for hunting are kept in packs. The size of the pack, and the number of hounds that are hunted, depends upon a variety of circumstances, and these include financial considerations and also whether the Master hunts more than once a week. Hare and foxhounds are always counted in couples, and some hunts take out their dog pack separately from the bitch pack.

A certain amount of tradition is connected with hunting, and there are rules that followers must obey. Although the field is normally composed largely of

mounted riders when hunting the fox, there are always a few faithful sportsmen known as the 'foot-sloggers', staunch supporters who can often be relied upon to give the first 'view holloa' when a fox has broken cover. Foxhounds run fast when on the scent, however, and the followers on foot are unlikely to see much of the hunt, unlike the Beaglers.

Most hunts breed their own replacements for the pack and it is customary to put promising hound puppies 'out to walk' with local hunt subscribers and farmers. This not only cuts down the cost of rearing but helps to separate the growing youngsters at a time when puppies are susceptible to epidemics or infections.

The puppies are called in at about the same time as a Puppy Show is organized and prizes awarded to the best dogs. As the manner in which the puppies have been 'walked', that is fed, exercised and trained, plays a part in impressing the judges, there is keen competition and the 'walkers' are encouraged to give the young hounds special care throughout their growth period.

Hound puppies are lively, noisy, destructive and, like all young dogs, attractive, but they are really too boisterous for the average household and there must be many families who see them go off to join the pack without many regrets no matter how great an attachment has sprung up between them. Foxhounds often have to be drafted because, for one reason or another, they do not reach the high standards required by the Masters of Hounds, but regretfully it is rare for one to find a home as a pet and pack rejects are usually destroyed.

Anyone who 'walks' hound puppies is advised not to make pets of them, since it is hard for such animals to return to pack life. The young hounds need good food, kind handling and scrupulously clean quarters, but the important thing is to accustom them to livestock.

Pack hounds inevitably find their way leading through farmlands and even farm yards since one never knows the route the fox will decide to take. A 'riot' amongst poultry or sheep or a chance encounter with someone's pet cat or dog must at all costs be avoided, and this is where early training can help young hounds to adjust to pack discipline.

Pack hounds are trencher fed—not for them the individual dish of the house pet. The food is poured into huge troughs and the pack held up at the gate by a hunt servant or kennelman. The leaner hounds are let in first and directly they have helped themselves, the rest may follow.

The standard hound food is horse flesh mixed with a sticky mush made of cooked oatmeal and called 'pudding'. Hounds are not fed the day before they are to hunt.

# The Bloodhound

THE lugubrious expression of the Bloodhound has earned the breed a regular place in cartoons, jokes and advertisements which detract from the breed's true qualities. Even among dogs, whose sense of smell is perhaps one million times better developed than our own, the breed is quite outstanding in its ability to detect and to follow the most difficult of trails. In fact, its accuracy is legendary, and it can be relied upon to such an extent that the evidence of a Bloodhound has been accepted in court cases. Thus the breed has earned the respect and admiration of all who are interested in the work of hounds, and it is this ability which allows the breed to retain its place as a working dog.

The breed lays claim to an ancient and aristocratic lineage; the very name refers, not as is popularly supposed, to a savage nature, but to the breed's aristocratic 'blood' in the same sense that blood or thoroughbred horses are differentiated from their more common counterparts. The history of the breed can be traced back to the Mediterranean countries of Egypt, Greece and Italy before the birth of Christ, and it is the ancestor of all the hounds. References to and descriptions of a lugubrious hound with an unusually good scenting ability are to be found in the works of such authors as Claudius Aelianus in his famous *History of Animals*, in the third century AD, and these strongly resemble the modern Bloodhound. The dog he describes was first brought to Europe from Constantinople and it became very popular with hunters. By the twelfth century, the breed had become well established in the courts of barons and kings in Europe, as well as in the monastic establishments of the bishops. They became an important part of medieval monastery life. It is very likely that the black St Hubert hounds living in Hubert's Abbey in the Ardennes were, in fact, Bloodhounds.

The Bloodhound was probably introduced into Britain at the time of the Norman Conquest. The breed was valued by the sporting gentry, to whose slow and patient methods of hunting its qualities were ideally suited. When fox-hunting became popular and with it the need for greater speed and dash than the Bloodhound possessed, its position was lost to breeds of hounds specially developed for the new sport, and by the middle of the nineteenth century, this ancient breed was very nearly extinct. It was, perhaps, saved from extinction and certainly its popularity was revived by the growing popularity of dog shows which provided enthusiasts of the breed with a means of introducing it to a wider public, able to recognize and respect its inherent qualities as a hunting dog. However, its main disadvantage when kept solely as a pet is this very hunting instinct that the breeders were to strive so hard to retain when they attempted to make the breed more popular. It will always need something to do and if a scent is picked up, it will be very difficult to dissuade a Bloodhound not to trail it.

Although these breeders were interested in the breed as a show dog, they were careful not to lose its traditional qualities and were quick to seize any opportunity to demonstrate its scenting ability. Some breeders, notably Lord Wolverton in Savernake Forest, returned to the slow, traditional pattern of hunting deer. Lord Wolverton's pack was admired and described by Whyte-Melville as 'of the finest breed, stand seven or eight and twenty inches, with limbs and frames proportioned to so gigantic a stature. Their heads are magnificent, solemn, sagacious eyes, pendant jowls, and flapping ears that brush away the dew. . .' Their voices he describes as 'full, sonorous and musical. . .' and compares them favourably with 'the peal of an organ in a cathedral'.

The modern Standard of the breed stresses the importance of retaining the breed's ancient points and the characteristics of those dogs which hunt together by scent. The skin should be thin and loose, particularly on the head, where it hangs in deep folds. While recognizing that much of the breed's typical expression and appearance is derived from this feature it must also be realized that it may contribute to some of the eye troubles to which the breed is prone. Bloodhounds, along with some other large breeds such as Great Danes, are also more likely to die from an infection such as distemper, than some of the terrier breeds, so it is extremely important to ensure immunity by having your puppy vaccinated.

Modern Bloodhounds are slightly smaller than those described by Melville, ranging from 23 to 27 inches. The average height of dogs is 26 inches and of bitches 24 inches, though large rather than small hounds are still preferred, providing that their essential quality is not thereby lost. An adult hound may attain a weight of over 110 lb and this great size, combined

*The Bloodhound has gained a worldwide reputation for its ability to detect and follow an extremely faint scent trail*

with its desire to hunt in order to exercise its remarkable qualities, means that the breed needs a very great deal of free and vigorous exercise. Certainly, the Bloodhound should not be the choice as a pet of someone of a sedentary nature, or of those living in a confined urban situation. It is certainly not to be recommended for flat life.

The dog's expression is described as noble and dignified. Traditionally, the breed was used to follow and seek out quarry and not to attack it. It is not now in general use as a police dog but it has been widely used in the USA on long and difficult trails. One famous dog successfully tracked a wanted criminal on a line some 105 hours cold. It has also worked as a police and army dog in Britain. Its attitude towards children and other animals is fatherly and gentle.

The conscientious owner will see to it that his Bloodhound is bathed at least every three months. If a dog is to be entered for a show, do not bath it in the week before the event as bathing takes some bloom out of the coat.

Any dog which is required to follow a quarry must be strong and active and the Bloodhound should be physically capable of undertaking this traditional role. It must therefore have sound legs with strong, well-knuckled feet. Forelegs should be straight and set in muscular and well-laid shoulders, and its hind quarters too, should be muscular with well-bent stifles. Back and loins should be strong, and its general appearance should be one of great strength, and its movement elastic, swinging and free.

One of the bonuses the Bloodhound owner can claim as a result of his choice of breed is that he can enter the dog for Field Trials. Not only does this bring an added interest to the dog lover's life; it is a way of forming new friendships among the Field Trial fraternity and of improving one's knowledge of hound breeds. Once a puppy has been shown the way to hunt – and this calls for thorough training involving time and energy – then it can be trained further with a number of possibilities in view. Competing at Field Trials is perhaps the most common of these possibilities. But the Bloodhound is also a dog in considerable demand to do a job of work, perhaps for the police, where its extremely acute sense of smell can be put to good use. Thirdly, your dog can be trained to hunt man just for the fun of it. Being an unaggressive breed there is no danger of the human quarry being attacked, as there might be with some other breeds. The Bloodhound is satisfied with the tracking and finding alone. When exercising your dog, remember that it will enjoy time off the lead, when it can wander freely after scents.

The first steps of puppy training are connected with the dog's mealtimes. Allow him to smell and taste the food in his dish, then remove it out of sight, hiding it behind some object. Do not distract the puppy until he has found the food and eaten it. If he catches sight of where you have hidden the food it does not matter; the next day a different hiding place can be chosen and this time it should be hidden from the puppy's gaze. Increase the distance at which you hide the food. It may happen that you increase the distance too much, causing the puppy to lose interest. Then lead him quietly to the hiding place. Should the puppy be out of sorts the the training game that day can be omitted, because loss of appetite takes away the incentive for seeking out the food.

When the game is fully understood by the puppy who is showing obvious enjoyment, introduce some hindrances or distractions. For under working conditions such hindrances will be commonplace, and the dog must learn to ignore them. They can consist of noise – people clapping hands, a transistor radio blaring – or an obstacle such as a low fence, or a barrier with a door in it some distance away from the scent line. At this stage of the training the owner should start using voice signals that will be used when the dog is fully trained and is 'working'. The voice should express confidence and should be clear and loud, whether you are directing the puppy where to go, cheering him on or rating him for some misdemeanour. Later the hunting horn can be used; the straight type, some ten inches long and made of copper, is the one generally bought for this purpose. The calls differ in the length of note and the pauses between the notes. You can either adopt the horn signals of a professional or make up your own.

Later, a butterfly type of harness made of webbing should be put on the puppy (the fully trained working dog will wear one of soft leather), for when competing or working, a harness is obligatory. A lightweight lead to the harness will also be needed, and this will give the owner control over the animal which in time comes to be exercised more and more.

Membership of the Bloodhound Club will help to provide the owner with advice on further training to help the dog reach competition level.

Perhaps because of the breed's great size and its need for vigorous exercise it does not enjoy great popularity, but for prospective owners who can accommodate these features, the Bloodhound's loyal, mild and affectionate nature will make it a good – although not the most jovial – companion.

# Breed Standard: the Bloodhound

## CHARACTERISTICS
**Possesses markedly every point of those dogs which hunt together by scent (Sagaces). Very powerful, standing over more ground than is usual with hounds of other breeds. Skin is thin and extremely loose, especially round the head and neck. Affectionate, neither quarrelsome with companions nor with other dogs; somewhat reserved and sensitive.**

## GENERAL APPEARANCE
**Expression is solemn and dignified. Elastic, swinging gait; the stern carried high.**

## HEAD AND SKULL
**The skull is long and narrow, with the occipital peak very pronounced. The brows are not prominent although, owing to the deep-set eyes, they may seem so. The foreface is long, deep and of even width throughout. Skin loose, falling into pendulous ridges and folds when head is carried low. Nostrils large and open. The dewlap is very pronounced.**

## MOUTH
**A scissor bite with the inner faces of the upper incisors touching the outer faces of the lower incisors.**

## EYES
**Deeply sunk in the orbits, the lids assuming a lozenge or diamond shape. Colour corresponds to general colour of the animal, varying from deep hazel to yellow.**

## EARS
**Thin and soft to the touch, extremely long, set on very low and falling in graceful folds.**

## NECK
**Should be long.**

## FOREQUARTERS
**The shoulders muscular and well sloped backwards. The forelegs straight, large and round in bone, with elbows squarely set. Strong pasterns.**

## HINDQUARTERS
**The thighs and second thighs (gaskins) are very muscular, the hocks well bent and squarely set.**

## FEET
**Should be strong and well knuckled up.**

## BODY
**Ribs well sprung; chest well let down between forelegs. Back and loins strong.**

## TAIL
**Long, thick and tapering, with some hair underneath. Carried high but not curled over the back.**

## COLOUR
**Black and tan, liver and tan (red and tan) and red, sometimes interspersed with lighter hair.**

## WEIGHT AND SIZE
**Average height for dogs: 26 inches; bitches: 24 inches. Average weight: between 80 and 90 lb.**

# Coonhounds

THE Coonhound is an entirely American development superbly bred for a specialised operation–the hunting by day or night of racoons. It is a hound of mixed blood compounded of foxhound and bloodhound strains and it can therefore trace its ancestry back to the famous French hounds bred by St Hubert, some of which were brought to England by William the Conqueror in 1066 and who were the forebears of the foxhounds brought to America in 1650. The bloodhound came to the United States a little over a century ago and it is to this breed that the 'cooner' owes his superb scenting power. The black-and-tan Virginian Foxhound is its immediate ancestor and the AKC recognised the black-and-tan Coonhound as a pure breed in 1945.

The racoon feeds on the ground and the Coonhound hunts on its foot scent. The hound is not fast but is very persistent. He does not give tongue while trailing and the hunt may last for hours before the racoon takes refuge in a tree. Then, and then only, does the cooner give tongue, his deep bark telling the hunters that it is time to move in for the kill.

# Breed Standard: the Coonhound

## GENERAL CHARACTERISTICS
The black-and-tan Coonhound is fundamentally a working dog, capable of withstanding the rigours of winter, the heat of summer and the difficult terrain over which he is called to work. Judges are asked by the club sponsoring the breed to place great emphasis upon these facts when evaluating the merits of the dog. The general impression should be that of power, agility and alertness. His expression should be alert, friendly, eager and aggressive. He should immediately impress with his ability to cover the ground with powerful rhythmic strides.

## HEAD
The head is cleanly modelled with a medium stop and should measure 9–10 inches in males and 8–9 inches in females. Viewed from the profile the line of the skull is in an almost parallel plane to the foreface or muzzle. The skin should be devoid of folds or excessive dewlap. The flews should be well developed with typical hound appearance. Nostrils well open and always black. The skull of the Coonhound should tend towards an oval outline.

## EYES
Should be round and not deeply set; hazel to dark brown in colour.

## EARS
Low-set and well back, hanging in a number of graceful folds and extending well beyond the tip of the nose.

## BODY
The back is level with a slope from withers to rump, the forelegs straight and the feet catlike. The quarters must be muscular and the tail set slightly below the level of the backline and carried free. The stride of this breed is easy and powerful and shows plenty of reach in front and thrust behind.

## COAT
Short and dense.

## COLOUR
Coal black with the markings above the eyes, the sides of the muzzle, chest, legs and breeching being a rich tan. There are black pencil markings on the toes.

## SIZE
Measured at the shoulders, the size for dogs should be 25 inches to 27 inches; for bitches, 23 inches to 25 inches. The height should be in proportion to the general conformation so that the dog appears neither leggy nor close to the ground. Dogs which are oversized should not be penalized when general soundness and proportion are both favourable.

## FAULTS
Judges should penalize undersize, elbows out at shoulder, splay feet, lack of depth in chest, a sway or roach back; yellow or light eyes, shyness or nervousness. White on the body is highly undesirable.

# The Dachshund

THE Dachshund has for so long been familiar to people in the UK and USA as a family pet and as the canine butt of cartoonists, that it tends to be taken for granted. Little thought has been given, for example, to its origins, and precisely when the breed materialized is uncertain. Some claim that it dates back as far as ancient Egypt, pointing to possible replicas of the breed on royal monuments. Others, however, choose a much later date, tracing the Dachshund's origins as a definite breed to the sixteenth century. German woodcuts of that time depict a similar type of dog, and in the following century copper plates confirm the breed's role as a badger fighter.

Whatever the truth, it should be remembered that until about a hundred years ago all dogs were bred, more or less, for a specific purpose: gundogs for hunting, hounds and terriers to kill vermin and toy

*Above, right: a fine example of the Longhair Miniature Dachshund; centre: the Standard Wirehair Dachshund; below: the Standard Smooth Black and Tan. Dachshunds originally hunted badgers*

dogs as companions. This particular one was developed to deal with the local badger plague, but, as happened with most other breeds, the German Dachshund was the product of trial and error.

Whatever the purpose for which it was needed, a male which had proved itself particularly adept at its job would be mated to a large number of bitches within a given locality. The features which made it outstanding were thus passed on, until breeders came to realize that certain points were essential for the specific task entailed. In this manner a type, rather than a breed, gradually evolved, and it would be crossed with dogs of other types that had also proved their worth. In the case of the Dachshund outside blood ceased to be introduced only when breeders realized that it was sufficiently skilled in the purpose for which it had been developed – badger digging – and that no other type had anything new to offer that development.

In the course of the evolution of the Dachshund, the French Bracke, the German Pinscher and the eighteenth-century Basset Hound (a rather different dog then) all played their part.

Dachshunds first came to Britain in about 1845, introduced by Albert, the Prince Consort, who imported several from Prince Edward of Saxe-Weimar. Queen Victoria and Edward VII kept a number in the Royal Kennels. The breed is one of the most popular in Britain and likely to increase in favour. The USA knew the Dachshund long before dog shows or Stud Books were introduced and several were entered in the AKC Stud Book in 1885. Although lacking badgers or other animals suitable for Dachshunds to hunt, field trials were introduced in 1935 and run under AKC rules, thus encouraging the original instincts of the breed.

In both countries, the breed has had its successes and reverses. World War One in Britain led to the unreasoning destruction of all things German, but fortunately World War Two had a far less disastrous result and the Dachshund soon regained its popularity. In the USA the breed also lost ground during the wars, but under the auspices of the Dachshund Club of America it has since reached a high place in both public esteem and AKC registrations.

There are, in fact, six distinct breeds of Dachshund. They are identified by coat type – Smooth-haired, Long-haired and Wire-haired – each in a Standard and a Miniature size.

There have always been Smooths and Longhairs during the known history of the breed, with a preponderence of the former. At one time they could be bred together, in Germany and still later in Britain. Germany outlawed this practice in 1924 but through Longhairs being born to Smooth parents, which presumably had some longhair ancestry, the longhair was established in Britain, together with imports from its native land. Wirehairs are believed to be the result of eighteenth-century crosses of Smooths with Dandie Dinmont Terriers and Schnauzers. They were very much the poor relation in Germany as recently as 1888 when only three were registered with the then newly formed Teckel Klub. By 1948 more than 2,000 were being registered annually with that organization.

The Miniatures are a comparatively recent innovation. Like their larger relatives, they were brought into being for a purpose. Towards the end of the nineteenth century, German sportsmen recognized the need for a breed capable of going to ground after small quarry such as rabbits. It was after World War Two that Miniatures were introduced into Britain. Although a Standard Dachshund may weigh up to 25 lb, the Miniature is expected to weigh not more than 11 lb. In the USA the Miniatures are not classified separately, but provision is made in shows for an open

## Breed Standard: the Dachshund

**GENERAL CHARACTERISTICS**
The long-haired and short-haired Dachshunds are old, well fixed varieties, but into the wire-haired Dachshund other blood has been introduced. Nevertheless, care has been taken to keep this variety in conformity to the true Dachshund type. Low to ground, short-legged, long-bodied but with compact figure and robust muscular development, the breed carries its head boldly and with confidence and has an intelligent facial expression. A Dachshund should be clever, lively and courageous to the point of rashness, persevering in his work both above and below ground. His build and disposition qualify him for hunting game below ground.

**HEAD AND SKULL**
Long and uniformly tapered. The stop not pronounced, the skull slightly arched in profile. The jaw should be strong.

**EYES**
Medium in size and set obliquely.

**MOUTH**
Teeth well fitted with scissors bite.

**NECK**
Sufficiently long, muscular and clean with no dewlap. Carried well up and forward.

**EARS**
Broad, of moderate length and well rounded. High and well set on.

**BODY**
Long and muscular, the line of the back slightly depressed at the shoulders and slightly arched over the loin.

**FEET**
The front feet should be full, broad and close-knit, the hind feet being smaller and narrower.

**TAIL**
The tail should be set on fairly high and should be strong and tapering.

**COAT**
There are three coat types. Smooth or short-haired: short, dense and glossy. Wire-haired: hard with a good undercoat. Long-haired: the hair resembles that of an Irish Setter. The greatest length is on the tail.

**COLOUR**
Any colour other than white: red, black-and-tan, chocolate-and-tan and dapple. In chocolate and dapples, the nose may be either brown or flesh-coloured.

**WEIGHT AND SIZE**
Dogs not to exceed 25 lb, bitches 23 lb. Miniatures in all three coats must conform to the Standard except for size. In Britain, a Miniature should not weigh more than 11 lb. The USA Standard permits Miniatures of under 9 lb and twelve months old or over to compete in shows as Miniatures; there is no separate classification.

class division for dogs under 9 lb and twelve months old or under, permitting winners to compete for championship points in each coat variety.

Apart from these variations in coat and size, Dachshunds come in an attractive range of colours. Red, black and tan, and chocolate and tan are all popular colours, but possibly the most fascinating, and

certainly the most unusual, is the type of coat marking known as dapple. There are three different forms of dapple: silver, chocolate and red. The first is shown as a ground colour of silver-grey, with patches

*The Longhair Dachshund is full of character, quick in attack and defence, and very obedient and faithful*

of black. The basic colour of the second type is provided by an intermixture of chocolate and white hairs, with patches of solid chocolate, and the third is a combination of red and white hairs, with red patches.

A detailed description of the Dachshund – a universally popular breed of long standing – is surely unnecessary, but there can be a world of difference between the reality and the ideal. The regrettably overindulged pet Dachshund is far removed from the type of dog which breeders had in mind when aiming to produce improved representatives of the breed.

The Kennel Club Breed Standards – a counsel of perfection – require all types of Dachshund to be 'long and low' with a 'compact and well-muscled body . . . but despite its short legs not crippled, cloddy or clumsy, with bold, defiant head carriage and intelligent expression.'

Such an appearance immediately recalls

*The Wirehair is believed to be the result of eighteenth-century crosses of Smooths with Dandie Dinmonts and Schnauzers*

the original purpose for which the Dachshund was bred. Lowness so that it might easily go to earth, and length for manoeuvrability below ground, were important. Only if compact and well muscled could it gain an advantage over its adversary, bearing in mind that death was the only outcome for a dog incapable of doing its job. Bold, defiant head carriage is often indicative of well-laid shoulders, another essential for the work in hand.

Although the Kennel Club, in its Breed Standards, uses different wording for the various coat characteristics, the Dachshund is basically described as 'first and foremost a sporting dog'. The Smooth is 'remarkably versatile . . . equally adept as a house pet; its smooth, close coat . . . impervious to rain and mud.' The Longhair is 'full of character, quick in attack and defence, faithful when properly brought up and very obedient . . . It has the reputation of being extraordinarily intelligent and easy to train.' The Wire is 'clever, lively, courageous to the point of rashness, sagacious and obedient.'

In short, the Dachshund, in spite of its

sporting past, is an ideal family companion. Yet it is not a pet best suited to life of indolence. Chasing the cat away i order to eat its food, then making sure tha nobody else steals the meal is not what intended as 'quick in attack and defence Unfortunately, this is the fate of many a p Dachshund, as is evident from its port shape even when young. To indulge th dog in this manner is unnecessary an unkind, and it is certainly not the treatmer recommended by those who drew up th Breed Standards when they described th Dachshund in the following terms: 'In th field of sport it is unequalled, combinin the scenting powers of a Foxhound wit unflinching courage, and will go to groun to fox, otter or badger . . . Its build an temperament fit it to hunt quarry bot above and below ground; its eagernes keen sight and hearing and its sonorou bark make it especially suitable for track ing . . . In following a trail its highl developed sense of smell stands it in goo stead . . .'

The Dachshund is not a pack anima but prefers the company of people or small number of its own kind. For thi reason it adapts better to family life tha do many hound breeds. (Though by th very nature of its underground work, i which certain terrier traits are required i addition to scenting ability, it is somethin of an odd man out in the hound group. It will not accept all and sundry as friends reserving judgment until it knows then better – an aloof attitude which gives mistaken impression of timidity to thos not well acquainted with the breed. Onc accepted as a friend, however, you are friend for life. Moreover, this seemingl aloof air makes the Dachshund an out standing house dog, with loud and earl notice being given of the arrival of an stranger.

Town life and small gardens may appea to be restrictions that are impossible t reconcile with the active needs of th Dachshund, but this is not necessarily th case, provided an intelligent view is take and, if need be, a satisfactory compromis worked out. Thus a careful check must b kept on feeding, both with regard t ingredients and quantities, so that the do remains well covered but not in flabb condition. Sufficient exercise must b guaranteed, whether in the park or in th street, not only as a general conditione but also in order to provide variety an interest in the dog's life, enabling it t utilize the intelligence developed over man generations. Any Dachshund, whethe Standard or Miniature, can adapt from sporting past to a more sedate present But do not forget that it is essentially sporting dog, not a toy, and that it mus be given every opportunity to lead a lif free from the evils of over-indulgence.

# Elkhound and Finnish Spitz

INDEPENDENT, hardy, clean cut and handsome is a fitting description of both the Elkhound and the Finnish Spitz. A more correct name for the Elkhound is Elghund, which literally means 'moose dog'. It is not strictly a hound breed although it is classified as such in Britain. It originates from Norway and in the USA it is called the Norwegian Elkhound. This breed is not the result of cross-breeding, but has evolved naturally to suit its environment.

Exclusively a working breed until comparatively recent times, the job from which it took its name, elk (moose) hunting, requires two different approaches. The 'loshund', running free, locates the elk by scent, and by barking guides the

*The ancestors of the Finnish Spitz were hunting companions and guard dogs*

hunter to where it has the quarry at bay so that it may then be shot; the 'bandhund', on the other hand, is kept by the hunter on a long leash, and after trailing the elk is not required further. It is a dangerous operation because of the elk's great stamina and strength, qualities the Elkhound must match in order to first find its target and then keep free of the massive antlers and fast-flying hooves. The Elkhound's sense of smell is so acute that it can detect the presence of an elk two or three miles away.

Other tasks have also been expected of the Elkhound in the past, notably that of a guard dog for livestock and people against bears and wolves. In his book on the breed, Olav Wallo describes the night of February 14th, 1842 in southern Norway as 'Wolf Night', following the slaughter of 27 wolves by an Elkhound, Fanorok the Fearless, and several of his fellow Elkhounds. Bird hunting is another natural tendency of the Elkhound. It is both an exceptionally versatile breed as well as an extremely brave one.

One of the first impressions a good Elkhound gives is of great strength and firm, well-muscled solidity, far more than is suggested by its size, which is around $20\frac{1}{2}$ inches at the shoulder for dogs, and slightly less for bitches. Weight for a dog should be 50 lb and 43 lb for a bitch.

## Breed Standard: the Elkhound

**CHARACTERISTICS**
The Elkhound is a hardy sporting dog of Nordic type and of a bold and virile nature. Its disposition should be friendly and intelligent.

**GENERAL APPEARANCE**
It has a compact and proportionately short body, a coat thick and abundant but not bristling, and prick ears; tail tightly curled over back.

**HEAD AND SKULL**
Broad between the ears; the forehead and back of the head are slightly arched with a clearly marked but not large stop. Muzzle moderately long, broader at the base and gradually tapering – whether seen from above or from the side – but not pointed; bridge of the nose straight, jaw strong with lips tightly closed.

**EYES**
Not prominent, in colour brown and as dark as possible, giving a frank, fearless and friendly expression.

**EARS**
Set high, firm and upstanding, height slightly greater than their width at the base and pointed.

**NECK**
Of medium length, firm and muscular.

**FOREQUARTERS**
Legs firm, straight and powerful with good bone; elbows closely set on.

**BODY**
Short in the couplings; back wide and straight from neck to stern; chest wide and deep with well-rounded ribs; loins muscular; stomach very little drawn up.

**HINDQUARTERS**
Legs straight at the hock and when viewed from behind. There should be no dewclaws on the hind-legs.

**FEET**
Compact, oval in shape and not turned outwards; toes tightly closed; toe-nails firm and strong.

**TAIL**
Set high, tightly curled over the back but not carried on either side; hair thick and close.

**COAT**
Thick, abundant, coarse and weather-resistant; short on the head and on the front of the legs; longest on the chest, neck, buttocks, behind the forelegs and on the underside of the tail.

**COLOUR**
Grey, of various shades with black tips to the long outer coat; lighter on the chest, stomach, legs, and the underside of the tail.

**WEIGHT AND SIZE**
For dogs, the height at the shoulder is about $20\frac{1}{2}$ inches, and for bitches, about $18\frac{1}{2}$ inches. Weight approximately 50 lb and 43 lb respectively.

It has a keen and alert expression, which strongly suggests its great courage and stamina. Another distinctive feature is its colouring. This can be different shades of grey with each hair black-tipped; it is darker on the body and head, with a lighter coloured harness effect and lighter legs, breeching and tail. The tail is conspicuous, being carried in a double curl on the back rather than to either side. The hair on the tail is thick and dense, whereas on the body it is coarser and longer, especially on the chest, forelegs and buttocks.

The Elkhound is not a dog which can be recommended for people who want slavish, fawning devotion, but it is ideal for those who lead the sort of life that will give rein to the breed's natural energetic activity and curiosity, and who want an innately clean animal and one which is strong enough to prove it means business as a guard, though only when it is really necessary. The breed is very bold and aggressive and is a fierce barker. It will be devoted both to its master and to the hunt at which it excels. This dog makes a great friend and is both loyal and trustworthy. It learns quickly, provided it has firm training. Its strong will requires an equally strong-willed owner who knows how to train dogs well and who can give the Elkhound puppy the constant supervision it needs if it is to become an obedient adult.

Given a sensible diet and sufficient exercise, the Elkhound remains in good health for the whole of its long life. But it is inclined to put on excess weight if kept in any other way. So if you choose an Elkhound as a companion, be kind and do not let this happen. There is no sight more pathetic than a potentially active dog weighed down by fat.

The coat requires a minimum of attention except when moulting; the sooner the old hair can be removed at this time, the faster a new coat will take its place. Again a sensible diet – any good breeder will supply details when selling a puppy – counts for much in keeping the coat in pristine condition. The Elkhound's coat should be smooth, hard and very dense.

Being also a member of the spitz group, the Finnish Spitz has many features broadly similar to the Elkhound: small erect ears on a wedge-shaped head, an overall square build, great activity and independence of character. But the Finkie, as it is often called, is more lightly built. It sports a slightly longer, but still weather-resistant, coat of shades varying from either brilliant red or bright reddish brown, to brilliant gold or yellowish-red, and its expression is somewhat more penetrating. Dogs measure about 17½ inches at the shoulder, bitches about 15½ inches.

As a working dog, its duties are very similar to those of the Elkhound, except that the quarry is mostly game birds. Hunting is carried out in forests where the dog uses both scent and sight to track its quarry and then, having located the target, drives it up into the branches of a tree. By barking the Finnish Spitz lets its master know its whereabouts, at the same time keeping the attention of bird (or squirrel) riveted on the dog. That way the hunter's arrival is unnoticed and makes for a quick despatch of the prey.

This has been the Finkie's duty for centuries in Finland and Lapland. But at the end of the last century it looked as though the breed might become extinct in pure form, since many crosses took place with other breeds. By getting together a nucleus of pure-bred animals and continuing to use it for hunting, Finnish sportsmen not only saved the breed but developed its sporting instincts still further. Many imports to America and Britain have been made, the first in 1927 and, because the working side is still emphasized in its native land, present-day Finnish Spitz here have lost nothing of their keenness for hunting.

While the Elkhound and the Finnish Spitz have a dedicated following, numbers remain low, a rather surprising fact considering the beauty and intelligence of these Northern breeds. Affectionate and easily trained, both breeds are good with children and it is to be hoped that, before too long, their excellent qualitie come to be more fully appreciated to pre vent any possibility of their becomin rarer or even extinct.

A coat that is easy to care for, clea habits and a suspicion of strangers he make the Finnish Spitz an ideal hous dog. It is remarkably free from the usua canine odour. It is a very adaptable do and its love of children makes it an idea family pet. It is an extremely handsom and loyal dog too. Because barking is pa of their working duty, care must be exe cised in rearing puppies not to let th trait get out of hand. If the puppies ar brought up to appreciate there are goo causes for barking but that not everythin is a 'good cause', no difficulty should b experienced. As a puppy the Finnish Spit is exceptionally lively and independent, s it must be handled gently but firmly i its rare intelligence is to be fully appre ciated. Being natural, physically unexag gerated breeds, Elkhounds and Finnis Spitz are comparatively straightforwar to breed where whelping and rearing ar concerned. They are also very hardy ani mals, and this combined with their hand some appearance and sporting nature makes these breeds companions wel worth owning.

*Elkhounds are the dogs of the Norwegian Vikings, used for hunting elk and moose*

# Irish Wolfhound and Deerhound

DARWIN once said of the whole canine race, 'We shall probably never be able to ascertain their origin with certainty'. So it is not surprising that attempting to trace the origins of individual breeds is so difficult. In the case of the Irish Wolfhound and the Deerhound, there is no doubt that both breeds share a common ancestry. Their purpose in life was similar: coursing. The Irish Wolfhound was the bane of wolves, and the Deerhound of Scotland's magnificent red deer.

There are many ancient descriptions of the Irish Wolfhound, which is Ireland's greyhound. All portray the same dog that today is officially described as 'of great size and commanding appearance, very muscular, strongly though gracefully built, movements easy and active'. It is the tallest and possibly the most powerful of dogs, standing at least 31 inches at the shoulder. The Irish Wolfhound is the great heroic dog of Ireland, with an ancient history which goes back even further than the establishment of that country. It is depicted in many stories, legends and paintings, which tell us that the dog was brought to Greece by the invading Celts in 279 BC. As far back as the second century AD, the Greek writer Flavius Arrianus, in his manual on coursing, gave four different methods of coursing the Wolfhound. All hold true today. There were two ways of slipping hounds from horseback after hired beaters or the horsemen themselves had evicted the quarry. One was to go on foot with beaters, and the other involved using other breeds to flush the pursued animal before slipping the hounds. For centuries the hunt has been an important part of life to many of the Irish, who hunted hares, wolves, deer and wild boar with equal enthusiasm. They used the same breed of dog to cope with them all.

Legend sets the Wolfhound apart. One story tells of the time when Queen Maive in Connacht and King Conor in Ulster each offered a vast sum for a Wolfhound, Ailbhe, said to be the envy of all Ireland. Deadlock resulted and the dog, Ailbhe, took the side of Ulster, only to have its head cut off while trying to overturn Queen Maive's chariot. Ailbhe's grip was so firm that even when dead it refused to release its hold on the chariot. In gratitude, Ulstermen named the place where this happened the Plain of Ailbhe. Such legends are many, and there are more about the bitch Bran than any other. Lough Bran is a memorial to her great deeds.

The Wolfhound's status may be gauged by the number given as presents to people of high rank. In 1200 AD Gelert, the dog which in Spencer's poem lost its life by saving its master's child from a wolf, was given by King John to Llewellyn, Prince of Wales. Much later in the same century, Edward I sent to Ireland for wolfhounds. Henry VIII and Elizabeth I followed the tradition, so did a King of Denmark, Cardinal Richelieu and countless others. There has even been a sonnet written to the Wolfhound by the great Spanish poet and playwright, Lope de Vega, in 1596.

No legends would have been created and no high status could have been achieved, had the Wolfhound not been an incomparable opponent of the much-feared wolf. But the last wolf in Ireland was reputedly killed by a pack of Wolfhounds at Myshall in 1786, so, although the legends have persisted, the Wolfhound's status has diminished since then. For quite some time, before the wolf and the elk (also hunted by Wolfhounds) disappeared in Ireland, its lack of numbers seemed to sound the death knell for the Wolfhound. They could only be used for lesser sports. By the beginning of the nineteenth century the breed had reached so low an ebb that one great dog, another Bran, was used to resurrect the Wolfhound. Recourse was also made to a similar breed, the Scottish Deerhound, which held sway as the great gazehound of Scotland, but whose quarry was the red deer.

Lighter in frame than the Wolfhound, the Deerhound, or the 'Royal Dog of Scotland', was none the less peerless at its task. The kernel of that occupation is well described in a book on deerstalking by Augustus Grimble where he says 'To see a good dog slipped at a deer is indeed a sight to remember. To watch him overtake and place himself alongside of a galloping stag and then to see him seize the foreleg, roll the stag over, shift his hold in a movement and fix his teeth in the throat, and kill quickly, is indeed a fine spectacle.' In fact, the Deerhound is capable of bringing down a Scottish deer

*Both the Scottish Deerhound (left) and the Irish Wolfhound (right) were originally used for coursing; the Deerhound for the red deer of Scotland and the Irish Wolfhound for wolves*

eighing about 250 pounds. It also has a ceen scent and is an excellent tracker.

The Deerhound has always been associated with medieval tales of chivalry, where knights in plumed helmets jousted for the hand of a lady, and where the old ideas of honour and courtly love dominated the life of the time. In those days men thought nothing of living and dying only for the glory and splendour of battle or a duel over some minor (to us) point of honour. The breed's history goes back to the early sixteenth century, and it was so greatly favoured by the Scottish chieftains that a brace of these hounds was considered as valuable as a nobleman. Minor battles were fought over this breed which was considered to be a great servant and friend of mankind: in one incident 160 men died following an altercation concerning the restoration of a stolen Deerhound to its owner. And, as with its Irish cousin, gifts were made of it, but only to the fortunate few.

With the break-up of the clan system in the mid-eighteenth century, the breed suffered a huge drop in popularity, but was restored to its previous position as a status symbol in about 1840. This was only after a great effort on the part of two men to save the breed. Technological progress had meant that in the early nineteenth century, improved sporting rifles made deer stalking possible without using dogs, whereas the old rifles had been too heavy, inaccurate and of insufficient range. The increased financial benefits to landowners of this mode of sport, as well as the changing emphasis in parts of Scotland towards agricultural use of land instead of giving it over to vast forests, robbed the Deerhound of the principal purpose of its life. In 1838 hardly more than a dozen pure representatives of the breed were said to exist. It was then that Lord Colonsay and his brother Mr Archibald M'Neil decided to save the pure breed from extinction and to work it as before. They were successful on both counts; to them must go much of the credit for a breed now so much admired in Britain and the USA, many being coursed on hare and other game. But both hounds are equally happy in urban surroundings providing they can have a daily gallop.

As with so many breeds this century, the show ring has saved both the Scottish Deerhound and the Irish Wolfhound from oblivion, after they were abandoned for the task for which they were created. But both breeds will always be essentially sporting. Though not normally used

singly for hunting, neither breed is a pack hound. As such they are both good-natured with other dogs and make wonderful companions for humans, being devoted to their owners. Indeed, the Deerhound's desire for its master's love seems to be insatiable; it will never abandon its family, and for this reason should be rewarded with plenty of attention and affection. It will not be happy if brought up in kennels. It is easy to train and is completely stable, and makes an ideal pet.

The Wolfhound also makes an excellent companion, fitting into family life very well, and being very good with young children. It is a reliable and dependable breed, but not easily adaptable to new situations; once established in a home, the Wolfhound prefers to stay there. This is nevertheless an intelligent, courageous dog which need fear nothing, since it is the tallest of all dogs. Thus it makes a good guard. Though dignified, the Wolfhound also makes a good playmate, and, like the Deerhound, it has an even temperament.

'Gentle giants' is an apt description of these members of the greyhound family which have so much to offer as pets. Apart from their biddable temperament, unswerving loyalty and gentle approach to life, they have easily-managed coats of a rough, wiry texture that does not harbour dirt. They come in colours which are

always attractive, if not showy. The Deerhound can be different shades of grey, but dark blue-grey is to be preferred for show purposes. The Wolfhound also is shown in shades of grey, and black, white, red, wheaten and brindle are more frequently met with in this breed than in its Scottish cousin.

Big dogs which carry the sort of history belonging to these hounds are obviously not suited to homes where they will be unable–especially as young adults–to exercise themselves to the full in a regular run. Only one way exists of learning whether these aristocratic animals will fit into your life: this is by putting yourself entirely in the hands of a reputable breeder. Fortunately, such dedicated people are the majority in both breeds. Wolfhounds have seen an upsurge in their popularity during recent years and 500 and more are now registered annually. There is no shortage of people with good advice for would-be owners to trust when making a decision. Puppies of such large and rapidly growing breeds–the smaller Deerhound is seldom under 28 inches at the shoulder–do need great care in their upbringing to avoid a disastrous end result. The experienced breeder alone can guide you on the right path; if you take the course advised, you need never regret the addition of an Irish Wolfhound or a Deerhound to the family circle.

*If you decide to have either the Deerhound or Wolfhound as a pet you should take expert advice from the breeder first and then undoubtedly the dog of your choice will be a lovable friend and companion*

# Two Sporting breeds from Africa

TWO remarkable dogs from Africa are big favourites in the UK and America. The Basenji is the famous barkless dog; the Rhodesian Ridgeback is the brave and fearless dog that is still used for hunting lions.

The Basenji is a handsome dog which is almost identical to the dogs of ancient Egypt depicted in tomb paintings. They were probably the first domesticated dogs of the Egyptians, of the dingo-pariah type. Known as 'Khufu' dogs, they were depicted in the tomb of the Pharaoh Khufu of the Fourth Dynasty about 2,700 BC. These dogs had tightly curled tails, which is not a characteristic of the dingo, and some experts believe that the Egyptians practised selective breeding in producing this tail feature. Among wild dogs a tail carried low suppresses the scent from the peri-anal glands, and this is a useful function as the smell can create hostility and aggression in other dogs in certain circumstances. When the dog wishes to be recognized by another dog the tail can be raised, releasing the scent. This function is now lost to the Basenji because of the selective breeding already referred to.

The shape of the Basenji skull is another feature that has led experts to assert that the breed–along with huskies, dingos and pariahs–is descended from canid ancestors including wolves and coyotes. A skull in the British Museum, taken from a first-century BC tomb at Denderah, Egypt, is probably that of a domestic dog akin to the Basenji. Two of the incisor teeth had been knocked out of the skull during the lifetime of the dog, but the remaining teeth are still present. The suggestion is that the two incisors were lost as the result of an injury sustained while hunting a large animal. It points to the conclusion that Basenji-type dogs were used in packs for hunting, and this was one stage towards complete domestication. Although at various times since then the dingo-type dogs like the Basenji have been regarded as untrustworthy, and therefore not to be recommended as domestic pets, today the concensus of opinion is quite the opposite. Basenjis have become increasingly popular.

The Basenji was unknown outside Africa until about a hundred years ago, although early explorers had recorded their curious lack of a bark. Attempts were made to introduce them to Europe in 1895 and again in the 1920s but the breed had no resistence to distemper and the imported dogs all died. Finally, a litter imported into Britain from the Katanga (then the Belgian Congo) in 1929 survived. And all British Basenjis were bred from that family.

Two specimens were brought to the United States in 1927 and a litter was born. Unfortunately, with the exception of the sire, the mother and puppies died from distemper. The dog was subsequently mated to a younger importation and the puppies were raised to maturity. Further imports came from Canada and in 1924 the Basenji Club of America was formed, the AKC granting recognition in 1943. The breed is now firmly established in America and growing in popularity.

The Basenji is still a common dog in the forests of the Congo and the swamps of southern Sudan, where it is used for hunting. A handsome dog, the Basenji makes a good house pet. In countries with a temperate climate it is not wise–because of its tropical background–to keep the breed in an outside kennel in winter, unless you can provide an infra-red heater.

The Basenji is a smallish, elegant dog, slim and gazelle-like, and weighing about 24 lb. It stands 17 inches at the shoulder. The ears are erect, the eyes dark and almond-shaped and the curly tail sits upright over the short sleek coat of the spine. The most popular colour is an

*The Rhodesian Ridgeback (left) is a strong, muscular dog whose main feature is a ridge of hair along its spine, growing the opposite way to the rest of the coat. The Basenji (right) was probably the first domesticated dog of the ancient Egyptians*

# Breed Standard: the Basenji

## CHARACTERISTICS

The Basenji does not bark but is not mute; its own special noise is a mixture of a chortle and a yodel. It is remarkable for its cleanliness.

## GENERAL APPEARANCE

The Basenji should be a lightly built, finely boned aristocratic looking animal, high on the leg compared with its length, always poised, alert and intelligent.

## HEAD AND SKULL

The skull should be flat, well chiselled and of medium width, tapering towards the nose, with a slight stop. Fine and profuse wrinkles should appear on the forehead when the ears are pricked.

## EYES

Dark, almond-shaped, obliquely set.

## EARS

Small, pointed, erect and slightly hooded, of fine texture, set well forward on top of the head. The tip of the ear should be nearer the centre of the skull than the outside base.

## MOUTH

The mouth should be level, with scissor bite.

## NECK

Strong and of good length, without thickness, well crested and slightly full at the base of the throat. It should be well set into laid-back shoulders so as to give the head a lofty carriage.

## FOREQUARTERS

The shoulders must be well laid back, muscular but not loaded. The forelegs should be straight with fine bone and very long fore-arms.

## BODY

Balanced with short, level back. Ribs well sprung, deep and oval, and the loin short-coupled.

## HINDQUARTERS

Strong and muscular, with hocks well let down, turned neither in nor out, with long second thighs and moderately bent stifles.

## FEET

Small, narrow and compact, with deep pads, well-arched toes and short nails.

## TAIL

The tail should be high set with the posterior curve of the buttock extending beyond the root of the tail. The tail curls tightly over the spine and lies closely to the thigh with a single or double curl.

## COAT

Short, sleek and close, very fine. Skin very pliant.

## COLOUR

Pure bright red, or pure black, or black and tan, all with white feet, chest and tail tip.

## SIZE AND WEIGHT

Ideal heights: dogs 17 in at shoulder; bitches 16 in. Ideal weights: dogs 24 lb; bitches 21 lb.

The Rhodesian Ridgeback is a strapping great dog that was used by the native warriors of Southern Africa to hunt lions and was first described in Europe in 1505. The appearance of the breed has changed over the years as it was crossed with greyhounds, pointers, and other breeds introduced by Europeans into Africa. But the main feature of the Ridgeback—the prominent ridge of hair along the spine which grows in the opposite direction to the rest of the hair—has remained. Without it a Ridgeback is not a Ridgeback.

As a hunting dog the breed is able to hold big game, including lions, at bay. In fact, for many years this animal was known in Africa as the Lion Dog. The breed was finally standardized in Rhodesia 50 years ago, and the name Rhodesian Ridgeback was chosen because breeders felt Lion Dog suggested a ferocious animal. In fact the Ridgeback is tremendously devoted to its master and family and is a remarkably gentle pet.

Ridgebacks have been bred in Britain since 1928, but the first importations to America did not take place until shortly before 1950. The characteristic colour of the Ridgeback is a light golden shade, and it often has a little white on its chest and toes. The dark muzzle, ears and nose helps give the dog its characteristic expression.

orangey-red with white chest and white feet, but there are also black Basenjis, black and white, and tan and white. A few are born with curious tiger stripes.

The breed needs a great deal of daily exercise and a diet containing plenty of fresh meat. Curiously, all Basenjis eat grass regularly and should be given a chance to do this.

Although the Basenji has no bark it does express itself with a variety of yodels and growls. Some experts believe that the bark disappeared through hundreds of years of selective breeding to produce a dog that would hunt silently. Others suggest that the Basenji cannot bark because of its oddly-shaped larynx.

As a pet the breed is intelligent and impish, with a keen sense of fun. It is affectionate, but no one could say it is an over-obedient dog. Most Basenjis need firm handling from an early age.

Although a good town pet, the Basenji loves the country and is specially happy trotting along after horses. But it hates the rain, and if it does get wet it must be dried off with a towel. One advantage of owning a Basenji is that its short coat stays very clean and it has no smell.

*Basenjis (right) are smart, neat-looking dogs which are both charming and full of fun. The tail is carried tightly curled over the spine*

# Unusual hound breeds

FOR more than 700 years the Otter-hound has been used to control the population of otters as a means of protecting fish. Its form must have been established in Britain even in the reign of Edward II (1307–27) when it was des-cribed as a 'rough sort of dog, between a hound and a terrier'. Otter hunting was never a popular sport. It reached a peak during the last half of the nineteenth cen-tury, when up to 20 packs were in use.

Since exceptional scenting ability is es-sential, over the years the blood of various breeds – notably that of the Bloodhound – has been introduced to make the Otter-hound better at its work. A big dog at up to 27 inches at the shoulder, the Otter-

hound needs to be immensely strong, well boned and muscled for endurance, yet in no way cloddy or clumsy as this would detract from the speed required of the breed. The head is on the same lines as the Bloodhound, without as much exag-geration in occiput and flews (the hanging parts of the upper lip). A rough, double, water-resistant coat is necessary, for much of its work takes place in water.

The Otterhound of today has probably had more strains from other breeds in its ancestry than any other breed of dog. Experts say that it descended in its ori-ginal form from the now extinct St Hubert Hound. Later it is thought that the blood of the Griffon Vendeen was introduced,

and still later that of the Southern Har-rier, English Water Spaniel and the Bloodhound. In the last century and a half, the Otterhound has been bred with care to keep its extremely keen nose for scent and its outstanding swimming ability, and it is known for certain that blood of the Welsh and Dumfriesshire Foxhounds (the last-named being a smooth-haired hound), the Staghound and the Kerry Beagle have been intro-duced. King John was known to have a pack of Otterhounds in 1212, six couples being the extent of the pack. Edward II also had six couples in 1307. Elizabeth I

*Above: a pack of Otterhounds*

74

is reported to have been the first Lady of Otterhounds.

The Otterhound is not a domestic pet, nor is it available as such. While specimens are seen on the show bench in America, they are rarely shown in Britain. It is possible that unless the breed is taken up for show purposes in Britain it may eventually become extinct.

Swedish hounds are found in three different forms: the Hamiltonstovare, Schillerstovare and Smalandstovare. In Sweden the Hamiltonstovare is popular as a hunting and show dog, but only a handful are to be found in Britain.

All three breeds are long in the leg and lighter-boned than their English counterparts, the Hamiltonstovare coming closest to the British Harrier. But Swedish hounds do not hunt in packs. Their quarry of fox or the like is hunted over snow and through forests. For this pur-

pose, strength and endurance are necessary, as is a loud, melodious voice, since the thickness of the forest makes it impossible for huntsmen to keep up with their hounds. The fox is driven towards the huntsmen by the hounds and then shot.

While basically similar, the older Smalandstovare is the smaller breed at 19½ inches, whereas the Hamiltonstovare can be up to 24 inches at the shoulder. It is of medium build, and its colour is black with tan points. Either a very short or a very long tail is equally correct. A heavier build, tricolour (black, tan and white) markings and a more hound-like head with greater flews distinguish the Hamiltonstovare from the Schillerstovare, which is black, blanketed over tan.

Primarily hunting breeds that need to be able to indulge their hunting instincts, the smooth-coated and easily maintained

Stovare will obviously present problem for anyone unable to provide sporting ou lets. However, the temptation of ownin them is so limited by lack of numbers i many countries outside Sweden that it not worth considering.

Think of a rather large smooth Chihua hua with a head which is too long an flatter in the skull than that breed; i many ways the result will look like th smallest version of the Portuguese Warre Hound.

There are three sizes of this breed whic was developed as a rabbit hunter, thoug the largest variety is used to catch hare as well. The biggest (the Grande) stand from 21 to 27 inches at the shoulder, th smallest (the Pequeno) 8 to 10 inches, an the one in between (the Medio) from 1 to 21 inches.

The Podengo, as it is known in Portuga is of indefinite ancestry. Skill at hunting

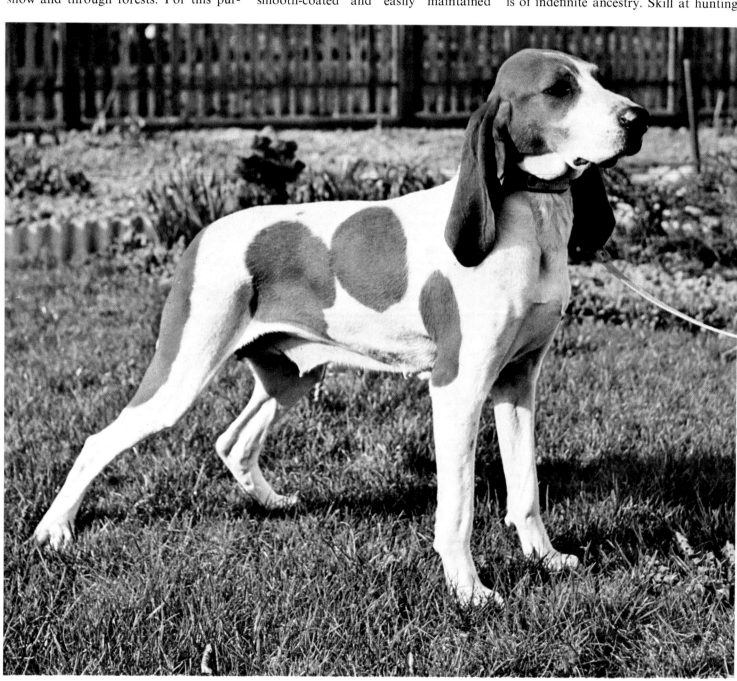

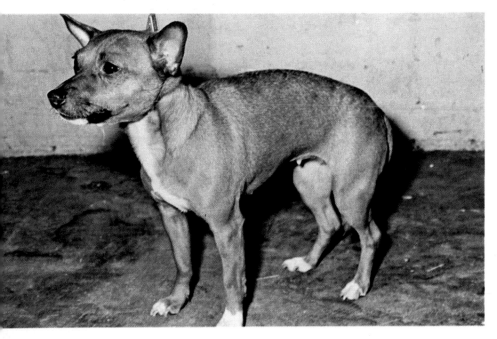

By contrast, the Bruno type is racier in its appearance. Lighter all through, it lacks nothing in bone and muscle development, but the body is longer in relation to its height. The Bruno's head is long, with the planes of skull and muzzle nearly on the same line, divided only by the stop. It is altogether a cleaner head than the St Hubert, with little dewlap. The ears are long and low-set.

Both types sport a medium length of tail. The St Hubert's is carried higher but in conventional hound fashion, never right over the back. Minimum height at the shoulder for both is $17\frac{1}{2}$ inches.

Developed entirely as hunting dogs, the Jura hounds have an almost fanatical sense of the chase, as all good hounds must. Their ability to keep on the track of their target is exceptional. This inevitably causes problems in keeping this breed of dog as a companion.

which is done both alone and in packs, has always been the main criterion in the past, though the dogs were of a basic type. Since being taken up for exhibition purposes, greater conformity has been achieved within each variety.

There is a wire-haired version of the Podengo but this is not found in the smallest variety. Racy build is a keynote of the appearance of the two larger breeds, together with strength in bone and muscle. Fawn is the principal colour. A distinguishing feature is the tail carriage; the tail sweeps over the back.

Only the small variety, the Pequeno, exists in Britain, and there is probably only a handful of them. The Grande and Medio are unknown here. Like all hounds they are hardy, and can adapt from a sporting life to one that is less active.

The Bruno de Jura or Swiss hound is a scent hound, that is one that hunts by its nose, not its eyes. It is recognized in two forms, the Bruno type and the St Hubert type. Both hunt the hare.

The most obvious similarity between the two is their black-and-tan colouring. In build they vary considerably, the St Hubert type being constructed on heavier lines, with very strong bone, a powerfully made body and well-muscled hindquarters. Its head is distinctly of Bloodhound type—both breeds being descendants of the St Hubert hound—without being so exaggerated in loose skin. But it does have a pronounced occiput, long low-set ears and great depth of flews with corresponding throatiness.

# Whippets and Greyhounds

THE Greyhound, the most famous of all sporting dogs, can be claimed to be one of the oldest breeds of all dogs and is even mentioned by Solomon in the Old Testament who refers to it as one of the 'four things which are comely in going'. It is generally thought that this dog originated, as did all the other greyhound-type dogs, in the Middle East and that in its various forms it was used for hunting by the nomadic Arab tribes in conjunction with the hawk. During the time of the great Roman Empire, hundreds of these dogs found their way across northern Europe and became firmly established among the Celtic nations, quickly adapting themselves to the different climates. On the dissolution of the Roman Empire, these dogs were taken in their thousands to the southern parts of Europe where they quickly established themselves as great favourites. Of all countries perhaps none quite so readily accepted the Greyhound as England, where the breed was held in great esteem.

Through the ages the English monarchy has always been associated with this handsome breed; mention is made of the Greyhound as far back as King Elfric of Mercia when the dog was an inmate of Anglo-Saxon kennels. King Canute, Henry II, King John and Edward I and II were others who kept large kennels of these dogs. Edward III was so fond of the breed that he took sixty couples of them with him when he went to war with France. Charles I favoured them as much as his son Charles II, and in later times Queen Victoria kept many of them, some kennelled and some in the palace as companions. Today HRH the Duke of Edinburgh owns a number of racing Greyhounds.

Some experts believe that the first dogs of greyhound type found their way into southern Europe about 300 years before Christ, and through the years many variations in the coat took place, according to the terrain and climate. In Scotland, the Highland Greyhound came into being, a breed now popularly known as the Scottish Deerhound. And the Irish Wolfhound is also thought to have Greyhound blood in its veins. However, it was the smooth-haired hound that was always held in the greatest esteem and this was confirmed by the desire to cross the rough-coated specimens with the smooth coats whenever they could be im-

ported from other parts of the world. However, the results were not altogether pleasing, and in Britain it was left to a dedicated Greyhound enthusiast, Lord Offord, in the 1750s, to bring about the attractive smooth, silky coat as we know it today. This he achieved by crossing a smooth-haired Greyhound with the English Bulldog and he continued with this cross for seven generations until he found himself in possession of 'the best greyhounds ever known'. He now had a hound with the characteristic small ear, a fine, silky coat and possessing tremendous courage. This crossing also introduced the brindled coat, a colour that remains popular to this day.

The sport of coursing using the Greyhound has been carried on for over 2,000 years and some of the rules as we know them today were perfectly described by the Greek historian, Arryan, in the second century BC. It was not, however, until 1776 that Lord Offord formed the first official coursing club, the Swaffham Club in Norfolk. Coursing greyhounds after live hares is now an organized sport—though very controversial—with numerous clubs in operation. There is a considerable body of public opinion which condemns the sport as extremely

*Right: Whippets, which are the result of crossing Greyhounds with terriers. Below: a Greyhound, which is thought to have originated from the Middle East*

# Breed Standard: the Greyhound

## CHARACTERISTICS
The Greyhound possesses remarkable stamina and endurance; its straight through, long-reaching movement enables it to cover ground at great speed.

## GENERAL APPEARANCE
The general appearance of the typical Greyhound is that of a strongly built, upstanding dog of generous proportions, muscular power and symmetrical formation, with a long head and neck, clean well-laid shoulders, deep chest, capacious body, arched loin, powerful quarters, sound legs and feet, and a suppleness of limb, which emphasize, to a marked degree, its distinctive type and quality.

## HEAD AND SKULL
Long, moderate width, flat skull, slight stop. Jaws, powerful and well chiselled.

## EYES
Bright and intelligent, dark in colour.

## EARS
Small, rose-shape, of fine texture.

## MOUTH
Teeth white and strong. The incisors of the upper jaw clipping those of the lower jaw.

## NECK
Long and muscular, elegantly arched, well let into the shoulders.

## FOREQUARTERS
Shoulders: oblique, well set back and muscular; forelegs: long and straight.

## BODY
Chest: deep, providing adequate heart room; ribs: deep and well sprung; flanks: well cut up; back: broad and square; loin: powerful.

## HINDQUARTERS
Thighs and second thighs: wide and muscular; stifles: well bent; hocks: well let down. Body and hindquarters should be of ample proportions and well coupled.

## FEET
Moderate length, with strong pads.

## TAIL
Long, set on rather low, tapering to the point, carried low, slightly curved.

## COAT
Fine and close.

## COLOUR
Black, white, red, blue, fawn, fallow, brindle, or any of the colours broken with white.

## HEIGHT
Dogs: 28–30 inches; Bitches: 27–28 inches.

## WEIGHT
Dogs: 75–90 lb; Bitches: 60–65 lb.

cruel. The premier event in the English calendar is the Waterloo Cup held early each year at Altcar and many winners of this classic event have gone down in history for their spectacular achievements.

Early in this century a new sport of greyhound racing after a dummy hare was introduced in America and, after enormous progress had been made, the sport was brought to Britain in 1926, quickly spreading to other parts of Europe and later to other continents as well. From the opening event which was held at Manchester, the popularity of this new craze grew so rapidly that after only six years the total attendances at all tracks in Britain amounted to a staggering 20 million. During the last few years, however, attendances have stabilized at about 15 million.

Greyhounds are beautiful, graceful dogs and, although the majority of people associate them only with racing and coursing, they should not be despised as pets and companions. Nor are they devoid of intelligence as most people would have you believe. When they are on the track or the field they are not required to stop and think, or show anything like the sagacity of a well-bred and trained dog. It has been proved many times that their intelligence and capability for reasoning are of no mean order.

They are extremely affectionate and make really excellent house pets and companions, although as King Charles I once said, 'they have not got court manners!' Greyhounds can be taught a certain amount of obedience and can show great love for their owners, while at the same time not being too flattering. They make very good mothers, being extremely fond of their offspring. A word of warning: Greyhounds are avid eaters and require a substantial amount of food. To keep one in peak condition, at least one pound of meat should be fed each day, together with cereal, biscuit and milk. Grooming is easy and is the same as is recommended for its smaller cousin, the Whippet.

The Whippet is essentially a sporting breed. Although it possesses all the characteristics to make it a most delightful and faithful companion and pet, it does, in many people's eyes, still retain its early identity as a 'poor man's Greyhound'. This image came into being early in this century when the Whippet was used extensively by the working-class, in the industrial parts of the North of England, purely for the sport of racing. However, over the years numbers of people have grown to appreciate its excellent qualities, and its status in the canine world has risen rapidly. The Whippet now stands close in popularity to the Afghan hound which leads the Hound Group.

It is thought that this enchanting breed was evolved around 1850 by crossing small Greyhounds with Manchester Terriers, Bedlington Terriers, the now extinct English White Terrier and the very similar Italian Greyhound. The crosses proved very successful. After only a few generations the resultant progeny started to breed true, and the Whippet became firmly established.

Retaining the elegance of the Italian Greyhound and most of the speed of the Greyhound, the Whippet quickly gained in popularity and soon this handsome little sporting dog became a firm favourite with the British miners who exploited it to the full by racing dogs over sprint distances of 200 yards. In early Whippet racing no mechanical or live hares were used to excite the dogs to compete but they were taught to run to the 'rag', and with all their hearts going into their racing they could easily cover the 200 yard track in 12 seconds, a speed which compares very favourably with that of the Greyhound.

Without doubt, amateur Whippet racing was the forerunner of the professional and highly industrialized and organized Greyhound racing, and after the introduction of the latter in 1926 Whippet racing fell from popularity. However, it was soon realized that in more than one respect Whippet racing had its own advantages,

one being an individuality of which the other sport is deprived. With Whippets, not only does the man have charge of his own dog instead of it being passed over to a recognized trainer to whom a weekly fee is paid, but he has the interest of training it himself, looking after its feeding, general welfare and exercise. When these facts were realized, Whippet racing gradually became more popular again and is now well organized throughout Britain and the Continent, with a great number of non-profit-making clubs in operation.

This graceful breed also became a firm favourite of show enthusiasts and great numbers are exhibited all over the world at all types of shows. The Breed Standard requires that the head be long and lean, rather wide between the eyes and flat on top. The jaws should be powerful, the teeth level and white, the eyes bright and fiery, and the ears small and fine. The neck should be long and muscular, shoulders oblique, and the chest deep and capacious. The back should be broad and square, rather long, and slightly arched over the loin which should be strong and powerful. The forelegs should be rather long, well set under the dog, possessing a fair amount of bone. The hindquarters should be strong and broad across, stifles well bent, thighs broad and muscular, and hocks well let down. The feet should be

*Far left: Greyhound. Above: Whippet. The controversial sport of coursing, using Greyhounds, has been known for over 2,000 years, and the first official club came into being in 1776*

round but well split up. The tail should be long, tapering and nicely carried, the coat fine and close. There is a great variance of colour which can be black, red, white, brindle, fawn, blue or any mixtures of these. The ideal weight for a dog is 21 lb and for bitches 20 lb. The ideal height should be 18½ inches for dogs and 17½ inches for bitches.

Whippets, although giving the appearance of being delicate animals, are in fact a very hardy breed and can withstand the winter months in outside kennels as well as any other smooth-coated dog of their size. They make excellent pets and thrive better when allowed to live in the house and treated as part of the family. They have numerous advantages, for as well as being relatively cheap to purchase as puppies, they are also inexpensive to keep and feed, only requiring about half a pound of meat per day plus the usual biscuit cereal and additives. Being smooth-coated they require the minimum amount of grooming and a quick brush daily will suffice, together with a weekly examination of toe-nails, teeth and ears which will need attention when and where necessary.

# Chapter III
# Sporting Dogs
# Gun Dog Group

# Continental gun dogs

OVER a thousand years ago the Magyar hordes invaded Central Europe and settled in Hungary. With them came their hunting dogs. Many primitive stone etchings have survived to prove that this early breed was, without doubt, the root stock from which the modern Vizla has descended. It is one of the purest breeds in the world, perhaps because of the great care taken by the Magyar nobles who avoided introducing any kind of out-cross.

The Vizla is a medium-sized dog of 22 to 24 inches at the shoulder, the bitches being an inch or so smaller. The skull is moderately wide between the ears, which are thin, silky, set rather low and hanging close to the cheeks. The nose is brown in colour with slightly open nostrils. The eyes must not be yellow, and must harmonize with the coat.

The body is well proportioned and strong with a short back, the chest being deep and moderately broad. The feet are round and compact and the toes close. The Vizla's coat is short and dense, smooth and close-lying without any kind of woolly undercoat. The colours are solid

and may be rusty-gold or dark sandy yellow in various shades. A gun dog of outstanding ability, the breed has a wonderful nose and excels as a retriever – a truly all-purpose worker in the field. At the same time the Vizla is a splendid companion which will settle down quite happily as a family pet.

The Pointing Wire-haired Griffon was developed about 1870 by a Dutch sportsman named Edward Korthals. A breeder of very considerable knowledge and experience, he managed the kennels of a German prince for many years and was determined to breed a dog which would combine all the virtues of tenacity, pluck and love of hunting, so important in a sporting breed. He selected a number of German, French and Belgian gun dog breeds and experimented until he produced a Griffon which was a first-class water dog as well as a swift pointer.

The breed is of medium size, measuring 22 to 24 inches at the withers, bitches

*Right: the Italian Spinone is a pointer used as an all round sporting dog. Below: the Small Musterlander is about 20 ins high*

eing a little smaller. The head is large with a long and square muzzle. It has beard and thick eyebrows, and the nose broad and brown in colour. The ears re medium in size and lie flat. The eyes re large and can be brown or yellow. hey must not be concealed by the shaggy yebrows. The body is very strong and owerful, the back is short and straight, nd the chest deep.

The coat is distinctive and is shaggy, ough, hard and wiry. It should not be urly or woolly in any way. The colour an be steel-grey, white and brown, white nd fawn, or all brown mixed with grey.

The Large Munsterlander is a German etter breed which has descended from the ld German spaniels and sporting dogs. is a handsome medium-sized dog with long coat and a long, heavily feathered il. It is from 23 to 25 inches at the ithers, swift moving but quiet in oper- ion, and possessing a very keen nose.

The head is long and the skull slightly omed, the ears set on high and well inged, thus giving the ears a long ppearance although, in fact, they are dis- nctly broad. The body is strong and uscular, the croup slanting slightly and he docked tail set on high. The feet are nportant for a gun dog; the Large Mun- terlander must possess hard pads.

The coat is slightly wavy, long, and with he legs and tail well feathered. The colour s black and white, the head being black vith large black patches on the body var- ed with smaller markings and spots. The arge Munsterlander is a very tough dog nd has proved itself to be a very steady nd reliable worker. It will retrieve well nd is a good water dog. Easily trained, is a dependable house dog and will rove an obedient and faithful pet.

The Small Munsterlander is a medium- ized dog, but it is distinctly smaller than he Large Munsterlander and is not so trongly built. It is from 18 to 22 inches t the shoulder, bitches being 17 to 20 nches. It shares a common ancestry with he larger variety, both having descended rom the old German spaniels and some rench breeds. It is impossible to say with ny certainty what breeding plans were ollowed, but there is no doubt that both Munsterlander breeds have an affinity vith other European sporting dogs.

In a more leisurely age, the duties of gun dog were very clearly defined. ointers and setters were not expected to etrieve nor was a spaniel blamed for fail- ng to point game. A retriever knew its ob was to retrieve, and that was that. he Italian Spinone is a pointer but it s able to perform as an all-round sporting log. As with some other breeds, the intro- luction of gun dogs from other countries hreatened this fine native breed with xtinction. It was saved by a number of

*Above: two Pointing Wire-haired Griffons; below: the Hungarian Vizla is a quiet, good- natured pointer of outstanding ability*

faithful admirers who recognized that shooting men prefer an all-round dog.

The Spinone is a big dog measuring from 23 to 28 inches at the withers and weighing 70 to 80 lb. Bitches are some two inches shorter with a corresponding decrease in weight. The breed has a square appearance, since length is equal to height. It has a very sturdy stance, but is quite alert and very active.

The coat is rough, hard and thick, with a dense weather-resistant undercoat. It may be pure white, or white with lemon, orange or brown markings. The tail is docked to a length of 6 to 10 inches and is set on level with the croup. Intelligent, docile and with an excellent temperament, the Spinone makes an ideal companion.

# Pointers

I N recent years the American expression 'bird dogs' has come into use for a subdivision of the gundog group of dogs. Like many Americanisms it is quite appropriate, for it applies to those breeds which work on game birds, principally grouse and partridge but also on pheasant when in the open, though this last-named is really a bird of the covert. Originally the group consisted of Pointers and English, Irish and Gordon Setters, enlarged after World War Two by the inclusion of German Pointers and Weimaraners.

Pointers and Setters were the sole exhibits at the first dog show, which was held at Darlington at the end of the nineteenth century, even before the creation of the Kennel Club. Since those early days they have been accepted by non-shooting people for their sheer beauty of outline, equable temperament and adaptability. Classical Pointer work is regarded as the very height of perfection in gundog work, and the bag (the quantity of birds shot) is a very secondary consideration. In fact, at field trials for Pointers, held every year in this country in the spring and autumn, no birds are shot, although a gun is discharged to show that the contestant is not gun-shy, and will drop to shot and birds going away (known as 'flushing').

Pointers are worked two at a time: one is sent off to the right and one to the left of the ground to be covered. They are trained to work to the extent of the beat and then to turn inwards until meeting up with their opposite number; then they turn away again until one of them, scenting birds ahead, comes to a halt in classic pose with head held high, foreleg raised and tail rigid, 'pointing' towards where the covey is lying. Staunchness on point is an essential. The second dog, on seeing this 'point', will also come to a halt in a similar pose, this being known as 'backing'. The gun or handler then goes up to the dog on point, which then advances slowly towards the hidden birds. This is known as 'roding'. On the birds flushing, the dog drops, so that it does not interfere with the shot.

The breed in its early progress fortunately attracted the attention of a wealthy sportsman, William Arkwright of Sutton Scarsdale. He travelled the world, studying the history and evolution of the breed. It is accepted that they originated in the

*Pointers are a subdivision of the gundog group which the Americans call 'bird dogs'. The large picture shows a German Shorthair Pointer, the top insert a Pointer, and the bottom insert a Weimaraner*

# Breed Standard: the Pointer

## CHARACTERISTICS
The Pointer should be symmetrical and well built all over. Alert, with the appearance of strength, endurance and speed.

## HEAD AND SKULL
The skull should be of medium breadth and in proportion to the length of fore-face; the stop well defined, pronounced occipital bone. The muzzle somewhat concave, and ending on a level with the nostrils.

## EYES
The same distance from the occiput as from the nostrils. The colour of the eyes either hazel or brown according to the colour of the coat. Should be bright, not bold or staring.

## MOUTH
Scissor bite, neither under- nor over-shot.

## NECK
Long, muscular, slightly arched, springing cleanly from the shoulders and free from throatiness.

## EARS
The ears should be set on fairly high, and lie close to the head, they should be of medium length, and inclined to be pointed at the tips.

## FOREQUARTERS
The shoulders long, sloping, and well laid back. The forelegs straight and firm, of good oval bone, with the back sinews strong and visible.

## BODY
Well-sprung ribs, gradually falling away at the loins, which should be strong, muscular and slightly arched.

## HINDQUARTERS
Well turned stifles. The hock should be well let down, and close to the ground.

## FEET
The feet oval, with well-knit, arched toes, well cushioned underneath.

## GAIT
Smooth, covering plenty of ground with each stride. Driving hind action.

## TAIL
The tail of medium length, thick at the root, growing gradually thinner to the point. It should be well covered with close hair, and carried on a level with the back, with no upward curl.

## COAT
The coat should be fine, short, hard and evenly distributed, and perfectly smooth.

## COLOUR
The usual colours are lemon and white, orange and white, liver and white, and black and white. Self colours and tricolours are also correct.

## SIZE
Dogs 25–27 inches. Bitches 24–26 inches.

East, and were valued in Italy where they are numerically strong to this day. They came westward to Spain where what is termed the 'Spanish' head was developed with a very deep stop between the eyes creating a 'dish' face with a distinct lift towards the nostrils, which should be large and flared. From Spain they came to England, and, it was believed, were also taken to South America. Arkwright spent a lifetime in the study and propagation of the breed. However beautiful the dog he produced, if it showed no aptitude for work it would be put down, rather than allowed to get into other hands and be used for breeding with an adverse effect on the breed.

He finally produced privately possibly the greatest book on an individual breed, profusely illustrated by various members of the Earl family. *Arkwright on Pointers* comes occasionally on the market at prices ranging from £50 to £125 a copy. Dog pictures by any of the Earls have appreciated so much in value that they sell at anything from a hundred to two thousand pounds. Anyone interested in Pointer research should visit the British Museum, where one can see preserved the Field Trial Champion Sea Breeze presented by William Arkwright in 1905. Today the Pointer is a fine, fast gundog noted for its ability to stand rigidly on scenting a bird, with the nose, body and tail of its lithe body in a straight line. The ideal height for this breed is 24 to 27 ins; weight is 50 to 55 lb.

As household companions Pointers are quite charming. They are fond of their home and will guard it without being vicious. They require no special feeding and only a light regular grooming. An essential is that they are regularly and well exercised. All English gundogs are 'soft-mouthed' and not destructive. Pointers are mostly liver and white with some black and white; occasionally a wholly black one appears, looking very handsome.

On the Continent there is a wide range of gundogs. Germany has three distinct breeds of Pointer; the Drahthaar, the Kurzhaar and the Langhaar. It is the Kurzhaar or German Shorthaired Pointer which attracted the interest of gundog lovers in Britain. The GSPs (as they are known colloquially) are also firmly established in America and are particularly popular as field dogs. They originated in Germany about 300 years ago, descended from Spanish Pointers which were imported to Germany in the seventeenth century. These were crossed with Bloodhounds in order to produce a dog with greater intelligence, more 'nose' and a

*The German Wirehaired Pointer is a dog that can operate on any type of terrain*

etter instinct for trailing. But it also resulted in a dog with less speed. Foxhound blood was then introduced, and while its speed was greater, its pointing instinct was lost. Finally, the English Pointer was used to restore this, and the German Shorthair Pointer was the result.

In its homeland the GSP, whether Wirehaired or Longhaired, works on pheasant, partridge, woodcock, rabbits, fox, deer and duck. There is on record a GSP which tracked down a wounded fox, killed it, and retrieved it to hand. In the early days of the breed the GSPs were run with English Pointers, but as the Continentals differ considerably the Kennel Club has granted them separate field trial status; in addition to acting as Pointers they also retrieve, are good swimmers and excel at water tests, even in icy conditions. In fact, this breed is a good all-round hunting dog, although it should not be used for a very long hunt, as it is not particularly fast. With strangers the GSP tends to be somewhat reserved, and takes some time to make friends. With its owner, however, the breed is extremely loyal, affectionate and playful, and is good with a family and children. The GSP is happiest when used as a hunter as well as a family pet; city life does not suit this dog's need for plenty of space and exercise.

The recognized Standard for GSPs is 55 to 70 lb in weight and 23 to 25 inches in height. Their smooth, glistening coat may be solid liver, liver and white ticked, or black and white. Other colours are not permitted, and unlike the English Pointers, their tails are docked to two-fifths of the original length. For those who like Pointer work, the GSP is a great one-man dog and a good all-rounder.

The German Wirehaired Pointer Club was founded in 1902 with an original stud book entry of four only. Sixty years later they were Germany's strongest hunting dog with a club membership of 3,500. The breed was recognized in America in 1959.

A rapidly progressing breed is the Weimaraner, used as a hunting dog by the nobles of Weimar, Germany, in the early nineteenth century. It is almost certain that one of its ancestors was the bloodhound. Originally a tracking dog, it was trained to hunt wildcats, deer, mountain lions and even bears. These animals disappeared from Germany and it now hunts, points and retrieves most game. The breed was granted Kennel Club Challenge Certificates in England in 1960.

Weimaraners are 22 to 27 inches in height, and dogs weigh 55 to 65 lb and bitches 45 to 55 lb. They are a silver-grey colour which has led them to be christened by Americans as 'The Grey Ghost',

and the term is often used in Britain. Their coat is smooth and sleek. As well as an all-round shooting and sporting dog, the Weimaraner has been trained for police work on the Continent because of its marvellous scenting powers and tracking ability. Being highly intelligent, it has done well in many obedience competitions. It is a loyal companion and vies with the GSP as an all-round shooting dog. The Weimaraner is an extremely individualistic dog and must receive very careful and firm training when a puppy, if it is to learn to respect authority. It is a very active dog and must be given plenty of exercise to keep it busy. It adapts very well to any climate and living conditions. The Weimaraner is a fearless, courageous dog and can be very aggressive towards intruders, although with its owner and family it will be gentle.

For best results, the training of a sporting dog must start when it is very young, ideally when the puppy is about six months old. It is important not to start training before this age, as the dog is most likely to become tired and confused. It is a good idea to take the puppy out with an older, fully-trained dog.

*Below: Davian Titus Lartius, a show champion that finished second at Cruft's in 1973 as best exhibit of all breeds*

# Retrievers

AS the name implies, Retrievers were bred originally with the sole object of retrieving game during a shoot. In most instances, therefore, the early retrievers were to be found on the larger estates belonging to the aristocracy. Many of these dogs have been sent to all parts of the world, and wherever they have gone these Retrievers have proved themselves to be excellent ambassadors for the British canine world.

Several different breeds are classified under the heading of Retrievers, namely the Labrador Retriever, the Labrador Flat-coated Retriever, the Golden Retriever, the Curly-coated Retriever and the Chesapeake Bay Retriever. Numerically the Golden and the Labrador breeds now far outnumber the others, but fashions change and the position could well be reversed. Both the lovable and playful Flat-coated Retriever and the more sedate but extremely elegant Curly-coated Retriever are likely to become very popular. The Chesapeake relies on its strength and kindliness to achieve recognition, and this has been forthcoming in America but not as yet in Britain.

The origin and history of the Labrador

*Left: Golden Retriever, which with the Labrador Retriever, is by far the most popular of the Retriever breeds*

is a little obscure. That it was used extensively in Newfoundland and Labrador in the seventeenth and eighteenth century is well known. The chroniclers of the day describe and discuss two dogs which they call the Greater and the Lesser Newfoundland. From their descriptions it is assumed that the two breeds to which they refer are the predecessors of the breeds known today as the Newfoundland and the Labrador Retriever respectively.

In these old articles, great admiration is expressed at the capability of the smaller dogs to retrieve from the icy waters surrounding Labrador. Apparently the dogs accompanied the hardy fishermen of the region, and dived into the sea when required to retrieve any fish lost. This was no mean feat in those waters, and one for which the dogs were justly famous. There are conflicting views on where the Labrador first appeared in England; some say it was first seen at Poole in Dorset, while others believe that it was in the border country between England and Scotland.

Another group of experts believe that the Labrador came to Britain in about 1800, when a number of dogs were brought in by the 2nd Earl of Malmesbury, and that the breed as we know it today owes much to these early specimens. The breed is not so coarse as it was in the early nineteenth century; even so it has not been spoilt by

undue efforts to produce exaggerated points for the show bench.

The origin of the Golden Retriever is almost as obscure as that of the Labrador, but does not go back quite as far—just over 100 years if the researchers are correct in their findings. Credit for starting the breed by crossing a Yellow Retriever with a Water Spaniel, and then line breeding from this mating using a similar cross and introducing Setter and Bloodhound blood, is given to Lord Tweedmouth. His carefully kept records of the matings were produced by one of his successors in the early 1950s. This theory has many followers. There is, however, a more direct theory held by many reputable breeders that the breed was imported from Archangel in Russia where it had been used as a cattle dog. Supporting this theory is the way a Golden Retriever sniffs the air to find its game. Attention is drawn to its wonderful range of hearing, both points lending credence to this argument. Like the Labrador, a Golden Retriever is a great character, with a style and elegance all its own.

The Flat-coated Retriever, normally black or liver brown, is yet another type of Retriever with obscure ancestry. Newfoundlands, Setters and Cocker Spaniels are credited with a part in its make-up and from these origins today's breeders have established a great breed of dog.

The Flat-coated Retriever is a very handsome dog, intelligent and strong. It has the most expressive face; it looks up at you very often with an expression of mischief, tolerance and kindness very difficult to define. The Flat-coat seems to possess a sense of humour which is without a rival among dogs but this does not detract from its working capabilities.

The Curly-coated Retriever is possibly the oldest of the five breeds of Retrievers; certainly it has been winning on the show-bench since the middle of the nineteenth century. There is doubt about its ancestry. Was it a cross between the English or Irish Water Spaniel and the small Newfoundland that started the breed, or was it a cross between the Retriever and the Poodle? No one is quite certain. What is certain, however, is that here is probably the most elegant of the Retrievers. A big dog standing 25 to 27 inches at the shoulder, covered in a mass of tight curls of either black or liver brown, makes a very handsome animal indeed.

Unlike the other Retrievers the Curly-coated is rather aloof and, when mature, very sedate. It is not as extrovert as most breeds and appears to appraise carefully all factors of a situation before making up its mind. Once it accepts someone, that person could not wish for a truer or more loyal friend in any situation. It's steadfastness is quite remarkable. In the field, as elsewhere, its training requires much

# Breed Standard: the Labrador Retriever

### GENERAL APPEARANCE
The Labrador should be a strongly-built, short-coupled, active dog, broad in the skull, broad and deep through the chest and ribs, broad and strong over the loins and hindquarters. The dog must move neither too wide nor too close in front or behind.

### HEAD AND SKULL
The skull should be broad with a slight stop so that the skull is not in a straight line with the nose. The head should be clean cut without fleshy cheeks. The jaws should be powerful and free from snipiness, the nose wide and the nostrils well-developed.

### EYES
The eyes should be brown or hazel.

### EARS
Should not be heavy, and should hang close to the head.

### MOUTH
The mouth should be level with strong and regular teeth.

### NECK
Should be powerful, set into well-placed shoulders.

### FOREQUARTERS
The shoulders should be long and sloping, the forelegs well-boned and straight from the shoulders to the ground. The dog must move neither too wide nor too close in front.

### HINDQUARTERS
The loins must be wide and strong with well-turned stifles; hindquarters well-developed and not sloping to the tail. The hocks should be slightly bent and the dog must not be cow-hocked.

### FEET
Should be round and compact with well-arched toes and well-developed pads.

### TAIL
The tail should be very thick towards the base, gradually tapering towards the tip, of medium length and practically free from any feathering, but clothed thickly all round giving a rounded appearance which has been described as the 'otter' tail. Carried gaily, but should not curl over the back.

### COAT
It should be short and dense and without wave, with a weather-resisting undercoat, giving a fairly hard feeling to the hand.

### COLOUR
The colour is generally black or yellow—but other whole colours are permitted. The coat should be free from any white markings but a small white spot on the chest is allowable. The coat should be of a whole colour and not flecked.

### WEIGHT AND SIZE
Desired height for dogs, 22–22½ inches; bitches, 21½–22 inches. In USA, dogs 22½–24½ inches; bitches 21½–23½ inches.

understanding and patience because by nature it will not be 'pushed around'. This type of Retriever has to be trained properly by someone who understands the breed. Then it becomes a dog of exceptional merit in any sphere. It has one other attraction: it does not shed its coat like most breeds.

The Chesapeake Bay Retriever is rarely seen in Britain although it is one of the finest bird dogs ever bred in any country. The roots of the breed go back to England, but America must be given the entire credit for developing these fine dogs to the present high standard.

The breed has a romantic history which stems from the wreck in 1807 of an English sailing vessel off the coast of Maryland. The crew were rescued by an American ship which also took off two Newfoundland puppies, a black bitch and a red dog—both the latter of no particular breed. The puppies form no part in the subsequent events but the two adult dogs were presented by the crew to the Americans who were so hospitable to them while they were waiting for another ship. The dogs were found to be superlative retrievers (it must be remembered that this was an age when the value of a dog was measured by its working qualities, appearance coming a bad second). The two were never mated together, but both were paired with the local retrievers which were a very mixed batch indeed. In spite of this, their progeny retained the ability to retrieve anything under the most difficult circumstances.

The time came when breeders began to take more interest in the appearance of their dogs and so attempts were made to develop a standard type of retriever. As in many other breeds, different outcrosses were introduced, some known and others now forgotten, according to the theories of the breeder. It can be safely assumed that Curly-coated and Flat-coated Retrievers were the most successful, since both served the dual purpose of improving appearance and retaining the hereditary instinct to retrieve. By 1885 the type was fixed and development has continued right up to the present time. First used to retrieve duck, the breed has lost none of its hardy characteristics and it can work all day in the cold and rough waters of Chesapeake Bay and come back for more.

The Chesapeake is a sturdy dog weighing 65 lb to 75 lb, bitches 55 lb to 65 lb. The height at the withers is 23 in to 26 in and 21 in to 24 in respectively. It is a happy dog, intelligent and willing to work. It has a broad skull with a medium stop, a muzzle which is of medium size and not pointed. The ears are small, set high and hanging loosely. The eyes are yellowish and wide apart. The body is muscular with a deep barrel, of medium length with the flanks

well tucked up. The hindquarters are powerful since these are the motive power for swimming. The tail is of medium length and sometimes has moderate feathering.

The coat is most important, the outer coat being harsh and oily because the animal will have to work in the roughest weather. The inner coat must be thick and helps to shed the water after swimming. The breed is used mostly to retrieve duck, so the colour of the coat should blend as much as possible into the scenery. The colour can range from a dark brown to a faded tan sometimes known as deadgrass. This can be any shade from tan to a dull straw colour. A white spot on the breast and white on the toes is permissible.

All Retrievers are extremely adaptable animals and make wonderful family pets. But these dogs must be properly exercised and looked after if owners are to have a happy and healthy dog that is a joy to own. As a group the bitches are all good and easy whelpers, usually having litters of between six and ten without any undue trouble. Many owners of bitches assert that they seem to become more mature and intelligent after they have had a litter than they were before.

For anyone who is looking for a companion that is equally at home in a house, in the field or in water, one which is thoroughly adaptable and trustworthy, then a Retriever of one type or another can

*The Chesapeake Bay Retriever is strong and active, and can make a good guard*

be recommended without hesitation.

It is a good idea for would-be purchasers to contact the secretary of the local canine society and ask him to supply the names and addresses of reputable breeders of the Retriever of your choice. He will be delighted to do this and will be almost as anxious as the prospective owner to ensure that the right choice of dog is made.

*The Flat-coated Retriever is a very handsome dog which makes a good family pet*

# Setters: always in search of game

THE Setter now exists in three distinct breeds: English, Gordon and Irish (Red). It was evolved from the large Land Spaniel (usually referred to as the setting or index dog) as a game-finding dog. The development of guns and gunpowder, which occurred towards the end of the seventeenth century, made it possible to shoot birds on the wing, whereas previously game birds had been taken with a net. This was a rather hit-and-miss method. The sportsman would encourage his setting dog to range, on a zigzag course, over the ground where birds might be expected to be found. If the dog scented game it would halt and raise one front leg to indicate the presence of birds: hence the name 'index'. It would then worm its way slowly on its belly towards them and, when quite close, would lie down quietly. The sportsman would then throw a net over both dog and birds, although, as might be imagined, the quarry would frequently escape.

Later, when it became possible to 'shoot flying', as the modern practice came to be termed, the need arose for a dog that worked rather differently. What the sportsman now required was a dog that would stand up to indicate the presence and whereabouts of game and draw towards it, instead of crouching and crawling. Such a dog was eventually produced by cross-breeding with the Spanish Pointer, and it was in this way that the setting breeds as we know them today were originated.

At that period the population of Britain was comparatively small (probably under six million), communications were poor, and the breeding of game-finding dogs was confined to the landed gentry. This resulted in individual types and strains, each breeder endeavouring to produce the sort of setting dog best suited to his particular needs; it explains why the three breeds of Setters that are recognized today came to acquire special, individual characteristics.

The English Setter, which comes in a variety of parti-coloured forms with a white base, is the smallest and least volatile of the three. If any one individual is to be given credit for the breed's improvement, it is Edward Laverack, who died in 1877 and who bred extensively during the preceding half-century. The English Setter was produced from a combination of the Spanish Pointer, the Large Water Spaniel and the Springer Spaniel.

The English Setter is a beautiful dog, with a stable, mild and sweet disposition. Its great need for love and affection make it an ideal pet. Nor does being kept as a pet affect its hunting ability. It is an open, friendly dog, of little use as a guard dog, as it will welcome strangers as long-lost friends.

The English Setter reacts extremely well to obedience training. It does, however, need a great deal of exercise – at least two hours daily – so cannot really be recommended for life in a town flat.

Its coat colour can be any one of the following: black; white and tan; black and white; blue; lemon and white; orange and white; liver and white. The coat should be long, flat or slightly wavy, but not curly. It should not be soft or woolly.

The Gordon Setter, a black-and-tan dog, originated as a distinct breed at Gordon Castle, the Banffshire seat of the

*The Irish or Red Setter is the most high-spirited and lively of all the Setter breeds, which means that it is far more demanding in matters of training than its two relatives. Furthermore, as it is a large dog, it is expensive to feed.*

Duke of Richmond and Gordon. It is the biggest and heaviest of the three breeds; although not quite as fast as the other two, it possesses plenty of stamina. It is a beautiful and highly intelligent dog, absolutely loyal and devoted to its family, but particularly to one member of the family. It is a perfect one-man shooting dog. The Gordon is extremely good with children and soon becomes part of the family. It is much less friendly towards strangers than the other Setters, and will make a better guard dog. It is not a kennel dog, and should not be kept together with many other dogs. It needs a great deal of exercise, and will be much happier living in the country.

The Gordon is a rich black colour with tan markings on the throat, chest, inside of hind legs and thighs. The coat should be soft and shining, slightly waved, but not curly. A dog should be 26 inches high at the shoulder and weigh 65 lb; a bitch should be 24 inches high and weigh 56 lb.

The Irish Setter was evolved in Ireland where game was not as plentiful as in the United Kingdom, where the weather is inclined to be more inclement and the going correspondingly rougher and more tiring. Because of these factors the breed, broadly speaking, is inclined to be more high-spirited than the other two, even meriting the description 'headstrong'. It is more demonstrative and less easily discouraged. It therefore demands more understanding in the matter of training, whether as a gun dog or companion dog.

From the above remarks it will be appreciated that the Setter is, or should be, a dog with the natural capacity of ranging widely in search of game (the Irish being the widest ranger) and to respond to training. The dog will obviously show to best advantage, therefore, if its owner is able to give it free-ranging exercise as frequently as possible, and if he is also prepared to take the trouble to train it to fit into the family.

Any breed of Setter will, if necessary, adapt itself to conditions of urban life, but it is ideally a dog of the open spaces. Success depends entirely on the owner, who must have a great deal of patience and be ready to take great pains over initial training. It is emphatically not a dog for the elderly, for anyone of limited mobility, for a person who is away from home all day, or for the housewife whose family takes up most of her time and attention. Furthermore, being a dog of some size, it is not the cheapest to feed, and therefore it cannot be recommended to a dog-lover of limited means.

The Setter is normally of equable temperament and good with children. As a dog evolved for the silent tracking of game, it is not given to barking and is not a fighter. Although it will usually give

# Breed Standard: the Irish Setter

**GENERAL APPEARANCE**
Must be racy, full of quality, kindly expression. An elegant, aristocratic dog.

**HEAD AND SKULL**
The head should be long and lean, not narrow or snipy. The skull oval (from ear to ear), and with well-defined occipital protuberance. From the stop to the point of the nose should be long, the nostrils wide, and the jaws of nearly equal length. The colour of the nose: dark mahogany, or dark walnut, or black.

**EYES**
Should be dark hazel or dark brown.

**EARS**
The ears should be of moderate size, fine in texture, set on low, well back; and hanging in a neat fold close to the head.

**MOUTH**
Not over or undershot.

**NECK**
Should be moderately long, very muscular, but not too thick, slightly arched.

**FOREQUARTERS**
The shoulders to be fine at the points, deep and sloping well back. The chest as deep as possible, rather narrow in front. The fore legs should be straight and sinewy, having plenty of bone, with elbows free and well let down.

**BODY**
Should be proportionate, the ribs well sprung.

**HINDQUARTERS**
Should be wide and powerful. The hind legs from hip to hock should be long and muscular; from hock to heel short and strong.

**FEET**
Should be small, toes close together and arched.

**TAIL**
Should be of moderate length, tapering to a fine point; to be carried as nearly as possible on a level with or below the back.

**COAT AND FEATHERING**
On the head, front of the legs, and tips of the ears, should be short and fine, but on all other parts of the body and legs it ought to be of moderate length, flat, and as free as possible from curl or wave. The feather on the upper portion of the ears should be long and silky; on the back of fore and hind legs should be long and fine; a fair amount of hair on the belly, which may extend on chest and throat. Feet well feathered between toes.

**COLOUR**
The colour should be rich chestnut, with no trace whatever of black; white on chest, throat or toes, or a small star on the forehead, or a narrow streak or blaze on the nose or face not to disqualify.

*Above: The English Setter is the smallest of the three breeds. It makes a delightful pet, but a prospective owner should bear in mind that it needs plenty of exercise. Left: The Gordon Setter is the heaviest of the three breeds and has great staying power*

warning of a stranger entering the home, it must not be expected to do the work of a genuine guard dog.

To appear at its best, a Setter should be groomed regularly, which means that its owner must be prepared to devote at least a quarter of an hour each day to this task. Constitutionally, it is a tough dog, and, provided it is given proper food and accommodation, is unlikely to become seriously ill.

As already stated, the Setter originated as a game-finding dog and only began to be considered as a show dog a little over a century ago. Because of changes in shooting practice (such as grouse shooting from butts) and as a result of farming methods which led to the gradual disappearance of long stubble and hedges, the 'dogging' of game birds declined. Consequently, the demand for the Setter as a practical shooting dog waned.

On the other hand, the introduction in 1865 of field trials created an interest in

Setters on the part of owners who wished to enter them for competition. The outcome has been that breeders of Setters nowadays approach their work from three distinct angles and tend to concentrate on any one of these three objectives—a dog capable of winning at shows, of competing successfully at field trials, or of serving as a general utility gun dog. Consequently, each of the three breeds has tended to be divided into show and working strains, the division being least marked in the Gordon Setter. A prospective buyer must therefore decide what purpose a dog is to serve. He cannot, for example, expect to get a high-grade worker from a kennel breeding for show.

The English Setter, as a result of selective breeding for field trials both in Britain and the United States, is today the best worker of the three breeds. It has a better nose than the Irish Setter and is more easily trained. However, it is not as tireless as the latter and is more inclined to get discouraged in bad weather or by the scarcity of game. The best working strains of Irish Setters are now to be found in Ireland.

The Irish Setter is the most popular show dog and the Gordon Setter the least favoured of the three. Relative interest is

shown by these figures of breed registrations at the Kennel Club of Great Britain in 1971: Irish 3,764, English 996, Gordon 114. Irish Setters now rank twelfth in the list of registrations of all dog breeds. The general show level of the breed in Britain has never been higher. Stock bred in this country is in demand from all over the world. Even in the United States the breed is based on dogs originating in the United Kingdom or Ireland. The English Setter is not far behind in its standing as a show dog, its popularity increasing every year.

Clubs exist to further interest in each breed, and anyone who contemplates buying or showing a Setter is well advised to visit a few shows where the breed is scheduled. Particulars of forthcoming shows appear in the weekly canine journals. Much can be learned by observing the dogs in the show ring, and from the manner in which they are prepared and presented for competition. Similarly, anyone intending to take a serious interest in the working side of these breeds should go and see field trials. The Kennel Club is able to supply details of future trials. At shows and trials alike there are always 'old hands' who will be able to give valuable advice to the novice.

# Clumber, Field, Sussex, Irish Water and American Water Spaniels

THERE are seven breeds of spaniel in the Gundog Group recognized by the English Kennel Club, since the American Cocker has been officially accepted as a gundog, an agreement being reached on the restriction of its amount of feathering. This excessive feathering on the legs, as carried by the show dogs, was considered too great a handicap in the penetration of rough cover, which is the speciality of the spaniel.

In the beginning, spaniels fell into two divisions: those for land work and those for water work. As the retriever population grew, the water spaniels declined in number until the breed was maintained only in Ireland and America. Inevitably, the survivors became known as field spaniels. Gradually, sub-divisions were evolved (with the exception of the Clumbers which were an imported breed), among which was the Field Spaniel, now breeding to type and once very popular with shooting men.

When the English Kennel Club was formed in 1873 the only spaniel breeds registered were Clumbers, Sussex and Fields. In another ten years Irish Waters were added to the list, and the first Stud Book printed that year listed Clumbers, Irish Water Spaniels, Water Spaniels other than Irish, Fields, Cockers and Sussex. The next official step came in 1905, when the official classification read: Spaniels, Irish Waters, Water other than Irish, Clumber, Sussex, Field, English Springer, Welsh Springer, Red and White Cockers. A forewarning of things to come was in the introduction of the Springers, whose prowess in the field brought about a decline in a number of other breeds. Water Spaniels as such became extinct, and Red and White Cockers (known as Welsh Cockers) became extinct around the time of the First World War.

That serious breeders were aware of the danger of exaggerating certain characteristics such as feathering is shown in an article in the Kennel Gazette of February 1900. By this time the tendency to elongate the body was apparent. The Gazette article said of the Field Spaniel: 'He is being dragged in opposite directions, as it were, on the rack of fadism. Some of his admirers seize him violently and stretch him out until he assume the guise of the Basset Hound, whereby he loses

*Far left: the Clumber (above), well established in Britain, is slow compared with lighter gundogs, as is the Sussex (below). Centre: the Field Spaniel is threatened with extinction, but the Irish Water (below) is still often used*

# Breed Standard: the Field Spaniel

**GENERAL APPEARANCE**
That of a well-balanced, noble, upstanding sporting dog; built for activity and endurance.

**HEAD AND SKULL**
Skull well developed, with a distinct occipital protuberance; not too wide across the muzzle, long and lean, neither snipy nor squarely cut, and in profile curving gradually from nose to throat; lean beneath the eyes; a thickness here gives coarseness to the whole head. Nose well developed, good with open nostrils.

**EYES**
Not too full, but not small, receding or overhung, colour dark hazel or brown, or nearly black, according to the colour of the dog. Grave in expression and showing no haw.

**EARS**
Moderately long and wide, sufficiently clad with nice Setter-like feather and set low. They should fall in graceful folds, the lower parts curling inwards and backwards.

**MOUTH**
Level and strong; neither overshot nor undershot.

**FOREQUARTERS**
The shoulders should be long and sloping and well set back, thus giving great activity and speed. The forelegs should be of fairly good length, with straight, clean, flat bone and nicely feathered. Immense bone is not desirable.

**BODY**
Should be of moderate length, well ribbed up to a good strong loin, straight or slightly arched. The chest, deep and well developed. Back and loins very strong and muscular.

**HINDQUARTERS**
Strong and muscular. The stifles should be moderately bent and not twisted in or out.

**FEET**
Not too small; round with good, strong pads.

**TAIL**
Well set on and carried low, if possible below the level of the back, and nicely fringed with wavy feather of silky texture.

**COAT**
Flat or slightly waved, and never curled. Silky in texture, glossy and refined. On the chest, under the belly and behind the legs, there should be abundant feather.

**COLOUR**
Should be a self-coloured dog: Black, Liver, Golden Liver, Mahogany Red, Roan; or any one of these colours with Tan over the eyes, on the cheeks, feet and pasterns. Other colours, while not debarring a dog, are a fault.

**WEIGHT AND SIZE**
From about 35 to 50 lb. Height: about 18 inches to shoulder.

much of his native character for activity and stamina. Others look on horror struck, with eyes agog, and when the sworn torturers have ceased, they pounce on the victim and proceed to shorten him up and elongate his legs until he resembles the Setter. Between the two extreme parties the working spaniel proper is in peril of being improved off the face of the earth!' However exaggerated this may sound, the truth is that exhibitors bred them long in body, low on the leg and so heavily boned that they lost their ability to work in the field.

This was unfortunate for the breed after a good start. Indeed, in the USA there was some difficulty in establishing the breed, since Cocker and Springer blood was introduced in order to breed out the exaggerations.

For a number of years, in the annual Spaniel Championship no other breed has challenged the supremacy of the English Springer at work, and the Cockers have now their own Breed Championship. Added to failure in the field, Field Spaniels began to lose their variety of colour, the roans reverting to self-coloured black or liver. In the meantime, the gay, handy-sized Cocker in many colour combinations captured the imagination of owners who wanted a dog for companionship, and the Cocker still stands supreme in this sphere.

During World War One the Field Spaniel breed suffered a great deal, and worse was to come following World War Two, until in 1949 came the devastating report that only one Field had been registered in the Stud Book that year. However, at Crufts Show the following year, seven dogs were entered and thus another revival of the breed was begun. Today, Field Spaniels have the lowest registrations of any of the spaniel breeds, but the Field Trial Society is very active, and 31 Field Spaniels were registered in 1971. The modern Field Spaniel is between a Cocker and a Springer in size, and is a lively, biddable dog.

Another grand old breed which has suffered fluctuating popularity is the Clumber Spaniel. Clumbers first appeared in this country as big-bodied white dogs of spaniel character; they came as a present from the Duc de Noailles to the Duke of Newcastle towards the end of the eighteenth century and took the name of Clumber from the Duke's family seat in Nottinghamshire. Apart from their striking appearance, to which their massive build and lemon markings on the white coat contribute, they have a strong appeal to sportsmen.

Today much of the exalted patronage of Clumbers is missing, but a new generation of owners has yielded to their undoubted charm, and the breed is becoming a feature of the big show. Portly, comfortable and obedient in the field and at home, they are very affectionate companions.

Although the English Water Spaniel are now extinct, the Irish Water Spaniel still survive. In fact, these dogs more resemble a Curly-coated Retriever than a spaniel, and in the Irish Field Trial they run in competition with the retrievers. They are very loyal animal but of such independence as to amount almost to unruliness.

In this country, between the wars, strain of dark-coloured dogs with tightly turned curls was perfected and proved unbeatable at the shows, so much so that they drove other breeders from the show ring. However, in Ireland they preserve both their show and field trial entries. Their chief work is retrieving from water however, turbulent it may be, and thus they are trained as much to hand signal as to the whistle. They are full of courage and vigour. As an instance of swimming prowess, a Champion Irish Water Spaniel bitch swam at night from the mainland across the Race of Man to the Calf of Man. The breed stands about 20 to 2 inches high and, not surprisingly, its coat is almost totally waterproof.

The origin of the American Water Spaniel is a mystery. It is suggested that it was evolved from the Irish Water Spaniel the Curly-Coated Retriever and the old English Water Spaniel. Whatever it ancestry, there is no doubt that it is a very capable working dog. He has an excellent nose and will spring game from the thickest covert. Retrieving present no problems whether on land or in water.

The American Water Spaniel is of medium size, standing 15 to 18 inches at the shoulder. It is solid liver or chocolate in colour and its distinctive coat is closely curled or has a marcelled effect. Dense but not coarse, it is all but entirely waterproof. Recognized by the AKC in 1940, its working qualities are jealously maintained by the American Water Spaniel Club.

The Sussex Spaniel appears to be on the way to extinction; only 34 were registered with British Kennel Club in 197. Perhaps it is surprising that the breed has existed so long, for even a century and a half ago when the Sussex was originated it did not fill a need. Other breeds, in existence at that time, were doing all that was required of them as gundogs. Standing at 14 to 15 inches high, the great attraction of the Sussex, to those who are looking for a companionable dog, is its golden-liver colour which proves an ideal background for the hazel or amber eyes.

*The Sussex Spaniel (right) is a breed which is unfortunately dying out*

# The Cocker Spaniel

THE Cocker Spaniel, or English Cocker Spaniel as it is known in the USA, is the direct descendant of the first spaniels, so called because of their Spanish origin. Nowadays it is one of the most popular sporting dogs. It is robust, eager, cheerful and tireless. For those who know how to train and to utilize this breed, and so can take advantage of its intelligence and inborn aptitude for work, the Cocker becomes the ideal sporting companion.

The Cocker Spaniel is not a pointing dog but a hunter, and as such it finds and flushes all the game it can. It is very fast, so it is necessary for the owner to keep his dog under control at all times in order to prevent it from getting out of hand.

The Cocker likes all types of terrain, even the most difficult, but is really in its ideal element on marshland. Being an excellent swimmer it throws itself into the water with great impetuosity to retrieve game.

Because of its lively, affectionate temperament, its gentle yet proud eyes and its compact size, it has today become predominantly a family pet. This fact has made the breed more widely known, but it may not have been a good thing with regard to selection and breeding. The Cocker Spaniels seen today in the show rings of the world are certainly very beautiful dogs, but it can be argued that they are further away from the ideal of the breed which at one time required a balance between beauty and function.

When deciding on a Cocker Spaniel as a pet it should not be forgotten that the dog is by heredity a hunter. So its life should include plenty of exercise in the open air, and runs in the fields and woods, where its hunting instincts can be allowed a certain amount of play. Too often the Cocker kept as a pet is overweight, due to enforced inactivity. A fat dog is not a beautiful one, nor is it healthy.

Perhaps because of the breed's pendulous ears, the Cocker is more likely to suffer from ear complaints than other dogs. The owner will soon become aware that something is wrong when he sees his dog holding its head on one side, or shaking its head, or scratching one ear. The cause may not be serious, but it may be a condition known as canker—an inflammation of the outer ear canal. Usually this occurs through an accumulation of wax brought on by dirt or ear mites. But as

there are several causes it is essential to get the advice of your veterinary surgeon, since until the cause of the canker is known the correct treatment cannot be given.

The first mention of the name 'spaniel' in English appears in Chaucer's *Canterbury Tales* written in the fourteenth century, and by the seventeenth century there were many types of sporting dogs in existence called spaniels regardless of their size and shape, but all clearly derived from the Spanish spaniel. Slowly the different varieties emerged, varying in size and conformation according to the type of sporting work they carried out.

The Cocker Spaniel is a cheerful dog that traces its descent from the King Charles Spaniels which were imported from France and Italy and which were greatly beloved by Charles I and Charles II. In those days, the dogs were long-nosed— the short nose being bred in much later.

The Duke of Marlborough experimented with spaniel breeding and crossed the King Charles with his own strain of red-and-white Blenheim spaniels. These were larger than the modern King Charles Spaniels and were used to flush woodcock —hence the name 'Cocker' which derives not from the name of the bird but the expression 'to cock' or drive game from cover. A periodical published in 1820 reported that the best breed of Cockers in England were bred by the Duke of Marlborough and that puppies of this strain were eagerly sought by the sportsmen of the period.

During the nineteenth century the practice of holding dog shows was introduced. The first appearance of the Cocker Spaniel in British show rings was at Birmingham in 1859 where one of the classes was for 'Clumbers' and another for 'Cockers, or Other Breeds'. British

*The American Cocker (right) and the English Cocker (far right) make good companions and fine gun dogs*

# Breed Standard: the Cocker Spaniel

**GENERAL APPEARANCE**
The Cocker Spaniel should be well balanced and compact and should measure about the same from the withers to the ground as from the withers to the root of the tail.

**HEAD AND SKULL**
There should be a good square muzzle with a distinct stop which should be mid way between the tip of the nose and the occiput. The skull should be well developed, cleanly chiselled, neither too fine nor too coarse. The cheek bones should not be prominent. The nose should be sufficiently wide to allow for the acute scenting power associated with this breed.

**EARS**
Lobular, set on low, on a level with the eyes, with fine leathers which extend to but not beyond the tip of the nose; well clothed with long silky hair which should be straight.

**NECK**
Neck should be moderate in length, clean in throat, muscular and neatly set into fine sloping shoulders.

**FOREQUARTERS**
The shoulders should be sloping and fine, the chest well developed and the brisket deep, neither too wide nor too narrow in front. The legs must be well boned, feathered and straight and should be sufficiently short for concentrated power but not too short to interfere with the tremendous exertions expected from this grand little sporting dog.

**BODY**
Body should be immensely strong and compact for the size and weight of the dog. The ribs should be well sprung behind the shoulder blades, the loin short, wide and strong, with a firm topline gently sloping downwards to the tail.

**HINDQUARTERS**
Hindquarters should be wide, well rounded and very muscular. The legs must be well boned, feathered above the hock with a good bend of stifle and short below the hock allowing for plenty of drive.

**FEET**
Feet should be firm, thickly padded and catlike.

**TAIL**
Must be merry, carried in line with the back and never cocked up.

**COAT**
Flat and silky in texture, never wiry or wavy, with sufficient feather; not too profuse and never curly.

**COLOUR**
Various. In self colours no white is allowed except on the chest.

**WEIGHT AND SIZE**
The weight should be about 28 lbs to 32 lbs. The height at the withers should be approximately 15 inches to 15½ inches for bitches and approximately 15½ inches to 16 inches for dogs. In USA, dogs 16–17 inches, bitches 15–16 inches.

dogs went abroad to appear in foreign shows, and in Paris in 1863 a dog listed as 'Mr. Heath's Cocker, No. 486' gained the top award in its class. A few years later Field and Cocker Spaniels became distinct groups, the Field Spaniel being over 25 lb in weight and the Cocker under this weight. But it was not until 1892 that the British Kennel Club acknowledged the Cocker Spaniel as a separate breed, and the further development of the breed dates from 1901 when the weight limit was abolished.

The English Cocker Club of America was founded in 1935 with the object of promoting the breed and discouraging inter-breeding between the American and English Cockers. A speciality show was held shortly afterwards and then, in 1936, the British Standard was adopted.

The American Cocker Spaniel traces its descent from the Cocker Spaniels imported from England around 1880. The American breeders thought they could improve the type and develop a dog which was more suited to American sporting needs. To this end a number of selective breeding operations were undertaken with the result that a very beautiful animal was produced. It is true that the English Cocker and the American Cocker were once interbred but this practice has now stopped and both varieties can now be considered pure. The American Kennel Club has

given both a separate registration.

This attractive dog is about five pounds lighter than its English cousin, the legs are slightly shorter and the eyes more prominent. The coat is lustrous, very full, and the ears and legs well feathered. It created a record for all breeds by once heading the Registration Tables for seventeen consecutive years. Still one of the most popular dogs in the United States, it is now making headway in Britain where its beauty, intelligence and docility have assured it a welcome as a companion dog capable of settling down in either town or country.

The American Cocker is a serviceable-looking dog with a refined chiselled head, standing on straight legs and well up on the shoulders. It has a compact body and wide, muscular quarters. It is a dog capable of considerable speed coupled with endurance. Free and merry, it should be well balanced and indicate a keen inclination to work. The temperament is good and there should be no trace of nervousness.

The head is rounded with no tendency to flatness, or pronounced roundness of the crown. The muzzle is broad and deep, the jaws even and square. The nostrils must be well developed, the nose being black in blacks and black-and-tans. In other colours it may be black or brown, the former for preference. The eyes are

round and full and set to give the eye a somewhat almond shape. The ears are lobular and set on high but no higher than the lower part of the eye. The hair should be long and silky and either straight or wavy.

The body of the American Cocker is short, compact, and firmly knit, giving an impression of strength. The shoulders are deep and sloping and the forelegs strongly boned and muscular. The rear legs are also muscular, well boned and with well-turned stifles and clearly defined thighs. The tail is set and carried on a line with the top-line of the back.

The coat is of medium length and silky in texture with sufficient undercoat to give protection in bad weather. It can be flat or wavy but never curly. The ears, chest, abdomen and posterior sides of the legs should be well feathered but must not disguise the dog's true lines or movement. There is a choice of approved colours. The blacks must be jet black. The tan in black-and-tans should have clearly defined tan markings, at specified locations, on a jet black body. The tan locations are: a clear spot over each eye; on the sides of the muzzle, where the tan should not extend over or join; on sides of cheeks and undersides of ears; on all legs and feet, and on the underside of the tail. Solid colours, other than black and tan, should be of sound shade. Parti-colours should have one or more colours appearing in well-defined markings on a white background. Roans may be of any of the accepted roan patterns of mottled appearance, or alternating colours of hairs distributed throughout the coat.

The ideal height at the withers is 15 in to 15½ in, bitches 14 in to 14½ in.

The English Cocker has long been dubbed 'the merry cocker' and the American variety shares this carefree attitude to life. It is interesting to note that in the stage and screen productions of the famous play 'The Barretts of Wimpole Street', an American Cocker took the part of Flush, Elizabeth Barrett's pet dog.

Cockers are undoubtedly one of the most intelligent of dog breeds. Cocker owners often vie with one another with stories that reveal the cleverness of their dogs. Veronica Lucas-Lucas, an authority on the breed, tells the story of a red Cocker bitch named Plum who showed great intelligence when nursing a litter. It was a very hot summer's day and everybody was perspiring—yet Plum's puppies were always cool. How did it happen? Plum's owner, on one visit to the puppies and their mother, saw the method in operation. Plum was dipping each puppy in turn in the water bowl, and finally made herself as wet as possible. Here is just one example of the Cocker's power of thought. There are many others.

# Welsh and English Springer and Brittany Spaniels

MANY years ago, when our various gun dog breeds were being developed, the smaller medium-coated multi-coloured ones were known as spaniels, and they were eventually split into two sections on a weight basis. The smaller ones became known as Cockers, either English or Welsh, and they were used a great deal for woodcock shooting. The English Cockers were produced in self colours, and in many colour combinations, and remain so to this day. The Welsh Cockers were all red and white but they became extinct shortly after the turn of the century. However, the larger red-and-white spaniels survived and are known today as Welsh Springer Spaniels.

From the family of the larger type of spaniel there gradually emerged a dog that was principally liver and white. Through the years its inherent aptitude for work has been developed until the English Springer Spaniel stands unchallenged as the best worker of all the spaniels, and one of the best utility gun dogs of all the breeds. At the same time, selective breeding by those who appreciated a good-looking animal has ensured that the type is fixed; so the English Springer, in addition to being a hard worker, is also a beautiful, well-balanced dog. It can be seen in show rings throughout the world. In Britain's dog world, 1973 is known as the Year of the Springer, because of the great win by the liver and white Sh.Ch. Hawkhill Connaught, which took the title 'Top Dog of the Year' in a competition promoted by the magazine *Dog World*. The title is awarded on the number of points won at championship shows during the year, with all breeds competing against one another. The winner was so outstanding that it won by a clear 16 points.

There are many Springers which are champions in the show ring, and others which are champions at Field Trials, but the competition today in each section is so strong that there is no joint champion and in fact there have only been three in the history of the breed.

The various titles awarded to championship spaniels, which, incidentally, apply to all gun dogs, can be confusing to the layman, and therefore require an explanation. In the days when Springers were increasing in numbers as show dogs, the Kennel Club decided on a means of preserving their working instincts. It ruled that when a dog had won three Challenge Certificates under three different judges it had to go to a Field Trial and obtain a working certificate before it could claim the title of Champion, which was given to all breeds (other than gun dogs) with the appropriate show qualifications. But more and more people bred Springers for companionship and exhibition only, and they became so powerful numerically that they persuaded the Kennel Club to give them a title of their own. Thus the title of Show Champion was created.

A dog holding this title is of course typical and good looking, but it may never have been worked and could actually be gun-shy. If an owner wishes to discard the word Show, he can apply for a working certificate at any time he likes. If granted, his dog has the simplest but most highly creditable title of all, that of Champion.

To become a Field Trial Champion, a dog must win an open stake in its breed class and another open to all dogs of its group. There are also various types of obedience and working competitions for which owners can enter their dogs, whether they are pedigree champions or mongrels. These obedience trials have become very popular with the owners of gun dogs and other working dogs; they like to think that their pet could, given the opportunity, do the work for which it was originally bred. These competitions are the next best thing to Field Trials.

The English Springer Spaniel was known in the USA before the breed was recognized by the Kennel Club of England. A few Americans had a high regard for the sporting qualities of the dog and found it an excellent all-round bird dog. However, generally speaking, it was not until the formation of the English Springer Spaniel Field Trial Association in 1924 that the Springer became better known to the sportsmen of America. Field Trials were organized and in 1927 the Association became the parent club of the breed. This resulted in a Standard being drawn up which was approved by the AKC. The Standard was formulated in such a way that the natural abilities of the breed would be given every attention by serious breeders who were, of course, anxious that the Springer should continue to be a real working gun dog and not merely a show bench ornament.

The Standard has contributed noticeably towards the uniformity of the breed and this is very obvious when watching Field Trials and the dogs on the show benches. The Springer is firmly established in the USA and it seems likely that it will not only retain its standing as an excellent hunting dog but will increase in popularity as more and more people see it at work. It is a dog that responds well to training.

The name Springer indicates the age of the breed and it is thought that the title originated from the time when the bow and arrow was the only device for

*The origin of Welsh Springer Spaniels, shown here in an attentive group, is the cause of much speculation among experts*

# Breed Standard: the English Springer

## CHARACTERISTICS

The English Springer is the oldest of our Sporting Gundogs and the taproot from which all of our sporting land spaniels (except Clumbers) have evolved. It was originally used for the purpose of finding and springing game for the net, falcon, or greyhound, but today is used to find, flush, and retrieve game for the gun.

## GENERAL APPEARANCE

That of a symmetrical, compact, strong, and active dog, built for endurance and activity. The highest on the leg and raciest in build of all British land spaniels.

## HEAD AND SKULL

The skull should be of medium length and fairly broad and slightly rounded, rising from the foreface, making a brow or stop. The cheeks should be flat, the foreface fairly broad and deep without being course. Nostrils well developed.

## EYES

Neither too full nor too small but of medium size, well set in, of an alert, kind expression. The colour should be dark hazel. Black and deep brown in the black and white dogs.

## EARS

Lobular in shape, set close to the head. Should be in a line with the eye.

## NECK

Strong and muscular, of nice length and free from throatiness, arched and tapering towards the head – this giving great activity and speed.

## FOREQUARTERS

The forelegs should be straight and nicely feathered, elbows well set to body and with proportionate substance to carry body; strong, flexible pasterns.

## BODY

Strong and of proportionate length, the chest deep and well developed with plenty of heart and lung room, well sprung ribs, loins muscular with slight arch and well coupled, thighs muscular.

## HINDQUARTERS

The hindlegs should be well let down from hip to hocks. Stifles and hocks moderately bent, inclining neither inwards nor outwards.

## FEET

Tight, compact, and well rounded with strong pads.

## TAIL

The stern should be low and never carried above the level of the back, well feathered and lively.

## COAT

Close, straight and weather-resistant without being coarse.

## COLOUR

Any recognized land spaniel colour is acceptable, but liver-and-white, black-and-white, or either of these colours with tan markings, preferred.

## WEIGHT AND SIZE

Approximate height: 20 inches. Approximate weight: 50 lb.

---

killing at a distance–an obviously inefficient weapon for winging a rising bird. The spaniel was used to find and "spring" game for the nets or the falcons carried by the hunters.

Two schools of thought exist about the origin of the breed. One maintains that the English Springer came from Norfolk and was known in the early days as the Norfolk Spaniel. The other maintains that it took its name from the Norfolk family.

The approved Standard for the English Springer states that any recognized land spaniel colour is acceptable, but liver-and-white and black-and-white, or either of these colours with tan markings, is preferred. An early breed patron, Sir Hugo FitzHerbert, produced some chestnut-and-white spaniels. It was at his home, Tissington Hall, just before World War One, that the cobby little red-and-white Welsh Cockers were worked in competition.

The Welsh Springer Spaniel was introduced to the Kennel Club register of breeds in 1902. There has often been speculation as to the consistency of the colour breeding in Welsh Springers, and there is a theory that they are not related to English Springers, but descend from the orange-and-white Brittany Spaniel. The term 'orange' is American; the British terms are lemon for pale markings and

red for deeper markings.

Rich red-and-white is the only colour allowed in the British Kennel Club Standard, but there is a deviation with regard to the nostrils, which may be flesh-coloured or dark. The name 'Starter' is an old and unofficial term for the Welsh Springer Spaniel. A breed difference between the English and the Welsh is also found in the shape of the ears, which, in the Welsh, are comparatively small, instead of being lobular, set moderately low and hanging close to the cheeks, gradually narrowing toward the tip.

There is also a difference between the two Springers in action. All spaniels are required to stride out smoothly with a powerful drive in the hindquarters, but, when moving slowly, the English Springer may revert to a 'pacing' stride, which is typical of the breed. This means that instead of the legs moving individually in sequence, the nearside and offside pairs are moved in unison.

A Welsh Springer dog should not exceed 19 inches at the shoulder, and a bitch should be approximately 18 inches. Although the modern Kennel Club Standard does not specify any definite weight, the old Welsh Springer Club Standard gives the weight as 33 to 40 lb.

The possible connection between the Brittany and Welsh Springers can be

judged more clearly in America where Brittanies are numerous and well respected as working dogs, where their Field Trials are always well supported, while the Welsh Springers are comparatively few in number. English Springers, however, are growing in number, and championship shows and field trials are strongly supported by their owners.

The Brittany Spaniel is an old French breed which, judging by its size and method of working, is more like a Setter. The basic stock originated in Spain and much development took place in Britain and various other European countries. All this went on so long ago that no one really knows what happened in those early days. It has been said that the breed was related to the early Irish red-and-white Setters.

The Brittany Spaniel has no tail or, at most, a stump of 4 inches or less. It is a dog of compact build, leggy and able to cover the ground at speed. The head is of medium length, slightly wedge-shaped, the ears being short and leafy. The coat is dense and flat or wavy, and the colours should be dark orange and liver or liver and white.

Almost unknown in Britain, the breed was imported into the USA in 1931 where it has achieved a large following and many Field Trial successes.

All spaniels are most companionable, and these two breeds are no exception. They will find a niche in any sort of establishment, are biddable, and need no special attention, as a run through the coat with brush and comb will keep it in pristine condition. Two important points are worth mentioning: firstly, give spaniels all the exercise you can, for they are contented dogs and are inclined to become fat; secondly, never overfeed. This may be difficult advice to follow, for many spaniels have voracious appetites, but it is important in order to avoid obesity.

The Springer Spaniel is certainly a breed that needs and responds to correct training. With so many established training classes all over the country there is really no excuse for a dog owner to allow his pet to remain untrained. Being a sporting dog, the Springer possesses instincts that can make it a nuisance, unless those instincts have been refined and channelled into correct behaviour patterns. For example, it is to be expected that an untrained Springer will chase livestock and poultry. Therefore at a very early age it is advisable to put it on a lead and to walk it among farmyard animals. Immediately it shows interest and pulls forward it must be taught 'No', and if this is repeated often enough your pet will get used to the sheep and poultry, and remember that chasing them is forbidden.

Even so, with a Springer—even if it has been trained—it is inadvisable to let it roam at will without a lead. Its natural instincts may reassert themselves and then your seemingly well-trained dog will be reckoned a nuisance by neighbours.

The ideal, of course, is for every Springer to be allowed to do field work for which it is so admirably suited. Training for this can begin indoors when your pet is only three or four months old. First the dog must learn to sit quietly by you when you, perhaps, are resting in a chair. Then an element of play can be introduced into the proceedings, by you producing an old woollen hat or sock which has been stuffed with some soft material such as cotton wool. You throw this into a corner and send the puppy to fetch it.

Then comes the first difficult phase: to teach your dog not to fetch the stuffed sock until you tell him to do so. Throw the sock into a corner, but as you do so keep a strong grip on his neck and say 'No'. Hold this position for several seconds, with the sock lying in the corner and the puppy restrained by your chair. Then give the command 'Go fetch!' and reward the puppy with a tit-bit or make

a fuss of him when the procedure has been gone through correctly. In training, be sure to show your pleasure; dogs respond to appreciation. This is just one reason why extroverts make good dog trainers—they are not afraid to show their feelings.

This 'fetch the sock' routine should be gone through every day until the puppy is thoroughly accustomed to it, and is, in fact, very much looking forward to the game it can share with its master. A variation should be introduced when the puppy is thoroughly trained in the initial procedure. You hide the sock behind some item of furniture in the room, taking care not to let the puppy see you do it. Then give the word 'Go find!' To do this your pet must use its nose to sniff out the object.

When the weather is fine enough, transfer the game to out of doors. There is the possibility that, with all the space of garden or park to explore, the puppy will chase the sock and carry it off, instead of bringing it back to you. When this happens do not run after your dog. After you have called to him, walk backwards. This will make him come towards you with the sock—assuming he has heard your call. The final stage is to have someone trail the sock through long grass or behind bushes while you hold the puppy on the lead. Then release him with 'Go fetch!' and after he has found it, recall him and walk backwards so that he brings the sock to your hand. This is ideal early training for a Springer.

*Facing page: The English Springer is said to be the oldest of our sporting gundogs. Right: In Britain the only colour allowed for Welsh Springers is rich red and white*

# Chapter IV
# Sporting Dogs
# Terrier Group

# Airedale, Irish, Welsh and Lakeland terriers

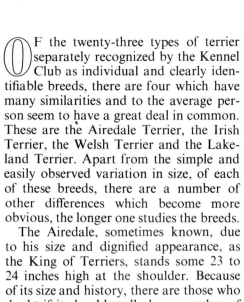

OF the twenty-three types of terrier separately recognized by the Kennel Club as individual and clearly identifiable breeds, there are four which have many similarities and to the average person seem to have a great deal in common. These are the Airedale Terrier, the Irish Terrier, the Welsh Terrier and the Lakeland Terrier. Apart from the simple and easily observed variation in size, of each of these breeds, there are a number of other differences which become more obvious, the longer one studies the breeds.

The Airedale, sometimes known, due to his size and dignified appearance, as the King of Terriers, stands some 23 to 24 inches high at the shoulder. Because of its size and history, there are those who doubt if it should really be a member of the terrier group at all. The word terrier comes from the Latin 'terra', meaning the earth, and these breeds were originally intended to be earth dogs–going to ground after vermin of one sort or another in order to 'bolt' or chase them out from their hiding places. The Airedale is obviously much too large ever to have performed such a function. However, it originated as a result of a crossing between terrier-type dogs on the one hand and Otter Hounds on the other. As far as is known, this crossing took place around the middle of the nineteenth century in the Aire and Wharfedale regions of Yorkshire, and since that time the breed's popularity has never really been in doubt. The name of the breed originated in 1879 at an agricultural show in Bingley, Yorkshire. A large group of 'Waterside Terriers' so impressed the judges that they named the breed after the show, which was called the Airedale Show.

Airedale Terriers were used quite extensively during the First World War for the carrying of despatches from one part of the battlefield to another. The Airedale is generally a friendly dog, yet makes a really good guard dog. Like all terriers it is aggressive, but since it has been bred as a working dog it is never highly strung. It is a very efficient hunter and a good retriever of ducks. It is easy to train, loyal and devoted to its master and good with children. The symmetrical and powerful make-up of its conformation, coupled with an undeniably appealing, and at the same time very alert, head and expression, all contribute to its present status as the most popular of the four terriers under discussion. The coat of the Airedale, which is hard, dense and wiry in appearance, is no harder to look after than that of most of the 'trimmed' terrier breeds, except that there is a good deal more of it. This naturally makes adequate care a little more time-consuming for many breeders. However, anyone who falls for the noble and powerful appearance of the Airedale Terrier and who decides upon this breed as a pet, must surely not grudge the extra time that grooming will undoubtedly take.

The Irish Terrier shares certain characteristics with the Airedale, although it is about six inches shorter to the shoulder than its larger cousin. The head and skull shape are similar. As far as the history of the Irish Terrier is concerned, its origins are even more steeped in uncertainty than are those of the Airedale, and it was not until around 1870 that the breed emerged in any sort of standard form, or indeed that there was any agreement that a certain breed should be known as the Irish Terrier. Undoubtedly, at that time the breed was somewhat longer in body than it is today, and there is evidence to suggest that the ears of the Irish were originally cropped until the practice became illegal in this country. The Irish Terrier was developed to be a hunter. It is an excellent hunter of rabbits and other small game. It is a superb ratter and retriever.

The official Kennel Club Standard of the breed is careful to stress how good-tempered the breed should be, especially with people, though it has to admit that the Irish is not too keen on any interference on the part of other dogs. This is perhaps a simple way of pointing out that they can really be quite aggressive with other dogs. The Irish Terrier is a fearless, brave, little dog. It is devoted to its owner and his family but can be aloof with strangers. It can adapt to both town and country and is unaffected by cold and heat. Coats are not really difficult to manage and, of course, the real red colour is much desired by breeders. These factors, coupled with the smartness and alertness of the breed, all go to make the Irish Terrier good to look at and a pleasure to own. The breed has a steady number of annual registrations with both the English and American Kennel Clubs.

The third dog–the Welsh Terrier–is an even smaller breed, also of Celtic origin, and whose working history, at least, is perhaps older than that of the two previous breeds. Although it was not until 1886 that the Welsh Terrier Club was founded (the breed being offered its first Championship Class by the Kennel Club in the following year), the working history of the Welsh Terrier–assisting hounds in the sporting districts of Wales–can be traced back well into the eighteenth century. There are even those who claim to be able to prove that the Welsh Terrier was in existence in the eleventh century. About equal in popularity to the Irish, this breed

*The Irish terrier has been given the nickname 'red devil' because its coat is red and it is aggressive towards other dogs*

# Breed Standard: the Airedale Terrier

**CHARACTERISTICS**
Keen of expression, quick of movement, on the tip-toe of expectation at any movement.

**HEAD AND SKULL**
The skull should be long and flat, not too broad between the ears, and narrowing slightly to the eyes. The skull to be free from wrinkles, with stop hardly visible, and cheeks level and free from fullness. Upper and lower jaws should be deep, powerful, strong and muscular. Lips to be tight. The nose should be black.

**EYES**
Should be dark in colour, small, full of terrier expression, keenness and intelligence.

**EARS**
Should be "V" shaped with a side carriage.

**MOUTH**
Teeth strong and level being capable of closing together like a vice.

**NECK**
Should be clean, muscular, of moderate length and thickness.

**FOREQUARTERS**
Shoulders should be long, well laid back, and sloping obliquely into the back, shoulder blades flat. Forelegs should be perfectly straight, with plenty of bone. Elbows should be perpendicular to the body, working free of the sides.

**BODY**
Back should be short, strong, straight and level, with no appearance of slackness.

**HINDQUARTERS**
Should be long and muscular with no droop. Thighs long and powerful with muscular second thigh. Hocks well let down.

**FEET**
Should be small, round and compact, and the toes moderately arched, not turned either in or out, and well cushioned.

**TAIL**
Should be set on high and carried gaily, but not curled over the back.

**COAT**
Should be hard, dense and wiry; the outer coat of hard, wiry, stiff hair, the undercoat should be a shorter growth of softer hair.

**COLOUR**
The head and ears, with the exception of dark markings on each side of the skull, should be tan, the ears being of a darker shade than the rest. The legs up to the thighs and elbows also should be tan. The body to be black or dark grizzle.

**WEIGHT AND SIZE**
Height about 23 to 24 inches for dogs, and bitches about 22 to 23 inches. Weight to be commensurate with height and type.

deserves greater recognition than it presently enjoys. The Welsh is a loyal, affectionate dog and very good with children. It is very high spirited, with boundless energy and aggressive towards other dogs.

Its short back should have a strong and straight topline to give it as smart an appearance as possible, but the head should be stronger than that of the more popular Wire Fox Terrier, without being in any way coarse. The foreface should not be as long as that of the Wire Fox Terrier but somewhat longer than that of the Lakeland Terrier. The colouring of the Welsh is of some importance, and at its best make the breed extremely appealing. The head, ears and legs should be of as deep and rich a tan as is possible and the rest of the body should be a raven black colour. Black-grizzle and tan is permitted but is not nearly so attractive. The Welsh coat should be wiry and hard in texture. There has been an increasing tendency in the show ring since World War Two towards showing Welsh Terriers with a good deal of leg hair, thus approaching closer to the previously mentioned Wire Fox Terrier mould. In size the Welsh stands around 15½ inches at the shoulder, and this makes it an admirable house dog, easy to handle and quite adaptable for both town and country life.

The Lakeland Terrier is the smallest of the four breeds covered here. As its name suggests, it originated in the fells of the Lake District in the north-west of England. Although it was only recognized as an individual breed by the Kennel Club in 1931, and is therefore a relatively young breed as far as the show ring is concerned, its working ancestry is a long one, almost as old as that of its Welsh cousin. The Lakeland has been developed from the same family as the Bedlington and the Dandie Dinmont and descends from the Black-and-tan Broken-haired Terriers. It was bred to be tough and courageous. The breed was, and indeed some of the working strains still are, used by those packs of hounds which hunt the Lakeland Fells, their supporters following on foot, since the countryside is unsuitable for horses to be ridden there.

The breed's size, shape and temperament are designed to enable it to fulfil this role adequately in the conditions prevailing in its native haunts. It is extremely strong for its size, with great endurance and determination. When battling with a fox or otter, it will utterly disregard danger. It is an extremely hardy little dog, seemingly unaffected by bad weather or the roughest terrain. It is not surprising that the breed has developed along similar lines to the Welsh Terrier, since the types of country in which the two are worked—the Welsh Mountains and the Lakeland Fells—are in many ways alike. There is

is in many ways distinct from every other terrier head, and a muzzle which must not be too long or like that of a Fox Terrier. The average weight of a male is 17 lb, and a female 15 lb. The Lakeland's coat can be a combination of blue and tan, black and tan, red and grizzle, or plain red, wheaten, liver, blue or black. Contrary to what is acceptable in the Welsh breed, a deep tan colour is not considered to be typical of a Lakeland Terrier and should be discouraged.

These four breeds clearly have much in common and a good deal to recommend them. None of them requires a great deal of grooming to maintain ordinary condition, but such is the competition in the show ring that each requires a great deal of careful preparation if there is to be any hope of gaining top honours. All are fairly adaptable and all have a smart, alert and game appearance, combined with that hardy and robust constitution so necessary in terrier breeds if they are to be good workers and companions.

*The Lakeland Terrier (facing page) is a friendly dog. Its harsh coat needs frequent grooming to keep it neat. The Welsh Terrier (above) is similar to the Lakeland, except for its trimmed coat. The Airedale Terrier (below) is the largest breed in this group and makes a good guard dog*

no doubt that the compact size and easily maintained coat of this terrier has made it quite popular in recent years. Nevertheless, the original fears of those who worked the breed, namely that Kennel Club acceptance would mean the eventual emergence of two distinct strains—the working strain and the showing strain—may prove to have been well founded. For a working Lakeland seldom does consistently well in the show ring, and a show Lakeland will rarely do any form of regular work. This is a great pity.

The original working temperament of the Lakeland Terrier should make it suitable for town life in general and to home life in particular. Although it will be friendly towards its master's family, it is essentially a one-man dog and all its devotion will be directed towards its master. The aggressive spirit of the Irish Terrier would not meet with the approval of the Lakeland enthusiast, for any terrier which is intended for work with hounds cannot afford to be quarrelsome if it values its own life. The Lakeland makes an excellent guard dog as it has extremely good hearing and a loud bark. It fearlessly tackles any intruders. This terrier needs firm training when young as it has a will of its own, but if properly brought up, makes an obedient companion.

The Lakeland, standing about $14\frac{1}{2}$ inches at the shoulder, has a head which

# Tenacious Bull Terriers

THE Bull Terrier family cannot claim an ancient lineage, since it is the descendant of the bulldogs which were once used to bait bulls and other unfortunate animals. When this cruel sport was banned by Parliament in 1835, it deprived thousands of working men of their favourite sport, and it became essential for them to find an outlet for the bloodthirsty tastes prevalent in that day and age. What seems to us to be abhorrent now, was then a commonplace sport.

Deprived of bull-baiting, they had to evolve another sport. This took the form of dog fighting. The bulldog was taken to the fighting pits, and it should be noted here that the fighting bulldog was quite a different creature from the modern product which is physically incapable of the feats performed by its ancestors. The modern bulldog is also less aggressive and more placid than its forebears.

It was found that the bulldog was too slow when fighting another dog, and so many owners began to look round for a cross-bred which would combine the pluck and tenacity of the bulldog with increased agility. The choice fell upon many game terriers which abounded in every district, and it is said that the Black-and-Tan and the English White Terrier figured largely in the transformation of the bulldog into a fast, plucky fighting machine, the Bull Terrier. Courage was all-important and any puppy which failed to prove sufficiently game was quickly disposed of.

The new breed, known variously as the Bull-and-Terrier, the Half-and-Half, the Pit Dog, and later the Staffordshire Bull Terrier, proved ready to attack anything and was almost impervious to pain. In 1825, several were matched against a lion and showed no hesitation in going into the attack. Once they had tasted blood they would fight to the death. At this time there was a considerable variation in size. The smaller dogs were not wasted: they were superb as rat killers and one terrier named Billy is reputed to have killed one hundred rats in just over six minutes, an amazing feat of courage and skill.

*The Bull Terrier was originally bred for bull baiting and dog fighting*

However, although it is necessary to mention the fighting history of the Staffordshire, it must be stressed that this is part of its past and no one should be deterred from buying a puppy on this account. The modern Staffie (as it is popularly known) is a dog with a great deal of courage, but it will not attack other animals unless forced to defend itself against aggression. Although primarily a peaceable dog, it can fight extremely fiercely if provoked, and only a very bold intruder will face a Staffie in its own home. It makes a tenacious and devoted guard dog. It should be noted that it is a mistake for a puppy, of any breed, to be encouraged to attack, to 'go for him', even in fun. Any fool can teach a dog to bite; the wise owner will train it to be docile and obedient. Not only will the dog benefit, but the owner will reap the rewards of the Staffie's loyalty.

If a Staffie appeals to you, then buy a puppy without hesitation, provided you are prepared to give it careful training. The money buys affection, intense loyalty and the companionship of a lifetime. It is best to choose a puppy from a breeder so that one has a chance to see the dog's parents, and so assess the temperament of the stock. The Staffordshire will not fawn upon strangers but neither will it show hostility. Those forward-looking eyes are very direct and it will size up people and offer its friendship in its own good time. As a family dog, it is safe with children and will allow them to take liberties which would not be tolerated if taken by adults. The Staffie is a dog of character and due regard should be paid to its sense of dignity. It takes life seriously but this will not prevent it from taking part in family games. Thriving in either town or country, it is an ideal all-purpose dog. It must, however, receive plenty of exercise to stay in peak condition. With its short, smooth coat, the Staffordshire requires little in the way of grooming. A regular brushing session to keep the coat neat, and periodic inspection of teeth, eyes and ears are all that is needed.

The Staffordshire Bull Terrier is a very strong dog, well muscled but agile, active and alert. Standing quietly by its owner, one can be deceived into thinking that its reactions are slow, but nothing is further from the case. Given good reason, it will move with the speed of a whip-lash generated by the power bequeathed to the breed by its fighting ancestors.

A short, broad skull with pronounced cheek muscles and a distinct stop is a characteristic of the Staffie. The nose is black, and a pink (or Dudley) nose is a bad fault. The eyes are dark for preference, round in shape and set to look straight ahead. The ears are medium in size, half-pricked or rose. Full prick or

# Breed Standard: the Bull Terrier

## GENERAL APPEARANCE
The Bull Terrier is the Gladiator of the canine race and must be strongly built, muscular, symetrical and active, with a keen, determined and intelligent expression, full of fire and courageous but of even temperament and amenable to discipline. Irrespective of size, dogs should look masculine, and bitches feminine.

## HEAD
The head should be long, strong and deep right to the end of the muzzle, but not coarse. Viewed from the front it should be egg-shaped. The profile should curve gently downwards from the top of the skull to the tip of the nose, which should be black and bent downwards at the tip.

## EYES
Should appear narrow, obliquely placed, and triangular, well sunken, preferably black.

## EARS
Should be small, thin and placed close together.

## MOUTH
The teeth should be sound, clean, strong, of good size and perfectly regular. The upper front teeth should fit in front of, and closely against, the front teeth. Lips should be tight.

## NECK
Should be very muscular, long, arched, tapering from the shoulders to the head, and free from loose skin.

## FOREQUARTERS
The shoulders should be strong and muscular but without loading. The forelegs should have the strongest type of round quality bone; they should be moderately long and perfectly parallel.

## BODY
Should be well rounded with marked spring of rib and great depth from withers to brisket.

## HINDQUARTERS
The hindlegs should be parallel when viewed from behind. The thighs must be muscular and the second thigh well developed. The stifle joint should be well bent and the hock well angulated, with the bone to the foot short and strong.

## FEET
The feet should be round and compact, and the toes well arched.

## TAIL
Should be short, set on low, and carried horizontally. Thick at the root, it should taper to a fine point.

## COAT
Should be short, flat, and harsh to the touch.

## COAT
For white, pure white coat. Skin pigmentation and markings on the head should not be penalized. For coloured, colour (preferably brindle) to predominate.

The modern white and coloured Bull Terrier owes its existence to James Hinks of Birmingham who, in 1850, decided to try and produce a more refined type of Bull Terrier. In spite of the civilized appearance of the modern Staffie, it must be admitted that it was once a rather grim animal. With its cropped ears, fighting stance, and generally bellicose expression it was not the sort of canine companion which the respectable gentry of the era cared to have trotting at their heels. Mr Hinks decided to alter the appearance of the breed and concentrated on breeding a dog which would be all white, free from cloddiness, and fit to be exhibited and owned by the most particular member of the population.

It was an uphill struggle, not only to produce the right type, but to overcome the objections strongly put forward by interested breeders who said that the fighting qualities of the breed would be lost in the process of amending the type. Undeterred, Mr Hinks tried many crosses and used the old English White Terrier (now extinct) and the Dalmatian to refine the breed. He eventually succeeded and the Hinks terriers became very popular winning at many shows, and proving that they possessed all the courage and tenacity of the fighting dogs. It took time to produce a strain which would breed true

dropped ears are undesirable. (A prick ear is carried stiffly erect; a rose ear folds backwards exposing the inner ear.) The mouth is level and the lips tight and clean. The neck is rather short, gradually widening towards the shoulders.

The body is close-coupled, wide-fronted, the brisket deep and the ribs well sprung. The tail should be of medium length and set low. It tapers to a point and is carried low. The coat is short, smooth and close to the skin. There is a choice of colours which can be red, fawn, white, black or blue, or any of these with white. Black-and-tan or liver colours are undesirable. The weight is from 28 to 38 lb, and height from 14 to 16 inches at the shoulder. Bitches should be some 4 lb lighter.

The breed was recognized by the British Kennel Club in 1935 and has since acquired a sizeable following. It came to the United States in 1870 where it was first known as the Pit Dog, the American Bull Terrier and the Yankee Terrier. The American Kennel Club recognized it in 1935 and it is now known as the Staffordshire Terrier. The Standard of Points is much the same in both countries but the Americans prefer a dog some 10 lb heavier than the British version.

*The Staffordshire Bull Terrier has a history of fighting but makes a lovable pet*

or colour and type, but the final result was the ancestor of the dog which we see today, bearing the name Bull Terrier.

The white Bull Terrier, now known as the White Cavalier, became very popular with the young men of the pre- and post-war generations of the First World War. The breed's popularity spread to India and Africa and to other countries of the Commonwealth, from whence it travelled to the United States and elsewhere. At one time disaster threatened the breed when it was discovered that some strains suffered from congenital deafness but, fortunately, the Bull Terrier Club took strong action and breeders not only refused to breed from affected stock but ruthlessly put down animals known to carry this factor.

In 1913, it was suggested that a coloured Bull Terrier would prove to be a welcome alternative to the whites. Many breeders bred back to Staffordshire Terriers and some very curious results were achieved. This was not very surprising when one considers exactly how the bull terriers descended from the bulldog and the subsequent experiments undertaken to produce the original fighting dogs. However, success was attained at last. Both the British and American Kennel Clubs have recognized the new type. The preferred colour is brindle but other colours are not considered a fault.

The Bull Terrier has never been at the top of the dog popularity stakes, but it is favoured by many thousands of people all over the world. It is a handsome animal with its long, strong head, and observant pin-point eyes full of intelligence. The muscular body is ready to spring into instant action with every muscle taut and responsive. This dog has a very strong constitution and many have been known to survive attacks of distemper of an intensity that would have been fatal to many other breeds. The Bull Terrier stands extremes of heat very well, and for this reason was very popular with the British Civil Service in India. It is a very hardy dog, and can take the rough with the smooth. It is truly termed the 'gladiator of the canine race', and some consider it to be one of the most handsome dogs ever bred.

The coat is short and easy to groom. It should be flat and harsh to the touch. The tail should be set on low and carried horizontally, thick at the root and tapering to a point. The white variety should have a pure white coat but markings on the head are permissible. The coloured variety should preferably be brindle, but colour should predominate. Skin pigmentation must not be penalized. There are neither height nor weight limits but there must be an impression of substance according to the size of the dog.

The Bull Terrier needs a good deal of exercise, so should not be kept in the city unless its owner is prepared to take it for long daily walks. It is very energetic and needs to be given more food than is normal for a dog of its size. This breed is not an ideal choice for those who have never kept a dog before. A Bull Terrier must be carefully and strictly trained as it is such a powerful dog. If such training is rigorously carried out then it will make a good pet. The female is often considered preferable to the male because it is slightly more gentle and easier to house-train. The Bull Terrier is famous for its benevolent attitude to children. It never seems to become snappy and bad-tempered, no matter how rough the games. However, the children of the family should always be taught to respect a dog's need to rest, particularly while the dog is still a puppy.

The third breed of bull terrier is the Miniature. It differs from the Bull Terrier only in size. The weight must not exceed 20 lb and the height should be not more than 14 inches. Apart from these, the Standard of Points is identical to that of the Bull Terrier. In all respects but size the Miniature variety should be a real replica of the larger dogs, possessing the same courage and tenacity as its big brothers. It makes an ideal pet for town dwellers as well as for country dwellers.

*The modern Bull Terrier is docile and not at all vicious like its ancestor*

# The Cairn, Australian and West Highland White terriers

TERRIER lovers may differ on many facts concerning these dogs, but all are agreed upon one point, that a terrier, whatever the breed, must be fearless, alert, and fully alive from the tip of one whisker to the last hair on its tail. Provided this condition is satisfied, terriers can differ widely in appearance, and there are certainly enough varieties to suit every taste.

The Cairn Terrier, the smallest of the working terriers, is one of the most fearless of dogs and it is for this reason that it stands so high in the esteem of terrier owners all over the world. This little dog, weighing around 14 lb, is a merry fellow, always ready for a game, a hike in the country or, given the opportunity, a rat or rabbit hunt. Its bright eyes, set in a 'foxy' head, and alert, pointed ears, together with its jaunty tail and compact body, give it a very debonair appearance. Its coat can be red, sandy, grey, brindle or nearly black, often with dark colouring on the ears and muzzle. It will adapt itself to all conditions and climates and its hard, rainproof coat is easy to groom and keep in good condition, and is not prone to shedding. It has, in fact, a double coat with a profuse, hard, but not coarse, outer coat. The undercoat resembles fur, and is short, soft and close. An independent little dog, it will stand and look the world straight in the eye. A Cairn is utterly devoted to its owner and family and is always a splendid watch dog, ready to raise the alarm at the slightest sign of a night prowler. It will adapt easily to any surroundings.

The Cairn Terrier is one of the most ancient breeds in Britain, with its ancestry going back many centuries. It is the direct descendant of the Highland Terrier and is believed to be the ancestor from which all the other varieties of Scottish terrier have sprung. Dr John Caius, in a book written in Latin in about 1570, makes special mention of the prowess of the Highland Terrier as a killer of vermin, and James VI of Scotland so admired the breed that he ordered six of the 'earth dogges' to be sent to France as a present.

*The West Highland White or 'Westie' has been extremely popular since the turn of the century because of its lively nature*

Life in the Highlands has never been easy for man or animal and the rugged terrain has always provided refuge for many species of vermin preying upon the flocks. Fox hunting in Scotland developed in a completely different way from the chase in England. The local farmers hired a professional fox hunter who would own a couple of hounds and a small pack of terriers—real little 'varmints' who feared nothing. The hounds would trail the fox to its lair, often many feet underground in the crevices of rocks which were honeycombed with passages, and the terriers would then be sent in to bolt the fox. The job was dangerous, and many a terrier was trapped underground, never to be seen again.

Such is the background of the Cairn, and the modern dogs have inherited all the pluck and tenacity of their ancestors. Once known as the Skye Terrier, because authorities believed the Isle of Skye to be the homeland of the breed, the Kennel Club ruled in 1910 that the official title should be Cairn Terrier. The breed has been fortunate in that the Cairn Terrier Clubs stipulated that breeding for show points must not take precedence over the working qualities. The welfare of the breed is in the hands of the following organizations: the Cairn Terrier Club, founded in 1910; the Southern Cairn Terrier Club, founded in 1913; the Cairn Terrier Association, formed in 1925, and the Cairn Terrier Club of America.

The West Highland White Terrier is a little dog with a sense of humour and a happy disposition. With a twist to its lips which is a kind of canine grin, the Westie (as it is known) is the most carefree of all the Highland breeds. It has an affectionate nature but, make no mistake, retains all the determination and swift reactions of its hunting ancestors. Standing some 11 inches at the shoulder, the breed is very compact but big enough to accompany its owner over many miles of country before flagging. Indeed, it is more than likely that the owner will give up first. On the other hand, for the town dweller a free run on the common or in the park will ensure enough exercise for health.

The West Highland is a handsome dog and its dark, slightly sunken eyes are

# Breed Standard: the West Highland White

**GENERAL APPEARANCE**
The general appearance of the West Highland White Terrier is that of a small, game, hardy-looking Terrier, possessed of no small amount of self-esteem, with a varminty appearance, and exhibiting in a marked degree a great combination of strength and activity.

**HEAD AND SKULL**
The skull should be slightly domed and when gripped across the forehead, should present a smooth contour. There should only be a very slight tapering from the skull at the level of the ears to the eyes. The head should be thickly coated with hair, and carried at a right-angle, or less, to the axis of the neck. There should be a distinct stop formed by heavy, bony ridges, immediately above and slightly over-hanging the eye, and a slight indentation between the eyes. The nose must be black.

**EYES**
Should be widely set apart, medium in size. Slightly sunk in head, sharp and intelligent.

**EARS**
Small, erect and carried firmly, terminating in a sharp point.

**MOUTH**
Should be as broad between the canine teeth as is consistent with the sharp varminty expression required. The teeth should be large for the size of the dog.

**NECK**
Should be muscular and gradually thickening towards the base allowing the neck to merge into nicely sloping shoulders.

**FOREQUARTERS**
The shoulders should be sloped backwards. Forelegs should be short and muscular, straight and covered with short hard hair.

**BODY**
Compact. Back level, loins broad and strong. The chest should be deep and the ribs well arched.

**HINDQUARTERS**
Strong, muscular and wide across the top. Legs should be short, muscular and sinewy.

**FEET**
The forefeet are larger than the hind ones, are round, proportionate in size, and strong.

**TAIL**
5 to 6 inches long, covered with hard hair, no feather, as straight as possible, carried jauntily, not gay nor carried over the back.

**COAT**
Colour pure white, must be doublecoated. The outer coat consists of hard hair. The under coat, which resembles fur, is short, soft and close.

**WEIGHT AND SIZE**
Size about 11 inches at the withers.

brilliant and full of intelligence. It has a sturdy, muscular body covered with white coat of hard hair about two inches long, which, contrary to some opinions, is just as easy to keep clean as a coloured coat. Daily grooming with a brush and comb will ensure that the coat is kept in good condition. The Westie has no fads or fancies and will thrive on a plain, balanced diet. The bitches make good mothers and considering these various advantages, it is a breed which is likely to maintain its popularity for a very long time.

It has been said that the West Highland White is the result of a cross between a variety of Cairn and a Sealyham terrier but there is no evidence whatever for such an assumption. In any event, there would have been no necessity for such an out cross, since occasional white puppies have always tended to show up in Highland terrier litters. The old fox hunting fraternity of Scotland, which valued terriers with courage above all else, were prejudiced against white pups and destroyed them at birth, believing that their colour denoted a lack of gameness. This was a completely mistaken assumption, and the Malcolms of Poltalloch, who did not subscribe to it, collected all the white pups they could find and sought to establish a white breed of their own. True whites were produced after some years of selective breeding, and all the Poltalloch terriers were noted for their work in the field. Another white strain was bred by the Duke of Argyll at Roseneath, by which name his strain was known. These were unrelated to the Poltalloch dogs, but it can safely be assumed that Cairns and Scottish Terriers were used by the breeders of white dogs to improve the strain.

West Highland Whites were used to hunt badgers as well as foxes. This is a task which requires great endurance and pluck. The terrier must follow the badger deep into its earth, baying and sniffing at it all the time to prevent it from digging itself further down into the ground and so eluding capture. At the beginning of this century, many of the terriers exhibited were also veterans of many a badger hunt and it was considered that a terrier's working qualities were just as important as its appearance.

It would seem that the Westie made its first appearance in the show ring at Birmingham in 1860. Classes for 'Scotch Terriers' were included, and a 'White Skye' was among the winners. At the Crystal Palace Show in 1899, a team of Roseneath Terriers was shown. The first show where West Highland White Terriers were classified separately was at the Annual Show of the Scottish Kennel Club held in Edinburgh in October 1904.

An English Club was formed in 1905, and the breed was admitted to the Kennel lub Stud Book in 1909. It became opular soon after the first shows and is ill a favourite in Britain and the United tates, as well as being exported to most ther dog-loving countries. Three societies ere formed to further the interests of the reed in Britain: the West Highland White errier Club, the West Highland White errier Club of England and the West Iighland White Terrier Club of Northern reland. In the USA this work is under-aken by the West Highland White Terrier lub of America.

The Australian Terrier is a happy little og and a true native of Australia. Sharp, etermined, and as plucky as they come, his terrier is equally at home roaming the tockyards or living in the heart of a big ity. It is loyal and affectionate, and can vithstand any weather and any hardship. t is a mixture of many breeds and it has een said that it was evolved from the ydney Silky Terrier. This is quite in-orrect since there can be no doubt that he Silky was derived from a cross between he Australian Terrier and the Yorkshire Terrier, hence the long silky coat and blue-nd-tan coloration.

Many different breeds of terrier were rought to Australia, and the Australian Terrier is a mixture of most of them. Over 100 years ago there existed on the sheep nd cattle stations a dog known as a Broken-Haired Terrier, which had a repu-ation as a first-class destroyer of vermin nd a faithful and dependable guard. It vas essentially a sporting dog without any pretensions to good looks, and lacking a consistent breed Standard. The time came when breeders determined to fix a type which would appeal to the eye, without loss of the sporting instinct and sound temperament. The Broken-Haired Terrier must be regarded as the rootstock of the modern Australian Terrier, and the breed was moulded by introducing the blood of almost every terrier breed which was known in that country.

The early breeders, as usual, kept few records and every man had his own theory as to the best blood for the various crosses. It is impossible to determine with any accuracy exactly what proportions of the various breeds were used before a satis-factory fix was obtained. It is sufficient to say that the Australian has the harsh coat of a Scottie, a Dandie Dinmont topknot, the erect ears of a Cairn, the long body of a Skye and the blue-and-tan coloration of a Yorkie. It is very probable that an Irish Terrier contributed to its tempera-ment and it is claimed that the Norwich Terrier was also used. This latter assertion is very doubtful since the pure Norwich was first introduced into Australia some five years after the Australian Terrier, under the name of the Australian Rough, and was first shown at Melbourne in 1885.

*Facing page: the Cairn Terrier was a favourite of James I. Above: the Australian Terrier was first shown in Melbourne, Australia in 1885. It is very adaptable and is suited to both town and country life. Right: the Westie has a lively intelligent expression*

The Australian Terrier is rather low-set in appearance, being about 10 inches in height at the shoulder and weighing from 10 to 11 lb. The head is long, with a flat skull, and the eyes are dark, small and keen. It has a topknot and small ears which may be pricked or dropped towards the front. It is a muscular dog with straight forelegs, the hindquarters possessing strong thighs, and the hocks being slightly bent. The body is rather long in proportion to height, the back straight, the feet small, neat, and well padded. The tail is docked.

The breed was recognized by the Kennel Club in 1933 and recognition was granted by the American Kennel Club in 1960. It is known in Great Britain, New Zealand, South Africa and Canada, and although it has never headed the list of popular breeds outside its native land, there have always been a consistent number of ad-mirers to ensure that the breed will never die out.

The Australian Terrier is a splendid companion, loyal and affectionate, frien-dly to humans and other dogs, but death

to vermin. It is quiet and not prone to unnecessary barking. It does not need a great deal of exercise, so will adapt to city life quite readily. Its hard coat does not scatter a profusion of loose hairs—a point which will appeal to prospective owners. It can be had in two main colours. Those with a blue or silver-grey body have tan on the legs and face, and the topknot should be blue or silver. The coat can also be sandy or red with a soft topknot. It is a hardy breed, able to thrive in almost any climate. It is easy to feed, and for breeders there are no abnormal difficulties in whelping.

These three breeds all make delightful pets, and both the Australian and Cairn Terriers are suitable for flat dwellers, and are best for a single person or a couple who want a small, energetic, high-spirited dog.

# Contrasting Terrier Breeds: Dandie Dinmont, Glen of Imaal

THREE of Britain's native terrier breeds have their origins in the wild country along the north-eastern boundary between England and Scotland. The Border terrier, as its name suggests, was the terrier favoured by the Border pack of hounds, though it was also used by the two neighbouring packs. In the heart of Border country lies the village of Rothbury which was the birthplace of the Bedlington terrier and which originally gave its name to the breed.

Not far from Cognetdale, on the border between England and Scotland, is the remote homestead of Hyndlea where James Davidson lived, a border man who appears to have resembled the character of Dandie Dinmont in Sir Walter Scott's novel 'Guy Mannering'. Davidson kept a strain of terriers well known for their sporting prowess and his dogs were

*The Dandie Dinmont is a terrier with a very strong character, and is an ideal pet*

named after the character Scott had created. It is the only breed to be named after a literary character. That these three terrier breeds share a common ancestral stock cannot be disputed. Even today, when they are quite distinct breeds, they share characteristics which betray their common ancestry. Even at the end of the last century it was still possible for pups from the same litter to win prizes as either Dandie Dinmont or Bedlington terriers. At that time, Dandie Dinmonts were longer in the leg, shorter in the back and smaller than the modern breed – if the evidence provided by Sir Edwin Landseer's well known portrait of Sir Walter Scott's dogs is to be accepted. The breed is also portrayed in Gainsborough's portrait of the third Duke of Buccleuch, painted in 1770.

In Manchester, England, in 1861, and the following year in Birmingham, show classes were being provided for Dandie Dinmont terriers. By the 1870s the breed

was beginning to make an impression a a show dog, and Robert and Paul Scott' dog, Peachem, made regular and success ful forays from its home in Jedburgh Peachem has been described as an idea Dandie Dinmont, 'not too big, not too little, good in coat, colour and topknot nicely domed in skull, shapely, wel arched in body, and not too crooked ir front.'

Since those days the Dandie Dinmon has remained a dog appreciated by a dis criminating minority. It has never achieved or, perhaps, aspired to grea popularity but it remains an ideal companion. The Dandie Dinmont train easily, but it should be trained when i is young or else its behaviour will never be perfect. It is game and intelligent, fond of children and with an amiable disposition. Often it is found that, although the dog is friendly to all, it will single ou one member of the family to whom i gives its undivided loyalty. Perhaps its short legs and fairly thick coat make i more in need of regular grooming than longer-legged, shorter-coated breeds, but a good and regular brushing is all that is required to keep it smart and presentable. However, the dog must be brushed every day and should not be kept in a warm room. There is no elaborate or expensive trimming to be undertaken. Unfortunately, because of its rough coat, the Dandie Dinmont, like other rough-coated terriers, is susceptible to skin ailments such as summer itch and nonspecific dermatitis. However, if given a sensible, balanced diet and good treatment, the Dandie Dinmont will prove to be a long-lived, very healthy dog, capable of living happily in town or country.

The modern Dandie Dinmont has lost none of the gameness or sporting characteristics of its ancestors; it remains a courageous foe and a trustworthy friend. The appearance of the breed is distinctive, even singular. It has a strong, rather large head with a broad, domed skull. The head is furnished with very soft silky hair, and the mouth has unusually large and strong teeth. The dark eyes are large, full and round, expressing great determination, intelligence and dignity. The ears are pendulous, set low on the skull. In build the Dandie Dinmont has a long, flexible body with an arched back and a round, well-sprung ribcage, set on short, muscular and heavily boned forelegs and longer hindlegs.

# Breed Standard: the Dandy Dinmont Terrier

**HEAD AND SKULL**
Head strongly made, the muscles showing extraordinary development, especially the maxillary. Skull broad between the ears, forehead well domed. Soft, silky hair on head; muzzle deep, about 3 in long. The nose black.

**EYES**
Set wide apart, large, full, round but not protruding; expressive. Colour, rich dark hazel.

**EARS**
Pendulous, set well back, wide apart and low on skull, tapering almost to a point. Should harmonize in colour with body; all should have a thin feather of hair; skin should be very thin; length 3–4 ins.

**MOUTH**
Inside of the mouth dark or black; teeth very strong, especially the canines which are of great size for such a small dog. Teeth level in front, the upper ones slightly overlapping. Under- or overshot mouths are objectionable.

**NECK**
Muscular, strong, and well developed; well set into shoulders.

**FOREQUARTERS**
Forelegs short, muscular, wide apart but not bandy. Colour of forelegs of pepper dog should be tan; of mustard dog a darker shade than its head, which is creamy white. Feather about 2 ins long, lighter than hair on front of leg.

**BODY**
Long, strong and flexible; ribs well sprung and round, chest well developed and let well down between forelegs. Back low at shoulders, arching over loins; gradual drop to root of tail.

**HINDQUARTERS**
Hindlegs a little longer than forelegs, set rather wide apart; thighs well developed; no feather.

**FEET**
Not flat. Claws dark; feet of pepper dog tan; of mustard dog darker than head.

**TAIL**
8–10 ins, with wiry hair darker than that of body on upper side, lighter underneath. Feather about 2 ins long. Tapering at tip; curved; neither set too high or too low.

**COAT**
About 2 in long; a mixture of hardish and soft hair, but not wiry. Hair on belly lighter and softer.

**COLOUR**
Pepper or mustard. Pepper ranges from dark bluish to silvery grey, gradually merging into leg colour. Mustards vary from reddish brown to pale fawn, head being creamy white, legs and feet a shade darker.

**WEIGHT AND SIZE**
Size 8–11 ins to top of shoulder. Weight as near 18 lbs as possible.

valley from which the name of the breed is derived. The fame of the courage of the breed had spread well beyond its native heath before it was officially recognized as a breed by the Irish Kennel Club in 1933. The breed was, and still is, used as a working terrier to hunt badger and fox. Its courage and qualities as a working terrier are jealously guarded to the present day, and terriers which meet with the high standard of gameness set by the Glen of Imaal Terrier Club are awarded the coveted 'Teastors Misneac'.

In common with all terriers which have retained an association with their original purpose in life, Glen of Imaal terriers usually have an extremely affectionate nature, becoming very attached and faithful to their masters. With children they are reliable and playful. When at work, however, they tackle badgers with great courage and tenacity. They are rarely seen in the show ring.

The breed is very heavily boned, with great strength and stamina. It stands no more than 14 inches at the shoulder and weighs up to 35 lb. The drop ears are set high on the strong, broad skull. The heavily boned legs are short and the forelegs are slightly bent. The gaily carried tail is docked short. The coat, which may be blue, blue-and-tan or wheaten, is harsh but not wiry.

*The Glen of Imaal Terrier, a working dog, is very good with children*

The rather short scimitar-shaped tail is carried a little above the level of the body, and furnished with wiry hair which is a shade darker than the colour of the coat. The coat itself is of great importance. The hair should be about two inches long. It is a mixture of hard and soft hair of a pepper or mustard colour, the pepper ranging from dark bluish black to a light silvery grey, the mustard from reddish brown to a pale fawn. Nearly all Dandie Dinmont terriers have some white on the chest and some have white claws. However, white on the feet is considered to be a fault.

A Dandie Dinmont ranges from 8 to 11 inches in height to the shoulder, the length of its body being slightly less than twice its height. A Dandie in good working condition weighs about 18 lb.

The breed is not numerically large in England (about 200 registrations with the Kennel Club each year) or America. Thus pedigree puppies are not in abundant supply. But prospective owners who want a loyal, game and distinctive sporting companion will find it worthwhile waiting and searching for a puppy of this breed.

The Glen of Imaal terrier is an indigenous Irish terrier originating in the south-western county of Wicklow, in the

# The Fox Terrier

# Breed Standard: the Wire Fox Terrier

**GENERAL APPEARANCE**
Height at withers should be the same as length of body; movement of legs should be straight forward, the forelegs swinging parallel to the sides. Main propulsive power is from hind legs which should have long thighs and muscular second thighs well bent at the stifle. Should be alert, quick of movement, and keen of expression.

**HEAD AND SKULL**
Top line of skull should be almost flat, sloping slightly and gradually decreasing in width towards the eyes, not exceeding $3\frac{1}{2}$ in wide. Length from occiput to nostrils should be $7-7\frac{1}{4}$ in. Well-developed jaw-bones. Nose should be black.

**EYES**
Should be dark, moderately small and not prominent; circular and not too far apart.

**EARS**
Should be small and V-shaped, the flaps neatly folded over and dropping forward close to the cheeks. The top line of the folded ear should be well above the level of the skull.

**NECK**
Should be clean, muscular, of fair length, and with a graceful curve when seen from the side.

**FOREQUARTERS**
Shoulders should be long, well laid back, and sloping obliquely from points to withers. Chest deep and not broad. Legs should be straight.

**BODY**
Short, level back; loins muscular and very slightly arched; deep brisket; front ribs moderately arched and back ribs deep and well-sprung.

**HINDQUARTERS**
Strong and muscular, stifles well curved, hock-joints well bent and near the ground; hocks parallel when viewed from behind.

**FEET**
Round, compact, not large. Toes moderately arched. Pads hard and tough.

**TAIL**
Set on high and carried gaily; should be a three-quarters dock.

**COAT**
Should have a broken appearance as the hairs tend to twist; has a dense, wiry texture, harder on back and quarters than sides.

**COLOUR**
White should predominate.

**WEIGHT AND SIZE**
A dog should not exceed $15\frac{1}{2}$ in at the withers, and weigh 18 lb. A bitch should be proportionately smaller, and weigh about 2 lb less.

**FAULTS**
White, cherry, or spotted nose; prick, tulip or rose ears; mouth undershot or overshot.

THE title 'Terrier' was derived from the French *terre* and the Latin *terra*, both meaning 'earth', and therefore a terrier is the name for a dog with a propensity for digging and literally 'going to earth' in order to 'bolt' or destroy vermin. The name 'Fox Terrier' was first used in about 1790 when fox hunting became popular, but the small terriers then in use bore no resemblance to our present-day dogs. They were, in fact, a very mixed strain, sharing but one characteristic – complete fearlessness – standing them in good stead to tackle anything above or below the ground.

The modern Fox Terrier has existed in roughly the same form for some 100 years, and it has a band of fanciers all over the world who are prepared to swear that there is no other dog to equal it. Certainly, few animals have so smart and neat an appearance as a Fox Terrier. Poised on its toes, its eyes shining with the desire for action, it has been likened to a little hunter and there is certainly an element of truth in the description, as horse and dog alike demonstrate the unmistakable stance of the true thoroughbred.

A pedigree Fox Terrier is a well-balanced dog weighing up to 18 lb, and is therefore small enough to insert itself into tight corners and restricted spaces, should this be necessary. It has an affectionate nature but this generosity naturally does not extend to rats, mice and other vermin. It is true that the modern family dog is no longer required to root out the rodents from the stable yard, but it retains the spirit and determination of its ancestors. It is a fast mover, with lightning-quick reactions, a reminder of those early days when survival underground against an animal larger than itself depended on its ability to strike swiftly or retreat rapidly if threatened.

It is extremely important to take particular care when walking a Fox Terrier in town, and to keep it on a lead in busy streets. A terrier only has to have something catch its eye to spring into action, and another dog on the opposite side of the road is a strong temptation for an unleashed terrier to dash across, regardless of traffic.

There are times, however, when a terrier must be allowed to run free. It will be happiest in the country but it can enjoy itself equally in a city park where every hedge and path will be inspected in a hopeful search for vermin. As it sniffs at a drain or hole, the deep-set eyes are alert and concentrated, the body tense and ready to pounce. If there is nothing there, off it will bound again.

*Facing page: Wire-haired fox terrier. This page: Smooth-haired fox terrier, which was the first to evolve*

*The Wire-haired fox terrier is by far the most popular of the two breeds*

When its daily run is over, the Fox Terrier will be quite happy to go home and sleep, suggesting by its little growls and twitches that perhaps it may be dreaming of the rabbit that got away, yet still ready, at the least unusual sound, to leap up, eager to defend its owner's family and his property.

There are two varieties of Fox Terrier, the Smooth- and the Wire-haired. The Smooth was the first to evolve, but both were bred from the working terriers whose coat colours were sometimes reddish, black-and-tan, or pied. The reds were not liked because of their resemblance to foxes with which they could easily be confused. Bulldog blood was introduced with a view to supplying additional fighting spirit but this resulted in many whelps showing brindle patches which proved very difficult to breed out. In 1860, Beagle blood was introduced and this resulted in very handsome black-and-tan markings. This was followed by a concentration on the breeding of smooth black-and-tan terriers and this successfully refined the breed to an extent not previously believed possible. Mating with the Bull Terrier resulted in still further improvement, and there can be no doubt that white Bull

Terriers played a great part in forming the modern Fox Terrier.

The breed grew rapidly in popularity; a show held in Birmingham in 1862 put on a class for 'White and other smooth-haired English Terriers except Black-and-Tan'. Several Fox Terriers were entered and they won every prize. (This was the way it all started.) The leading hunt kennels bred strains which produced many outstanding specimens of the breed, while a succession of dog shows scheduled classes which were filled to the limit. Ordinary citizens, who had never seen a fox outside a picture book, became proud owners of a Fox Terrier or two, and prices of up to 500 guineas were paid for a brace of bitches.

The Fox Terrier Club was formed in London in 1876 and it is interesting to note that the Standard for the breed, with a few minor exceptions, is the same today as it was when drawn up by the original committee.

The Fox Terrier also became a favourite in Europe and the colonies, as well as in Britain. Clubs were formed in France and Germany and many fine specimens were bred in both countries. The United States imported many terriers, and the popularity of the breed grew to such an extent that the American Fox Terrier Club was founded in 1885.

The Wire-haired Fox Terrier was some nine years behind the Smooth-haired in its rise to popularity. First shown in Birmingham in 1872, it was far less popular than the Smooth for many years. Then the position was reversed: the Smooth-haired lagged behind while the Wire-haired was top of the list of Kennel Club registrations, where it remained for several years. It is still one of the most popular breeds, with an annual registration more than double that of the Smooth-haired variety. Wire-haired terriers were no newcomers to Britain, since both types of coat have existed for centuries. The Wire-haired Fox Terrier was chiefly derived from the rough-haired terriers of Wales, the Derbyshire countryside and the Durham district. There was some interbreeding between 'Smooths' and 'Wires' but this gave no great advantage to either and the practice has now been discontinued. The Wire-haired is a hardy dog, intelligent, determined and handsome. It has much in common with the Smooth-haired, although the latter was evolved from a greater variety of breeds.. Whether you choose a 'Wire' or a 'Smooth' is a matter of personal preference, although the Wire is still the most popular. The Smooth-haired, however, is supported by a devoted band of enthusiasts and there is no danger of it ever disappearing.

# Four Terriers

UNIQUE in shape among terriers, the Bedlington originated in that area of Northumberland known as Rothbury Forest. Indeed it was called the Rothbury Terrier until some time in the 1820s when Joseph Ainsley, a resident of the village of Bedlington who had for some time specialized in breeding dogs of a type, decided that the breed should be known as Bedlington Terriers.

Racy-looking animals that are often likened in appearance to lambs, the Bedlington colouring is limited to blue, liver, blue and tan, liver and tan, and sandy. Puppies are born very dark, but lighten with age.

The differences between Bedlingtons and all other terriers lie mainly in their considerably roached back, horseshoe-shaped front and a coat which has a kind of linty feel to it. About 16 inches high at the shoulder, this is a handy-sized dog with all the energy and spirit of other terriers, despite its rather fey appearance. This latter feature is largely produced by trimming, which is a job for the expert if an immaculate showpiece is the aim. But for everyday purposes a serviceable but typical effect can be achieved by the pet owner after a little tuition from someone more experienced. Otherwise the maintenance of a Bedlington poses no special problems.

As long as can be remembered, blue terriers have been known in Ireland, even if the name Kerry Blue Terrier was universally accepted only in the 1920s. And while they were no doubt always spread wide over Ireland, one area – County Kerry and particularly Tralee and Castleisland – was the hotbed of enthusiasm for the breed and produced its best representatives in days when the rest were a very mixed lot.

It is to the needs of Irish farmers that the Kerry Blue owes its existence. It was bred as a vermin killer, sheep herder, retriever of shot wildfowl, and guard, and to provide sport by way of the once-popular, but now illegal, sport of dog fighting.

A medium-sized dog, some 18 to 19 inches high at the shoulder, its most striking feature is a soft and abundant coat in glorious shades of blue-grey, varying between dark and light. This colour is not

*Above: the Kerry Blue has a soft, silky coat.*

## Breed Standard: the Scottish Terrier

### GENERAL APPEARANCE
A Scottish Terrier is a sturdy thick-set dog of a suitable size to go to ground, placed on short legs, alert in carriage, and suggestive of great power and activity in small compass. The body is covered with a close-lying, broken, rough-textured coat. In spite of its short legs, the construction is such that it is a very agile and active dog. The movement of the dog is smooth, easy and straight forward, with free action at shoulder, stifle and hock.

### HEAD AND SKULL
Without being out of proportion to the size of the dog, it should be long, the length of skull enabling it to be fairly wide and yet retain a narrow appearance. The skull is nearly flat and the cheekbones do not protrude. There is a slight, but distinct, stop between skull and foreface just in front of the eye. The nose is large.

### EYES
Should be almond-shaped, dark brown, fairly wide apart and set deeply under the eyebrows.

### EARS
Neat, of fine texture, pointed and erect.

### MOUTH
The teeth large, the upper incisors closely overlapping the lower.

### NECK
Muscular, of moderate length.

### FOREQUARTERS
The head is carried on a muscular neck of moderate length, showing quality.

### BODY
The body has well-rounded ribs, which flatten to a deep chest and are carried well back. In general the top line of the body should be straight and level.

### HINDQUARTERS
Remarkably powerful for the size of the dog. Big and wide buttocks. Thighs deep and muscular, well bent at stifle. Hocks strong and well bent.

### FEET
Of good size and well padded, toes well arched.

### TAIL
Of moderate length to give a general balance, thick at the root and tapering towards the tip; set on with an upright carriage or with a slight bend.

### COAT
The dog has two coats, the undercoat short, dense, and soft; the outer coat harsh, dense and wiry; the two making a weather-resistant covering.

### COLOUR
Black, wheaten, or brindle of any colour.

### WEIGHT AND SIZE
Ideal weight from 19 lb to 23lb. Height 10 to 11 in.

omplete before the dog is about 18 months old. Puppies are born black and become blue gradually. Trimming the coat brings out the best colour as well as making for a smart finish and accentuating the true Kerry Blue features. These are strength of jaw and a fair length of a not too narrow head, straight limbs, and powerful hindquarters.

Keeping a Kerry Blue as a pet can be recommended for those who want a breed which is both beautiful and courageous. But that recommendation can only be made to people prepared to remember that the Kerry, despite being mainly a show breed today, has inherited much of the gameness it was created for. A firm but kind upbringing is necessary if it is not to become a wilful adult. And while feeding and exercising are matters of commonsense in following the breeder's instructions, coat care requires a lot of time and effort or an expert's attention.

An ancestor of the Irish terrier and next of kin to the Kerry Blue, the Soft-coated Wheaten Terrier is the least known of the three. For example, only in 1975 is it possible for members of the breed to become British champions, although recognition was made in Eire 38 years ago.

The Soft-coated Wheaten Terrier came into being as an all-purpose farmers' dog for cattle work, vermin killing and as a gun dog. It belongs to Southern Ireland. Unspoiled by extensive trimming or by being bred in very large numbers, it still has the advantage of a breed which, at least until recently, saw only the survival of the fittest.

In appearance the Soft-coated Wheaten is completely unexaggerated. Medium in size at 18 inches high, with a fair length of leg, the head looks powerful but is neither wide or narrow, nor too long. The jaw must be strong for its work. The same applies to other features: all strong and powerful but in no way exaggerated. Its crowning glory is a soft, abundant, wheaten-coloured coat.

Because their numbers are small it is not easy to buy a Soft-coated Wheaten Terrier unless one is prepared to wait. For those who like a typical terrier that is one of the most adaptable of the terrier type, and is an attractive and natural breed, the wait will be very worthwhile.

Scotland has been the cradle of many short-legged terrier breeds, most known as Scotch terriers at some time in their history. But one alone emerged as the national rather than a regional breed. It is now known as the Scottish Terrier, although at one time it was referred to as the Aberdeen Terrier.

Formerly a light-coloured breed, darker shades—black and dark brindle—have increasingly predominated since the Scotch Terrier was taken up by exhibitors.

This breed is thick-set and low on the ground, and was originally used for the control of vermin in the Highlands. It should give an impression of strength and substance without loss of activity.

Inclined to be a one-man dog, the Scottish terrier is a devoted companion, able and willing to accompany its owner on strenuous hikes or equally happy to stay at home. And that home can be small yet still provide adequate accommodation, so long as exercise is not forgotten.

*The Scottish terrier is a sturdy, thickset dog, but is very active*

Coat trimming is essential, not only for appearance, but for the dog's comfort. Not all trimming establishments know what is required of this breed, so if in doubt go to a local breeder. There is certainly no shortage of these.

*The Soft-coated Wheaten, originally a farm dog, will easily adapt to town life*

# Two working Terriers

THE Jack Russell Terrier is a true working terrier with the will and ability to tackle any adversary, irrespective of size, either above or below ground. There are many varieties of working terrier, such as the Border and Lakeland breeds–including the Patterdale–widely used in the North of Britain, and there are also the Scottish Terriers, noted for their tenacity in hunting hill foxes. None of these are true Jack Russells, although the name has been wrongly applied to some types of terrier found on the Scottish border and in the north of England.

Neither must the Jack Russell be confused with the Smooth and Wire Fox Terriers, although the Russell has sprung from the same rootstock. The modern Fox Terrier is a beautiful animal but generations of breeding for exhibition has diminished its working qualities, although some strains will show that it has by no means lost its gameness.

Jack Russell Terriers are a type of dog which cannot be classed as a breed, since no Kennel Club in the world will recog-

nize them as such. There is no official Standard of Points and Jack Russells conform to none. Indeed they have never been bred to any specific standard–but the experienced eye will readily identify an authentic specimen.

These game little terriers are small dogs of about 12 lb in weight. The body is muscular, well ribbed, the tail docked and almost always in constant motion. Movement is swift and the dog should appear vibrant with life. The legs are short and strong, with wide paws suitable for digging. The pads and nails are hard and close. The legs, although on the short side, must not be confused with those of a Dachsund or Sealyham. The Jack Russell is by no means a leggy dog but there must be sufficient length of leg to enable it to run with hounds. The coat may be rough, smooth, or something between the two. The colour is predominately white but the coat may have black or tan markings which are very often found over one ear and one eye, and at the base of the tail. The ears are V-shaped and responsive to

every sound, the jaws are very strong with sharp teeth and the eyes are dark and brilliant. The general impression is one of a terrier ready and alert to deal with any emergency.

The Jack Russell is first and foremost a country dog which delights in exploring the hedgerows. It will hunt happily for hours, and any rat, polecat or weasel it unearths will be dealt with decisively. Any kind of earth, burrow or hole in the ground is an invitation to make a thorough investigation. Two dogs working together are a delight to watch: Jack Russells have an inherited tendency to cooperate with each other.

Loyal and affectionate, the Jack Russell is courageous and will defend its home to the death. As a rule it is good with children and other animals, although it must be said that a Jack will not allow itself to be pushed around by other dogs, and it needs no encouragement to defend itself, should the necessity arise.

Jack Russells are named after a sporting clergyman in Devon who was reputed o spend more time in the hunting field han in church. His ambition was to breed strain of working terrier which would ace anything on four legs. It was said hat a terrier with three long legs and short one was unblemished in his eyes o long as it kept up with hounds and earlessly went to earth. It is certain that is terriers were outstandingly game and he same can be claimed for their modern descendants.

A Jack Russell bitch should not be mated to any sort of terrier in the mistaken belief that the progeny will be of he correct type and temperament. Choose a known Jack Russell dog to be he sire of the puppies. This is easy advice, but the novice breeder is immediately aced with the problem of which type of stud dog to choose. Should it be a rough- or smooth-coated, or something between he two? Should it be short- or medium-egged? All sorts of small physical differences will come to mind, and it is at this point that the breeder of standardized pedigree dogs has to consider so many different factors, but the Jack Russell breeder is more fortunate. There is just one important factor to be decided: is the terrier a real worker? Is it game and prepared to face any enemy? Is it friendly towards humans and other dogs? Does it show the bright-eyed intelligence and swiftness which are two of the essential characteristics of the working terrier?

Almost as famous as the Jack Russell as a working terrier, the Patterdale Terrier takes its name from Patterdale, an extremely rugged and rocky valley in the heart of the country hunted by the Ullswater Foxhounds. Patterdales trace their ancestry back to the terriers used by the Patterdale hunt before it amalgamated with the Matterdale hunt, to become the Ullswater Foxhounds. These terriers are extremely hard and tough and have been bred for many years to follow the huntsman of the Fell Foxhound packs, which hunt in Lakeland. Their origins are more or less the same as those of the present-day pedigree Lakeland Terrier, except for the introduction of Bedlington Terrier into the Patterdale strain. The difference is that the Patterdales were bred for gameness rather than looks, and still are.

The job required of the Patterdale is o follow the huntsman (who is on foot, not mounted on horseback) in couples over the fells. These are extremely steep and rocky and need a very active and sure-footed terrier to traverse them. Finally, hey have either to bolt or kill the fox which will have 'holed' in what can be very difficult and dangerous rocky terrain. The Patterdale has to be able to jump up and down rock ledges to get to its quarry. The Lakeland fox is a force to be reckoned with at close quarters, weigh-

ing anything from 17 to 22 lbs. These little dogs work at some 2,000 feet above sea level in mid-winter, and the weather conditions at the top of the fells at this time can be near-Arctic.

For this extremely tough life, the terrier needs to be constructed with a narrow front, but not tied-in at the elbow, and with enough room for action of heart and lungs. Its legs should be long enough for it to travel freely across the fells, more often than not through snow, and it has to be absolutely sound in its feet so that the rocks do not cause 'knocked-up' toes. It must be very strong in the loin and with powerful hindquarters so that it can jump onto and climb off rocky ledges. Its coat should be hard, dense and wiry, and very weather-resistant. It has small, neat ears to avoid unnecessary punishment from the fox. It has a very powerful and functional, but not over-long jaw with large strong teeth. Above all, it possesses inborn courage, brains and tenacity.

The Patterdale weighs around 15 to 16 lb. Its colour can be black, liver, red, blue, black and tan, or any colour except white. Occasionally there is a topknot on the head which is a relic of its Bedlington ancestry. The tail is docked.

A good Patterdale is the pride and joy of its owner and there is much competition to obtain puppies from a good, well-trusted bitch. Puppies are disposed of more as a favour to the recipient than as a commercial transaction.

It is a memorable sight to see these grand terriers present at a meet of the Fell packs. Many of the followers will have a couple with them, as well as the Hunt terriers with the huntsman. The Patterdale is usually shown in classes for 'working Lakeland Terriers'. A good number of the breed is exhibited, all looking gay and fearless, many bearing the scars of past encounters with foxes on their faces.

Like the Jack Russell, the breed is not recognized by the Kennel Club, as technically it would be more a 'strain' than a breed. Pedigrees are not recorded on paper, although many can be traced back by word of mouth to the famous Patterdales owned by a great huntsman, Joe Bowman, the 'flying whip' Brett Wilson, and through the famous strain of Joe Wear (who was also a great huntsman). These terriers are very much of a type, as can be seen at a Hunt Terrier show, and are instantly recognizable as Patterdales by those who are familiar with the breed.

*Above and top centre: these two Jack Russells show how the breed has varying physical characteristics, as does the Patterdale Terrier (bottom centre and below)*

# Manchester and Border Terriers

FOR as long as can be remembered there have been black-and-tan terriers; their purpose in life was to kill rats and other vermin. Not until the last century were they of any particular type; all that mattered was the number of rats a dog could kill.

Quite which breeds were used in its evolution can never be known for certain. There was no Kennel Club and no Stud Book to chart its progress. There is no doubt that the old black-and-tan terrier formed the basis of the breed. Whippet blood seems likely to have been added, otherwise there is no explanation for the transformation of what was an ordinary-looking terrier, to a sleek-coated dog with more than a touch of class.

Before 1895, the Manchester terrier, then known as the Black-and-tan terrier, (the name reverting to Manchester in the 1920s) always had its ears cropped, some say to prevent rats holding on to its folded-over ears, but it is just as likely that the reason was the extra smartness a cropped ear gives to a dog. After 1895, when cropping was outlawed in Britain, the Manchester terrier lost many of its supporters. Now less than 100 are registered with the British Kennel Club.

A handy-sized animal, some 15 or 16 inches high at the shoulder, the Manchester has much to recommend it as a companion. It has the same game spirit that was such a success in the rat pits of days gone by. As it has a short smooth coat, a minimum of dirt is brought into the house.

In America it was also once known as the black-and-tan terrier, but in 1923 the USA reverted to Manchester Terrier by which name the breed is still known. The miniature variety, registered in England as the English Toy Terrier, is known in America as the toy Manchester Terrier, the show classes being divided into standard and toy sections, the toys not to weigh more than 12 lb. The Club may consider this being altered to 7 lb and under, and over 7 lb but not exceeding 12 lb.

*Top: a Manchester Terrier. Right: Border Terriers. It is not known precisely when either breed came into being, but both were originally used for ratting and hunting*

# Breed Standard: the Manchester Terrier

**GENERAL APPEARANCE**
The dog shall be compact in appearance, with good bone, and free from any resemblance to the Whippet.

**HEAD AND SKULL**
Long, flat in skull and narrow, level and wedge-shaped, without showing cheek muscles; well-filled up under the eyes, and with tapering, tight lipped jaws.

**EYES**
Small, dark and sparkling, oblong in shape, set close in head, not prominent.

**EARS**
Small and V-shaped, carried well above the top line of the head and hanging close to the head above the eyes. If cropped, carried erect. Cropped ears disqualify Toys.

**MOUTH**
Should be level.

**NECK**
The neck should be fairly long and tapering from the shoulder to the head; and it should be slightly arched at the crest.

**FOREQUARTERS**
The shoulders should be clean and well sloped. The chest narrow and deep. The forelegs must be quite straight, set on well under the dog, and of proportionate length to the body.

**BODY**
Short with well-sprung ribs, slightly roached and well cut up behind the ribs.

**HINDQUARTERS**
The hind legs should be neither cow-hocked nor with the feet turned in, and should be well bent at the stifle.

**FEET**
Small, semi-harefooted and strong, with well-arched toes.

**TAIL**
The tail should be short and set on where the arch of the back ends, thick where it joins the body and tapering to a point, carried not higher than the level of the back.

**COAT**
Close, smooth, short and glossy and firm.

**COLOUR**
Jet black and rich mahogany tan which is distributed on the head, muzzle, cheeks, over each eye, the under-jaw, throat, legs (from the knee downwards), inside the hind legs, under the tail and on the chest. The colour divisions should be clearly defined and not merge.

**SIZE**
Desired height at the shoulders 16 inches for dogs, 15 inches for bitches. Weight to be over 12 lb but not exceeding 22 lb.

If you want frills and furbelows do not buy a Manchester terrier. If you want a good old-fashioned sort of dog, unspoiled by the show ring, ready to go anywhere but happy to stay at home, a good ratter and rabbiter, there is no need to look beyond this breed that has one other advantage. Its ancestry is British through and through.

Of all the sporting breeds of dog in existence, probably no other has been so little changed or spoiled by the cult of dog-showing than the Border terrier. It is still worked with hounds, and this applies to many which are shown as well.

Like most terrier breeds, the Border had no precise, traceable ancestry before two centuries ago. Terriers were developed in a locality to suit the particular hunting needs of that area. Border terriers were created to fill a need in country on the Scottish and north of England borders, though the name, dating from 1870, was taken from the Border pack of hounds.

The Breed Standard stipulates that the Border terrier should have a head like that of an otter, moderately broad in the skull, with a short, strong muzzle. A black nose is the most desirable, although a liver- or flesh-coloured nose is not considered a serious fault. The eyes should be dark with a keen expression, and the ears should be small and V-shaped, of moder-

ate thickness and dropping forward close to the cheek. The teeth should have a scissor-like grip, with the top teeth slightly in front of the lower ones. The tail should be moderately short and fairly thick at the base, then tapering towards the tip. It should be set high and carried gaily but not curled over the back. Border terriers appear in a variety of colours, the most predominant of which are red, wheaten, grizzle-and-tan or blue-and-tan. There should be no white on the feet. Dogs weigh between 13 and 15½ lb, and bitches between 11½ and 14 lb.

Each part of a working dog is developed for a particular purpose. In relating this to Borders one has to remember first that they are used as hunt terriers for bolting fox or badger. They are usually expected to run with the hounds rather than be taken by other means, so without a fair length of leg they cannot keep up with the hounds. And no Master of the Hunt wants to wait an age to begin terrier work, which is in any event not the most exciting part of hunting. Having arrived at the earth the terrier must enter, find its quarry and attempt to make it bolt. For those purposes it has to be game and supple, and a strong jaw is needed in case it has to do more than worry the fox. A harsh, weather-resistant coat is needed for work in foul weather.

There are several advantages in keeping such a hardy, unexaggerated breed as a companion, especially when it is small enough to live without disadvantage in a household of any size. However, it must be remembered that it is a working dog and should not be pampered.

Given a sensible diet and accommodation, its hardiness makes it most unlikely to need more than a minimum of basic veterinary attention in its usually long life. Brought up properly, the Border is not quarrelsome so it can easily be kept in towns where the presence of other dogs will not cause trouble, though if attacked first the breed is not cowardly and can give a good account of itself. This grand companion for all members of the family has an easily maintained coat. Any breeder selling a puppy will explain how to strip the coat, or arrange to do this if the buyer can take his puppy back.

Border terrier breeders are proud of the way they have maintained the breed's physical characteristics and sporting qualities almost unchanged for many generations. Registrations with the British Kennel Club have risen to more than 1,000 each year. Therefore, in order to get the best from this small, rough-coated terrier with a head like an otter, it is essential that puppies are bought from genuine breeders who are best able to advise buyers whether their way of life will suit the breed they know so well.

# Norfolk and Norwich Terriers

NORWICH and Norfolk Terriers share a common heritage and until 1964 were known only as Norwich Terriers, but in that year the prick-eared and the drop-eared varieties were given official recognition by the British Kennel Club as separate breeds. The prick-eared breed retained the old name of Norwich Terrier and the drop-eared breed took the name of Norfolk Terrier.

Although these dogs have been in existence for a hundred years or more, it was not until 1932 that the Kennel Club accepted the application of Mrs Normandy Rodwell to recognize Norwich Terriers as a breed. The Norwich Terrier Club had been formed at the Richmond Championship Show held in July the same year, in order to protect the breed and to further public interest in it. However, these dogs had been well known and respected as sporting little terriers since the last half of the nineteenth century, in the eastern counties of England. At that time, the small, red terriers, seldom weighing more than ten pounds, with their hard, red coat, their keen, dark eyes, short legs and rather cobby appearance and pricked or cropped ears, were well known among sporting Cambridge undergraduates. From 1870 these terriers were being exhibited at shows.

There is disagreement between experts concerning the origin of the Norwich Terrier. Some believe that a Colonel Vaughan of Ballybrick, in Southern Ireland, laid the foundations of the breed. In the 1860s he hunted a pack of Foxhounds consisting of small red terriers with drop-ears, which were descended from the Irish Terrier. There were many different out-crosses at this time and both drop- and prick-eared terriers were produced. Since they were primarily working dogs, the breeders were not then concerned about this difference in appearance, and they cropped the ears of the dogs whose ears were not naturally

*The Norfolk was not recognized as a separate breed in Britain until 1964. In America, it is still called the Norwich*

erect, until this became illegal. When they stopped this practice of cropping, the breeders belonging to the newly formed Norwich Terrier Club disliked the carriage of the drop-ear so much that when the Kennel Club granted the breed recognition in 1932, they asked for a Standard requiring only erect ears. This was the beginning of a controversy between the two types, which raged until the Standard was eventually set out accepting both types of ear carriage.

Other experts say that a Mr Jodrell Hopkins, a horse dealer of Trumpington, Cambridge, played a major part in the 'construction' of the Norwich Terrier. At the time of the Boer War at the turn of the century Hopkins had acquired a smooth-coated terrier bitch which was an enthusiastic chaser of vermin. Her offspring were much sought after by sporting undergraduates from the university. One of Hopkins' employees, named Frank Jones, had several of the pups and crossed them with various small terriers of other breeds, notably Glen of Imaal and Irish Terriers. He took care to select only small specimens of these other breeds. The resultant offspring were sometimes called Jones Terriers, sometimes Trumpington

Terriers. There was a ready market for them both in Britain and overseas, for these game terriers would keep up with a horse all day and would seek out a fox, rat or rabbit, when given the chance, either above or under the ground.

The link between these terriers, descendants of the Hopkins-Jones dogs, and today's Norwich Terrier is provided by a breeder, Mrs Fagan, who bred selectively and regularly from one of these Cambridgeshire dogs. She called her animals the Jericho Hill dogs and it is claimed that a direct line can be traced from the Jericho Hill stud and the Norwich Terrier of today.

When first shown, the Norwich Terriers displayed considerable variation in size and shape–something like that shown by the Jack Russell today which is bred for its working ability and not to a Standard. But breeders of the Norwich Terrier have now succeeded in breeding true to a Standard. The result is a dog full of 'bounce' and the joy of living, a dog with a lovable and loyal disposition and a dog with an extraordinarily hardy constitution.

The original terriers were of a size to work a six-inch drain, and they seldom exceeded 10 to 12 inches to the point of

*The Norwich Terrier (above) is distinguished by its erect ears from the Norfolk Terrier which has drop ears*

the shoulder. They achieved something of a reputation by hunting the fox and badger, although, because of their small size, it must be accepted that more usually rats or rabbits were their quarry. Their small size and their basic sporting characteristics have been retained.

During World War One the breed became almost extinct, and was revived and revitalized only by the use of small specimens of other terrier breeds, including Bedlingtons, Staffordshire Bull Terriers, Cairn Terriers, Irish Terriers and the now extinct Trumpington Terrier.

Today the two breeds are safely in the hands of dedicated and enthusiatic breeders, so their future is assured. However, neither breed has ever managed to win any real popularity with the general public. Neither breed is a prolific breeder and this factor protects them from commercial exploitation, as does the attitude of their adherents. Both breeds make charming companions, each having its distinct personality, and they are equally at home both in town and country.

# Breed Standard: the Norwich Terrier

### CHARACTERISTICS
The Norwich Terrier is one of the smallest of the Terriers. Of a lovable disposition, not quarrelsome and with a hardy constitution. Temperament–gay and fearless.

### GENERAL APPEARANCE
A small, low, keen dog, compact and strong with good substance and bone. Excessive trimming is not desirable. Honourable scars from fair wear and tear should not count against it.

### HEAD AND SKULL
Muzzle 'foxy' and strong; length about one third less than a measurement from the occiput to the bottom of the stop, which should be well defined. Skull wide (good width between the ears) and slightly rounded.

### EYES
Dark, full of expression, bright and keen.

### MOUTH
Tight lipped. Jaws clean and strong. Teeth strong, rather large, scissor bite.

### NECK
Strong, of good length, commensurate with correct overall balance.

### FOREQUARTERS
Well laid back shoulders, with short, powerful and straight legs; not out at elbow. Legs should be moving straight forward when travelling.

### BODY
Compact with good depth. Rib cage should be long and well sprung with short loin. Level topline.

### HINDQUARTERS
Strong and muscular with well-turned stifle and low set hock and with great powers of propulsion.

### FEET
Round with thick pads.

### TAIL
Medium docked, set on high to complete a perfectly level back and carried erect.

### COAT
Hard, wiry and straight, lying close to the body. It is longer and rougher on the neck and chest, forming a ruff to frame the face. Hair on the head, ears and muzzle short and smooth, except for eyebrows and whiskers.

### COLOUR
All shades of red, wheaten, black-and-tan and grizzle. White marks or patches are undesirable.

### SIZE
Height 10 inches at withers; weight 11–12 lb.

### FAULTS
Light bone; long weak back; over or undershot mouth; long narrow head; cow hocks; feet turned in; yellow or pale eyes; soft, wavy, curly or silky coat. In USA, cropped ears disqualify.

The modern Kennel Club Standards of the two breeds are similar except with regard to the ears. The Norfolk has neatly dropped ears carried close to the cheek and slightly rounded at the tip, while the Norwich has erect ears. The two breeds are the smallest in the Terrier Group. They have hardy constitutions and likeable, sporting, though not quarrelsome, dispositions. Their temperament is described as steady and fearless. Both breeds are strong, aggressive, hard-working and high-spirited. However, the Norwich is more lively than the Norfolk; the latter tends to be the more docile of the two.

In general appearance they are small, low and keen, with good substance and bone. Their skulls are wide and slightly rounded; the muzzle is strong with a well-defined stop. Their eyes are dark, intelligent, full of expression, bright and keen. The jaws are strong and clean with strong, rather large teeth meeting in a scissor bite. The neck is of medium length fitting into clean, powerful shoulders, with short, powerful, straight legs. The body is comparatively short and compact with well-sprung ribs. The hindquarters have a good turn of stifle, with well let down hocks and with great powers of propulsion. The feet should be round with thick pads. The tail is usually docked quite short, although a medium dock is called for in both the Standards. The coat is hard, wiry and straight, lying close to the body, except for the coat on the neck which is longer and which forms a distinctive mane. On the whole, the Norfolk's coat is shorter than that of the Norwich, although the Standard asks for the same type of coat in both varieties. It is usually red in colour, though black-and-tan, red-wheaten and grizzle are also allowed. This type of coat means that it can adapt to the worst weather conditions.

The Standards place great emphasis on power and substance, strength and endurance, but it must be appreciated that they are describing the smallest of the terrier breeds and that these terms must be applied in relation to the breeds' size.

As companions, both breeds have much to recommend them. Their temperaments are usually reliable, their dispositions gay and lovable, and their adaptability to any type of home pronounced. They are eager to please and are ideal as family pets. They are good with children if the children are considerate and do not tease them. They require neither elaborate grooming nor expensive trimming and their appetites for both food and exercise are commensurate with their small size. They are loyal and devoted to their owners, and make excellent watch-dogs.

*The Norfolk (left) has never been popular, but its future is assured by breeders*

# Skye and Sealyham Terriers

THE Sealyham Terrier is not a breed that can lay claim to an ancient history, but its ancestry is nevertheless very interesting. In the mid-nineteenth century, Captain John Edwardes, whose country estate, Sealyham, lies between Haverfordwest and Fishguard in Wales, became dissatisfied with the sporting performance of the local strain of terriers and resolved, therefore, to breed a strain which would meet his very high standards. Using the best of the local terriers as a basis for his breeding programme, he introduced the blood of an indigenous Welsh breed, the Corgi, and a northern terrier breed, the Dandie Dinmont, for whose working ability and courage he had great respect. In order to improve the hardness and pugnacity of his terriers, Captain Edwardes introduced some Bull Terrier blood, but with it came a tendency

to deafness, a degree of quarrelsomeness, and coats which are shorter than is considered desirable in a working terrier. Captain Edwardes did not record what other blood was introduced, but it is likely that Wire-haired Fox Terriers were used and possibly a West Highland White, in order to fix the white colouring which he wanted. Over a period of years, a strain began to emerge which was close to the Captain's ideal, but so that the terriers should not lack the courage which was required for their demanding work, he developed an equally demanding method of selection which was simply to try his young stock against a polecat. He discarded any pups which failed the test.

Eventually, the fame of this new terrier breed from Sealyham spread far beyond Wales and by 1910 it began to appear at Kennel Club shows, though under the name of Pembrokeshire Terriers at first. In 1911, the breed was awarded Championship status and were then called Sealyham's. The Sealyham's smart appearance and jaunty, devil-may-care manner very quickly brought it to the notice of enthusiasts whose prime interest was the show ring. In the period between the wars, the breed developed into a far more glamorous terrier and in the process lost a great deal of its value as a working dog, although it lost none of its un-

## Breed Standard: the Skye Terrier

**CHARACTERISTICS**
A one-man dog, distrustful of strangers but not vicious.

**HEAD AND SKULL**
Head long with powerful jaws. Nose black.

**EYES**
Hazel, preferably dark brown, medium size, close set and full of expression.

**EARS**
Prick or drop. When prick, gracefully feathered, not large, erect at the outer edges and slanting towards each other at inner edge, from peak to skull. When drop, larger, hanging straight, lying flat and close at front.

**MOUTH**
Teeth closing level.

**NECK**
Long and slightly crested.

**FOREQUARTERS**
Shoulders broad and close to the body, chest deep. Legs short and muscular.

**BODY**
Long and low. Back level. Ribs well sprung, giving flattish appearance to sides.

**HINDQUARTERS**
Well developed. Legs short and muscular.

**FEET**
Large and pointing forward.

**TAIL**
When hanging, upper part pendulous and lower half thrown back in a curve. When raised, a prolongation of the incline of the back, not raising higher nor curling up.

**COAT**
Double. Undercoat short, close, soft and woolly. Overcoat long, hard, straight, flat and free from crisp and curl. Hair on head shorter, softer, veiling forehead and eyes. On ears overhanging inside, falling down and mingling with side locks, surrounding the ears like a fringe and allowing their shape to appear. The tail should be gracefully feathered.

**COLOUR**
Dark or light grey, fawn, cream, black, with black points. In fact, any self colour allowing shading of the same colour and lighter undercoat, so long as the nose and ears are black. A small white spot on the chest is permissible.

**WEIGHT AND SIZE**
Height 10 inches, total length 41½ inches. weight 25 lbs. The bitch is slightly smaller in the same proportions.

**FAULTS**
Yellow eyes, tail curled over back or any deformity.

doubted charm or cheerful, swaggering manner. Nowadays the show Sealyham is not used for the work for which Captain Edwards developed the breed, but it has developed into a first class show dog, with its harsh, white coat and large, powerful head and gleaming black eyes.

The breed could very well have died out after the death of Captain Edwards had not a number of admirers kept it going. A club was formed in 1908, followed by Kennel Club recognition in 1911. The American Kennel Club recognized it later in the same year and public interest increased until checked by World War One. Breeding in both countries started again in 1918 and there was a boom in the breed in Britain and the USA.

The little terriers make excellent house dogs. They are naturally clean in their habits, able to distinguish between genuine callers and intruders, and are excellent with children. Affectionate and loyal, the Sealyham retains all the fire and pluck of its ancestors.

The Skye Terrier is something of a connoisseur's dog, arousing intense loyalty among its admirers but apparently lacking the sort of appeal to make a popular pet.

*Facing page: the Skye Terrier is a strong dog for its size, which is seldom more than 10 inches high. Sealyham Terriers (below) are a little smaller than Skyes*

Dr Caius, writing at the end of the sixteenth century, described the 'Iseland' dog in terms which identify it as a Skye terrier or something very similar to it, though the ancestors of the native Scottish terrier breeds probably also shared features with this ancient terrier. The breed was well established in the Scottish Highlands and Islands and was valued as a hunter and destroyer of vermin for many years, but it was not until Queen Victoria's affection for the breed became known that it began to attract wider attention.

From about 1876, the breed began to appear at dog shows, though at first under the broad generic name of Scotch Terrier, of which three distinct varieties were discernible. The dispute as to which of these three was the true Scotch Terrier was resolved in 1879 and the Skye Terrier was recognized as a separate breed, since which time its contact with its original purpose in life has been largely lost, and it has been bred as a show dog and as a companion. In order to achieve distinction in the show ring, a uniform type was quickly established and those features which breeders prized were enhanced. The hard, straight coat was grown long, parted centrally down its long back so that it swept the floor, and meticulously groomed to reveal its shine and colour. The breed is of an intelligent and enquiring turn of mind. As a companion, the

Skye is a one-man-dog *par excellence*, unreservedly loyal to those to whom it gives its affection, but reserved and distrustful of strangers. This great loyalty was recognized by the erection of a statue to Greyfriars Bobby, a Skye who was so disconsolate at its master's death that it guarded his grave night and day until its own death ten years later.

In return for such loyalty, the breed expects great affection, without the reassurance of which it may become introspective and surly.

The old sporting terriers bred in the rugged Isle of Skye were tough and fearless and expected to creep into rock crevices and burrows prepared to face whatever foe lurked there. The modern Skye may never see a fox but is loyal to the death, canny and also good-tempered unless provoked, when he will stand his ground and defy anything on two or four legs. Like the Sealyham, the Skye is game and hardy enough to enjoy the most vigorous exercise but is not so big that less energetic people would find it difficult to keep. Its weight seldom exceeds 25 lb.

For those who are able to handle the breed, are willing to give it the affection that it demands and to keep its profuse coat in good order the Skye can be a loyal and distinctive friend. And who would not allow such a friend to have and to exert its own strong personality?

# Chapter V
# Non-sporting Dogs
# Utility Group

Three Spitz breeds: the Akita, the Keeshond and the Iceland dog

ESSENTIALLY, the Akita, the Keeshond and the Iceland dog are all breeds which have been fostered and developed by man for working purposes: the first two as guard and hunting dogs, the Iceland dog for herding sheep. They all descend from the northern group of dogs, which embraces the Spitz and the dogs collectively known as Huskies.

Although classified as being of northern descent, the Akita has become the native dog of Japan, where it has been bred, in what is thought to be its pure form, since the seventeenth century. It originated, however, in the Polar regions. Rare in Britain, the Akita is best known, outside Japan, in the United States of America, as many specimens were taken there by American servicemen after World War Two. It is a registered breed with the American Kennel Club. In Japan it is the commonest and largest of that country's Spitz breeds, the others being Sanshu, Shiba, Shika and Ainu. In Japan the Akita is often called the Shishi Inu.

The owner of an Akita will find that it truly lives up to its original qualities of a guard dog, and that it is alert, courageous and intelligent. The Akita's liveliness makes it an ideal pet for someone who wants a dog to participate to the full in family activities, and the few breeders of the Akita in the West feel that the dog's assets have, to date, been singularly neglected. In addition to its qualities as a domestic pet, it makes an excellent hunting dog for deer, bear and wild boar, which has increased its popularity in America.

Akitas come in a whole range of colours including red, brown, cream-grey, black and silver, and may also be brindled. These colours may be solid or shaded. Like other northern breeds, the Akita has a double coat composed of a thick, soft undercoat and a harsher overcoat.

Standing some 21 to 24 inches high for dogs and 19 to 21 inches for bitches, at the shoulder, the Akita is the largest of the Japanese breeds. In the USA careful breeding has produced even larger dogs, males up to 27½ inches and females up to 24½ inches at the shoulder. The body is well knit and muscular, particularly round the shoulders, and the skull is wide, a feature accentuated by its flattened top, the presence of a well-defined 'stop', and small erect ears which tip slightly forwards over the triangular-shaped, dark eyes. Also characteristic of the Akita, and of other northern breeds, is the tail, which is carried over the back. In the Akita,

*Left: the Keeshond needs plenty of exercise and so is more suited to living in the country. Although recognized in Britain, the Iceland dog (right) is rarely seen outside its own country*

# Breed Standard: the Keeshond

**GENERAL APPEARANCE**
A short, compact body; alert carriage; fox-like head; small pointed ears; a well-feathered, curling tail, carried over the back; hair very thick on the neck, forming a large ruff; head, ears and legs covered with short thick hair. Dogs should move cleanly and briskly (not lope like an Alsatian) but movement should be straight and sharp.

**HEAD AND SKULL**
Head well proportioned to the body, wedge-shaped when seen from above; from the side showing definite stop. Muzzle should be of medium length, neither coarse nor snipy.

**EYES**
Dark with well-defined spectacles.

**EARS**
Small and well set on head; not meeting.

**MOUTH**
Should be neither over- nor undershot, upper teeth should just overlap under teeth and should be white, sound and strong (but discoloration from distemper not to penalize severely).

**FOREQUARTERS**
Forelegs feathered, straight, with good bone and cream in colour.

**HINDQUARTERS**
Hind legs should be straight, showing very little hock and not feathered below the hock.

**FEET**
Round and cat-like with black nails.

**TAIL**
Tightly curled, a double curl at the end is desirable. Plume to be white on the top where curled, with black tip.

**COAT**
Dense, and harsh (off-standing), dense ruff and well feathered, profuse trousers; a soft, thick, light-coloured undercoat. Coat should not be silky, wavy or woolly, nor should it form a parting on the back.

**COLOUR**
Should be wolf, ash-grey; not all black or all white and markings should be definite. Hind legs should be cream.

**WEIGHT AND SIZE**
The ideal height is 18 inches for dogs and 17 inches for bitches, but type is of more importance.

**FAULTS**
Light eyes; prominent eyes; curly or wavy tendency in coat; silky coat; absence of spectacles; nervous demeanour; drop ears; whole white foot or feet; black marks below the knee, pencilling excepted; white chest; apple head or absence of stop.

Note: male animals should have two apparently normal testicles fully descended into the scrotum.

the tail is very long and may curl in a complete or even a double circle, a feature made even more distinctive by its plumed hair. Its feet are fully webbed and this makes it an excellent swimmer. At the full run its hind legs move together and this enables it to spring on its quarry.

Like the Akita, the Keeshond is also a national dog, of Holland. Sometimes known as the Dutch Barge Dog, it was once employed on canal barges as a guard dog because its acute hearing made it ideally suited for this purpose. However, today it is more of a show dog than a working one. The Keeshond allegedly received its name from its use as watchdog and companion by the ordinary people of Holland, who adopted it during the eighteenth century as a symbol of the struggle between the Patriot party and the supporters of William V of Orange. Because Jan Kees was a common name (the equivalent, perhaps, of John Smith) the dog was duly called the Keeshond. Other experts believe the name was created because the dog was the favourite of Cornelius de Witt (Kees for short).

The Dutch took little interest in developing their native dog into a well-defined breed, until some specimens were taken from Holland to England in the early part of this century. The Keeshond has a direct line of descent from the Finnish Spitz and shares the bulky proportions of other Spitz breeds. A male stands some 18 inches at the shoulder, a bitch 17 inches, and the broad body is topped with a wedge-shaped head bearing a well-defined 'stop' and slightly domed muzzle. Also, like other northern breeds, the Keeshond has a luxuriant double coat. Colours are ash-grey, wolf, but not all black or all white. The black markings of the Keeshond's face give it a unique appearance of being 'spectacled', for the black coloration is pencilled in lines extending from the outer rim of each eye towards the base of each ear.

Alert and intelligent, the Keeshond excels as a watchdog, the purpose for which it was first employed, and will give warning of anyone's approach to the house. It is also a good house dog, although its long hair makes daily grooming an essential, and is liable to be deposited freely on clothes and furniture. A Keeshond will take readily to an energetic, outdoor life, so is far better kept as a country dog than as a flat or town-dweller. It has a large appetite and an adult will consume as much as, say a Labrador Retriever – about 1½ lb mixed meat and meal each day – though it does not tend to put on excess weight.

Although the Iceland Dog is recognized by the British Kennel Club, it is extremely rare in the UK and only seven were registered with the Kennel Club in 1972. It

appears in the 'Any Other Varieties' class at dog shows, and many have won prizes. It was introduced to this country in the 1950s by an Englishman who selected specimens very carefully, and the progeny have bred true to type. In the past, most Icelanders have not been interested enough in the Iceland Dog to start selective breeding, and this is why the pure type is seldom seen in Iceland today, except on farms in the remoter areas.

During the settlement of Iceland, which began in 874 AD, dogs came from Norway and became common on every farm. During the Middle Ages, when England traded with Iceland, many attractive Iceland Dog puppies were imported and became favourites with English ladies. In its native land, the Iceland Dog was used for guarding the tún (home meadow), rounding up ponies, and warning the farmer of any stranger's approach, as well as for sheep herding.

*The Akita (top) is the national dog of Japan. The Keeshond (below) is the national dog of Holland*

The general appearance of the Iceland Dog is of a Spitz type, slightly under middle size, lightly built and with a game temperament. The colours should be white with fawn markings, golden, and light fawn with black tips to the long hairs. The ears are erect and the tail is bushy and carried over the back. It is from 13 to 16 inches high, and weighs about 25 lb. This breed develops slowly and is not fully mature till it is about 18 months old. It needs to have strong ties with humans in order to mature, and is therefore a family dog in every way. It makes an ideal house pet, being both intelligent and affectionate. In 1969, the Iceland Kennel Club was formed, and since then its fame has increased so that it is no longer in danger of extinction.

# The Boston Terrier

THE Boston Terrier is an American creation, sometimes affectionately known as the 'American gentleman'. Smart and debonair, this dog weighs from 15 to 25 lb, and is compactly built, with a short, square head. The markings of its short, smooth coat are particularly eye-catching. Ideally, these are dark seal brindle (although lighter brindle markings are also permitted), with a wide, white blaze on its head, white collar and white stockings. The ears stand proudly erect. In the United States the ears are often cropped, which gives a sharper effect, but in Britain (where cropping is not practised) breeders have made an excellent job of producing dogs with an ear that stands naturally erect—so much so that the natural ear can now also be seen in America.

Although extremely lively and active, the Boston Terrier is the ideal pet for any town dog lover, even for people who live in flats. It is very adaptable and is not inclined to yap. In fact, it seldom barks without good reason, and when it does, it emits a bark which is surprisingly deep for its size. The dog's fine coat and dainty feet tend to be comparatively dirt-free, and loose hairs are unlikely to be found on the upholstery. Being a fun-loving dog, notable for its alertness and intelligence, the Boston will obviously appreciate the freedom of the countryside, but since it keenly enjoys a ride in a car, a town dweller can take it anywhere. It can be relied upon to guard the vehicle and will make itself inconspicuous under any hotel or restaurant table. In the United States it is one of the most popular of city breeds, but in Britain it has never been such a firm town favourite as the Poodle—surprising when one considers its delightfully clean-cut appearance and the fact that it is so easy to feed and simple to groom.

Unlike many other breeds, the origin of the Boston is quite well known. The father of the breed was a crossbred dog called Judge, who was imported to America from England in 1865. Judge's background consisted mainly of English Bulldog with a dash of terrier. So into the melting pot went this dog's progeny—English Bull Terrier and Staffordshire Bull Terrier blood being added, and the

*This Boston's ears have been cropped. This practice is illegal in Britain and dogs with naturally erect ears have been bred*

*The Boston is a smart compact dog and the markings of its short, smooth coat are particularly eye-catching*

mixture repeatedly refined, until at last the Boston Terrier emerged. The breed took its name from the city of Boston, in the neighbourhood of which it had been developed, and was finally recognized by the American Kennel Club in 1893. It is interesting to note that the sponsors of the Boston, when applying to the American Kennel Club for recognition of the breed, had called the breed the American Bull Terrier. This name met with several objections from other Bull Terrier clubs. It was James Watson, an American writer on dogs and an acknowledged authority who suggested that as the breed had been developed in and around Boston it should bear the name of that city.

Boston Terriers were imported into England from America around 1920. The early imports were mostly poor specimens, for the American home market was sufficiently large and wealthy to absorb all the top show specimens available. English breeders, however, with their usual skill, soon improved upon the original stock. Many of the early bitches were far larger than desired, but at least they proved to be good breeders. Eventually some small stud dogs were imported and, with selective breeding, the correct size

became more stabilized. The ears, which were at first inclined to be soft and droopy, in the absence of cropping as practised in America, gradually became stronger in muscle and texture, and eventually stood erect without artificial aid. Today the English-bred Bostons are successfully exported as potential prize-winners at shows all over the world.

The breed has two outstanding characteristics, the first being the unique head. This should be built up of squares—square skull, square muzzle, and all planes as flat as possible. The ears should be small and pointed, carried erect, and set on the top corners of the skull. The eyes are also most important; they should be large, round and lustrous, set wide apart and looking forward, the outside corners in line with the cheeks. The balance of all the separate parts of the head, plus a correct eye, combine to give the dog its characteristic expression—what one American expert has called the 'God-loving' look.

The other important and unique breed point is the white marking. The minimum marking required for the show ring is a nose band and white blaze, but a Boston with white head blaze, full white collar, white front legs and white back feet is termed 'fully marked' and is greatly admired if the markings coincide with the correct breed points. The addition, on a fully marked dog, of a brindle diamond on

top of the skull, separating the nose blaze and collar, makes the markings perfect. must be stressed that markings shoul never take precedence over correct bree type, but they undoubtedly make a stron impression on judges in the show ring The brindle colouration may be so dar as to appear almost black, but whe examined in good light the basic colourin will undoubtedly be seen to contain som brindling—rather like an artist's palett in which the impression of black is con veyed by using dark browns and umbe without touching the tube of ebony black

A Boston Terrier which lacks whit markings or possesses too much white i its coat is, of course, no less acceptabl as a companion. Such an incorrectl marked puppy will often be availabl relatively cheaply. It makes an ideal pe even if not suitable for the show ring.

The body of the Boston Terrier is fre from any exaggeration; short but neve chunky. The front legs are straight an strong; the back legs fairly well angulated The topline is a straight curve down ove the croup; the tail is short and set on low The neck must be of medium length, wel arched so that the head is carried high an proudly. This gives the essential elegan carriage when walking.

One of the most important features i any dog is temperament. In the canin world, temperament can be described a the dog's outlook on life and the way th animal responds to stimuli of variou types. Looking back at the origin of thi breed, it is interesting to note that it wa founded on the redoubtable gladiators o the fighting pit—dogs that feared nothin and would willingly fight to the death Some authorities consider that the earl Bostons were, in fact, bred as fightin dogs. However, the earlier breeders no only refined the dog's appearance but als improved its character, removing it instinctive ferocity while retaining its grea courage.

The Boston Terrier is truly a small do with a large dog's heart. Despite it battling ancestry, it was intended primar ily to be an ideal companion, smal enough to fit comfortably into the humb lest cottage and possessing an appeal fo owners of either sex. For men who fee slightly embarrassed to be seen walking a Poodle or a Pekingese, the Boston carrie a different status. Although small in stature, it is courageous and sporting, ar efficient killer of vermin, if given th chance, and an excellent guard dog Apart from these masculine qualities, th Boston is affectionate and loyal, easy tc train, and a delightful playmate for children. So it gains the approval of women as well.

Looking after the Boston is largely a matter of common sense. Being a hardy tle dog, all it requires is a warm, dry ace to sleep and regular meals of the ght kind.

Most people prefer to acquire a puppy the age of about nine weeks. Choose one hich looks sturdy, with good bone, a lid body and bright eyes. Check the mperament and try to select a puppy at trots to meet you with a lively, enuiring expression. Be wary, however, of e that crouches or runs away, for although such a puppy may have a very veet, gentle temperament, much care and fection are likely to be needed for it to alize its full potential. The bold puppy usually foolproof. Incidentally, marking an be assessed at this age, but the white eas tend to close up as the dog grows.

The puppy should be taught the meaning of 'no' by its owner, using a firm voice. ouse training is especially important. he puppy is simply put out of doors after eding, after a long sleep or when it arts running in circles, sniffing the round. Praise it lavishly when it performs nd it will soon learn; then you can scold whenever it forgets its good manners.

Feeding is also a question of common nse. As a small puppy, four meals should e given, two based on milk and two on eat. The former can be of warm milk and atmeal or baby cereals, the latter meals f minced meat and a little puppy-meal or rown bread moistened with gravy. The umber of meals will then be progressively duced until the adult dog is being given ne main meal a day, usually in the vening, with perhaps some hard biscuits nd milk in the morning. The quantity an be assessed for a growing dog by nsuring that it has just the amount it an eat at one attempt. As an adult the mount will be regulated by the dog's ondition. Never allow a dog to become verweight, for a fat dog is unhealthy.

Keep a puppy away from other dogs ntil it has been inoculated against infecions such as distemper. Most vets will dvise this to be done at an early age. The uppy should also be wormed. A reputable reeder will have attended to this before ale, but it is wise to ask about it at the ime of purchase.

Although you will naturally be anxious o show it off, do not over-exercise a young uppy. It will play just as much as it vants, and rest when tired. Children nust be taught to respect a dog's need for leep and should be discouraged from icking the puppy up. Parents should show hem the correct way to lift a dog which hould be picked up around the middle, ot by the front legs.

Some experts aver that the Boston Terrier does not like to live outside in a ennel; it prefers the same quarters as its wners and is not happy unless it has the un of the house or flat. As the breed does

## Breed Standard: the Boston Terrier

### GENERAL APPEARANCE
The general appearance should be that of a lively, highly intelligent, smooth-coated, short-headed, compactly built, short-tailed, well-balanced dog of medium size, of brindle colour and evenly marked with white.

### HEAD AND SKULL
Skull square, free from wrinkles; cheeks flat; stop well defined. Muzzle short and square. Nose black and wide; jaws broad and square.

### EYES
Wide apart, large and round, and dark in colour.

### EARS
Erect; small and thin. At times cropped in USA.

### MOUTH
Teeth short and regular, bite even.

### NECK
Of fair length, slightly arched and neatly set into the shoulders.

### FOREQUARTERS
Legs set moderately wide apart and on a line with the point of the shoulders; straight in bone and well muscled; pasterns short and strong.

### BODY
Deep with good width of chest; shoulders sloping, back short; ribs deep and well sprung; loins short and muscular.

### HINDQUARTERS
Legs set true, bent at stifles, short from hocks to feet; hocks turning neither in nor out; thighs strong and well muscled.

### FEET
Round, small and compact. Toes well arched.

### TAIL
Set on low; short, fine and tapering.

### COAT
Short, smooth, bright and fine in texture.

### COLOUR
Brindle with white markings. Ideal markings: white muzzle, even white blaze over head, collar, breast, part or whole of forelegs, and hind legs below hocks.

### WEIGHT AND SIZE
Weight should not exceed 25 lb divided by classes as follows: Lightweight, under 15 lb; Middleweight, 15 and under 20 lb; Heavyweight, 20 and under 25 lb.

### FAULTS
Solid black, black and tan; liver or mouse colour; docked tail; eyes small or sunken; light colour or wall eye; muzzle wedge-shaped or lacking depth; pinched or wide nostrils; protruding teeth; narrow chest; long or slack loins; roach back; sway back; long and weak pasterns; splay feet; long and coarse coat, lacking lustre.

not give off any doggie smell (or so little as to be hardly noticeable) there are no overriding objections to keeping the breed as a house dog in the truest sense. Furthermore, as has been said, the Boston's coat does not cause a great deal of trouble because of falling hairs. The Boston loves to play, and is delighted to have a ball which it can chase and bite. A word of warning here; if you do provide a rubber ball for your dog then you must keep a watchful eye to see that it is not chewed and bits of the rubber swallowed. To swallow parts of a rubber ball can be extremely dangerous to a dog; in some instances death has resulted. One can readily imagine the distress of owners who lose a dog in this way, for unwittingly they have been partly responsible.

It is not all that easy to breed Boston Terriers. This is because virtually all Boston puppies must be delivered by a Caesarian operation. Puppies that conform to the desired head structure are often too wide to pass out the uterus in the normal way. So that the mother and puppies survive, the birth needs the help of surgery. This makes breeding expensive and so it is important that good stock is used to make it worthwhile.

There have been many famous Boston Terriers in the show ring; in Britain Ch Erijo's Sir Galahad was Best of Breed at Crufts in 1971 and 1972, and was Boston

*The head of a Boston with its square skull and muzzle is a unique feature of the breed*

Terrier of the Year in 1971. He was the leading Boston in Ireland with nine COs, two reserve CCs and many other awards. In America, the home of the breed, an outstanding Champion was Star Q's Brass Buttons, owned and bred by Dr K. Eileen Hite of New York City. At two years of age Brass Buttons had been three times Best in Show, had been Best of Breed no less than 75 times, first in group 27 times and had had 32 group placings.

Anyone who buys a Boston Terrier and trains the dog well will have good reason to be proud of this delightful little 'American gentleman'.

# Dogs of the Bulldog breed

THE Bulldog and the French Bulldog are distinctive breeds with one common denominator: they both belong to the non-sporting group. This is perhaps a misleading classification, if taken to imply that these breeds lack all sporting characteristics; rather it is used to describe those dogs which are not specifically bred for hunting or for shooting purposes, but are intended to be kept for other work or as domestic pets.

In Britain this group is further subdivided into the working group (comprising breeds concerned with guard work or looking after cattle) and the utility group. This subdivision has come about fairly recently, whereas in the United States the working group has been in existence for some considerable time. The American non-sporting group is identical to the utility group in Britain. The Bulldog is commonly recognized as the national dog of England; but the French Bulldog cannot be said to have yet usurped the place of the Poodle as the national dog of France.

The Bulldog is certainly unique in appearance, with its massive head and large skull, its broad, blunt muzzle and prominent chin, its thickset, pear-shaped body and its powerful, wide chest. The great appeal of the breed, paradoxically, is the 'beauty' of its very ugliness. Its short, fine coat is easy to clean and groom.

As a puppy, the Bulldog is a great charmer and just as playful as any of the more active breeds. Its deeply wrinkled face, huge paws and chubby body make its youthful antics all the more entertaining. Solid, dependable and with a reliable temperament, it is an extremely satisfying family dog which loves being petted. With its relatively low stature and somewhat phlegmatic character, it will inspire confidence even in a small child, and although it will never bowl a youngster over, as some of the more boisterous, leggy breeds are sometimes inclined to do, the Bulldog,

*The great appeal of the Bulldog is the 'beauty' of its very ugliness*

with an undershot jaw was better able to grasp the bull by the nose and hang on, thus providing a new thrill for the sadistic tastes of much of society in those days. Bull-baiting was not abolished until 1835 and thereafter the breed was regarded as a companion rather than a fighter. The Standard for the Bulldog was drawn up as early as 1876, one year after the formation of the Bulldog Club, the first specialist club for any individual breed of dog. Since then the Standard has only been slightly revised.

The French Bulldog might be described as a smaller, more active version of the Bulldog, but there are a number of physical differences too, as stipulated in the Standard for the breed. Although the head of the French Bulldog is also massive,

*Above and below: the French Bulldog is thought to have been a mixture of a Toy English Bulldog and a small native French farm dog*

specially as a puppy, greatly enjoys games nd romps. Often stubborn, this breed demands great patience from its owners.

Although the Bulldog, with its pushed-back nose, is inclined to react badly to intense heat, it can be a very active dog. Many people believe that it is incapable of enjoying a long country walk, but this is not so. A Bulldog will be all the fitter for regular exercise, bearing in mind that a steady walking pace is more suitable than strenuous running. In fact, too little exercise and too much food are equally harmful to the dog's health. A mile-long walk each day is normally enough for this dog, but when fed sensibly and kept in good health, it is frequently capable of a short, brisk run. The breed is extremely long-suffering, putting up with pain and discomfort without complaint.

For the dog-lover who lives in a built-up area, the Bulldog has the double recommendation of not being noisy, but nonetheless being a good guard dog. Its aggressive appearance is usually enough to deter any would-be intruder. Although it is not inclined to fighting, it can do so when necessary. If provoked beyond endurance it can be very formidable, and if called upon to defend master and home, the Bulldog will show great courage. The Bulldog is unfortunately not usually a long-lived dog, though some do reach the age of ten or twelve years.

The origin of the Bulldog has been traced back to the reign of Queen Elizabeth I. References to the 'bulldogge' in those days were to be taken literally, for they describe the dog that was used for the popular but cruel sport of bull-baiting. The early specimens bred for this so-called sport were of Mastiff type, until it was recognized that a lower-slung dog

146

square and broad, with the lower jaw deep, square, broad, slightly undershot and well turned up, it does not have the exaggerated upsweep of the Bulldog. Perhaps the most eye-catching difference, however, relates to the ears. The Bulldog possesses 'rose' ears—soft ears with what is almost a pleat which folds over—whereas the French Bulldog has attractive 'bat' ears, carried erect like those of a Boston Terrier, although considerably larger and set much farther apart.

The French Bulldog is described as sound, active and intelligent. Although small and compact in build, it is an extremely lively dog. At the tender age of four months it will spring neatly onto the settee or armchair. Its hindquarters are strong and muscular, enabling it to clear obstacles with surprising grace and ease. This neat, compact little dog is highly suitable for town life. It is intelligent and has a calm disposition, not often disturbed by traffic or city turmoil. The French Bulldog is a delightful family pet which needs human companionship almost constantly. It does not occupy too much room enjoys adventure and will happily follow its owner anywhere.

The coat of the French Bulldog is smooth, fine and very easy to keep in shining condition. The most usual colour is brindle but pied also occurs. In the latter case the coat is basically white, but with brindle or black patches, which make an attractive combination. Fawn is another coat colour and this is especially striking when contrasted with a black or shaded mask. The ideal weight is 28 lb for the male, and 24 lb for the female.

The origin of the French Bulldog is not too clear. In spite of its name, there are theories that it may have come from Spain rather than France. Some claim that its ancestors were small specimens of the Bulldog, probably crossed with a small, prick-eared breed. However fashioned, the French Bulldog rapidly became popular on the Continent. The first specimens to reach England were imported from France around 1902, by which date the breed was also in the USA and although never one of the most popular breeds it has a very faithful following.

Perhaps one of the reasons why these two breeds are not seen in such large numbers as, say, Poodles or Cocker Spaniels, is that they have breeding problems and can be difficult whelpers. Because of the large square head, puppies do not arrive easily, and both breeds are notorious for the number of Caesarian sections used to ensure safe delivery. It is wiser, therefore, to leave the breeding of these two to the experts.

*Right: a Bulldog puppy, which makes a charming and entertaining pet*

# Breed Standard: the Bulldog

**GENERAL APPEARANCE**
The general appearance of the Bulldog is that of a smooth-coated, thick-set dog, rather low in stature, but broad, powerful, and compact.

**HEAD AND SKULL**
The skull should be very large—the larger the better—and in circumference should measure (round in front of the ears) at least the height of the dog at the shoulders.

**EYES**
The eyes, seen from the front, should be situated low down in the skull. They should be quite round in shape, of moderate size, neither sunken nor prominent.

**EARS**
The ears should be set high on the head. In size they should be small and thin.

**MOUTH**
The jaw should be broad and square.

**NECK**
Should be moderate in length (rather short than long) very thick, deep and strong.

**FOREQUARTERS**
The shoulders should be broad, sloping and deep, very powerful and muscular. The forelegs should be very stout and strong, set wide apart, thick, muscular, and straight, with well-developed forearms.

**BODY**
The chest should be very wide, laterally round, prominent, and deep. The back should be short and strong, very broad at the shoulders, and comparatively narrow at the loins.

**HINDQUARTERS**
The legs should be large and muscular, and longer in proportion to the forelegs.

**FEET**
The hind feet, like the fore feet, should be round and compact, with the toes well split up.

**TAIL**
The tail should be set on low, jut out rather straight, then turn downwards. It should be round, smooth and devoid of fringe or coarse hair. It should be moderate in length, and tapering quickly to a fine point.

**COAT**
Should be fine in texture, short and smooth.

**COLOUR**
The colour should be whole or smut (that is, a whole colour with a black mask or muzzle). The only colours which are whole colours are brindles, reds, with their varieties, fawn, fallows, etc., and white. Pied is also allowed.

**WEIGHT AND SIZE**
The most desirable weight is 55 lb. for a dog and 50 lb. for a bitch; in USA 50 lb. and 40 lb.

# Chow Chows

ONE breed of dog of which the Western world knew nothing until the late eighteenth century had been nurtured in Asia and the Far East for thousands of years – the Chow Chow. The name comes, it is believed, from the Chinese original, Chaou, 'a large, primitive, undomesticated, extraordinary dog of great strength'. Barbarian ancestors of the Mongols used enormous dogs with features like the lion, and black tongues, when they went to war against the Chinese 3,000 years ago. A certain authenticity is lent to the story by virtue of the fact that even today the Chow, among all breeds of dog, and, indeed, among all mammals but the polar bear, is the only one to have a blue-black tongue. Its gums are the same colour too.

The Chow therefore, was not originally a native of China. Indeed, for a long time it continued to be a breed of Mongolia

*Chow Chows are dogs with a fascinating history going back thousands of years*

# Breed Standard: the Chow Chow

**GENERAL APPEARANCE**
An active, compact, short-coupled and well-balanced dog, well knit in frame, with tail carried well over the back.

**HEAD AND SKULL**
Skull flat and broad, with little stop, well filled out under the eyes. Muzzle moderate in length, broad from the eyes to the point (not pointed at the end like a fox). Nose black, large and wide in all cases (with the exception of cream and white in which case a light-coloured nose is permissible and in blues and fawns a self-coloured nose); but in all colours a black nose is preferable.

**EYES**
Dark and small, preferably almond-shaped (in blue or fawn dogs a light colour is permissible).

**EARS**
Small, thick, slightly rounded at the tip, carried stiffly erect but placed well forward over the eyes and wide apart, which gives the dog the peculiar characteristic expression of the breed, namely, a scowl.

**MOUTH**
Teeth strong and level, giving scissor bite. Tongue bluish black. Flews and roof of mouth black. Gums preferably black.

**NECK**
Strong, full, set well on the shoulders and slightly arched.

**FOREQUARTERS**
Shoulders muscular and sloping. Forelegs perfectly straight, and of moderate length.

**BODY**
Chest broad and deep. Back short, straight and strong. Loins powerful.

**HINDQUARTERS**
Hindlegs muscular and hocks well let down and perfectly straight; these are essential to produce the Chow's characteristic stilted gait.

**FEET**
Small, round, catlike, standing well on the toes.

**TAIL**
Set high and carried well over the back.

**COAT**
Abundant, dense, straight and stand-off. Outer coat rather coarse in texture and with soft woolly undercoat.

**COLOUR**
Whole coloured black, red, blue, fawn, cream or white, frequently shaded but not in patches or parti-coloured (the underpart of tail and back of thighs frequently of a light colour).

**WEIGHT AND SIZE**
Minimum height for Chows to be 18 inches, but in every case balance should be the outstanding feature.

and later Tibet. But after so long a period of living in China it is not surprising that it is often considered to be native to that country. As far back as the seventh century BC, the Chow was classified as a hunting breed, used to attack wolves and leopards. So strong and wilful was the breed then that huntsmen, according to ancient records, were obliged to control them with a contraption of straps around the dog's body and neck. Guarding was another of the breed's occupations; so too was herding cattle and other livestock.

The Chinese have always been adept at selective breeding, moulding breeds of dog and other animals to their own extraordinary whims, and the Pekingese is just one example of this. The Chow Chow had already been developed as a breed; it was a strong dog with long hair and a broad head, and a suspicious, fierce, courageous nature.

A certain indication of the Chow's status was given when Han Dynasty pottery models of the breed, found in the graves of noblemen, were discovered. Laufer's *Pottery of the Han Dynasty* tells us this was done so that the dogs could 'guard their masters, and keep off the evil influences of obnoxious spirits'. Whenever the Chow is mentioned outside the circle of those people who show dogs, a usual response is 'Oh, the breed the Chinese

eat.' The comment is a true one, but it was not so when the Chow was at its height as a hunting dog; lesser dogs were used for food then. Only later, when the country became much poorer and hunting was restricted did the Chow become part of people's diet. At the same time its pelt was made up into fur garments. Only monasteries and the dwindling number of great noblemen maintained the breed in its former state.

How the breed arrived in England in the late eighteenth century, when it was apparently kept in zoos, is not clear. One hundred years later, when dog shows were becoming more popular, and when Chows were being imported from China (from 1880 onwards), they were shown in small numbers. Royal patronage was bestowed on the breed in 1881 by the Prince of Wales, later Edward VII, who exhibited a Chow called Chang. The first American Chow champion on record was exported from England in 1905; this was Mrs Garnett Botfield's Chinese Chum. During the years between the two World Wars the breed not only became popular in Britain and the USA, but established itself as a spectacular show dog. A price of £1,800 – a huge amount at that time – was paid for one well-known champion in 1925. This was Ch Choonam Brilliantine which was sold to America. Another, Champion, Choonam Hung Kwong, was Supreme Best in Show at Crufts in 1936. The breed has continued its show ring success since 1945. About 1,500 Chows are registered at the British Kennel Club each year.

Basically, the Chow Chow has not changed in appearance for many thousands of years, since it was first portrayed on pottery, till the present day. It remains a strong-looking, compact-bodied animal, broad and deep-chested, with a scowling face beneath small erect ears, a bushy tail curled over the back, cat-like feet, and those characteristics which are unique to the breed: the blue-black tongue and gums and the straight hind legs that make its movement stilted.

In the past, some breeders tended to produce dogs that were too heavy and too close to the ground. In general these specimens had exaggerated bone and the arch of the neck was not sufficiently pronounced. Consequently the dogs had a somewhat squat appearance. Fortunately for the breed these tendencies have largely disappeared and the Chow of today is a beautifully proportioned dog.

The original colours were red and black. Blue was highly prized, too. Now there are also creams and fawns, but they

*Of all the breeds of dog, only the Chow Chow has a blue-black tongue and gums. It has a dignified, leonine appearance*

are not common. A smooth-coated Chow is also to be found, though in small numbers.

Temperamentally the Chow has stayed much the same as ever, suspicious and courageous, though not actually fierce; it is just its scowl that makes it seem so. Like most Oriental breeds, it is very strong willed; it is therefore hardly a breed that an impatient person who expects unquestioning obedience at all times would consider as an ideal companion. Its characteristic aloofness makes the Chow inclined to be very much a one-family, even a one-person dog, although there are exceptions.

The diet of the Chow does not correspond exactly to that of other breeds. For one thing, the Chow does not need so much fresh raw meat, and if the percentage of meat goes much above half of the total diet it is likely to have an adverse effect. Some experts recommend that the Chow's diet should consist of 50 per cent cooked offal with which are mixed wholemeal biscuits and offal gravy, and the rest to be raw lean beef or lamb. Some suet from the meat can be added to the meal as well as fresh vegetables, milk and eggs.

No would-be owner need be put off by the breed's profuse coat. It is easily maintained in good condition (so long as the dog is itself in good health) by a few minutes' brushing each day. Experts do not always agree on the method of grooming the Chow. 'Brush' is emphasized by some authorities as they say the use of a comb should be restricted to moulting time, otherwise the undercoat, which contributes so much to the breed's appearance, may be dragged out. Other authorities use the comb to loosen and lift the dense undercoat whose function is to cushion the harsher hair of the outer coat. Use the fingers to remove any dead hairs. Trim away any tufts of hair that grow around and under the feet and between the toes. It is likely, too, that you will have to pay some attention to straggling ends of hair around the neck and ears, and between the front legs. If any of the feathering on the legs grows unduly long this must also be trimmed.

Thus it would seem that ownership of the Chow has no drawbacks for those prepared to take the trouble to understand its unique approach to life. Yet it would hardly be fair not to mention one drawback that can easily be overcome. Entropion, or ingrowing eyelashes, is a hereditary condition common in this breed. A simple operation will effectively deal with the problem which is not, in any case, universal. This is a small price to pay for a dog that has so much to offer in the strength of its devotion, its inborn qualities as a guard, and its extremely handsome appearance.

# Dalmatians

DALMATIANS are a friendly, hardy breed with boisterous, extrovert dispositions, a love of the open air and free, vigorous exercise. A well-kept, fit Dalmatian is a handsome sight running freely through open country with its black or liver spots sparkling against a pure white coat. It is not difficult to imagine the breed in its traditional role of coach or carriage dog trotting alongside or between the wheels of its master's carriage, which it would, if the need arose, defend with very great courage.

As late as 1851, the year of the Great Exhibition, a single coach was still plying between London and Brighton, taking a route through Dorking, Horsham and Henfield, a distance of seventy-two miles. There is a record of a Dalmatian guard making the journey on eight occasions in eight days, which well illustrates the breed's hardiness as well as its love of and need for free exercise.

The unique spotted coat of the Dalmatian makes the breed instantly recognizable and has brought it fame as the spotty dog, the currant-cake dog of nursery days, as a film star and, less desirably, to the attention of advertisers who see in the breed's distinctive appearance a means of boosting the sales of their particular product. However, the breed did not come into being merely in order to act as a decorative adjunct to nursery stories or as an advertiser's prop; it has a noble history during which it has performed valuable services for its masters.

The breed's early history seems to indicate that at one time it was valued as a gun dog, from which pursuit its very sensitive nose, its ability to hunt by scent rather than by sight, and its very soft mouth, are legacies. Pointing still appears to come quite naturally to the breed, and several modern-day Dalmatians have been successfully trained to the gun. In fact, in several Breed Standards of the late nineteenth century, notably that of the Dalmatian Club founded in 1890, the Dalmatian is described as in many respects resembling the Pointer, particularly in shape and build.

It is an accepted fact that Dalmatians are a very ancient breed, though a certain amount of mystery surrounds the actual

*The origin of the Dalmatian is uncertain, but it was once thought to have come from Dalmatia, hence the name*

# Breed Standard: the Dalmatian

**GENERAL APPEARANCE**
The Dalmatian should be a balanced, strong, muscular, active dog, symmetrical in outline and free from coarseness and lumber.

**HEAD AND SKULL**
The head should be of fair length, the skull flat, reasonably broad between the ears but refined and exhibiting a moderate amount of stop. The muzzle should be long and powerful, but never snipy. The lips are clean and fit the jaw moderately closely. The nose in the black spotted variety should always be black; in the liver spotted variety it should always be brown.

**EYES**
The eyes, set moderately well apart, should be of medium size, round, bright and sparkling, with an intelligent expression. Colour is dark in the black spotted and amber in the liver spotted variety.

**EARS**
The ears should be set on rather high and of moderate size. They are rather wide at the base and gradually taper to a rounded point.

**MOUTH**
The teeth should meet. The upper jaw should slightly overlap the lower jaw (scissor bite).

**NECK**
The neck should be fairly long, nicely arched, light and tapering.

**FOREQUARTERS**
The shoulders should be moderately oblique, clean and muscular. The elbows should be close to the body, the forelegs perfectly straight, with strong round bone down to the feet.

**BODY**
The chest should not be too wide but deep and capacious. The ribs well sprung, well defined wither, powerful level back, loins strong, clean and muscular.

**HINDQUARTERS**
Rounded muscles, clean with well developed second thigh. Hocks well defined.

**TAIL**
Should be free from coarseness and carried with a slight upward curve but never curled. Should reach approximately to the hocks.

**FEET**
Round, compact, with well arched toes and round, tough elastic pads. Nails should be black or white in black variety, and brown or white in liver variety.

**COAT**
The coat should be short, hard and dense, sleek and glossy in appearance. The ground colour should be pure white.

**SIZE**
Dogs 23–24 inches, bitches 22–23 inches.

place or country of their origin. It seems more than likely that several countries scattered all over the Old World are involved and that a number of different breeds of dog contributed to the make-up of the modern breed. From Bengal a lightly spotted hound is thought to have been used in the breed's development and from Europe an ancient Pointer breed, itself spotted as are some modern Pointers, also made its contribution and may have been responsible for the breed's ability as a gun dog. Dalmatians have also

*Below: a liver spotted Dalmatian. Spots can be black or liver brown, and should be equally spaced and of similar size*

been used at various times as war dogs, sentinels, draught dogs, herding dogs, guide dogs and as stable dogs.

From Germany it is likely that Great Danes of the harlequin variety were used in order to enhance the breed's outstanding characteristic of spotted patterning, and Youatt, a nineteenth-century canine historian, even goes so far as to suggest that the breed originated in Denmark and ascribed a far greater influence to the Great Dane than now appears to be likely.

From Britain the ancient Talbot, a guard dog which sadly now only survives on inn signs and perhaps in the blood of some of the heavily ticked Welsh foxhounds, is likely to have been responsible for the breed's natural guarding instincts. The Talbot was used as a guard for the trains of pack horses which carried merchandise throughout Britain, and this breed may well also have been the source of the Dalmatian's remarkable affinity with and love of horses.

Another English breed, the Setter, may also have contributed both to the Dalmatian's ability as a gun dog and to its characteristic markings. It is interesting that English Setters, though often quite heavily ticked as adults, are, like Dalmatians, pure white at birth and the markings emerge slowly as the puppies grow. English Setters, too, have a combination of blue, almost black, markings

with tan spots scattered mainly on the limbs. A similar combination of colour also existed in Dalmatians and was at one time accepted, though now the spots must be all of one colour, either liver or, more commonly, black.

The breed's name is derived from the fact that early authorities argued that its origins were in Dalmatia and that it had only been introduced into Britain in the early eighteenth century, but in reality is uncertain when the breed was first introduced into Britain. Certainly there are illustrations of Dalmatians by seventeenth-and-eighteenth century Dutch and Italian artists, as well as an engraving by the Northumbrian artist, Thomas Bewick which demonstrate how very little the appearance of the breed has changed in the last two or three hundred years.

The modern breed retains many of its ancient characteristics: its guarding instincts, its fidelity, its love of horses and its strong, robust constitution. Modern breeders have respected the breed's qualities and have not sought to change them and, by placing great importance on the breed's unique spotted coat, have improved the size, uniformity and depth of colour of the spots. This is particularly true of the liver variety.

The Dalmatian should be a strong, muscular and active dog, symmetrical in outline, free from any degree of coarseness and capable of great endurance with a fair degree of speed. The head should be fairly long, with a broad, flat skull, moderately defined stop, and free from wrinkle and loose skin. The neck should be long and arched, not thick but light and tapering, and set well into clean, sloping shoulders. The chest should be deep and capacious and the hindquarters powerful, muscular and strong with a long, gradually tapering tail carried with a slight upward curve but never curled. The dense, fine and glossy coat needs very little grooming; the Dalmatian is a healthy, neat and clean dog.

The well-defined spots on the short hard coat are an important feature of the breed; they should never intermingle, but should be round, evenly spaced and evenly sized. Dogs should weigh about 55 lb and bitches 50 lb.

The Dalmatian is an active, intelligent dog, and is easily trained. A good all-round pet, it is best suited for the suburbs or the country. It is neither a noisy nor a quarrelsome dog, but is extremely good-natured and makes friends easily. However, its loyalty lies with its master and family; the breed is an excellent playmate for children. It makes an affectionate and loyal companion as well as a fearless guard. Above all, the breed has an enormous appetite for free and vigorous exercise which should not be denied.

# Three little-known breeds of dog

THE Canaan Dog is of two kinds, a medium-sized collie type of dog and a dingo type, both of which are reputed to have existed 3,000 years ago in the Land of Canaan mentioned in the Bible. The Hebrews were forced to abandon their dogs when they were dispersed, and the breed reverted to the wild. Some were domesticated and trained as guards and herding dogs by the nomad tribes. Even today, some Bedouins trap young puppies and use them for the same pur-

poses, sometimes cutting off their ears in the belief that this makes the dogs keener on watch, a useless and cruel custom born of ignorance.

Their re-domestication was started in 1934 by Professor Rudolfina Menzel who was requested by the Israeli authorities to create a centre which would concentrate on training dogs for use with the Israeli army. She captured specimens of the wild dogs and began breeding operations which resulted in a supply of animals

which have been successfully trained for Army use as well as for guide dogs for the blind.

The Canaan is a rather square dog with a strong body; the head is blunt and wedge-shaped with dark, slightly slanting eyes which are intelligent in expression and very watchful. The ears are short and pricked or semi-pricked, except in the case

*The Leonberger is recognized in Europe, but little known in Britain or the USA*

of the dingo-like type which is usually button-eared. The coat should be harsh and of medium length, and the tail plumed. Colours can be sand to red-brown, white or black; large areas of white are permissible, as are harlequins of any description. Markings like those of the Boston Terrier are common.

There are now some 200 Canaans in the USA, and the breed is slowly becoming more popular in Britain. It was recognized by the British Kennel Club in 1971.

The Leonberger originated in Germany and was the product of a cross between a Newfoundland and a St Bernard. It is now recognized as a separate breed on the Continent but, so far as is known, there are no specimens in Britain, although one or two were imported around 1948. The breed is equally rare in the USA. It is a powerful dog with a height of some 27 inches at the shoulder, a few specimens being as much as 30 inches, and it has a very strong and muscular body. It weighs about 120 lb. It was

*The Canaan dog was first registered in Britain in 1971 and so is a relatively new breed to this country. There are, however, over 200 registrations of the breed in the USA. The Schipperke (far right) originates from Belgium where it was first shown in 1690.*

originally used to pull small carts and as a guard dog, but today its use as a draught animal is illegal in many countries. However, its docile and affectionate nature has led to its becoming a family pet.

This handsome dog has a long, soft coat of medium length, which lies close to the body, the colours of which may be grey, black, tan, black-and-tan, or any other dark shade with white markings. Grey and fawn are the most common.

The Schipperke is Belgian in origin, coming from the Flemish provinces of that country. The breed's history goes back to the first of all the dog shows, held in Brussels in 1690, which was organized for the special benefit of these little dogs. The name came into use in 1888; previously the breed had been known as Spitz or Spitzke, since it somewhat resembles members of the Spitz family of dogs. In fact, it is actually a small version of the old Belgian Sheepdog. This Sheepdog when bred larger produced the Groenendael, and when bred smaller the Schipperke. Its duties were to protect the barges which plied along the Flemish waterways. The word 'Schipperke' is Flemish for 'Little Skipper' or 'Little Captain' and it is certain that the dogs gave every appearance of being in sole charge of the craft. The breed increased rapidly in popularity when Queen Marie

Henriette of Belgium bought one as her personal pet.

It is probably the hardiest of all the small dogs, able to adapt easily to any climate and weather. It can sleep almost anywhere, so long as a draught-proof shelter is provided.

The breed is cobby in appearance and its foxy head gives it a very keen expression which is helped by the sharp and stiffly erect ears. The coat is abundant, dense and harsh and usually black although other whole colours are permitted. It is easy to groom. The tail is docked to within one inch of the rump. The body is muscular with a deep brisket, the back short and the loins well drawn up. Its weight is from 12 to 16 lb, dogs being heavier than bitches.

The Schipperke is a plucky, intensely lively little dog and an alert guard. An enthusiastic ratter and hunter of moles, it loves the company of other domestic animals and will not fight unless it is provoked. Its sharp expression emphasizes its watchfulness and spirited nature.

Combining all the qualities of a ratter, a watchdog, and a pet, the Schipperke should be given plenty of work to do. It should never be pampered or overfed. Hardy and active, its appearance is distinctive, since it looks unlike any other breed, while its excellent temperament

# Breed Standard: the Schipperke

**GENERAL APPEARANCE**
A small cobby animal, with a sharp expression, intensely lively, presenting the appearance of being always on the alert.

**HEAD AND SKULL**
Head foxy in type, skull not round, but fairly broad, flat and with little stop. The muzzle should be moderate in length, fine but not weak, and should be well filled out under the eyes. Nose black and small.

**EYES**
The eyes should be dark brown, small, more oval than round and not full; they should be bright and full of expression.

**EARS**
Sharp, of moderate length, not too broad at the base, tapering to a point. Carried stiffly erect and strong enough not to be bent other than length-ways.

**MOUTH**
Teeth strong and level.

**NECK**
Strong and full, rather short set, broad on the shoulders, and slightly arched.

**FOREQUARTERS**
Shoulders muscular and sloping. Legs perfectly straight, well under the body, with bone in proportion to the body.

**BODY**
Chest broad and deep in brisket. Back short, straight and strong. Loins powerful, well drawn up from brisket.

**HINDQUARTERS**
Fine compared to the foreparts, muscular and well developed thighs; tailless rump well rounded. Legs strong and muscular; hocks well let down.

**FEET**
Should be small, cat-like, and standing well on the toes.

**COAT**
Abundant, dense and harsh, smooth on the head, ears and legs, lying close on the back and sides, but erect and thick round the neck, forming a mane and frill and with a good culotte on the back of the thighs.

**COLOUR**
Should be black, but other whole colours are permissable, except in the USA.

**WEIGHT**
Weight about 12 to 16 lb; up to 18 lb in USA.

**FAULTS**
Drop or semi-erect ears. Dudley noses in the coloured variety. A light-coloured eye. Head narrow and elongated, or too short. Coat sparse, wavy or silky. Absence of the mane and 'culotte'. Coat too long, and white spots.

makes it an ideal family dog. It is especially fond of children and the smallest child may be left safely in its charge. Although needing plenty of exercise, it will adapt readily to either town or country.

In 1930, creams and greys were bred in addition to blacks, and these colours are now recognized by the British Kennel Club; however, black only is recognized in Belgium, the USA, and many European countries. It is classed in the utility group of non-sporting breeds, as listed in the Kennel Club classification.

In Britain the number of Schipperke owners is growing. The breed show organized by the Schipperke Club in July 1974 attracted 150 dogs–the highest number since the breed was first introduced into this country. The Club is one of the best organized breed societies in existence, efficiently run by Dr R Comerford, its secretary. Anyone wishing to buy a Schipperke is advised to write to him first to obtain a list of approved breeders. The club, which boasts many overseas dog-lovers in its numbers, has a library service which supplies books on the breed to members. This is especially valuable as the number of books on the breed published in Britain is minimal. In addition the Club has some 50 cups which are competed for by breed entries at shows all over the country.

The Schipperke first came to the USA in 1888 but it was not shown until several years later. A club, started in 1905, faded out during World War One and it was not until 1929 that the Schipperke Club of America was founded. The Schipperke Club Standard insists on the distinctive ruff and fairly heavy body coat, to prevent the breed degenerating into the "black wire-haired terriers" considered undesirable. American hunters have found the little dogs eager for sport and the breed has been used on coons and possums as well as being a useful ratter when required. Although never likely to head the list of AKC registrations, the breed has a steady following.

Dog-lovers attending a show for the first time are often fascinated by the Schipperke, for this dog has a silhouette unlike any other breed. Its chest is broad and deep in brisket, and its harsh smooth coat forms a splendid ruff. The culotte on the back of the thighs adds to the overall impression of a distinctive dog that could never be mistaken for any other breed.

Its reputation as a guard dog is well known, for this was the original intention of the Belgian breeders. The guarding instinct is retained in the dog now largely kept as a pet, and any intruder trying to break into a house in which a Schipperke lives is in for a rough time.

So intelligent and alert is the breed that its devotees say it can tell if any household object or ornament has been misplaced, if a cupboard door is open that should be shut, if, in fact, there is anything unusual in the domestic scene. It shows that it has noticed these happenings by a swelling up of the ruff around the neck, and by uttering a sharp bark.

Schipperke owners emphasize that the breed should never be kept in kennels with other dogs. Being a one-man dog and such an excellent guard, its place is in the home. It gets on well with children and so makes an excellent family pet. The Schipperke lives on average until it is 14 or 15 years of age; Dr Comerford, secretary of the Breed Club, owned a much-loved pet which lived to be 19, a really great age for a dog.

# Three miniature breeds from Tibet

THREE small dogs from Tibet, a mountainous state between China and India, have become popular in the western world. They are the Tibetan Spaniel, the Tibetan Terrier and the Lhasa Apso. All of them can be confused by laymen with the Pekingese. But if you make this mistake with a real fancier of any of the breeds he will be most unhappy, since similarities between the Tibetan and Pekes are penalized at shows.

All the breeds are gay and fearless. None of them likes strangers although they are not aggressive. All of them make splendid house pets even in quite small homes. The Tibetan Terrier and the Lhasa Apso are frequently confused and when they first came to the West they were regarded as the same breed. Now they are clearly defined by Kennel Club Standards in America and Britain.

The Tibetan Spaniel is a small, hardy, cheerful dog; it was first bred in Tibet and China where it was the most popular monastery dog. The monks found this intelligent little animal an ideal companion and early-warning system against intruders. In the monasteries of Tibet the Spaniel was also regarded as a sacred animal, and was trained to take part in re-

*The Tibetan Spaniel (right) and the Tibetan Terrier (facing page) make excellent pets*

# Breed Standard: the Tibetan Spaniel

### GENERAL APPEARANCE
Should be small, active and alert. The outline should give a well-balanced appearance, slightly longer in body than height at withers.

### HEAD AND SKULL
Small in proportion to body and proudly carried giving an impression of quality. Skull slightly domed, moderate width and length. Stop slight, but defined. Medium length of muzzle, blunt with cushioning, free from wrinkle. The chin should show some depth and width.

### EYES
Dark brown in colour, oval in shape, bright and expressive, of medium size set fairly well apart but forward looking. Eye rims black.

### EARS
Medium size, pendant, well feathered, set fairly high.

### MOUTH
Ideally slightly undershot, the upper incisors fitting nearly inside and touching the lower incisors. Teeth must not show when mouth closed.

### NECK
Moderately short, strong and well set on. Covered with a mane or 'shawl' of longer hair.

### FOREQUARTERS
The bones of the forelegs slightly bowed but firm at shoulder. Moderate bone.

### BODY
Slightly longer from point of shoulder to root of tail than the height at withers, well ribbed with good depth, level back.

### HINDQUARTERS
Well made and strong, hocks well let down and straight when viewed from behind. Stifle well developed, showing moderate angulation.

### FEET
Harefooted, small and neat with feathering between toes often extending beyond the feet. White markings allowed.

### GAIT
The gait should be quick moving, straight, free, and positive.

### TAIL
Set high, richly plumed and carried in a gay curl over the back when moving. Should not be penalized for dropping tail when standing.

### COAT
Double coat, silky in texture, smooth on face and front of legs, of moderate length on body, but lying rather flat. Ears and back of forelegs nicely feathered, tail and buttocks well furnished with longer hair. Should not be overcoated and bitches tend to carry less coat and mane than dogs.

### COLOUR
All colours and mixtures of colours allowed.

ligious services and rituals. One such duty was to turn prayer wheels. The Tibetan lamas used these revolving cylinders, containing prayers written on parchment, to send their requests to heaven, each turn of the wheel giving propulsion to the prayer on its journey. So the Tibetan Spaniel became known as the 'Prayer Dog'. Another more earthly use for the dogs was to provide warmth for their owners. The monks used them as hot-water bottles or muffs: the Spaniels were held inside the wide sleeves of the monks' robes.

Although the Tibetan Spaniel has been bred in Western countries for more than forty years, it is still a comparative rarity; however, the breed has been steadily increasing in number since the 1950s. An amusing, slightly scowling face with an undershot jaw gives the Tibetan Spaniel an interesting look. Its jaunty walk and intelligent eyes give it a saucy, fun-loving appearance and help to explain why the Tibetan Spaniel was the favourite breed of the last Dalai Lama. It was his interest that led to the introduction of the breed to America, for he gave several pairs to breeders in the USA. Breeders who want to invigorate their stock still send to Tibetan monasteries for new blood.

The Tibetan Spaniel's fine, silky coat is one easy way of distinguishing the breed

from the Pekingese. The breed also has longer legs and a lighter and slimmer body than the Peke. There is a wide variety of colour: white, creamy-fawn, red, and dark sable, all with white markings. There is also a black and tan line; the nose is usually black but a brown nose is considered equally aristocratic. The eyes are always dark brown. The ideal height for a Tibetan Spaniel is 11 inches at the shoulder for dogs and 9½ inches for bitches. It weighs about 11 lb.

The name 'Lhasa Apso' means 'goat' in Tibet, and this charming, long-haired little dog does look a little like the small shaggy goats found in Tibet. The breed came out of Tibet in the early 1900s, brought back to the West by missionaries and explorers. The breed, like the Tibetan Spaniel, was also bred in monasteries, but was not held in such veneration as the Spaniel. There was a belief that the souls of those lamas who did not lead such good lives as was expected of holy men, entered the bodies of the dogs on death.

The Apso is a lively, assertive, jaunty dog but tends to dislike strangers. Bred in the cold, high ranges of Tibet, this lithe little creature is surprisingly tough and can travel well in rough country. In fact, although the Apso makes a fine pet in a small city home, it is also happy in the country. It stands up to 11 inches tall and

has a fine, feathery tail which is curled high over its back. Its coat is heavy and coarse, not woolly or silky, and it has a dense undercoat which is shed in hot weather. This breed does need frequent grooming in order to maintain its coat in immaculate condition. The Lhasa Apso is a friendly dog with those it knows, especially with children; it is intensely loyal, intelligent, adaptable and long-lived, but can create problems because it is so independent and strong-willed.

In Tibet the most popular colour is golden and in this form the Lhasa Apso is often called the 'Lion-dog'. Other colours are sandy, honey, slate, smoke, black, brown and brindled white. The rib cage of the Apso is said to expand more than that of other dogs. The reason for this, it is thought, is that it allows the dog to take in extra oxygen in the high altitudes of its native country.

The Tibetan Terrier is the largest of the three breeds. In its native country, it is a no-nonsense, no-frills working dog where it is used to herd goats. It is not strictly a terrier at all but, because the breed is squarely-built, intelligent, alert, tough and brave, the western countries saw it as a terrier-type.

In spite of the superior claims of the Tibetan Spaniel to be the holy dog of Tibet, there are still some experts who

*The delightful Lhasa Apso, bred in the Tibetan mountains, is tough despite its size*

believe that in fact the Tibetan Terrier holds this distinction. These dogs were said to accompany the caravans taking tributes from the Dalai Lama to the Chinese Emperor, and to act as protectors. This was not because of their ferocity but because no thief would lay hands on a holy dog or the goods it guarded.

The breed looks a little like a small version of the Old English Sheepdog. It has a merry, bouncing character. Although large specimens sometimes stand as high as 17 inches, 13 to 16 inches is normal. The double coat (to keep out the wind and cold) is composed of a short down undercoat and a long, coarse outer coat. The feet are very big, flat and round. It is said that this feature was developed to give the animal extra braking power on snowy slopes. The dog is hardy and agile, a fine pet and companion and good both in town and country. It will bark at strangers but is not fierce or pugnacious. Colours are cream, white, gold, grey, smoke and black. Occasionally a chocolate-coloured Tibetan Terrier does turn up in litters but this colour is frowned upon by breeders and, although such a dog looks well enough to most of us, it never wins prizes at dog shows.

# Two unusual dogs: Mexican Hairless and Shih Tzu

THE Shih Tzu is of Tibetan and Chinese origin, the Chinese influence being dominant. The name is pronounced 'Sheed Zoo' and it is classified as a non-sporting utility breed by the British Kennel Club, although the Swedish and American Kennel Clubs term it a toy breed and it is registered in the Companion Dog Class in Denmark. It is a small dog weighing from 9 to 16 lb, and measuring some 10 to 12 inches at the shoulder, thus qualifying for either the title of toy dog or utility dog, according to personal preference.

The breed is very ancient and its ancestry is aristocratic. For several centuries it was the custom of the Dalai Lama of Tibet to bestow exceptionally fine specimens of the Lhasa Apso on the Emperors of China, and these valued gifts were immediately recognized as members of the Royal Court and accorded all the privileges belonging to their rank. This seems to have been the extent of the Tibetan influence on the shaping of the Shih Tzu, the credit for the breed going almost entirely to the Chinese breeders who were adept in producing small short-faced dogs and others different from the norm.

It is not, of course, possible to know exactly which breeds were used to evolve the Shih Tzu, but it may be assumed that the Pekingese and Lhasa Apso influence was considerable and the progeny of these two royal breeds formed the root stock of the modern Shih Tzu. As in the case of the Pekingese, the Chinese were reluctant to allow any specimens to leave the country, but a few were imported into Britain between the wars.

The Shih Tzu is a dog of character and great sense of personal dignity. It has a round, broad head with a shock of hair falling over the eyes and a plentiful beard and whiskers. The skull is wide between the eyes, which should be large, dark and round and not prominent. The hair grows upwards on the nose giving the effect of a chrysanthemum. The muzzle is short and square but not wrinkled, as in the case of a Pekingese. The ears are large and should be carried drooping. They are so heavily coated that they appear to blend with the hair of the neck. The legs are short and well boned, any sign of 'legginess' being considered a fault. The legs appear to be very thick because of the large amount of hair covering them. The body is sturdy, well coupled and rather long. The back should be level.

The tail is a major feature of the breed. It is set on high, heavily plumed, and carried gaily and well over the back. The coat is long and dense but not curly, with a thick undercoat. A dog with a sparse coat would not be considered a good specimen of the breed. While any colour is permissible, both a white blaze on the forehead and a white tip to the tail are most desirable. Dogs with liver markings are allowed a dark liver nose, and the eyes may be a little lighter in colour. Pigmentation on the muzzle should be as unbroken as possible.

A narrow head is seen to be a fault in the Shih Tzu. Nor should the muzzle be snipy, that is to say, weak, pointed, long and narrow. Pale pink noses and eye rims are considered a fault.

Although small, the Shih Tzu should not be fussed over or pampered. It has not the lightly triggered agility of a terrier but it is active and capable of accompanying its owner on long walks. It has a somewhat oriental sense of humour and, at times, an inscrutable expression, gazing out into the far distance as though engaged in deep meditation. Perhaps this characteristic is inherited from its Lhasa Apso forebears which spent their days in Tibetan monasteries. The Shih Tzu is very loyal and affectionate and readily settles down to become one of the family. It is peaceful and not given to quarrelling with other animals, preferring to go its own way in dignified silence. The breed has a real affection for children.

Daily grooming is a necessity if the shaggy coat is to be kept free from tangles. Particular attention should be paid to the long featherings on the ears, legs and tail. After grooming, a final rub down with a chamois leather will give a fine gloss

*Below: the Mexican Hairless is thought to be of Chinese origin*

# Breed Standard: the Shih Tzu

**GENERAL APPEARANCE**
Very active, lively and alert, with a distinctly arrogant carriage. The Shih Tzu is neither a terrier nor a toy dog.

**HEAD AND SKULL**
Head broad and round; wide between the eyes. Shock-headed with hair falling well over the eyes. Good beard and whiskers; the hair growing upwards on the nose gives a chrysanthemum-like effect. Muzzle square and short, but not wrinkled like a Pekingese; flat and hairy. Nose preferably black and about 1 inch from tip to stop.

**EYES**
Large, dark and round, but not prominent.

**EARS**
Large, with long leathers, and carried drooping. Set slightly below the crown of the skull; so heavily coated that they appear to blend with the hair on the neck.

**MOUTH**
Level or slightly underhung.

**FOREQUARTERS**
Legs short and muscular with ample bone. They look massive because of wealth of hair.

**BODY**
Body between withers and root of tail longer than height at withers; well coupled and sturdy; chest broad and deep, shoulders firm, back level.

**HINDQUARTERS**
Legs short and muscular with ample bone. They should look massive on account of the wealth of hair.

**FEET**
Firm and well padded. They should look big on account of the wealth of hair.

**TAIL**
Heavily plumed and curled well over back; carried gaily; set on high.

**COAT**
Long and dense but not curly, with good undercoat.

**COLOUR**
All colours permissable, but a white blaze on the forehead and a white tip to the tail are highly prized. Dogs with liver markings may have dark liver noses and slightly lighter eyes. Pigmentation on muzzle as unbroken as possible.

**WEIGHT AND SIZE**
10 to 18 lbs. Ideal weight 10 to 16 lbs. Height at withers not more than 10½ inches; type and breed characteristics of the utmost importance and on no account to be sacrificed to size alone.

**FAULTS**
Narrow heads, pig-jaws, snipyness, pale pink noses and eye-rims, small or light eyes, legginess, sparse coats.

---

to the coat. Despite a little extra care in this respect, the breed will thrive in any environment, being able to adapt to city life, and requires no special feeding. It is an ideal dog for people of discernment who would prefer a pet of unusual distinc-

*The Shih Tzu needs daily grooming to keep its coat in good condition*

tion to the more popular breeds.

In contrast to the shaggy coat of the Shih Tzu, the Mexican Hairless dog is almost completely nude. The breed is very similar to the Chinese Crested dog and sometimes has a crest of hair on the top of its head, as with the Chinese dog. However, unlike the Chinese dog, this is not a fault. The tail may also have a little

hair at the tip, but the feet must be completely hairless.

It is said that the breed has been known for centuries in Mexico, even as far back as the Aztecs. Although it is a quite separate breed from the Chinese Crested dog which is almost completely hairless, there is reason to believe that both breeds are Chinese in origin. But in the case of the Mexican Hairless, there are some Mexican authorities who believe that does not go back to the Aztec era, but was brought to Mexico by the sailors of the trading vessels sailing between the Orient and the Western countries. Hairless breeds are also found in Africa and Asia and the theory has been proposed that this dog originated in Africa spread from there to Guinea, Manila and China, and thence to America.

There are two types of Mexican Hairless dog, the larger of which is almost entirely confined to Mexico where breeding is strictly controlled by the authorities. There are very few of those left and, outside Mexico, the breed is represented by a smaller, more refined type, about the size of a small terrier. It was once recognized by the American Kennel Club but recognition was withdrawn owing to the small number of registrations.

The Mexican Hairless is an active little dog, keen, alert and intelligent but inclined to be obstinate—a trait which shared by many other breeds and so should not be held against this one. There is often a nervous tremor which seems characteristic of the breed. The head slender and narrow with a long and pointed muzzle. There is often a tuft of coarse hair on the top of the head. The eyes are yellow, hazel or dark. The back is level but the rump should be slightly rounded while the tail is long, smooth and hairless except that a little tuft or fuzz may be permitted at the tip. The usual height is between 16 and 20 inches and it normally weighs between 25 and 36 lb.

The skin is important. It must be smooth and soft and there must be complete absence of hair. The skin must not be wrinkled and can be of any colour. The colours most usually seen are bronze, elephant grey, greyish black and black. It should be warm to the touch. Care needed to keep the skin in condition, and baby oils should be used to keep it supple and free from irritation. Apart from this no extra care, special diets or exercise plans are required.

There are a few specimens in Britain and more in the United States—no doubt because that country adjoins Mexico and so the importation of the breed does not present so many difficulties.

*Right: the Shih Tzu is an ancient breed of dog of Tibetan and Chinese origin*

# The Poodle

THE Poodle is one of the world's most popular breeds. There are three basic characteristics which make this dog such a universal favourite. In the first place, the Poodle's coat does not undergo the periodic moulting process typical of so many breeds. Consequently it does not cover everything with a fine layer of hairs. Even so, the coat does need regular and careful grooming if it is to be kept in good condition and free from tangles and parasites. Regular and skilful clipping is also essential if the dog is to remain comfortable and look tidy and attractive.

Another advantage which the Poodle enjoys over most other breeds is that it is relatively free from the characteristic 'doggy' smell that can be so objectionable in the case of an old or neglected pet.

The third advantage of the Poodle is that the breed comes in three sizes: the Toy Poodle, perhaps weighing no more than 10 lb; the Miniature Poodle, at about 15 lb; and the big Standard Poodle, weighing up to 50 lb. The dogs also come in a wide range of very attractive and

*Left: a Toy Poodle. Poodles are very intelligent and can be very highly trained*

sometimes unusual colours, from dense black to pure white, with many subtle shades of silver, cream, blue, brown and apricot between these extremes. This range of colours has been inherent in the breed for many years and so it has not had to face the difficulties involved in introducing new colours from outside sources. Black is the dominant colour; it is from this colour that the most outstanding specimens tend to emerge. Any pups with one black parent will themselves be black and blacks appear to breed very true to type.

In addition to these qualities, the Poodle, at its best, is a highly intelligent animal, always anxious to please. Because of its cooperative attitude, it can be trained to a remarkably high standard of obedience, both in the performance of tasks that demand intelligence and in the course of developing into a friendly and tractable companion.

The guardian instinct is also a distinctive feature of the breed. Both the Toy and the Miniature Poodle are prepared to do their utmost to protect anything that is clearly of value or importance to their masters, even though they are not really physically equipped to be effective guard dogs. The Standard Poodle is much more formidable in this respect because of its larger size.

A good Poodle is a hardy dog, tough, proud and active in a way that often belies its delicate, fashionable air, although a small Poodle will obviously have less strength, stamina and resilience than a large one. Unfortunately, one of the penalties of great popularity is that a Poodle will not always conform to the highest standards. Too many people, who do not have the best interests of the breed at heart, have bred from inferior stock. Tempted by the all-too-easy profits to be made by foisting poor-quality animals on unsuspecting customers, who are ready to buy puppies simply because they look attractive, they have used physically or mentally unsound adults to produce puppies which are no credit either to the breed or the breeders. No matter how attentively and lovingly they are cared for, these sub-standard dogs must inevitably become a source of trouble and expense to their owners and will probably spend their lives in a state of nervous agitation or in constant physical pain.

For humanitarian and practical reasons, therefore, puppies should only be purchased from genuine and reliable breeders whose high reputation is their best recommendation. The old legal precept of *Caveat emptor* ('Let the buyer beware!') is valid in any transaction that involves livestock; it is especially important in the case of a would-be buyer, lacking both knowledge and experience, who sets out to buy a puppy belonging to one of the more popular breeds. It is always advisable to seek expert advice.

The earliest illustrations of dogs bearing a marked resemblance to Poodles appear on various Roman carvings which date from about 40 AD. After the middle of the fifteenth century one comes across paintings of clipped Poodles. Various names were used for these dogs–barbet, canicue, monton, moufflon and pudel. The name 'pudel', from which the modern name is clearly derived, is of German origin, and it seems likely that the breed itself also originated in Germany, although since the fifteenth century it has been the national dog of France and is now generally associated with that country.

There can be little doubt that even before the breed was sufficiently standardized to be given an all-embracing name, its value as a water dog, particularly as a retriever of waterfowl, was appreciated. It is likely that a great many of these sportive dogs found their way to Britain and that they were the ancestors of our Curly Coated Retrievers and Irish Water Spaniels, both of which, to some extent, retain the characteristic Poodle coat.

From the very beginning the breed has displayed a wide divergence in size and weight. This has now become standardized in the three previously mentioned sizes, Toy, Miniature and Standard. As

## Breed Standard: the Poodle

**GENERAL APPEARANCE**
That of a very active, intelligent, well-balanced and elegant-looking dog with good temperament, carrying itself very proudly.

**HEAD AND SKULL**
Long and fine with slight peak at the back. The skull not broad and with a moderate stop. Foreface strong and well chiselled.

**EYES**
Almond-shaped, dark, not set too close together.

**EARS**
The leather long and wide, low set on, hanging close to the face.

**MOUTH**
Teeth white, strong, even, scissor bite.

**NECK**
Well proportioned, of good length and strong to allow the head to be carried high and with dignity. Skin fitting tightly at the throat.

**FOREQUARTERS**
Shoulders strong and muscular, sloping well to the back, legs set straight from the shoulders, well muscled.

**BODY**
Chest deep and moderately wide. Ribs well sprung and rounded. Back short, strong, slightly hollowed, loins broad and muscular.

**HINDQUARTERS**
Thighs well developed and muscular, well bent stifles, well let down hocks.

**FEET**
Pasterns strong, tight feet proportionately small, oval in shape, toes arched.

**TAIL**
Set on rather high, well carried at a slight angle away from the body, thick at the root.

**COAT**
Very profuse and dense, of good harsh texture without knots or tangles.

**COLOUR**
All solid colours. White and cream poodles to have black nose, lips and eye-rims, black toe-nails desirable, brown poodles to have dark amber eyes, dark liver nose, lips, eye-rims and toe-nails. Apricot poodles to have dark eyes with black points or deep amber eyes with liver points. Black, silver and blue poodles to have black nose, lips, eye-rims and toe-nails. Cream, apricot, brown, silver and blue poodles may show varying shade of the same colour up to 18 months.

**SIZE**
Standard: Britain 15 inches or over; USA over 15 inches. Miniature: Britain under 15 inches but not under 11; USA 15 inches or under but minimum height 10 inches or even less; Toy: Britain under 11 inches; USA 10 inches or less.

a result of this peculiarity, there have been none of the problems customarily associated with the process of reducing the size of a breed, in order to produce an acceptable miniature form.

The necessity of clipping a Poodle's coat regularly should not deter anyone from becoming the owner of such a captivating dog. A properly clipped, regularly groomed Poodle presents a truly elegant picture, and the dog's appearance can be totally spoilt if it is badly clipped. Unfortunately, this can happen all too easily, for any person with a pair of clippers, though little knowledge and skill, is entitled to open a so-called Poodle Parlour. It is worth going to some trouble to find an expert clipper with a genuine concern and interest in the breed.

There are three basic clips, one not being acceptable in the show ring, one confined to show puppies and pets and one used exclusively on show dogs. The two clips employed on pets are the Dutch clip and the Lamb clip. The Dutch clip, which is not acceptable in the show ring, leaves the coat long on the legs but close-clips the body; the topknot, tail and muzzle may or may not be clipped. The Lamb clip reduces the entire coat to a uniformly short length over the legs and body; it is used for pets, show puppies and retired show dogs. The Lion clip (and its increasingly numerous variations) is used only on show dogs, the coat being left long in front of the last ribs, the legs and tail being close-clipped except for pompoms on the ankles and at the tip of the tail. The hindquarters may be clipped in various ways according to the preference of the owner and the virtue of the dog. In the English version the coat remains short over the hindquarters, but in the Continental version it is close-clipped except for pompoms on the hips.

A healthy Poodle is instinctively playful and can be taught many useful and amusing tricks. It is by nature clean and seems to take a pride in its appearance when newly bathed, clipped and groomed. Poodles, as a breed, are not greedy, although they should exhibit a healthy and constant appetite. Some of them, particularly Toys, are inclined to be rather fastidious about food and need to be coaxed to eat, a symptom which is sometimes, though not invariably, indicative of bad breeding, faulty rearing, ill-health or a nervous disposition. On the other hand, never allow a Poodle to become overweight, for this will reduce its vitality, endanger its health and shorten its life.

*These Poodles have the Lion clip used only on show dogs. Top right: apricot Miniature; Centre: black Miniature; Right: the beautiful Standard Poodle also makes a good guard dog*

Grooming is an essential and, ideally, enjoyable part of any dog's life. In the case of long-coated breeds, of which the Poodle is one, grooming is of particular importance. A Poodle is most easily groomed by being laid on its side with the feet pointing towards the person who is handling the dog. The coat should be carefully worked through, layer by layer, with brush and comb, removing all dead portions, tangles and dirt, until one side of the dog is completed. Then it should be turned over and the other side groomed in the same manner. A good nylon or bristle hairbrush will be suitable or alternatively, provided it is not too stiff, a rubber-cushioned wire brush. The comb should be a wide-toothed metal type especially for grooming long-coated dogs.

Every breed of dog is unique and each has its individual charm and peculiarities, as well as its devotees. The Poodle is elegant, alert and loyal, and an amusing clown. It is not a matter of mere chance that it is popular as a pet and companion all over the world.

# The Schnauzer trio

THE Schnauzer is quite an ancient breed which originated in Central Europe. It is claimed that specimens of the breed appear in paintings by Dürer dated as far back as 1492. In the early days the word 'pinscher' was used to describe terrier-type dogs in Germany; these were either black, tan or fawn, but later on there was a division of the term into rough and smooth-coated pinschers. It is

*The Schnauzer makes a good family pet, being happy in the company of children*

thought that the grey spitz and the old type of poodle were introduced and gave the salt-and-pepper colour which is a feature of today's Schnauzer.

Known as Wire-haired Pinschers, these early dogs were to be found herding cattle, or making themselves generally useful as guards and ratters. They were never designed as terriers and do not have the terrier temperament. In outline, perhaps, there is a similarity of make and shape to some of the English terriers, and in America the miniature of the breed is

classified as a terrier. However, in Britain, the continental conception of the breed has been retained and the breed is classified in the Utility Group.

The breed was first exhibited in Germany in 1879. A breed standard was agreed upon in 1880, but it was not until some years later that the German Pinscher Club was divided into the Pinscher and Schnauzer Clubs, the German word 'schnauzer' meaning muzzle or snout. It is always a sign of popularity when a breed of dog is eventually divided into different sizes. So it was with the Schnauzer, which now has three accepted sizes: the Standard Schnauzer, the Miniature Schnauzer and the Giant Schnauzer.

The Standard Schnauzer is a compact, strong, short-coupled dog with a hard, wiry coat. The head is strong, rectangular, diminishing from ear to eyes, and also to the tip of the nose. The skull is moderately broad, the forehead flat and unwrinkled, and the muzzle is strong and blunt with profuse wiry whiskers which are brushed forward. The body is nearly square, the height between 17 to 20 inches at the shoulder; the back is straight and the hindquarters well muscled; the whole dog is robust and sinewy. Its character combines high spirits, reliability, strength, endurance and vigour. The colour can be all shades of 'pepper and salt' in even proportions, or pure black. This neat, compact dog with its weather-proof coat makes an ideal family pet; it is gay and alert, very intelligent and really enjoys participating in all the family activities. It has protective instincts and makes a good guard, without being too aggressive.

The Miniature Schnauzer has the same conformation as its bigger brother. The difference in size is roughly 4 inches measured to the point of the shoulder. The ideal size for the Miniature is 13 inches for bitches and 14 inches for dogs. It is generally accepted that the Miniature was the result of crossing the Schnauzer with Affenpinschers. This latter breed was a small dog, usually black with a rather squashed-in face similar to the Griffon, but in the experimental stage there is the possibility of other breeds being introduced, such as the toy Spitz or Pomeranian, and one cannot rule out the potential of a Fox Terrier cross to improve head and coat requirements.

In 1928, the first Miniature Schnauzer was imported into Britain. This was a black bitch, and was followed by two salt-and-pepper Champions in 1930. In America, this dog quickly rose to popularity. The ears were cropped as on the Continent, and the bushy eyebrows and whiskers, the brushed up leg hair, and the smoother coat on neck and body made it a most attractive breed. Its temperament and size make it highly desirable

# Breed Standard: the Schnauzer

### GENERAL APPEARANCE
The Schnauzer is a powerfully built, robust, sinewy, nearly square dog whose temperament combines high spirits, reliability, strength, endurance and vigour. Expression is keen and attitude alert. Correct conformation is of more importance than colour or other 'beauty' points.

### HEAD AND SKULL
Head strong and elongated, gradually narrowing from the ears to the eyes and thence toward the tip of the nose. Upper part of the head moderately broad between the ears, with flat, creaseless forehead and well muscled, but not too strongly developed cheeks. Medium stop to accentuate prominent eyebrows. The powerful muzzle should end in a moderately blunt line.

### EYES
Medium sized, dark, oval, set forward, with arched bushy eyebrows.

### EARS
Neat and V-shaped, set high and dropping forward to temple.

### MOUTH
Scissor teeth, slightly overlapping from the top; with strongly developed fangs; healthy and pure white.

### NECK
Moderately long, nape strong and slightly arched, skin close to the throat.

### FOREQUARTERS
Shoulders flat and sloping. Forelegs straight viewed from any position. Muscles smooth and lithe rather than prominent; bone strong, straight.

### BODY
Chest moderately broad, deep, with visible strong breast bone reaching down to at least the height of elbow and slightly rising back to loins. Back strong and straight, with short, well-developed loins. Length of body equal to height from top of withers to ground.

### HINDQUARTERS
Thighs slanting and flat, but strongly muscled. Hindlegs vertical to the stifle; from hock, vertical to ground.

### FEET
Short, round, with close-arched toes, (cat's paws), dark nails and hard soles.

### TAIL
Set on and carried high, cut down to three joints.

### COAT
Hard and wiry, clean on neck, shoulder, ears and skull. Good undercoat is essential.

### COLOUR
All pepper and salt colours, or pure black.

### HEIGHT
For bitches: 18 inches; for dogs: 19 inches.

be found at Obedience and Working Trials. These trials include scent discrimination and 'man-work'–which mean tracking down a wanted man and attacking on command–and is part of the advanced training given to any guard dog. Here the Schnauzer takes its place with the other experts, such as Alsatians, Boxers and Dobermanns. Nevertheless, although it can be successfully trained for these duties, the biggest of the Schnauzer is really quite a gentle giant. These big dogs are to be found in America, Australasia and Britain, but are few in number. In their country of origin they are very popular as working dogs.

The Schnauzer is a very easy dog to keep. Like most dogs, it prefers to be in the house rather than outside. It is easy to house train and is not a fussy eater. It should be groomed at least once a week; the soft undercoat must not be allowed to matt or retain dead hair. The coat is stripped and trimmed at intervals. This can be done professionally, or at home with the help of the instructions found in any good book on the breed or with assistance from an experienced breeder. The Schnauzer has a very good life span, and anyone investing in a member of this breed can look forward to a happy companionship of 13, 15 or even 17 years.

*The strong, rectangular head and wiry whiskers are features of the Schnauzer*

in town or country. Today, the Miniature Schnauzer is numerically one of America's top breeds.

In Britain the climb to fame was considerably slower, because of the problems of the war years, but numbers finally grew sufficiently for the allocation of Kennel Club Challenge Certificates in 1935. Since then the breed has become more popular.

The third member of the breed is the Giant Schnauzer. This variety, similar in make and shape to the Standard Schnauzer, measures from 22 to 27 inches at the shoulder, the most common colour being black. While the enthusiasts were breeding down in size to produce the Miniature, the cattle dealers and farmers in the Bavarian highlands were using these dogs to herd their cattle. A thick, strong dog was required for this demanding work and a bigger dog was favoured. Some of them were probably used to pull miniature carts. At the Munich Show in 1909 there was an entry of thirty black dogs catalogued as Russian Bear Schnauzers. Shortly after this the Munich Schnauzer Club was formed, and in 1925 the breed was classified in Germany as a working dog. In Germany the Giant Schnauzer is recognized for its great intelligence and working ability, and several can usually

# Chapter VI
# Non-sporting Dogs
# Working Group

# The Alsatian: the greatest all-rounder

THE German Shepherd Dog was first introduced into Britain by ex-servicemen returning after the First World War, who called it the Alsatian. Originally bred as a sheepdog and known as the German Shepherd Dog in every country except Britain, the new name of Alsatian was chosen because it was thought the dog's German origin would kill any chance of the breed becoming established in Britain so soon after the end of the war between the two nations. Now known simply as the Alsatian, the title was originally Alsatian Wolf Dog. This was a most unfortunate choice of name which lent substance to the wild rumours concerning the origin of the breed. Indeed, it was sometimes asserted by people who should have known better that the German breeders frequently introduced wolf blood into the breed for some obscure reason of their own.

These stories were, of course, nonsense and in spite of its name the breed rapidly became one of the most popular dogs ever to head the list of Kennel Club registrations. This was not all to the good because many unscrupulous breeders 'jumped on the bandwagon' and foisted many hundreds of ill-bred puppies upon the public. Very high prices were paid until the bubble burst, and it was many years before the real lovers of the breed succeeded in restoring confidence in the Alsatian.

It is claimed that the Alsatian is the most intelligent dog in the world; it is certainly true to say that it can be trained to perform any task of which a dog is physically capable. It shows a certain reserve towards strangers but it is utterly devoted to its owner. The breed loves human company and many centuries of working with men as a shepherd dog has made it perceptive to an unusual degree. This trait accounts for its success as a police dog, a guide dog for the blind, a guard dog and for many other forms of service many of which—avalanche rescue dogs and army patrol dogs, for instance—have been directly responsible for saving human lives.

The German Shepherd Dog is a superb companion and worker; it was the introduction of the breed that led to the formation of the training clubs which are now such a feature in most large towns. Obedience training courses and field trials have added interest to dog owning, and the crowded ringsides at shows bear witness to the pleasure given to the public by the competing dogs. Other breeds are now

*The beauty of the breed is shown in these pictures; erect ears, brilliant eyes and strong muzzle. The Alsatian is highly intelligent and can be trained for numerous jobs*

# Breed Standard: the Alsatian

## GENERAL APPEARANCE
The body is rather long, strongly boned, with plenty of muscle, obviously capable of endurance and speed and of quick and sudden movement. The gait should be supple, smooth and long-reaching.

## HEAD AND SKULL
The head is long, lean and clean cut, broad at the back of the skull, tapering to the nose with only a slight stop between the eyes. The skull is slightly domed and the top of the nose should be parallel to the forehead. The cheeks must not be full and the whole head, when viewed from the top should be much in the form of a V. well filled in under the eyes. The nose must be black.

## EYES
The eyes are almond-shaped, matching the surrounding coat but darker rather than lighter in shade and placed to look straight forward. They must show a lively, intelligent expression.

## EARS
The ears should be broad at the base and pointed at the tips, placed rather high on the skull and carried erect. In Alsatian puppies the ears often hang until the age of six months.

## FOREQUARTERS
The shoulders should slope well back; a line drawn through the centre of the shoulderblade should form a right-angle with the humerus when the leg is perpendicular to the ground in stance. The forelegs should be perfectly straight viewed from the front.

## BODY
The body is muscular, the back is broadish and straight. There should be a good depth of brisket or chest.

## HINDQUARTERS
The loins are broad and strong, the rump rather long and sloping and the legs when viewed from behind, must be quite straight. The stifles are well turned and the hocks strong and well let down.

## FEET
The feet should be round, the toes strong, slightly arched and held close together.

## TAIL
When at rest the tail should hang in a slight curve. During movement it will be raised, but should not be carried past a vertical line drawn through the root.

## COAT
The coat is smooth, but is a double coat. The undercoat is woolly in texture, thick and close. The outercoat is also close, each hair straight, hard, and lying flat, so that it is rain-resisting.

## COLOUR
The colour is not important. All white or near white unless possessing black points are not desirable.

## WEIGHT AND SIZE
The ideal height (measured to the highest point of the shoulder) is 22-24 inches for bitches and 24-26 inches for dogs.

entered for these shows, but it was the Alsatian that started it all.

The breed possesses beauty as well as brains. The erect ears, brilliant eyes, strong muzzle and clean-cut skull combine to give a nobility of expression which cannot fail to convey the impression that here indeed is a real thoroughbred. The body is strong and lithe, the tail hanging in a curve which serves to emphasize its harmonious and graceful lines. The gait is smooth and produces the impression that the animal is flowing over the ground. Despite its size, the Alsatian is capable of adapting to any surroundings, and possesses the facility of taking up surprisingly little space, either at home or in a vehicle.

White is considered undesirable, since the Alsatian standard demands dark pigmentation. True whites with dark points are rare and tend to be confused with albinos. This confusion meant that those who drew up the official standard of points did not accept white as a legitimate colour. The coat can be black, iron-grey or ash-grey, either as the solid colour or with regular brown, tan or grey markings, and occasionally a black saddle. Dark sable is also permitted by the breed standard—this consisting of a black overlay on a grey or light-brown ground, with lighter markings to tone. Small white chest markings are allowed.

The German Shepherd Dog is of very ancient origin, its roots being buried deep in the first pastoral dogs of Europe. In common with most other breeds, it has varied in appearance over the centuries. Our ancestors were not greatly interested in appearance; working ability was the essential requirement, and so the ancient dogs bore only a superficial resemblance to the refined animals we know today. Gradually the dog began to take its place as a member of a family and became a pet as well as a working dog. Breeders came to realise that a handsome dog could work just as well as an ugly one; in short, there seemed no reason why a dog should not only be a capable worker but also be attractive enough to appeal as a pet.

So in 1891 a club was formed in Germany to combine the sheepdogs of Germany into one type which would combine the virtues of all. This venture did not succeed but in 1899 the *Verein für deutsche Schaferhunde* was founded under the presidency of a Herr Mayer who was later succeeded by the late Captain von Stephanitz, one of the greatest authorities on the breed. This club eventually grew until it had its own permanent headquarters and a staff qualified to give advice on all matters concerning the breed. The club organized shows, and police and herding trials. It introduced a system of breed surveys whereby Breed Masters inspected litters, advised on breeding plans and generally ensured that a high standard was maintained.

The modern dog has evolved from the working dogs of Thuringia, Franconia and Wurtemberg. The latter were big dogs, strong of bone, heavy of coat and usually with soft ears. The tail was carried low in a gentle curve and the gait was smooth and far-reaching—an important point in a sheep-herding dog since a flowing lope would not alarm the sheep in the same way as an approaching dog running with a jerky, stilted action. The Franconians and Thurigians were smaller usually wolf-grey in colour and with erect ears. They were also more agile. It seemed possible that a fusion of the three varieties would produce a working dog which would combine great intelligence with physical beauty.

Many breeding plans were made and put into execution. There were failures and successes but gradually the dream of von Stephanitz began to take shape. He lived to see his beloved shepherd dogs evolve into the lovely animals that are now so popular in every quarter of the world.

The Alsatian is a bold (rather than aggressive), calm and watchful animal whose strength of character makes it an excellent working dog in any capacity. It is a breed which loves to work and responds quickly to any form of training. The 'know-how' can be easily acquired by taking the trouble to join one of the many training clubs in every town. It is not enough for anyone to buy a puppy, lose interest after a while, and neglect to give it the companionship which will be so handsomely returned.

There are a great many clubs in Britain devoted to the interests of this splendid animal, governed by dog-lovers who have the welfare of the breed at heart, and who are always prepared to help the novice with advice. They are still known as Alsatian Clubs, although slowly the correct title of German Shepherd Dog is coming to be generally accepted in Britain. The British Alsatian Association (BAA) has branches in most parts of Britain where training instruction can be received. The Association organizes shows, obedience tests and competitions, and field trials for Alsatians only.

When the dog is thoroughly obedient the owner can then consider entering it for a show. Note at shows how the winning Alsatian stands. Note its erect ears, the way its tail hangs. When commanded, the dog trots on a loose lead without pulling, hanging back or rushing forward. It never gallops or leaps in the air. It stands quietly quite unresentful while the judge examines its teeth, feels its muscles and presses its back. When your dog is trained to do this then it is ready for exhibiting.

# The Boxer

THERE is a delightful fable which says that when God was modelling all the different breeds of dog, he finally came to the Boxer. 'And this dog', he said 'will be the most beautiful of all the dogs in the world'. On hearing these words the Boxer could not wait to see his image; before the clay was dry he ran headlong into the nearest mirror and his nose was squashed flat. This is the reason for the blunt, square muzzle of the Boxer.

The true history of the breed is that credit for its development must go to a Dr Toenniessen who lived in Munich in the 1890s. He mated an English bulldog named Tom to German bitches of a similar type. It was in Germany that the Boxer breed was refined to produce the elegant, long-legged dog we know today.

In January 1896 the Deutscher Boxer Club was formed and at the first show held in March, there were 20 entries. They were by no means a uniform collection of dogs by today's Standard. It has taken a great deal of hard work and patience to produce a standardized type of Boxer.

The Boxer was designed primarily as a superior guard dog. The head with its broad, square skull gives ample room for a superior brain, which possesses the intelligence vital for the work of a guard dog. The broad, deep, square muzzle with undershot mouth ensures a powerful, locking grip on any intruder. The dark keen eye denotes both intelligence and reliability. The strong neck and powerful body are essential to enable it to fulfill its duties as a guard dog. Well-sprung ribs allow plenty of heart room, strong hindquarters with well-bent stifle enable it to jump great heights. The shoulders should be well laid back to give the dog stamina in action. The dog should have a short, muscular and powerful back. The coat should be short and fine and the tail docked short. In Germany the ears are cropped, leaving a narrow erect ear.

The Boxer is a dog capable of tracking and holding the most cunning or dangerous miscreant. Imagine 68 lb of smooth muscular dog attacking you: no long fur, tail or ears to get hold of, a powerful jaw with a locking grip, and the courage of a lion. Such is the picture presented of the breed in Germany, where the Boxer is highly-trained for 'man work' and in which it excels over all other breeds.

There have been working trials in Germany where Boxers have taken the

*Boxer puppies are full of fun and even as adults retain much of their youthful charm*

## Breed Standard: the Boxer

**CHARACTERISTICS**
The boxer is renowned for its faithfulness, its alertness and its courage as a protector.

**GENERAL APPEARANCE**
Medium-sized, sturdy, smooth-haired with a short square figure and strong limbs.

**HEAD AND SKULL**
Should be in proportion to the body. The forehead should form a distinct stop with the topline of the muzzle. The mouth is normally undershot.

**EYES**
The eyes should be dark brown; not too small or protruding; not deep set.

**EARS**
Moderate in size; thin to the touch; lying flat and close to the cheek when in repose.

**NECK**
Should be of ample length, yet strong, round, muscular and clean-cut throughout.

**FOREQUARTERS**
The chest should be deep and the ribs should be well arched but not barrel-shaped. The loins should be short, close and taut and slightly tucked up. The shoulders should be long and sloping. The forelegs when seen from the front should be straight and parallel to each other. The pastern should be short.

**BODY**
Viewed in profile should be of square appearance. The torso rests on trunk-like straight legs with strong bones. The whole back should be short, straight, broad and very muscular.

**HINDQUARTERS**
Should be strongly muscled. Seen from behind the hindlegs should be straight.

**FEET**
Should be small with tightly-arched toes. Compact with tough pads.

**TAIL**
Should be docked so that it is not more than 2 inches long, and should be carried upwards.

**COLOUR**
The permissible colours are fawn and brindle; fawn in various shades from light yellow to dark deer red. The brindle variety should have black stripes on a golden-yellow or red-brown background. The black mask is essential.

**SIZE**
Dogs 22–24 inches at withers; bitches 21–23 at withers. In USA, dogs may grow up to 26 inches.

**FAULTS**
Viciousness; cowardice; plump, bulldoggy appearance; too low and broad in front; sway back; low-set tail; cow hocks; light eyes.

*Above: a brindle Boxer dog.*
*Facing page: two boxer puppies*

first five places over all other breeds. One demonstration showed a Boxer going through fire to rescue its master who was tied up with ropes. The dog bit through the rope, then climbed a high ladder, walked over a narrow plank and down another ladder, defied gunfire and attacked the hidden 'criminal', holding the man in spite of a fierce onslaught with a heavy stick.

It is the unequalled courage of the Boxer that makes it the pride of the German breeders; it will defend its owner with its life. Even in the show ring the emphasis is on courage and a bold temperament. Unlike in Britain and also America, in Germany Boxers are trained to stand out on the end of a long lead, usually roaring defiance to other Boxers. If when the judge approaches a dog in the ring the dog should take an apprehensive step backwards, this counts against it. Should it leap forward ready to attack, its owner will be delighted. However, these dogs are all highly trained. Outside the ring they will immediately obey the command of 'sit', 'down', and 'stay', and one can see a row of male Boxers which,

five minutes earlier, were almost at each other's throats, lying placidly within a few inches of each other.

Such is the great personality and tractable nature of the Boxer, that it will become the sort of companion each individual owner requires. As a puppy it is most appealing, with its square, slightly wrinkled head, expressive eyes, big bones and short powerful body, full of fun. Many people are captivated by the appeal of such a puppy, but then unfortunately fail to give it the training which it requires. The Boxer is a powerful dog when mature. If its owners do not school it to walk on a lead without pulling, to come when called and to obey other instructions, it can easily become uncontrollable, pulling small children over on the end of the lead, jumping up and knocking down the elderly, and generally behaving badly.

When someone decides he would like to own a Boxer, he is advised to find out as much as possible about the breed beforehand. He should visit shows and read the canine trade papers to find out who are the most reliable breeders. If he intends to breed from his pup, he should study the dog's pedigree carefully and chose only one which will be a credit to the breed. It is a dog best suited to people

who have strong personalities; the Boxer really enjoys being trained. It will even learn to love and guard its owner's car.

The Breed Standard of the Boxer, originally translated from German, is long and difficult for the layman to understand. All countries use the German Standard, although in America there have been a few alterations, for instance with regard to size. The British standard still reads: 'Dogs, 22 to 24 inches at the withers, bitches 21 to 23 inches at the withers. Heights above or below these figures not to be encouraged.' In America the height for males has now gone up to 26 inches, and the bigger dog is much in demand for the show ring. Of course, a big dog is always impressive as long as it remains typical, but the Standard also says that the Boxer is a medium-sized dog, and if one deviates too far from the original, the breed itself is in danger of losing its characteristics.

The German Boxer was shown in America several years before it was seen in England. Before the Second World War the Americans were shrewd enough to see the great potential of this very striking, smooth-coated breed as a spectacular show dog. It was not difficult for American enthusiasts to persuade the

*Above: A Boxer bitch. Boxers are one of the most popular breeds in the world*

German breeders, nearly all of whom were poor farmers or tradesmen, to part with the cream of this new breed. Sums which constituted a fortune in German eyes were offered. Consequently many of the top Boxers went to America, where the breed was quickly established, and become one of the most popular dogs. In the show ring there, the Boxer is prominent in winning Groups and Best in Show and at the Westminster (the top American show on a par with Cruft's), many Boxers have taken the top awards.

Boxers were first imported into Britain before the Second World War but were still identified by the general public as 'those big bulldogs'. The British Boxer Dog Club was founded in 1936 and became affiliated to the Kennel Club in 1937. Today there are Boxer clubs in all parts of the British Isles, the breed having increased rapidly in popularity since World War II. When the club was first formed, 80 dogs were registered, but by the end of the 1960s about 4,500 had been registered. The breed is now among the top ten in Britain and is well established throughout the world.

# The Briard

THE Briard is one of the most impressive of the Continental shepherding breeds. With the males often standing as tall as 27½ inches, and bitches only slightly smaller, these dogs can never be overlooked. Their coats are long, slightly wavy, but harsh, coarse and dry to the touch. Despite this the Briard is fairly easy to groom. Briards make excellent house-dogs; their presence is enough to frighten a stranger. However, they are very friendly and gentle with people.

This breed is one which must surely come from the same origins as so many of the other Continental herding breeds, such as the Puli and Komondor. It is the oldest sheepdog of France, going back to the twelfth century. The dog as we know it today is depicted on many tapestries of the 15th and 16th centuries. At this time the Briard's qualities as a fearless fighter and defender of livestock were used by the French farmers against both wolves and robbers. Today it is a much more peaceful dog, but is still used for herding and guarding flocks and for protecting farm property.

The way it is believed to have got its name is an interesting one. There is a French legend from the 14th century, which relates how Sir Aubry de Mont-didier was assassinated in the year 1371. His dog hunted down the assassin, a man named Macaire. The king ordained that a judiciary duel be staged between Macaire and the dog. This strange battle took place on the Isle of Notre-Dame and the dog, which from the description seems to have been very like today's Briard, was the winner. Macaire was astounded by his defeat, and as a result made a full confession of his crime. He was then beheaded for his treachery.

It is very probable that, from then on, that dog was known as the 'Chien d'Aubry'. To commemorate this event for posterity, a shield, sculpted in stone, was placed in the church at Montdidier. This shield bore a dog's head very similar to that of the head of the Briard today, plus the arms of the village. Sadly we can no longer see this, because the church was destroyed by enemy action in the 1914 war. There is little doubt that the shepherds using these dogs at the time, and who were very numerous in that area in the fourteenth century, almost certainly tranformed the 'Chien d'Aubry' into 'Chien de Brie', or Chien Berger de Brie.

*The Briard is adaptable and will make a suitable pet for the town or country dweller*

## Breed Standard: the Briard

**GENERAL APPEARANCE**
A dog of rugged appearance; supple, muscular and well proportioned, gay and lively.

**HEAD AND SKULL**
Head strong, carrying hair forming moustache, beard and eyebrows which slightly veil the eyes. The nose should be large and square, always black.

**MOUTH**
The teeth should be strong, white and well fitting in a scissor bite.

**EYES**
Horizontally placed, well opened and rather large, not oblique, dark brown, intelligent and gentle in expression.

**EARS**
Set on high. The ear should not lie too flat against the side of the head, and the ears should be fairly short. Covered with long hair.

**NECK**
Should be well muscled and arching, strong and carried well away from the shoulders.

**FOREQUARTERS**
Should be well angulated and well laid back, the forelegs well muscled with strong bone structure.

**BODY**
The back should be firm and level, the chest broad and well let-down.

**HINDQUARTERS**
Well angulated, with hocks set not too low, but the leg below the hock being not quite vertical. Double dewclaws on hind legs essential.

**FEET**
Strong and slightly rounded, about midway between a cat-foot and a hare-foot. Nails should always be black. Pads should be firm and hard.

**GAIT**
Should be effortless and, when the dog extends himself, should cover a great deal of ground. It should give the impression that the dog is gliding over the ground.

**TAIL**
Long, well covered with hair and with an upward hook at the tip. Carried low and deviating neither to one side nor the other. The bone of the tail should reach at least to the point of the hock.

**COAT**
Long (not less than 3 inches on the body), slightly wavy and very dry.

**COLOUR**
All solid colours are correct except those mentioned below. The darker shades are to be preferred. Incorrect colours are white, chestnut, mahogany and bicolour.

**SIZE**
Dogs, 23 to 27 inches. Bitches, 22 to 25½ inches.

The breed is comparatively new outside France, America having had specimens for about a decade and Britain since 1967. In recent years it has made great progress and is now well established in both countries. The dog's ears are cropped both in America and on the Continent; but in Britain they are left their natural length, as the practice of cropping ears is illegal. Les Amis du Briard is a society which was formed in France in about 1900, and it established the Standard for the breed which we have today.

The Briard is muscular and wiry, giving an impression of strength. It is protected from the elements by its stiff, long, slightly wavy 'goat's coat' which enables it to withstand any climate anywhere. The Standard of the breed asks for a sensible, rugged dog, of the height already indicated, with a strong head which is fairly long with a well-defined stop exactly halfway along the head. The muzzle should not be too narrow or pointed. The head carries hair which forms a moustache, beard and eyebrows, lightly veiling the eyes. The body is strong and deep-chested and the backline straight. The tail, set on low, must reach at least to the point of the hock, and have an upward 'crook' at the end. It must be carried low, never over the back. Double dewclaws on the hindlegs are required. The eyes must always be dark brown, round, large and with a kind, gentle expression. Although the Standard says that the coat can be of 'any whole colour except white, chestnut, mahogany or bicolour', dark colours are considered to be the best. In actual fact, one usually only sees black, fawn in all its shades, and, very occasionally, silver or pewter colours (light or dark grey). Puppies are never born this last-mentioned colour; they turn pewter later on in life. Bicolour should not be confused with the slightly lighter shadings which often occur at the extremities of the dog. This slightly lighter colouring is caused by uneven pigmentation, but it should, nevertheless, be of the same tone as the rest of the coat. A dark fawn dog should have light fawn markings; a dark grey dog should have light grey markings. White hairs which may appear in the coat of a black-coated specimen are acceptable and do not in any way designate a bi-coloured dog.

The Briard is a dog of exceptional intelligence and great sensitivity, forming a great 'rapport' not only with its owner but with other dogs; they are most affectionate towards one another. The breed does tend to be a slow learner, but having once learned something, it will never forget. It is a very hard and very serious worker. The Briard is normally very placid and good-tempered, but will fight to the death if provoked too far.

Briards are very good, easy whelpers, and make excellent mothers. They do tend to have rather large litters. The price of a Briard puppy varies according to sex, colour and show potential. In America $300 may be asked; in Britain the price ranges from about £40 to £100.

A Briard needs a great deal of food as a puppy. When purchased from a reputable kennel it should always be accompanied by full details of diet and rearing. Once the dog is adult, weighing between 70 and 80 pounds, it will need two to three pounds of food daily. It is not possible to estimate cost, for it depends where and what you buy. There are many proprietary foods on the market

*Although the Briard tends to have large litters, it makes an excellent mother*

today which are quite adequate, provided that the instructions for using them are closely followed. It is really up to the owner to make the choice.

Briards do not require an enormous amount of exercise, and they adapt themselves well to either town or country living. The prospective dog owner should consider this breed when thinking of buying a family dog, bearing in mind the fact that it tends to be a one-man dog. Provided that accommodation is a little larger than a two-roomed flat, the Briard will be happy wherever its owner lives.

# Continental Sheepdogs

## The Maremma

The Maremma, sometimes called the Abruzzi Sheepdog, is one of the most important of Italian sheepdogs. Descended from the Magyar pastoral breeds, it bears a distinct resemblance to the Hungarian Kuvasz. It is one of the most efficient sheepdogs in the world, and the Tuscany shepherds take great care to keep the breed pure. It is a handsome dog with a long, broad and flat head. The muzzle is clean-cut and the eyes black and round in shape. The ears are triangular, small, and carried folded over. The body is moderate in length with a straight back, the legs are well boned and the feet are of an oval shape with strong, tough pads. The tail is set on low and carried in a gentle curve, and has a plume of soft hair. The coat is short on the head and limbs but longer on the rest of the body. The colour is pure white, which contrasts strongly with the black of the nose and eyes. Sometimes a dog will be found with a little lemon, biscuit or fawn around the head and ears. The height for a dog is around 25 inches at the withers, bitches usually being about 24 inches; weights range from 70 to 65 lb.

The breed is recognized by the British Kennel Club and is gradually being seen more and more in Britain and the United States. It is essentially a working dog, clever and docile, and happiest when given a job to do. It should not be regarded as just a show dog, and should be trained to perform some sort of duty.

Exercise is essential to the Maremma. In its Italian homeland the breed would cover a much greater area in the course of its work than a British sheepdog, and would be left in charge of the sheep all day, responsible both for herding and guarding. So the breed is unsuitable for town life unless there is access to open parkland nearby. It is devoted to its owner and his family, and its guarding instinct makes it wary of strangers—at least until they have been accepted by the owner as well disposed. A fully grown Maremma needs about 1½ lb of raw meat a day, plus biscuits—but the meat need not be expensive; the breed has a great liking for sheep's paunch.

*The Maremma, one of Italy's best sheepdogs, also makes a splendid pet. It is affectionate and docile*

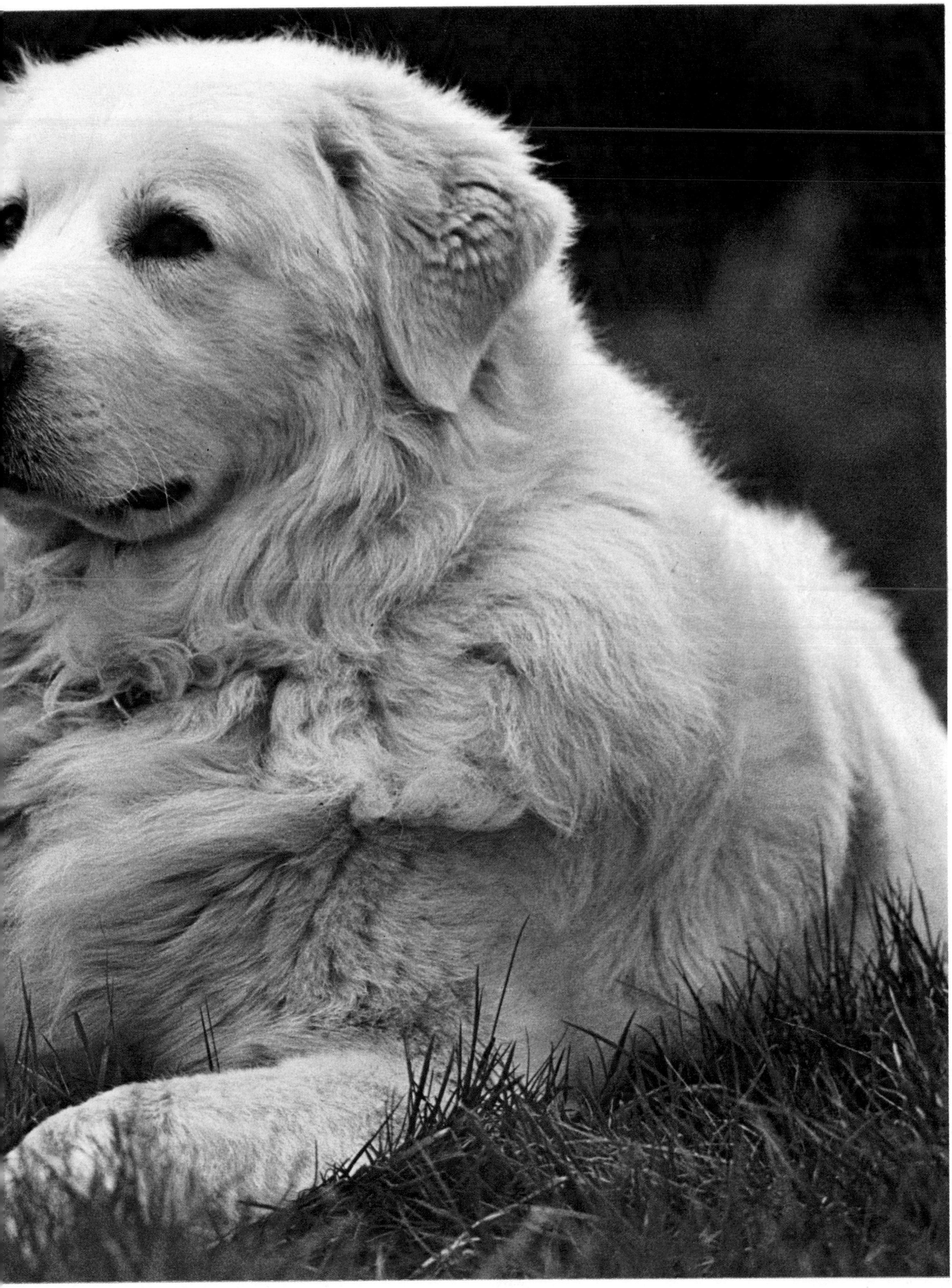

# The Groenendael

The Groenendael is one of the Belgian sheepdog varieties which takes its name from a village of the same name where a breeder called Rose first developed the type. Black dogs were at that time (around 1880) very rare, but the breeder determined to establish a strain which should breed true. He succeeded and finally produced a very fine variety which soon became famous all over the Continent. The breed bears a close resemblance to the German Shepherd Dog (known in Britain as the Alsatian), but there are important differences when the two are compared side by side. The body of the Groenendael is shorter than that of the German dog, and the hindquarters are not so well angulated. The coat, of course, is very much longer. The head is of medium width, tapering down to a strong muzzle. The ears are triangular, carried erect, and sensitive to the slightest sound. The eyes should be dark, almond-shaped, and shine with intelligence. The coat is long and water-resistant, and the undercoat is dense. The colour is black, but a small amount of white is allowed. The general appearance is that of a dog standing foursquare, well balanced, and with a noble, alert expression. The usual height is from 24 to 26 inches at the withers, with bitches some 2 inches less.

The Groenendael is an excellent working dog which has been trained for police work and for army service as a guard and patrol dog. It makes a loyal and affectionate companion. It has worked successfully as an avalanche rescue dog, and many lives have been saved as a result of its keen nose.

The breed is intelligent enough to be used either as a sheepdog or a shepherd dog. There is a difference. Among the people of northern Europe, working dogs were primarily trained to control and drive animals – sheep, cattle or reindeer. But in some areas something more than this was needed. The herds had to be protected from predators, such as wolves, and from thieves, cattle rustlers and bandits. Some dogs were bred and trained specifically for one or other of these tasks, but big, strong dogs of high intelligence could carry out both roles. The Groenendael is one of these, although under working conditions the majority were trained to guard and protect.

In Britain the Groenendael has established itself and there is a modest flow of annual registrations. The position in the USA is somewhat different since the Belgian sheepdogs bred between the wars were almost exclusively Groenendael. A few Malinois, the short haired black and fawn dogs, and a number of Tervuren, the long haired black and fawn dogs, were imported from 1954 and registered as Belgian sheepdogs. In 1959 the AKC decided to register them as separate breeds, the Groenendael alone being known as a Belgian sheepdog.

It is unfair on the breed to keep them in restricted surroundings such as a flat in town. They need a two-mile run every day, unless there is a large garden where they can have free range. For such large dogs they are relatively inexpensive to feed, thriving on a varied diet of raw meat, tinned and dry petfoods. The bitches make good mothers, usually bearing litters of six to ten puppies without any great difficulty.

In Europe the Groenendael has distinguished itself as an avalanche rescue dog, possibly the only canines to be annointed with automobile anti-freeze liquid which is used to prevent the snow from freezing on the long coat and impeding the work. In Britain it is likely that the breed will be selected for mountain rescue activities. In this regard a programme of dog training has recently been established by the Search and Rescue Dog Association, based on the experience the Association officials have already had, and on the experience of Continental rescue teams. Some 300 accidents a year occur on the fells and mountains of Britain, many of them fatal. A trained search and rescue dog can do the work of 20 men!

# The Tervuren

The Tervuren is another variety of Belgian sheepdog, and shares its origin with the Groenendael, which it resembles in everything but colour. The shepherd breeds were once judged solely by their ability to work, with the result that breeding was conducted on a haphazard basis. Physical differences such as colour and conformation were ignored, the sole criterion being the working reputation of the parents. This resulted in varying lengths of coat, a miscellany of shades and colours, and tails of different lengths.

In due course the dogs attracted the attention of breeders other than shepherds, and selective breeding was introduced. The Belgian Kennel Club eventually decided to register breeds with three kinds of coat. The Tervuren, which was one of those to be registered, takes its name from the town in which it was first bred and its coat is certainly very distinctive. The outer coat is long, straight and

profuse, the undercoat dense and weatherproof. The colour can range from rich mahogany to fawn, but the coat is double-pigmented, the tip of each hair being black, giving an attractive effect.

The Tervuren is of medium size, 24 to 26 inches at the shoulder, bitches being some 2 inches shorter, and weigh on average 55 lb. Some males go up to 65 lb. The head is broad, and the muzzle is moderately pointed and strong. The ears are erect and the eyes dark and watchful.

A graceful dog, the Tervuren is a tireless worker which responds well to any form of training. Already, selected members of the breed have started training in Britain for mountain rescue work. This is a long and arduous course lasting as long as four years.

Considering the Tervuren is not widely known in Britain—only 15 were registered with the British Kennel Club in 1973—the breed has made considerable impact. In addition to its mountain-rescue status, it has qualified for Crufts, and can also be

seen at important provincial shows such as Birmingham, Peterborough, Richmond, the Southern Counties and the Working Breeds' Show.

In America, the Tervuren is registered as a separate breed and a separate show classification is provided. The Malinois, a short-haired black-and-fawn which shares a common ancestry with the Tervuren and Groenendael, has made little impact in either country.

Tervuren breeders have proved that it is not an expensive dog to feed in spite of its size. It can live well and in good health on the pelletted 'complete' diet which contains all the essential vitamins, plus a feed of meat for pregnant and feeding bitches. The bitches make excellent mothers, bearing from eight to nine puppies. It is interesting to note that if the puppies are not removed from the bitch when they are three weeks old, the bitch will regurgitate her food for them in order that they progress from a milk diet on to solid foods.

# The Rough and Smooth Collies

EVEN those people who like many other breeds of dog very much, willingly agree that a really good specimen of a Rough Collie is one of the most beautiful canines. This time it is not a question of all beauty and no brains, for the Collie is also one of the most intelligent of breeds. The inherent instincts of the sheepdog seem most readily to adapt to modern life. The Collie quickly teaches itself that the 'herding instinct' can just as well be used on humans as on sheep. Where a Collie is a house-pet in a family of several children, it will watch them at play and, if a toddler appears to stray, will quickly return it to the group.

Because of its long association with humans, it is companionship with man that brings out the very best in the Collie. This is a dog which is happiest with a job to do. It will always try to find an outlet and frequently makes itself really useful about the home. Its great sense of property shows itself in the rôles of both watchdog and nanny to the family.

The Collie has a faithful, extremely affectionate and gentle character. As a rule it does not readily make friends with strangers, and needs time to accept a newcomer. The breed seems to have an almost telepathic power: it understands its owner's own moods, sometimes quite uncannily. One elderly Collie dog, the constant companion of its owner who owned a small kennel of Collies, was the only house-dog. If its owner was going out for a brief period the dog much preferred to wait alone in the house. If she was going to be away a long time, it preferred to

join the other Collies in the kennel. It would always know before its owner went out, that she was going and for how long. If it was to be for a long time it would know and put itself in the kennel, with no suggestion having been made and no word said. How did it know?

The Collie is a dog with a great sense of humour, and many Collies 'smile' in a way that resembles the human smile. It does not like being laughed at, but delights in being laughed with, and will often think of pranks to catch the attention of its owner. People often say that a dog with such a narrow head cannot have much room for a brain. This is completely false, since in all dogs the brain runs along the head, not across it, and

*The Smooth Collie (above) may have a less attractive coat, but has the same temperament as the Rough*

by this reckoning Collies should have more brain space than many other breeds.

The breed is of medium size, with a maximum shoulder height of 24 inches for dogs and 22 inches for bitches. It usually looks bigger than it is, because its huge coat makes it seem taller. But once the coat is thoroughly wet you can see that this is not a very big dog. Its head should be long and lean, with no bumps anywhere, and should appear as a wedge when looked at either from the top or in profile. It should move freely and easily, with no stilted up and down movement. The tail should be carried down when the dog is still, and never higher than the level of the back when it is in movement. The coat must be double: a harsh, straight outer-coat with a dense, fluffy one underneath. This dense undercoat should protect the dog from wet weather and also from extremes of heat. However, the undercoat is not usually evident in a baby puppy, so do not expect to find it when selecting one from a litter. The coat of the adult Collie should fit the dog; it should not stand away from the body, nor should it be floppy. Its ears must always be tipped over, with the top third of the ear falling forwards. Most puppies' ears need some training in this respect, usually until the teething period is completed. Eyes should be dark brown, almond in shape, and of medium size. A very tiny eye is highly undesirable, as often this causes problems connected with eyesight.

The Collie's coat is very easy to keep in good condition. A really good groom-

*The Rough Collie (below) is a dog said by its owners to have a sense of humour and it is also very playful*

# Breed Standard: the Rough Collie

**CHARACTERISTICS**
To enable the Collie to fulfil a natural bent for sheepdog work, its physical structure should be on the lines of strength and activity.

**GENERAL APPEARANCE**
A dog of great beauty, and impassive dignity, with no part out of proportion to the whole.

**HEAD AND SKULL**
The head bears a resemblance to a well-blunted, clean wedge, being smooth in outline. The skull should be flat. The sides should taper from the ears to the end of the black nose, without prominent cheekbones or pinched muzzle. The under jaw is strong, clean-cut and the depth of the skull from the brow to the under jaw is not excessive.

**EYES**
Of medium size, set somewhat obliquely, of almond shape and dark brown (except blue merles whose eyes can be blue or blue flecked). Expression full of intelligence and sweetness.

**EARS**
Small and not too close together. When in repose they should be carried thrown back, but when on the alert, brought forward and semi-erect.

**MOUTH**
Teeth of good size, fitting closely.

**NECK**
Muscular, of fair length and well arched.

**FOREQUARTERS**
Shoulders sloped. Forelegs straight and muscular.

**BODY**
A trifle long compared with the height, back firm with a slight rise over the loins; ribs well sprung, chest deep and fairly broad.

**HINDQUARTERS**
Muscular thighs, clean and sinewy below, with well-bent stifles. Hocks well let-down.

**FEET**
Oval; soles well padded, toes arched.

**TAIL**
Long, with the bone reaching at least to the hock joint. Carried low when the dog is quiet, but with a slight upward swirl at the tip.

**COAT**
Very dense; the outer coat straight and harsh to the touch, the undercoat soft, furry and very close. Very abundant mane and frill; the face smooth, also the tips of the ears. Forelegs well feathered, hind legs smooth below hocks.

**COLOUR**
Sable and white, tricolour and blue merle. All may carry white markings.

**WEIGHT AND SIZE**
Dogs 22–24 inches, bitches 20–22 inches. In the USA, 24–26 inches, bitches 22–24 inches.

ing with a stiff brush once a week is usually sufficient. The dog should not be combed except when it is casting its coat. Once this starts, then brush and comb your dog daily if you can afford the time, for the sooner the dead coat is got rid of, the sooner the new coat will grow in. Even when the Collie is casting its coat, the hairs are easy to deal with; whether they are left on your clothes or on the carpet, a damp brush will quickly get rid of them.

At one time the breed had a reputation for being snappy, and one sometimes hears this accusation today. It is absolutely untrue. It arose from the days when every farm had a Collie, and, except when it was working, it was kept chained up. A dog so treated has a right to become aggressive. It is an accepted fact that being chained increases aggression in a dog. Your Collie puppy, properly reared and never teased, will not become aggressive.

The breed's demand for food is not great. The growing puppy needs plenty of good food, but once it is adult it will need only about 1 lb to 1½ lb of meat daily, plus a breakfast of milk and cereals. If you have purchased your puppy, (as you will be wise to have done) from a reputable kennel specializing in the breed, you will have received a diet sheet with the dog. Usually this not only sets out the needs of the puppy but also of the adult dog. With the uncertainty of today's prices it is not possible to state how much per week the Collie will cost to keep; much will depend on where you live and what foods are available. Today there are many good quality prepared foods, so that you can give your dog variety if you think it is needed.

The cost of a well-bred Collie puppy will vary according to its show potential. It is advisable to buy from a reputable breeder to avoid later disappointment.

No one has been able to decide exactly on the origins of this breed. Almost certainly it evolved from a crossing of several breeds and of selecting those dogs which most nearly fulfilled the breeder's requirements. One thing is certain: the Collie was at first bred entirely for its working potential. Shepherds did not care what it looked like; its brain was much more important. It was not until the second half of the last century that any attention was paid to the looks of the breed, and this was when dog shows first came into being. The name 'Collie' does not help us in tracing the breed's origins, for we cannot trace the history of the word itself. Over the years it has been spelt in many different ways – Coll, Colley, Coally, Coaly, to mention just a few. The usually accepted derivation is that of the Anglo-Saxon word Col, meaning black, the dogs being so called either because in those days the majority of them were black, or because the most common of the Highland she[ep] were black-faced. By the end of the nin[e]teenth century the breed was well enou[gh] established to have a name, and the nam[e] was Collie, no matter how it was spe[lt].

There is one thing in which the Col[lie] is unique. This is a breed which is sprea[d] worldwide, and which is numerically ve[ry] strong, and yet every single Collie, do[g] or bitch, Rough or Smooth, in no matt[er] what country, traces its origins back [to] one dog only, a Tricolour called Tref[oil] that was born in 1873. No other bree[d] can claim such a descent. Both in the US[A] and in Britain, the Collie is among th[e] top ten breeds registered yearly by bo[th] the American and British Kennel Club[s], such is its popularity.

Today's Smooth Collie is so close[ly] allied to the Rough that until 1974 it di[d] not even have a separate standard [of] points; the only difference in the Britis[h] Kennel Club wording stated that 'Th[e] Smooth Collie differs from the Roug[h] only in its coat, which should be har[d], dense and quite smooth'. The underco[at] as found in the Rough should be prese[nt] also in the Smooth, but the top coat mu[st] be quite short and smooth. However, th[e] Smooth Collie now has a standard of i[ts] own.

The Smooths, too, all trace back to Tre[foil]. Throughout the breed's equally lon[g] history the Smooth has lagged behind th[e] Rough in popularity, both as a show do[g] and as a companion. The added beaut[y] of the coat of the Rough can be the onl[y] reason for this, since in every other respe[ct] the Smooth is identical, both physical[ly] and in temperament. In fact, through a[ll] its history, the Smooth has carried muc[h] of the blood of the Rough Collie and doe[s] so even today, for crossings between th[e] two coats are still made.

On several occasions over the years, th[e] Smooth has been on the verge of extinc[tion]. After the First World War, the bree[d] almost disappeared, and the state o[f] affairs was even worse in 1945. Both time[s] a small band of dedicated breeders save[d] the breed. On both occasions the crossin[g] with the Rough was absolutely essentia[l]. It is interesting to note that puppies fro[m] such a cross are always, in the first genera[tion] at least, either Rough or Smooth clearly defined and with no trace of [a] 'broken' coat in either type. Such puppie[s] are pure bred, and may be registered a[s] either Rough or Smooth, according to their coat.

Today the Smooths are increasing i[n] number and improving in quality, and ar[e] obtainable in all the three Collie colours[:] sable, tricolour and blue-merle. For thos[e] who do not want a long-coated dog, bu[t] still want the Collie character, a Smooth is undoubtedly the answer.

# The Bearded Collie

THE origins of the Bearded Collie are not fully known, but under one name or another this dog is probably the oldest of the British sheep-herding breeds. It has been known as the Highland Sheepdog, the Bearded Sheepdog, the Highland Collie and finally, the Bearded Collie. Many experts regret that the word Collie was ever used in its name; the breed is so different from the Rough or Smooth Collie, and at a glance so much more like the Old English Sheepdog. It seems certain that the Bearded Collie and the Old English Sheepdog must have had common ancestors, probably stemming from the blood of the Magyar herding dog, the Commondore, or the huge Russian Owtcharka.

The Bearded Collie is a medium to small dog with a long, lean body covered with a double coat. The top coat is harsh and strong and without any trace of curl; the undercoat is soft, furry and close, to protect against the extremes of weather. Its head is broad, and its ears should be set on high, falling along the side of its head. The short hair on the top of its nose lengthens as it goes down the side of the head until it becomes the beard which gives the breed its name. A Beardie should be 21 to 22 inches high at the shoulder for males, and an inch less for bitches. It can be black, slate grey, reddish fawn, all shades of brown, or sandy, with or without white markings on neck, chest, paws and tail-tip.

In the early part of this century, specimens of this breed were fairly numerous and, although rarely seen in the showing, were highly prized as working dogs. In 1912 an Edinburgh-based Bearded Collie Club was formed and this club drew up the first Standard for the breed, but few were registered by the Scottish shepherds who owned them.

Gradually the breed became less common until it was almost non-existent after the Second World War. Had it not been for a series of extraordinary coincidences, the Bearded Collie would surely be extinct today. In 1944, Mrs G Willison of the Bothkennar Kennels (now no longer in existence) obtained a Bearded Collie bitch puppy quite by accident. This puppy had at the time no pedigree, but it was established later that it was from working parents, and so was able to obtain Kennel Club registration. Many unsuccessful attempts were made to find a mate for her, until in 1949, Mrs Willison saw a Beardie dog playing with its owner on the beach at Hove. Its owner wished to sell the dog, so the dog joined the Bothkennar Kennels and later became registered as Bailie. It is from one litter (born in April 1950) from these two, Bailie and Jeannie, that all today's pedigree Bearded Collies are descended. It is remarkable that only 23 years later, in 1973, the breed had 661 representatives registered at the Kennel Club in Britain.

In 1955, the Bearded Collie Club was formed, and in 1964 this club revised the Standard drawn up by the Edinburgh Club in 1912. This is the official Kennel Club Standard of the breed today. In 1974, the American Kennel Club officially recognized the breed.

The Beardie is a dog of delightful temperament, great intelligence and is an instinctive herder. But it is so adaptable that it quickly enjoys home life. It is, of course, so full of energy that it needs at least one good free-running walk a day: simply going round the block on the end of a lead will not satisfy the Beardie. Its coat can be kept in good condition by a good brushing once or twice a week. You should not expect to buy a good quality Beardie puppy cheaply. Go to a breeder of repute and pay as much as you can afford.

*The Bearded Collie looks more like an Old English Sheepdog than a Collie*

# Cardigan and Pembroke Corgis

WHEN referring to Welsh Corgis one must realize that there are two types: the Pembroke Welsh Corgi and the Cardigan Welsh Corgi – much alike in many ways but different in others. The obvious difference is that the Cardigan has a tail which is like a fox's brush, whereas the Pembroke has none. The tail is docked when the pup is about three days old, at the same time as its dewclaws are removed. The novice should not try this without first having watched an expert.

There are other important differences but to the layman they may be of no great significance, as they apply mainly to the show ring. Cardigans, however, offer a wider choice of colour. The Pembroke is bred in red with or without white, sable with or without white, tri-colour (that is, black, red and white) and black and tan, the red or tan varying from pale to a deep mahogany. The Cardigan is additionally bred in two other colours: brindle, which is a mixture of black, brown and red, with or without white, and blue merle.

The general appearance of both types of Corgi is low set, strong and sturdy. They are alert and active dogs, giving an impression of substance and stamina in spite of their compact size. Their outlook is bold, and their expression is intelligent and workmanlike. Both types were bred originally for herding cattle and both types still work in this way in some parts of the world.

In both types the head should be foxy in appearance, the colour of the eyes to blend with the coat colour; ears should be pricked; the coat should be of medium length, dense and weather-resistant. A coat in good condition should carry a real gloss. A long, soft or fluffy coat is a bad fault, as is feathering on the ears and feet.

An adult Pembroke should weigh between 18 and 24 lb depending on sex, and should stand 10 to 12 inches at the shoulder. The Cardigan is a slightly larger dog, weighing from 20 to 26 lb; its height should be as nearly as possible 12 inches at the shoulder. One important point to be appreciated is that the Cardigan is not simply a Pembroke with a long tail. The Cardigan is a longer, slightly heavier dog than the Pembroke, with larger, more rounded ears, heavier bones, and with a distinct crook to the foreleg. The Pembroke's foreleg must be straight. The Cardigan has a cat-like foot but the Pembroke has a hare-like foot, the former being rounded whereas the latter is slightly tapered.

The origins and early history of the ancient Welsh Corgi are obscure but it has been known in Wales for hundreds of years, mainly as a companion and guard on farms where they worked the cattle, bringing them from the fields to the markets, which earned for the breed the descriptive name of 'heelers'. This old trait still remains with present-day Corgis and there are many, both Pembroke and Cardigan, who will 'herd' other livestock, not necessarily cattle, without ever having been taught to do so.

The earliest record of the breed appears to be around 900AD when Wales was governed by a great ruler called Howell the Good, 'the Great Law Giver'. One of these laws required the valuation of every domestic animal so that proper redress could be claimed and given in the event of it being stolen or killed. The value put on a 'cattle dog' was the value of a steer at 'current worth', which in those days must have been considerable. The opinion held in Wales is that the Corgi was the original British dog before the Roman invasion. There are also those who think the Corgi may be descended from dogs of the Spitz family brought into Britain by the Vikings. The Spitz family is one of the most ancient canine families and includes such breeds as Husky, Elkhound, Keeshond, Samoyed and Pomeranian. One authority, W. Lloyd Thomas, claims that the Cardigan Corgi was brought to Wales by the Celts around 1200 BC. Used as a general purpose dog, it was not until much later that the breed was trained to herd cattle. He also claims that the Pembroke Corgi was unknown in Wales until brought in by the Flemish in AD 1107. Cross breeding from both varieties resulted in the common name Corgi to denote both the Cardigan and Pembroke types.

The name Corgi itself is open to discussion: cor means dwarf and gi means dog, the plural being corgwn. In the South Wales area the word 'corgi' is also used to mean rascal – in a playful and affectionate sense – so did the dog get its name from the term or vice versa?

A Corgi, be it Pembroke or Cardigan, is one of the easiest dogs to manage. Coat trimming does not have to be taken into consideration; regular grooming is all that is required. The breed keeps itself remarkably clean, and will often wash its paws just like a cat. It is a grand companion and guard dog, appealing equally to women and to men. It is very adaptable, will walk for

## Breed Standard: the Pembroke Corgi

**GENERAL APPEARANCE**
Low set, strong, sturdily built, alert and active, outlook bold, expression intelligent and workmanlike. The movement should be free, elbows fitting closely to the sides, neither loose nor tied. Forelegs should move well forward without too much lift, in unison with thrusting action of hind legs.

**HEAD AND SKULL**
Head to be foxy in shape and appearance, skull to be fairly wide and flat between the ears; moderate amount of stop. Muzzle slightly tapering. Nose black.

**EYES**
Well set, round, medium size, hazel in colour.

**EARS**
Pricked, medium sized, slightly pointed. A line drawn from the tip of the nose through the eye should, if extended, pass through, or close to, the tip of the ear.

**MOUTH**
Teeth level, or with the inner side of the upper front teeth resting closely on the front of the under ones.

**NECK**
Fairly long

**FOREQUARTERS**
Legs short and as straight as possible. Elbows should fit closely to the sides.

**BODY**
Of medium length, with well-sprung ribs. Not short coupled or terrier-like. Level top line. Chest broad and deep, well let down between the forelegs.

**HINDQUARTERS**
Strong and flexible, slightly tapering. Legs short. Ample bone carried right down to the feet. Hocks straight when viewed from behind.

**FEET**
Oval, the two centre toes slightly in advance of two outer ones, pads strong and well arched. Nails short.

**TAIL**
Short, preferably natural.

**COAT**
Of medium length and dense; not wiry.

**COLOUR**
Self colours in Red, Sable, Fawn, Black and Tan or with white markings on legs chest and neck. Some white on head is permissable.

**WEIGHT AND SIZE**
Dogs 20 to 24 lbs; bitches 18 to 22 lbs. Height from 10 to 12 inches at shoulder.

**FAULTS**
White on the body or hound-like markings; long fluffy coat accompanied by feathering on ears and feet; over- or undershot mouth.

miles and live a rough outdoor life, yet i equally at home in a small house or fla with the run of a garden.

Never underestimate the intelligence o a Corgi; it is a very clever dog and wil understand and obey any reasonabl command in the shortest possible time. I is also very independent, so never reduc the self-respect of a Corgi by bullying o beating if you wish to get the best out of it You will never cow a Corgi in this way bu only make it bad tempered. People some times ask 'are Corgis snappy dogs?' Th reply should be 'there are no bad dogs only bad handlers' and this applies mor to Corgis and their owners than to an other dogs.

They are highly intelligent so the must be guided properly from puppyhood If you say 'no', then 'no' it must be, an this command must be carried through even if in the early days it requires patienc on the part of the owner. The Corgi, like : young child, quickly learns when it ca get away with naughtiness.

As a general rule, a Corgi bitch shoulc be asked to rear no more than four or fiv whelps with her first litter, and six to seve afterwards, although a big strong Cardigar can obviously rear more than the slightly smaller Pembroke. Breeding history mus also be a consideration: if a bitch is knowr to have had a difficult birth before, or if i is a long time since her last litter, then extra care must be taken. Normally, however Corgis give birth easily.

Although these dogs have plenty o stamina, it must be remembered tha young puppies of any breed need more care than adults, since they are easily tired and their bones are still soft. Bac management and faulty feeding at this ag can do a great deal of harm, and poo physique and general sickliness can be the result. It is also important to 'bring up' a puppy correctly: that is, to see that its temperament, and therefore its behaviour. is not ruined by unwise rearing. Many puppies have been ruined temperamentally by bad or irresponsible handling at this critical period of their life.

Corgis are not subject to any hereditary weaknesses or defects. In general they are very hardy and healthy, needing the minimum of fussing. The Pembroke has probably a more extrovert temperamen than the Cardigan, but a Cardigan, having once given its loyalty, will protect its ownei with its life. The Pembroke is better known than its Cardigan 'cousin', due mainly to Royal patronage of the former. This is perhaps unfortunate for the Cardigan, which is a lovely breed with its flowing tai and its great attachment to its owners.

*The Pembroke (top) is not such a heavy dog as the Cardigan, two varieties of which are shown here (centre and bottom)*

# The Dobermann

VERY few breeds can claim to have risen from obscurity to immense popularity in so short a space of time as the Dobermann.

German in origin and unknown even in that country until around 1899, the breed was not introduced into England until 1947, although by that time it was already achieving popularity in America, where serious breeding had commenced in the 1920s. Dobermanns rate high in the annual numbers registered with the American and British Kennel Clubs.

Perhaps, most surprisingly of all, this great popularity has been attained despite the fact that to the average man in the street the Dobe (as it is called by its admirers) is thought to be a vicious, snarling brute, forever on the lookout for something, or someone, to tear to pieces. This false image has probably arisen from the breed's film and television appearances, most of which depict it as tracking down and mauling its human quarry or, alternatively, frothing at the mouth and

*The Dobermann is an elegant dog of great strength and intelligence*

snarling with bared teeth at intruders to its domain. Its frequent use as a police dog may also have added weight to this erroneous impression.

Why should the Dobermann have been singled out for popularity in the canine world? It would be difficult to answer this question by giving one particular reason. It may well be because of the breed's immense adaptability and superior intelligence, both of which enable it to fulfil so many roles with ease. Its reputation as a guard dog, watchdog and Police dog are perhaps the attributes for which it is best known but it can be used with equal success to work sheep and cattle, as a gundog to scent, hunt and retrieve, as a guide dog for the blind, as a family pet, or as a loving and faithful companion. It is undeniably true that the breed's scenting powers are without equal in the canine world and tales of its uncanny tracking feats on scents which other breeds have found 'cold' are many.

In origin the Dobermann differs from many other breeds in that it is essentially a 'manufactured' breed, produced for a specific purpose, that of providing a perfect watchdog. The ingredients that went into the make-up of the breed are, however, purely a matter for conjecture as it was conceived and raised behind closed doors and no written records were kept of its evolution. The dog takes its name from the man who played the major part in its creation – Herr Louis Dobermann, a nightwatchman in the Thuringian village of Apolda. It is commonly believed that the Great Dane, Manchester Terrier, Greyhound, Rottweiler and German Pointer all contributed something towards the finished article but it cannot be too strongly emphasized that all this is a matter of guesswork and deduction. Herr Dobermann began his experiments in 1875 and was producing something close to his ideal by 1890.

In Great Britain the Dobermann differs in two important aspects from its American and Continental counterparts. Whilst almost everywhere in the world it carries the full title of Dobermann Pinscher, in Britain the word Pinscher was dropped officially some years ago and the breed therefore is known here as the plain Dobermann. In many Continental countries and parts of America, the Dobermann's ears are cropped during puppyhood to give it a sharp and alert appearance when mature but in Britain this practice is forbidden and the ears are allowed to grow naturally in a drooped position. The Dobermann is elegant and carries itself proudly. Its tough, compact build makes it capable of great speed. The head must be long and in proportion to the body. From above and from the side it should resemble a blunt wedge. There should be no wrinkle on the upper part of the head. The eyes should be almond-shaped, moderately deep-set and with a vigorous expression. It is a bad fault for black dogs to have light eyes. The ears can be either dropped or erect but erect ones are preferable. The body should be square, and the ribs deep and well sprung, with the belly fairly well tucked up. The hindquarters should be parallel to each other.

In intelligence the Dobermann is second to none but it would be foolish in the extreme to assume from this that it is an easy dog to train. On the contrary in fact, the dog's superior intelligence is such that having been taught to obey a command it will eventually want to know why. The Dobermann is essentially an individual and it has a mind of its own and the strength of will and character to try to impose it on you. The breed therefore demands the firmest discipline during the most impressionable growing period.

During early puppyhood there is perhaps no easier breed to train and such training can be carried out by any intelligent adult with the aid of a good text book on the subject. However, from about eight to twelve months of age, the Dobermann begins to show a marked resistance to commands of a repetitive nature.

It is at this vital stage in the dog's development that firm and determined discipline is necessary, to ensure that lessons already taught are obeyed promptly without question at all times. This, alas, is the stage where so many owners succumb and allow the dog to take over the role of master. With determination and firmness at this trying period the Dobe soon realizes that it is a servant and it is then that it begins to show that wonderful intelligence which, in America, has earned the breed the title of 'the dog with the human brain'.

The breed is equally at home in a city flat or country mansion. It is quite as happy with a daily walk 'round the houses' as it is being allowed to roam free at all times over the fields. It is a fallacy to subscribe to the view that because the Dobe is a fairly big dog it will always require a considerable amount of exercise. It requires precisely the amount of exercise that it has been brought up to expect. If therefore, as a puppy, the dog is taken for long daily walks, it will naturally expect this outing as a daily requirement throughout its life, whereas it can remain quite healthy and happy on a daily ration of a frolic night and morning in garden or park, if this has been its lot as a puppy.

A dog of any breed usually reflects in its adult behaviour its early upbringing. To this rule the Dobermann is no exception. It is therefore the wisest policy to acquire a young puppy rather than attempt a short cut by acquiring a young adult or an even older animal. A young Dobermann puppy brought up with a family of young children will guard those youngsters with its life. It will require no training in this respect as this guarding instinct is inherent in the breed, stemming from the character ingredients bred into the line by Herr Dobermann. As a faithful companion the Dobe is without equal and, once it has taken you over, it wears its heart on its sleeve and is happiest when in your company.

Having decided that the Dobermann is the breed for you, how do you go about obtaining one? In this connection the first consideration is that temperament and character are of paramount importance. It therefore follows that it would be very foolish to buy from a pet shop or dealer, as by so doing nothing can be learned of the puppy's background and heritage. The purchase must be from a reputable breeder, preferably one who is dedicated only to the one breed and who has a reputation for producing sound, good-tempered and intelligent stock. To trace such a breeder it is only necessary to write

# Breed Standard: the Dobermann.

## CHARACTERISTICS
The dog is of good medium size with a well-set body, muscular and elegant. He has a proud carriage and a bold alert temperament. His form is compact and tough and, owing to his build, capable of great speed. He is loyal and obedient.

## HEAD AND SKULL
Must be long, well filled under the eyes and clean cut. The upper part of the head should be as flat as possible and free from wrinkles.

## EYES
Should be almond-shaped, moderately deep set, with vigorous, energetic expression. Iris of uniform colour, ranging from medium to darkest brown in black dogs.

## EARS
Should be small, neat and set high on the head. Erect or dropped, but erect preferred.

## MOUTH
Should be very well developed, solid and strong.

## NECK
Should be fairly long and lean, carried erect and with considerable nobility, slightly convex and proportionate to the whole shape of the dog.

## FOREQUARTERS
The shoulder blade and upper arm should meet at an angle of 90°. The legs, seen from the front and side, should be perfectly straight.

## BODY
Should be square with a short back, the topline sloping slightly from withers to croup.

## HINDQUARTERS
The hindquarters should be well developed and muscular. While at rest, hock to heel should be perpendicular to the ground.

## FEET
Fore- and hindfeet should be well arched, compact and cat-like, turning neither in nor out.

## TAIL
Should be docked at the first or second joint.

## COAT
Should be smooth-haired, short and close-lying.

## COLOUR
Colours allowed are definite black, brown or blue with rust red markings.

## SIZE
Ideal height at withers: Males 27 inches; Females 25½ inches.

## FAULTS
Shyness or viciousness; head out of proportion to body; dish-face; light eyes in black dogs; overshot or undershot mouth; dewlap and loose skin; long, weak roach back; white markings of any kind; hair forming a ridge on the back of the neck and/or along the spine.

to the Kennel Club. The Kennel Club will be able to supply a list of all reputable Dobermann breeders in your particular area and the name and address of the secretary of the nearest Dobermann Club. The latter, in turn, can probably offer the name of a breeder near to you with young stock for sale and will most certainly be anxious to supply details of the club and its activities, of which you would be wise to take full advantage. By so doing you can gain much interesting information and useful advice from breed experts.

When visiting the breeder to select your puppy, ask to see the dam or the sire, or both. There is no finer way of assessing the probable temperament of the puppies, for it is safe to assume that, when dealing with temperament, like nearly always begets like. Ask to see all the puppies together and never be persuaded away from your determination to put good temper and character before all other requirements. Do not let your heart be stolen by that sweet, pathetic-looking pup that remains at the back of the kennel and cannot be persuaded to come out. Ensure that sudden noises are made during your inspection and avoid the pup that runs away when a feeding bowl or other object is dropped near it. Preferably, opt for the pup that is the first one out to greet you, that constantly demands attention and shows no sign of nervousness.

The ideal age at which to make this choice of dog is when it is between eight and twelve weeks. Prior to that age the dog's stomach is not strong enough to withstand the sudden change of diet, and after twelve weeks a Dobe pup becomes quite unruly and will be much harder to train. Ensure that full feeding and rearing instructions are given by the breeder. Finally, remember that good manners and obedience are henceforth a matter of training and upbringing and as such are your responsibility.

Never chain your puppy or confine him to a small kennel for long periods. Nothing is more certain to make a Dobermann bad-tempered than this practice. To the would-be Dobermann owner who fears for the safety of his children, it should be pointed out that, of the 2,000 or so Dobermanns that are registered annually, a substantial number go to homes with young children. I have yet to hear of a Dobe attacking a child with whom it has close associations.

As a daily companion, household pet, canine burglar alarm, trained watchdog or faithful servant, the Dobermann is without equal. To have been owned by a Dobermann is an experience never to be forgotten and it is true to say that once you have been owned by a Dobermann you would never be owned by any other breed.

# The majestic Great Dane

FOR centuries the Great Dane has been a favourite among the royal courts and great houses of Europe. If you want a large and truly aristocratic dog for your pet, you will find the Great Dane a very acceptable companion. This handsome well-built dog has an elegance all of its own. Its average weight ranges from 120 to 200 lb, and average height from 30 to 36 inches at the shoulder.

However much you may be attracted to one specific breed of dog, it is always important to remember that certain kinds of dog require certain kinds of conditions. For instance, if you are a flat-dweller in the middle of a big city where there are no open spaces, a Great Dane is hardly the pet for you. Another point to be borne in mind is how much will your pet cost and how much exercise will it require. On average, an adult Great Dane, although not greedy, will consume a lot of food and so a really important question is can you afford to keep such a large dog?

For exercise, the Great Dane should have two walks daily, each of about half an-hour and in addition a good gallop round a field. So another important consideration is whether you have the time to look after a pet of this type properly. Before buying a Great Dane a great deal of thought should be given to deciding if it is the right dog for you.

Having made the decision that the Great Dane *is* the dog for you, what do you look for in a puppy? It is important to establish that the puppy has been correctly reared, for if this is not the case defects of form may develop in your dog in later life. A puppy should look well balanced and sturdy with a squarish head. Its eyes should be dark and it should be well covered without being too fat. Good puppies are not cheap so beware of stock offered at bargain prices.

There are several different colourations for the Great Dane. The different types are: brindles, which range from a light

*This harlequin Great Dane has the typical grace and alert appearance of the breed*

yellow to a dark orange background with black stripes; fawns, which range from buff to dark orange and often have darker shadings on the face; blacks, which are completely black in colour; blues, which are anything from light grey to deepest slate; and finally harlequins, which have a white background with blue or black patches.

Up to the time of King Edward VII, Great Danes had their ears cropped, but this is now illegal in Britain. The practice started in the days when the Great Dane was a hunting dog; accidents often happened and the dog could become badly mutilated. Its ears were cropped as a preventive measure and in some cases were cut off completely. Cropping became common for artistic reasons later and today we have the 'long crop' which is greatly admired in America and on the Continent, although some states in America have also banned cropping.

The Great Dane is an intelligent dog with bright eyes and a keen expression. Despite its size, it will make a good household dog as it is essentially very gentle and good with children. By reputation this breed is thought to be aloof and, although this characteristic shows itself in the company of strangers, the Great Dane is very loyal and anxious to please its family. A dog fond of creature comforts, this addition to your family will make an excellent

*Above: this fawn Great Dane has darker markings round the muzzle. It is a magnificent dog combining strength and elegance*

fire screen in the winter! The Dane is also a good guard dog, and although it is a very peaceable dog most of the time, it will make a formidable enemy if it is provoked.

To keep your dog in good condition, proper feeding and grooming are essential. An adult Great Dane needs on average around 1 lb of meat per day with added biscuit meal. Fresh water should be provided at all times.

Attention should be given to its coat daily; the best method is to rub the fur up the wrong way for several minutes and then to smooth it down again with the palms of the hands. Regular daily grooming is essential to keep your dog's coat in top condition. As it is a short-coated dog, the Great Dane is an easy breed to keep clean and is remarkably free from the 'doggy' smell which is noticeable in dogs with longer coats. Grooming is important to stimulate the dog's skin, improve the blood circulation and contributes generally to the overall condition of the dog.

The Great Dane, generally speaking, is a very hardy breed of dog and suffers from few ailments. At one time, entorpion (in-

# Breed standard: the Great Dane

**GENERAL APPEARANCE**
Should be remarkable in size and very muscular, strongly though elegantly built. Elegance of outline and grace of form are essential and there must be alertness of expression.

**HEAD AND SKULL**
The head should give the idea of great length and strength of jaw. The muzzle is broad and the skull proportionately narrow. The whole head, when viewed from above and in front, has the appearance of equal breadth throughout. The skull should be flat and have a slight indentation running up the centre. The face should be well chiselled, well filled in below the eyes with no appearance of being pinched. The bridge of the nose should be very wide, with a slight ridge where the cartilage joins the bone. The nostrils should be large, wide and open, giving a blunt look to the nose. The lips should hang squarely in front, forming a right-angle with the upper line of the foreface.

**EYES**
Fairly deep set, of medium size, preferably dark. Wall or odd-eyes permissable in Harlequins.

**EARS**
Should be small and carried slightly erect with the tips falling forward.

**NECK**
Should be long, well arched, held well up, well set in the shoulders and the junction of the head and neck well defined.

**FOREQUARTERS**
The shoulders should be muscular. The forelegs should be perfectly straight with big flat bone.

**BODY**
Should be very deep with ribs well sprung and belly well drawn up.

**HINDQUARTERS**
The hindquarters and thighs should be extremely muscular. The second thigh is long and well developed, the stifle and hock well bent.

**FEET**
Should be catlike and should not turn in or out.

**TAIL**
Should be thick at the root and taper towards the end. It should be carried in a straight line level with the back.

**COAT**
The hair is short, dense and sleek-looking.

**WEIGHT AND SIZE**
The minimum height of an adult dog over 18 months must be 30 inches, that of a bitch, 28 inches. The minimum weight of an adult dog over 18 months should be 120 lbs, that of a bitch, 100 lbs.

**FAULTS**
Cow-hocks. Out at elbows. Straight stifles. Undershot or overshot mouth. Round bone. Snipy muzzle. Straight shoulder. Shelly body. Ring tail.

growing eyelids) was not uncommon in the breed but fortunately this is not found very often nowadays. This condition is hereditary and any dogs suffering from this complaint should not be used for breeding under any circumstances. The eyelid and lashes of the dog turn inwards, causing a watery discharge to come from the eye. In extreme cases this leads to ulceration of the eye and eventual blindness. The condition can be corrected with surgery.

Another vulnerable part in the make-up of the Great Dane is its tail. An excitable dog that wags its tail a lot can knock the tip off it. This is difficult to treat, as it is almost impossible to stop the dog wagging its tail, and the wound in consequence will keep reopening. In severe cases the tip of the tail can be amputated but this should not be done unless it is absolutely necessary. Daily dressing and thick padded bandages to cover the wound will in time help to ensure a complete recovery. If the treatment is applied carefully and for long enough, the end of the tail will form a thick skin or callous and no further damage will be done.

The Great Dane has a history that reaches back over the centuries to before the time of the Roman Conquest of Britain. This giant hound is thought to have descended from an amalgamation of the Wolfhound, Boarhound and Mastiff; breeds which were great favourites even in Roman times.

During the Middle Ages, Great Danes were utilized as working dogs for hunting wild boar, hence the name 'Boarhound'. During the fifteenth and sixteenth centuries, they were greatly esteemed by members of the aristocracy, especially by German princes and their followers. From this time until the nineteenth century, enthusiasm for this dog grew both in Britain and Germany. In fact, in Germany it was considered to be the national breed.

With a name like 'Great Dane', it would be fair to assume that this dog's history is connected with Denmark. But most authorities on the breed are not of this opinion and there is little evidence to support such a theory. The French naturalist Comte de Buffon (1710–1788) is thought to be the first person to have referred to the breed as 'Grand Danois', which translated means 'big Danish'. Whatever the reason for coining this name, it does not alter the fact that Germany must be given the credit for evolving this magnificent dog which has existed as a distinct breed for 400 years.

The Great Dane Club in England was started in 1883–five years before the Germans founded a similar club–and the breed was recognized by the Kennel Club in 1884. The Deutsche Dogge Club was formed in 1888 and about four years later an official standard for the breed was produced. Towards the end of the nineteenth century and before the First World War, the Germans were perfecting a strain of this dog that was coveted throughout the whole world. Between the two World Wars, progress in breeding continued in both Britain and Germany and the truly magnificent dog we know today as the Great Dane, the 'Apollo' of all breeds, finally evolved.

At the present time, the quality of Great Danes is higher in America than in Britain and Europe. Some bad faults commonly found in European dogs seem relatively rare in American animals. This is mainly owing to the fact that many superb German dogs were imported just before the Second World War. During the war breeding was not interrupted to such an extent as it was in Europe. The Americans were able to retain their stock and continue to improve their standards until they reached the overall high quality which exists today. The Great Dane Club of America was founded in 1891, the German Breed Standard being adopted.

Great Danes can be found all over the world, but it is in Britain, America and on the Continent that these lovely dogs are most popular.

*Below: Great Danes are very playful; their owners will need plenty of energy!*

# Three working dogs from Hungary: Komonder, Puli, and Kuvasz

FOR a thousand years the Komondor has served Hungary as a guard of its sheep and cattle. A massive, bizarre-looking animal, it is said by some to have originated in Russia, by others to have originated in Tibet about 2000 BC. It is certainly one of the oldest of European dogs.

The Komondor is one of the three herdsman's breeds in Hungary—the other two are the Puli and the Kuvasz—but it is used as a guard of flocks and herds rather than to round them up. It is ideally suited for this job, having the size, strength and courage to tackle predators such as the bear and wolf, and a thick heavy coat to withstand their attack.

Because the Komondor has not been crossed with other breeds in the past, today it has a unique appearance, the result of ten centuries of being developed for a particular purpose in life. It should give the impression of having great strength, bone and substance, unexaggerated conformation, and a fearless approach to any situation.

The chief distinguishing feature of the breed is its pure white coat which is long and corded. These cords are caused by the twining together of the coarse outer coat and the soft woolly undercoat which are both very dense; these combine to make long, felted tassels. Like the rest of the dog, the head is strong with a wide,

quite short skull and muzzle. The jaw is wide and the teeth strong. Its size alone—$23\frac{1}{2}$ to $25\frac{1}{2}$ inches at the withers—makes the Komondor a suitable guard dog.

Wariness of strangers, yet devotion to its master, makes the Komondor a good companion. The long shaggy coat may be a drawback in the house, and though pet animals can be shorn of this, they then lose much of their breed identity. Otherwise the breeder, when selling a puppy, should be asked to explain in detail what special care is needed.

*Above: the Puli's distinctive feature is its long, usually dark, corded coat*

# Breed Standard: The Puli

**GENERAL APPEARANCE**
The Hungarian Puli is medium-sized, nimble and extremely intelligent. In relation to its size, it is sturdy and muscular, with good bone. Viewed from the side, it must present a square figure.

**HEAD AND SKULL**
Disregarding the hair, the head should be fine and round, with a slightly domed skull. The head should have a well-defined stop and straight muzzle, bluntly rounded. The arches of the eye socket should be well defined; the nose relatively large and black; eyelids and flews black.

**EYES**
Should be of medium size and dark brown.

**EARS**
Set fairly high, 'V' shaped and pendant. Of medium size and covered with long hair.

**MOUTH**
Should be regular and strong with scissor bite.

**NECK**
The neck should be held at an angle of 45° to the horizontal, of medium length, tight and muscular.

**FOREQUARTERS**
The shoulder should be well laid. Elbows tight. The forelegs should be straight and muscular. The feet should be short, round and tight. The pads should be full, springy and dark in colour.

**BODY**
The withers should be slightly higher than the level of the back, which should be of medium length. The loin short, broad and tucked up. The ribs well sprung and barrel-shaped. The rump should be short and slightly sloping. The chest is deep and fairly broad.

**HINDQUARTERS**
Should be strong and well muscled, with well-bent stifles, and hocks set fairly low.

**GAIT**
The Hungarian Puli is a short-striding dog, the movement should always be nimble, quick and gay.

**TAIL**
Should be of medium length and curled over the back. It should be covered with long hair.

**COAT**
The coat is generally longest on the hindquarters and shortest on the head and feet. The coat should be corded and matting or felting should be avoided. Some dogs will grow a floor-length coat.

**COLOUR**
Acceptable colours are black, rusty black, various shades of grey, and white.

**WEIGHT AND SIZE**
Ideal height: dogs 16 to 18 inches; bitches, 14 to 16 inches. Ideal weight: dogs 29 to 33 lb; bitches 22 to 29 lb.

---

The smallest of Hungary's three traditional breeds used with livestock, the Puli is a worker among them rather than a guard. The Magyar shepherds are thought to have been responsible for introducing the breed to Hungary where it has been developed as a sheepdog.

It is usually dark-coloured, in contrast to the white of sheep-guarding breeds; there is good reason for this, since sheep are more easily controlled by dark dogs, and shepherds can better pick out the dog in a flock. The main colour is black but it is not very definite; bronze and rusty black hairs can be intermingled. Greys are also found, and occasionally white.

It is impossible to say now whether or not the Puli developed its unique form of movement from having to dart quickly in all directions to round up sheep. This seems the most likely explanation for its very fast, short-stepping stride which makes the dog look as though it is in a great hurry to get somewhere. Indeed, the Puli often controls the sheep by jumping over their backs or even onto their backs.

Its coat is one feature that makes the Puli different from other dogs. The soft undercoat and harsher, weather-resistant outercoat combine to form long cords; in mature dogs these often reach the ground. The effect is a rather bizarre, unkempt look and makes it difficult to dis-

*Like the Puli, the Komondor has a striking tasselled coat, but it is a much larger dog*

tinguish one end of the dog from the other since head and tail are both covered in cords, and the tail is carried over the back. Active, alert and hardy, the Puli is a naturally loyal and devoted companion. Its guarding instinct is well developed even if its size–about 17 inches–does not seem large enough to back up its protective instinct. It is not suitable for life in cramped conditions, and should be given the opportunity to use its instincts.

The Puli has been described as 'the shaggy dog to end all shaggy dogs'. This attraction could well take it from being a comparatively rare breed now (in Britain there were only 34 Kennel Club registrations for 1973) to a popular breed of the future. Its happy, bustling nature lends itself well to the role of house dog. It seems tirelessly energetic, and is also somewhat stubborn. But it presents no unusual problems except in coat care. Given a commonsense approach and the breeder's advice when buying a puppy, even the coat need not cause problems.

'Armed guard of the nobility' is what the original name of the Kuvasz meant. The breed is said to have originated many hundreds of years ago in Tibet or Turkey. But its identity and present appearance belong entirely to Hungary.

The Kuvasz has existed in its present form for 1000 years. In the days when the rulers and nobility of Hungary had good cause to fear for their lives at the hands of the populace or would-be assassins, dogs alone could be counted on for loyalty and protection. The Kuvasz became popular as the protector of the privileged classes. Only the fortunate few were permitted to keep them. During the fifteenth century, and especially when Matthias I was on the throne (1458 to 1490), the Kuvasz reached the height of its popularity as a guard dog, mainly because of the precarious way in which king and nobles held their positions.

Matthias gave the breed another purpose in life when he brought into being a large pack for use in hunting on his estates at Siebenbuergen. Long after his rule, when the Kuvasz had spread into wider ownership, it added one more role to its versatile repertoire–that of herder and guard of flocks and cattle. To see a Kuvasz is to understand why so much faith was pinned on its ability as a guard. It is sturdy and strong, yet active enough to make the best of those other qualities. Being 26 inches high at the shoulder it has the size of a good guard dog.

Although the Kuvasz has a thick, weather-resistant coat, this is not inconveniently long, and being white adds a

*The Kuvasz (above) was once kept by the Hungarian nobility as a guard dog*

spectacular touch. It is a breed unknown to a number of Western countries, including Britain, but its origins suggest there could be a place for the Kuvasz as a guard dog valued for its hardiness and looks.

It has been mentioned that some experts believe the Komondor originated in Russia and the Kuvasz in Tibet or Turkey. The evidence is slight, and many people prefer not to be dogmatic about such obscure matters. However, it should be said that there is a theory that both breeds came about as a result of crossing shepherd dogs of mastiff origin with some types of northern sheepdogs. The result has been dogs of fierce temperament and large size (qualities that make them good protectors) but which are not swift in movement like collie-type sheepdogs. Nevertheless, they are still able to control sheep effectively and to round them up.

One advantage of crossing these mastiff types with the northern sheepdogs (usually of the spitz breeds) is that, in addition to the sheep-herding qualities of the shepherd dogs, the shaggy, cold-resisting coats of the spitz type would be retained to some extent. The Old English Sheepdog has something in common with the Komondor, for the British breed has a shaggy, cold-resisting coat as well as a well-developed herding instinct. The introduction of the Tibetan mastiff types into Europe led in time to their appearance in Russia, and, it is thought, to the development of the Russian Owtchar, a dog of great size with corresponding fierceness in protecting flocks and capable of great endurance.

There is a distinction to be made between shepherd dogs and sheepdogs, although often the names are used as though synonymous. The Pyrenean Mountain Dog can be quoted as an example of a shepherd dog, not a sheepdog. It protects the sheep, very much as the shepherd does, but it has little value in rounding up and controlling the herd. Collies and the Old English Sheepdog are breeds that control and round up, and this quality—which comes from the northern spitz breeds—has also been passed on in the three breeds already mentioned. These are the Komondor, the Kuvasz and the Russian Owtchar.

The mastiff strain in these breeds gives them their fierceness in protecting the property of their owners. This fierceness was developed in mastiffs when they were used as dogs of war by the Assyrians of the ancient world, and for hunting animals such as wild horses and lions. But there is a great difference between these savage dogs and the domestic breeds of today, even though they are distantly related.

# War Dogs: Mastiffs, Bullmastiffs and Tibetan Mastiffs

IN Shakespeare's *Julius Caesar*, Mark Antony gives a grim warning of the dead Caesar's avenging spirit which 'Shall in these confines, with a monarch's voice, Cry "Havoc" and let slip the dogs of war.' Although this was probably the first reference in English literature to the Mastiff, this most noble of dogs has a history which stretches much further into the past.

There are many theories about the origin of the Mastiff. Some experts believe that it originated in Tibet many thousands of years ago and then spread to Persia, Egypt and Greece. However, the first record we have of the Mastiff is on an Assyrian bas-relief dated at about 2,200 BC, although the actual identity of the breed depicted is open to some doubt. More closely resembling the Mastiff we know today is the dog which appears on a Babylonian bas-relief at the palace of Assurbanipal, dating from about 700 BC. Babylon was a city of dog-lovers, and dating from approximately the same period are terracotta plaques that may be presumed to be Mastiffs, buried under the thresholds of many houses. Evidently the intention was that the spirit of the dog should help keep away evil spirits.

*The history of the Mastiff (facing page) dates back to 2200 BC. The Bullmastiff (below) dates from the 1850s*

From Babylon, the history of the Mastiff can be traced to Egypt and then to Greece, from which country the breed spread throughout Europe and even far eastward to the court of Kublai Khan, where 5,000 dogs were kept expressly for hunting lions and other big game. Rome, too, had its Mastiffs, and Shakespeare was not wrong in referring to their fighting qualities, for the Romans evidently used them in battle, though probably as much to deter the enemy as actually to attack him. Thus the Mastiff's early history portrays the remarkable courage, strength and guarding qualities of the breed.

Although its origins were in the East, the Mastiff has played a significant role in English history, and it is in England that the breed can be said to have been truly fostered and developed. In Norman times, for example, Mastiffs were the only dogs to be allowed in the forests, and in the reign of Henry V they accompanied knights into battle.

In addition to being employed for fighting, Mastiffs were widely used for wolf-hunting and bear-baiting in the Middle Ages, and their exceptional qualities were still highly valued in Tudor times. Henry VIII presented 400 of them specifically for use as fighters to Charles V on the occasion of the latter signing a pact with Francis I; and Shakespeare, this time in the person of

Edgar in *King Lear*, places the breed at the head of his list of hunting dogs:
'Mastiff, greyhound, mongrel grim,
Hound or spaniel, brach or lym,
Or bobtail tike or trundle-tail'.

At a later date, when dog-fighting developed into a fashionable pastime in English society, it was the Mastiff that was chosen as the premier breed, once again proving its power and courage.

The Mastiff's popularity, however, was not destined to last, and from the seventeenth century until the 1860s, the breed rapidly declined in numbers. There followed a brief revival, aided by the establishment of the breed in the United States, but with the outbreak of World War One, numbers decreased once more. Indeed, by the end of World War Two in 1945, the breed was in grave danger of dying out completely in Britain. It has only recently been restored to public favour by reason of the importation of dogs from the United States.

The massive, powerful Mastiff, as its history clearly denotes, is an excellent guard; yet despite its impressive proportions—it stands 30 inches at the shoulder ($27\frac{1}{2}$ for a bitch) and weighs 12 stone—it is surprisingly gentle and makes a wonderful family dog.

The short, dense coat of the Mastiff needs comparatively little grooming, but the dog does require plenty of exercise. Furthermore, it is not a cheap dog to own, for it will readily eat up to $3\frac{1}{2}$ lb of tinned food (alternatively 2 lb of meat or $1\frac{1}{4}$ lb of dry food) every day. It has to be remembered, too, that the energetic habits of the dog make it extremely demanding of space. A Mastiff will not thrive if confined to restricted quarters all day while its owner is out.

Ideally, the Mastiff should possess a well-knit frame and broad body, bearing a heavy head, broadly arched skull and clearly defined stop. The curved forehead shows marked wrinkles, and these are most clearly defined in a dog that is standing alert and at attention, ready for a command. Such an order, provided it is given by its master, will be obeyed to the letter. The Mastiff's small eyes, a feature which tends to reinforce its deceptively fearsome looks, are set wide apart, and the V-shaped ears, which are rounded at the tips, are characteristically thin in texture. The long tail of the Mastiff is held moderately high, but is never arched over the back. There are two acceptable colours for the Mastiff's coat—fawn and brindled. In either variety the muzzle must, in a perfect example of the breed, be black.

The Bullmastiff, as its name rightly indicates, owes its ancestry in part to the Mastiff. This dog is, in many respects, a smaller version of its blood relation, standing 27 inches high at the withers (24 inches

in bitches) and weighing between 100 and 130 lb. Not surprisingly, the Bullmastiff has an appetite to match, and although this is not as enormous as that of the Mastiff, the dog will demand some 3 lb of tinned food every day, and, like the Mastiff, it must have ample opportunity for exercise.

The Bullmastiff, like its cousin, is a powerfully built, first-rate house dog, with proven qualities of loyalty and affection. Its senses of sight and hearing are exceptionally keen, and it probably betters the Mastiff as a dog to choose for a household with children.

The history of the Bullmastiff began in the 1850s when the breed was developed from crosses between Mastiffs and Bulldogs. It is estimated that the modern Bullmastiff is sixty per cent Mastiff and forty per cent Bulldog.

The breed is popularly said to have originated as the result of efforts to produce a gamekeeper's ideal dog. At that period poaching was a serious problem in Britain, and poachers would be known to shoot gamekeepers without compunction, rather than relinquish their prizes or run the risk of being caught. In fear of their lives, therefore, gamekeepers desperately needed efficient dogs for guard purposes which could, if necessary, fight off intruders from their covers. The mastiff, though undeniably courageous, tended to be too slow in catching poachers and in consequence the Bullmastiff was developed (after a number of trial breedings using other dogs), coming to be known as the gamekeeper's night dog. The breed lived up to expectations, proving a fast, silent mover, with considerable powers of endurance, and capable of holding a poacher on command without mauling him. It could be counted upon to be absolutely obedient and loyal to its master.

Although initially employed in the field, Bullmastiffs were later adopted by breeders interested in standardizing this new breed. The first Bullmastiffs were shown in about 1900, although it was not until 1924 that they were officially recognized by the Kennel Club. The first show Challenge Certificates were awarded to Bullmastiffs in 1928. The United States granted the breed Kennel Club status in 1933.

The original coat colour of the Bullmastiff was brindle, and although this is still quite acceptable in the show ring, it has since been replaced in popularity by fawn. Another acceptable colour is red. In every case, however, a dark muzzle is preferred by judges. The coat is short and dense, which makes it easy to keep neat and smart without a great amount of effort. Hand-grooming will keep the coat shiny and in good condition.

Other important features are the broad muzzle, measuring approximately one-third of the total head length, the broad

# Breed Standard: the Mastiff

## GENERAL APPEARANCE
Large, massive, powerful, symmetrical and well-knit frame. A combination of grandeur and good nature, courage and docility.

## HEAD AND SKULL
Skull broad between the ears, forehead flat, but wrinkled when attention is excited. Muscles of the temples and cheeks (temporal and masseter) well developed. Face or muzzle, short, broad under the eyes, and keeping nearly parallel in width to the end of the nose; truncated, i.e., blunt and cut off squarely, thus forming a right-angle with the upper line of the face, of great depth from the point of the nose to under jaw. Under jaw broad to the end. Nose broad, with widely spreading nostrils when viewed from the front, flat (not pointed or turned up) in profile.

## EYES
Small, wide apart, divided by at least the space of two eyes. The stop between the eyes well marked but not too abrupt. Colour hazel brown, the darker the better, showing no haw.

## EARS
Small, thin to the touch, wide apart, set on at the highest points of the sides of the skull, so as to continue the outline across the summit, and lying flat and close to the cheeks when in repose.

## MOUTH
Canine teeth healthy; powerful and wide apart; incisors level.

## NECK
Slightly arched, moderately long, very muscular.

## FOREQUARTERS
Shoulder and arm slightly sloping, heavy and muscular. Legs straight, strong, and set wide apart. Elbows square. Pasterns upright.

## BODY
Chest wide, deep and well let down between the forelegs. Ribs arched and well rounded. Back and loins wide and muscular. Great depth of flanks.

## HINDQUARTERS
Broad, wide and muscular, with well-developed second thighs, hocks bent, and wide part.

## FEET
Large and round. Toes well arched up. Nails black.

## TAIL
Put on high up, and reaching to the hocks, or a little below them, wide at its root and tapering to the end.

## COAT
Short and close-lying, but not too fine over the shoulders, neck and back.

## COLOUR
Apricot or silver, fawn or dark fawn-brindle. In any case, muzzle, ears and nose should be black with black round the orbits, and extending upwards between them.

nostrils, a large skull over which the skin of the forehead is wrinkled when the animal is alert, and large canine teeth set wide apart. In a perfect Bullmastiff the eyes are dark, and the V-shaped ears are carried close to the cheeks. Another feature favoured by judges is heaviness of build on muscular foundations, but on no account any hint of overweight.

The Tibetan Mastiff is, at first glance, very different from its Mastiff namesake. Nevertheless, it is probably the breed which comes closest in anatomical features to the original Mastiff. Many historians uphold this view and believe that the Tibetan Mastiff was, in fact, the progenitor of the Mastiff breeds that are known today. It is not a common breed of dog; one or two have been imported into Britain and a slightly larger number into the United States. This may be due in part to its reputation for being a ferocious guard dog, which might deter people from owning one. In fact, its ferocity is more legendary than based on truth and a well trained Tibetan Mastiff will make a faithful companion.

The Tibetan Mastiff, unlike the other members of the Mastiff family, possesses a coat which ranges from long to medium in length and which is, above all, thick and weatherproof. This makes the dog well able to withstand the extremes of hot or cold weather which it would normally experience in its native environment.

Although not enormously popular outside its homeland of Tibet and India, the Tibetan Mastiff is a breed well worth choosing by anyone who has a hankering for an unusual dog. Since it is essentially an outdoor dog, the long coat will require special care and attention, and for the same reason it must be given plenty of vigorous exercise. It will venture out in the very worst type of weather, and is among the most assiduous of guard dogs into the bargain.

Other features which mark out the Tibetan Mastiff from its better known relatives are the plumed tail, carried high over the back, and the comparatively high-set ears. Black, black and tan, and any mixture of these colours are all acceptable in this breed, nor is there any demand for the muzzle to be of a different colour. The average Tibetan Mastiff measures 28 inches at the shoulder and weighs 130 lb, so, like other Mastiffs, it will make considerable demands at feeding time.

The Tibetan Mastiff, though perhaps a rarity in its own right, has found its way into the breeding lines of many other dogs. Indeed, Tibetan Mastiff blood features in the lines of such breeds as the St Bernard, the English Shepherd Dog, the Hungarian Sheepdog and the Newfoundland. The Mastiff breeds are thus 'founder members' of the canine race, as it has since been developed by human beings.

# The Neapolitan Mastiff

THE Neapolitan Mastiff is of Italian, and specifically Neapolitan, origin, and probably descends from those mastiffs which were brought by the Phoenicians to Italy. The earliest examples of the modern breed were first officially shown in Naples in October 1946. In 1949 it was officially recognized in Italy and has since been bred as a pedigree, retaining its centuries-old characteristics.

The name 'mastiff' appears to derive from the Latin for 'tame, domesticated', and therefore, like its English counterpart, it is a house dog whose purpose was to guard property and its inhabitants. Its great size and somewhat awe-inspiring appearance, combined with qualities of courage and power, make it ideal as a watch dog. It has also been used as a police dog and tracking dog.

Despite the fact that its appearance would seem to make it a daunting adversary, the Neapolitan Mastiff is most affectionate and gentle towards its owner. It is extremely intelligent and easy to train, having a stable, docile disposition. The breed is neither nervous nor aggressive, and is very good with children.

Its heavy, thick-set build (the length of the body is greater than its height at the withers), combined with its massive but well-proportioned head, gives this dog a plain and workman-like, but nevertheless majestic, appearance. The skin of the Neapolitan Mastiff does not adhere to the underlying tissues but is slack and plentiful, so that it can be lifted away from the body. This is particularly true of the head and neck, which have a great many loose folds and ridges. The general outline of the head is square when viewed from any angle, and the muzzle is also short and square, with a pronounced 'stop'. The ears are flat and triangular in shape, and small in comparison with the size of the head. The breed's coat is short, close and thick, and uniformly smooth with no fringing. The fine hairs should be less than an inch long and glossy throughout, giving a sleek effect. The preferred colours are black, dark grey, light grey (sometimes with white spots on the chest and tips of the paws), mahogany, and tawny. The colours can be either solid or streaked. The tail is broad at the base and tapers gradually to the tip. It is held in a scimitar shape when at rest, but is carried horizontally when the dog is in action; it is invariably docked to two-thirds of its natural length. The height to the withers is from 25½ inches to 29½ inches for dogs, and from 23½ to 26¾ inches for bitches. Weight

should be between 110 to 154 pounds. The breed's characteristic gait is a slow, lanky walk. When travelling at a faster pace, it trots, covering a great deal of ground with long strides. However, it rarely gallops.

The Neapolitan Mastiff should be vaccinated against disease after the age of two months. After the puppy stage is passed, at between 10 and twelve months, dogs of this breed will need two large meals a day. In the morning at least a pint of milk, mixed with raw egg and biscuits, should be given. The evening meal should consist of a pound and a half of raw meat, with rice, green vegetables, biscuits, vitamins and mineral salts.

The Neapolitan Mastiff belongs to one of the basic families of domestic dog, which includes some of the largest dogs in the world. In view of its great size, it is not a dog for the city, but should be kept on a farm or an estate. In such an environment it will certainly fulfil all the qualities attributed to the breed.

*The Neapolitan Mastiff, which is probably descended from the Phoenician Mastiff, is a member of the oldest family of dogs in Europe, as is the English breed*

204

# Old English Sheepdog

IT is a cold, wild day. The sheep are nowhere to be seen on the Yorkshire fell about the farm buildings. Moorland sheep stray for miles among heather, having no walls or fences to keep the different flocks apart. The busy farmer decides to send his Old English Sheepdog to fetch in the sheep. He gives an order and away goes the woolly bob-tailed character, departing over the rough terrain with alacrity. A short while later, sheep are heard bleating in the yard, and the dog comes in to tell its master that the flock is safely gathered in.

This is a typical example of a working dog, the more interesting because today the lighter Collie is much more in evidence at the shepherd's side. Nearly a hundred years ago, Bobtails (as Old English Sheepdogs were often called) were in common use as assistants in driving both cattle and sheep.

Old English Sheepdogs are generally blue or blue merle, or any shade of grey, and may be with or without white markings. They are tremendously strong, compact looking dogs of even symmetry and should be absolutely free from legginess. They should be thick-set, muscular, able-

bodied dogs, with a kind, intelligent expression. These splendid sheepdogs have a picturesque but dignified bearing, which is made all the more striking when they are found in the relatively humble surroundings of a farm.

Today, unfortunately, the showbench is where it is most often found, but the breed still exhibits so many of the qualities which it possessed as a working dog, that it is not uncommon to find an Old English Sheepdog among the last half dozen when the awards are being selected for the Best in Show. Although an excellent guard and house dog the Old English Sheepdog is not so popular as a pet as it might be, mainly because of its coat, which is supposed to require a great deal of attention.

In fact, the coat is more profuse today than in the specimens originally bred for work, and it seems a pity that breeders do not give more thought to the fact that quality and texture of coat are of greater importance than length. A good brushing and combing once a week does, in fact, keep the coat quite free of any tendency to matt or to harbour vermin. A little boracic powder dusted into the coat when grooming will keep it quite clean and

bright. The coat should always be brushed upwards from tail to head, using the comb sparingly. If straw or wood shavings are used for bedding it is wise to put them in a sack or large bag, because straw or shavings are inclined to stick to the coat; this detracts from the proud, natural bearing of the animal, making it look untidy and out of condition.

Fifty years ago, the combings from the dogs' coats were used for making woollen yarn and garments, but factories will not accept it now. There are some private firms, however, who might undertake to make the combings up as a private order. An article on this subject, published in 1926, stated: 'A bob-tailed sheepdog will yield from three to five pounds of wool a year so that, if you are lucky, you should get sufficient wool from the dog to make two coats reaching just below the knee.

Traditionally, this breed is docked; the operation is performed within a week of birth and preferably within four days. The tail is docked quite close to the rump, hence the description 'bob-tail'. A few strains are reputed to grow hardly any tail at all after whelping, but the average puppy is born with a normal dog's long tail. There is a story attached to the origin of this practice of docking the breed: that shepherds cut off their dogs' tails to distinguish them from non-working specimens, because shepherds' dogs were exempt from tax. But this theory is unlikely to be based on fact, judging by the long tails to be seen on other breeds of collies and sheepdogs. It is much more likely that it was a form of protection for the heavily coated tail may have impeded the dog in its work.

If you decide to breed the Old English Sheepdog then you must take this into account when buying the bitch, either as a puppy or as an adult. A dog which is perfectly acceptable as a member of the household and a family pet—and can be quite a good specimen of the breed—may nevertheless be quite unsuitable for breeding. The reason for this is that many buyers intend to show their dogs, hence they want first class animals. Secondly, if you want to establish a reputation as a breeder of the Old English Sheepdog you must be prepared to exhibit at shows yourself and to win some honours with your bitch before breeding from her. Prospective buyers will want to know what success the bitch has had at shows. In other words, the successful breeder is usually a successful exhibitor as well.

And just as you have taken care to get a first class bitch, you must also take great care to select a really first class dog to mate with her. Whatever price you pay for your bitch, she is still likely to have one or two weak points, as perfection is as hard to find in the dog world as it

## Breed Standard: the Old English Sheepdog

**GENERAL APPEARANCE**
A strong, compact-looking dog of great symmetry; absolutely free of legginess; profusely coated all over; very elastic in a gallop but in walking or trotting has a characteristic ambling or pacing movement. All round he is a thick-set, muscular, able-bodied dog.

**HEAD AND SKULL**
Skull capacious and rather squarely formed, giving plenty of room for brain power. The parts over the eyes should be well arched and the whole well covered with hair. Jaw fairly long, strong, square, and truncated; the stop should be defined to avoid a Deerhound face. Nose always black, large, and capacious.

**EYES**
Dark or wall eyes are to be preferred.

**EARS**
Small and carried flat to side of head.

**MOUTH**
Teeth strong and large, and evenly placed.

**NECK**
The neck should be fairly long, arched gracefully, and well coated with hair.

**FOREQUARTERS**
The forelegs should be dead straight, with plenty of bone, holding the body well off the ground, without approaching legginess; well coated all

round. The shoulders sloping and narrow at the points, the dog standing lower at the shoulders than at the loin.

**BODY**
Rather short and very compact, ribs well sprung, and brisket deep and capacious. The loin should be very stout and gently arched.

**HINDQUARTERS**
The hindquarters should be round and muscular, hocks well let down and the hams densely coated with a thick, long jacket in excess of that of any other part of the body.

**FEET**
Small, round; toes well arched, and thick pads.

**TAIL**
Puppies requiring docking should have the operation performed within a week from birth.

**COAT**
Profuse, and of good hard texture; not straight, but shaggy and free from curl. The undercoat should be a waterproof pile.

**COLOUR**
Any shade of grey, grizzle, blue or blue merle, with or without white marking.

**WEIGHT AND SIZE**
Twenty-two inches and upwards for dogs, slightly less for bitches.

s among humans. Suppose your bitch has less than good hind action; you must make sure, when selecting the dog for her mate, that he has an excellent hind action. All her weaknesses must be matched by excellence in the male. Failure to do this will result in some puppies being born in which the mother's fault has been magnified by a similar fault in the father.

How is one to find this perfect male? There are a number of ways. You can go to dog shows and observe the class winners. You can write to the Kennel Club for a list of breeders of the Old English Sheepdog or, on the other hand, you can visit shows and study the conformation and temperament of the winners. Judges are often pleased to give advice to novices. By studying the pedigree of show winners you will find out which sires produce winning offspring.

Usually bitches take about 63 days to produce their young after mating has taken place. The first 35 to 40 days do not call for any special diet, but the bitch must be helped in the remainder of the period if her bodily resources are not to be strained. Her diet must be enriched with the addition of such items as cod liver oil, milk and eggs. Several small meals are preferable to a few large ones

*This appealing shaggy-haired character is also a skilled working dog*

because the organs of digestion get squeezed as the uterus grows larger with the unborn puppies.

Rather surprisingly, the Kennel Club reports a rapid increase, during the last ten years, in the numbers of Old English Sheepdog puppies registered with it. During the 1960s there were only 600 registered; now, in the 1970s, the healthy figure of over 3,000 is reported. Clearly there are still many people who appreciate the breed for its fine qualities of intelligence, gentleness and splendid appearance.

One unique strain of this breed traces back to a sire who transmitted short tails to its offspring, and there was 'Wall-eyed Bob', who is still known by reputation to all enthusiasts of the breed. This dog became one of the most famous Old English Sheepdogs in the history of the breed, and was reputed to have been sold in a public house when a puppy, for the princely sum of twenty shillings. Subsequently, it sired many well-known puppies although was never a champion itself. One of its descendants is stuffed and now resides in the Natural History Museum.

Watching shepherds and their dogs at work in this country, it is sometimes apparent that the modern shepherd is too much in the habit of 'dogging' his flock into obedience by the employment of his swift and well-trained collie. The heartless

shepherd, at the slightest sign of confusion by a ewe or lamb, will, using his dog's speed and obedience, give the signal for his canine servant to drive the errant sheep back into the flock. The poor animal is often terrified and exhausted, as well as confused, and the rest of the trembling flock crowd together, dreading a similar fate. Witnessing the wise, albeit less agile, Old English Sheepdog at work, one is struck by the fact that sheep, like men, may be better led than driven, and one realizes that to harrass them, as some modern sheepdogs do, is both cruel and unnecessary.

It is always delightful to watch the Old English Sheepdog perform its duties. Intelligent and diligent, it watches the flock heedfully by the hour, using its power over the sheep without abusing them. The kind shepherd will be able to pass among the flock, examining them for injury, while his steady dog keeps them together, without terrorising them. Moving from place to place, the sheep follow the man obediently, one Bobtail walking silently behind its master and a second dog following close behind the flock, keeping strays up without alarming them in the least. This is indeed a sensitive and affectionate breed of dog which will guard house, cattle or sheep with spirit and vigilance, and an unshakable fidelity and is also a devoted companion.

# Four spitz breeds

NORTHERN Russia is the original home of one of the world's most spectacular breeds of dog, the Samoyed, which was named after the nomadic tribe that developed it as a herder of reindeer, as a guard, and for pulling sleds.

A typical spitz breed with a wedge-shaped head, small erect ears, a strong compact body and a tail carried over the back, the Samoyed is usually all white, each hair glistening as though silver-tipped. But it has not always been exclusively this colour. Original imports into England in the last century included black and solid brown dogs. Its crowning glory, a thick, harsh, fairly long double coat, was at one time cut down to the skin on working animals. The less useful dogs were killed for their hides which were worn by tribesmen.

The Nansen and the Jackson-Harmsworth Arctic expeditions in the 1890s both made use of Samoyeds as sled dogs. And in the Antarctic the Newnes-Borchgrevink

expedition used Samoyeds at the end of the last century. Shackleton took descendants of these dogs with him; they had been left on Stewart Island, off New Zealand, when Borchgrevink returned from his exploration.

A notable feature of Samoyeds is their smile. No other breed has an expression quite like it, and it is a true barometer of their suitability as companions. Easily adaptable to town or country life, they are not perhaps ideal for the houseproud person who does not like hairs on carpets during moulting time. The Samoyed has a great deal of hair and, when it begins to drop out, thorough grooming is essential. The sooner the old coat is removed, the faster the new one will grow. At other times, a few minutes spent on brushing each day will keep it looking good. Few breeds equal its striking beauty. For those who value that quality and appreciate a dog which responds to firm but kind treatment and will be a devoted friend but not a slave, the Samoyed is to be strongly recommended.

One of Norway's national breeds, the Norwegian Buhund–which means, literally, 'dog of the homestead'–is traditionally an all-purpose farm dog, mainly used for the control of sheep and cattle. Ancient though its history is, like all spitz breeds the Buhund came into the public eye, even in its native country, only recently. Its promotion began just before the First World War, but not until the mid 1920s was much progress made. It came to Britain in 1946, since when numbers have grown until in 1973 well over 100 were registered at the British Kennel Club.

The Buhund is quite a small breed, about 17¾ inches at the shoulder for dogs and rather less for bitches. It has all those features associated with spitz breeds: a wedge-shaped head with erect ears and bright eyes, a short, compact body, and a tail tightly curled over the back. Its coat is of the thick, double type but quite short. An especially attractive feature is the range of warm colours in which the Buhund is found; these are shades from light yellowy fawn through darker biscuit to tawny light red. Some specimens have black hairs interspersed with the main colour, others have a darker muzzle.

A busy, energetic and friendly dog, the Buhund's size and temperament make it

*Above: the Alaskan Malamute is an Arctic breed with striking colouring. Left: the magnificent head of the Samoyed is framed by a thick, long, double coat*

ideal for almost any household. Not a spectacular or glamorous breed, it will appeal to people who want an easily managed companion. A minimum of daily grooming plus a normally sensible diet will keep it fit and healthy as long as it has adequate means of expressing its love of life.

Originally developed for endurance as a sled dog for the Chukchi people of north-eastern Asia, the Siberian Husky was later utilized by its creators for pulling lightly loaded sleds at a moderate pace over vast distances. Its purity of race was always maintained. During the last century the breed was introduced to America where it became very popular. It is a comparatively recent import to Britain, where numbers are still very low.

An indication of the Siberian Husky' endurance may be given by the fact that in 1910 a team of the breed won the All Alaska Sweepstakes Race over 400 miles the first time Siberians competed. Later in 1925, when the city of Nome in Alaska was the centre of a diphtheria outbreak teams of Siberians were used to relay essential serums. It was this feat that contributed much to the breed's reputation

A beautifully constructed animal with no exaggerations, one of the Siberian' most striking qualities is its movement a free, easy, ground-covering stride. The head is typically spitz, but the eyes are sometimes of different colours, one brown, the other blue. Although the coat is thick and dense it is not long and in no way obscures the clean-cut outline. All colours are allowed by breed Standards among the most picturesque being blue and red, with paler markings on the head making a symmetrical pattern.

The Siberian Husky is not a guard dog it is friendly and gentle, and its innate tractability means that it is easy to train. Grooming and feeding pose no special problems in that it is essentially a hardy breed, and standing at about 23 inches at the withers, it is well suited to most homes if given sufficient exercise.

Power and substance are the essence of the Alaskan Malamute, a breed of sled dog named after a native tribe, the Mahlemuts. It is not known for certain from where the people of the tribe or their dogs came. But the Alaskan Malamute is obviously closely related to all other spitz breeds. It exhibits spitz features in the head and bushy tail though, unlike many members of the family, the tail is carried loosely over the back. In colour it is usually wolf-sable or black and white while size can be up to 25 inches.

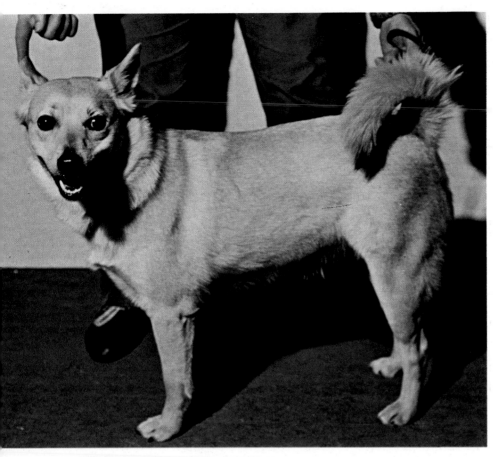

Having always been draught animals previously, Malamutes were used for sled racing in the early part of this century. Unfortunately, crosses were then made with other Arctic breeds in order to increase the Malamute's speed still further. However, breeders in America, also interested in sled racing, sought out pure Alaskan Malamutes and built the strains we know today. Many racing records have been set up by the breed, and it was used in the Byrd Antarctic expeditions.

Alaskan Malamutes are friendly and affectionate, hardy and easily maintained in good condition. But they are active and very strong and powerful, and so are not the sort of dog children or the elderly and frail should be allowed to take out on their own.

Numerically the breed is far stronger in America than in Britain. However, in the latter country the breed is in the hands of a few dedicated breeders who admire the imposing stature, dignity and temperament of the Malamute.

*Left: the Norwegian Buhund is a medium-sized dog with a short coat, and makes an ideal pet. Below: the Siberian Husky is both attractive and friendly*

# Mountain Dogs:
# St Bernard, Bernese
# and Pyrenean
# Mountain Dogs

FOR more than 800 years, the Hospice founded by Archdeacon Bernard of the St Augustine Cathedral (St Bernard) in 1050 provided welfare for the poor and needy, a House of the Lord for holy pilgrims, and a refuge for all from the elements and from bandits. For 250 of those years the dogs of St Bernard were one of its principal assets and later, attractions. Powerfully built animals with a distinctively marked, smooth coat which is white on a mainly mahogany or fawn ground, their very size and nobility of outlook gives the breed a dignity unmatched by any other.

St Bernards are descendants of a mastiff-type canine that originated in Asia, and their development as a species took place at the Hospice after which they were named. For anyone today wishing to understand those qualities of strength of character, sagacity and benevolence, it is necessary to consider for what purpose the breed was originally developed.

The Hospice was a lone settlement 8,000 feet up in the Swiss Alps on a principal pass between Switzerland and Italy. There was no tunnel as there is today, but only rock, snow and ice. Having reached the Hospice, travellers could be sure of safety, denied to the many who remained out in the blizzards and icy fog of this wild region. No human could survive in these conditions for very long, and so some way of rescuing those who had lost their way was necessary. A trained dog was the answer, but it would have to be a dog of great endurance, in order to keep looking for lost people in vile conditions. It would also need to have a keen nose to scent them if buried in snow, and strength to dig for survivors. These are the characteristics for which the St Bernard was bred for 250 years. Such qualities survive to this day, 100 years after the life-saving duties ended when the Simplon Tunnel was built in 1905, connecting Switzerland and Italy.

All the Hospice's dogs played their part in finding lost people. The most famous was Old Barry, outstanding as a representative of the breed and rescuer of more than 40 people. In 12 years of devotion to duty that ended with death in 1814, Barry's best remembered deed is the saving of a small boy found in the snow and carried to safety on his back.

The story goes that Barry was on his usual patrol with other dogs, accompanied by one of the monks. Suddenly the dog refused to move from a certain spot. The other dogs and the monk very naturally stopped too, for Barry's gifts of what often seemed like 'second sight' were well known. While they were still waiting for Barry to make a move, a terrific avalanche swept down the mountainside some 50 feet ahead of them. The monk then led the dogs on the way back to the monastery, as the way forward had been blocked by the fall of snow. But Barry did not return with them. Instead, he left the party, paying no heed to the monk who called to him and gave the whistle to return. Several hours went by, and at the monastery there was great concern over what could have happened to Barry, their most famous dog. A search party was sent out. Visibility was bad and there was no sign of the missing dog. Other travellers on the pass reported that a woman and child had been seen that day, near where the avalanche occurred. This was the only news that the search party carried on its return to the Hospice.

The storm continued, but shortly after midnight the keen-eared prior heard, above the noise of the storm, the whine of a dog. At the monastery door he found Barry, almost totally covered in snow. Strapped to the dog's back was a sleeping two-year-old boy. Who had strapped the child to Barry's back? The prior immediately realized that it must have been the boy's mother. But the search party led by Barry, that left immediately to try and find her, was only partly successful. The woman's body was there in the avalanche, but she was dead.

Barry had tunnelled through the avalanche, knowing by his 'second sight' that living creatures had been buried under the vast weight of snow. The mother must have been alive when the dog reached her and her son, but exposure to the elements while waiting for the rescue party had proved fatal.

Experts differ as to the exact nature of the 'second sight' shown by Barry and other dogs of the same breed. Some say that Barry possessed nothing more than the extraordinary gift given to all St Bernards – of being able to pick up the scent of a living creature several miles away – but that he had it to an amazing degree. Remember that these gifts operate when the man is buried in snow. There are other attributes besides that of an acute sense of smell. The working St Bernard has an excellent sense of direction which stands him in good stead when pathways are no longer visible, when swirling snow and mist obscure the customary landmarks, and when a cutting wind dispels what little scent there is.

Although the St Bernard may appear to be a very individualistic dog, in fact it works well with its fellows, and under working conditions is a pack animal. This has been demonstrated many times in mountain work. When a traveller suffering from exposure is found, the dogs will

*The handsome St Bernard (facing page) stands 36 inches at the shoulder and is a very expensive dog to keep*

# Breed Standard: the St Bernard

**GENERAL APPEARANCE**
Expression should betoken benevolence, dignity and intelligence. Movement is most important.

**HEAD AND SKULL**
Large and massive. Muzzle short, full in front of the eye, and square at nose end. Cheeks flat; great depth from eye to lower jaw. Lips deep but not too pendulous. From nose to stop perfectly straight and broad. Stop somewhat abrupt and well defined. Skull broad, with somewhat prominent brow. Nose large and black.

**EYES**
Rather small and deep-set, dark in colour, the lower eyelid dropping so as to show a fair amount of haw at the inner corner, the upper eyelid falling well over the eye.

**EARS**
Of medium size lying close to the cheeks, and not heavily feathered.

**MOUTH**
Level.

**NECK**
Lengthy, thick, muscular, and slightly arched, with dewlap well developed.

**FOREQUARTERS**
Shoulders broad and sloping, well up at the withers. Legs perfectly straight, strong in bone and of good length.

**BODY**
Back broad and straight, ribs well rounded. Loin wide and very muscular. Chest wide and deep. The lower part should not project below the elbows.

**HINDQUARTERS**
Legs heavy in bone, hocks well bent and thighs very muscular.

**FEET**
Large and compact with well-arched toes. Dewclaws should be removed.

**TAIL**
Set on rather high, long, and in long-coated variety well feathered. Carried low when in repose, and when excited or in motion should not be curled over the back.

**COAT**
Orange, mahogany-brindle, red-brindle; white with patches on body of any of the above-named colours. The markings should be as follows: white muzzle, white blaze on face, white collar round neck, white chest, white forelegs, feet and end of tail; black shadings on face and ears.

**WEIGHT AND SIZE**
The taller the better, provided that symmetry is maintained. Minimum at withers is 27½ inches.

**FAULTS**
Over- or undershot mouth; light or staring eyes; curly coat; open or hare feet; cow hocks.

big breeds, exercise is not much of a problem, and country life is not absolutely essential so long as sufficient living space is available and open ground within easy distance. At one time the St Bernard was the most popular dog in Britain.

The St Bernard may truly be described as a dog of the mountains. It is not the only Swiss breed able to make such a claim. The Sennenhunde—Swiss Mountain Dog—shares a common ancestry with the Hospice dogs, as both are descendants of the same ancient mastiff-type dog from Asia. The chief of the Sennenhunde dogs is the Bernese. Principally a herding and guarding dog, it was also used as a draught animal harnessed to a cart.

Apart from its obvious great strength and solidity, one of the Bernese's most arresting features is its colour which is mainly a lustrous raven black with the richest of brilliant tan markings above the eyes, on the cheeks and on the legs. A white chest, feet and blaze on the muzzle bring out the depth of the other colours in striking contrast, on a longish, slightly wavy coat.

The Bernese has the same placid friendly temperament which all the breeds of its type possess, and this makes it an ideal companion. It also has an inborn guarding instinct and is of considerable size (up to 27 inches at the shoulder).

work together to get him into a sitting position. They will lie alongside him, surrounding him with the warmth of their bodies. It is even said that, while the dogs of the Hospice were caring for a man, one member of the pack would return to the Hospice to bring help if, say a sled-stretcher was needed. Such behaviour clearly indicates that such groups of dogs have a leader who controls the rescue.

St Bernards have found their way to all parts of the world. Most of these are of the rough-coated type considered useless at the Hospice because such a coat soon became clogged with ice and snow. In any event, that coat was the result of the breed being crossed with Newfoundlands early in the last century when St Bernards risked extinction through a series of mishaps at the Hospice.

The role of the St Bernard today is that of a companion which is docile, wonderful with children, very patient and full of goodwill, ideally fitted for the sedentary existence it is often obliged and is happy to lead. This is a perfect pet for the fortunate few to whom the soaring cost of keeping a very large dog—up to 36 inches at the shoulder—is no bar, not forgetting the amount of room it needs. Unlike some

*The Pyrenean Mountain dog is rapidly growing in popularity, partly because of its spectacular white coat*

his makes it a breed of many possibilities, as a cattle and sheepdog, or draught dog.

It would be inappropriate to talk of the Bernese without mentioning other forms of Sennenhunde, the Appenzell and Entlebuch (both named like the Bernese after the districts where they were chiefly developed), and the Great Swiss Mountain Dog. All four breeds have points in common: their strength of build, basic head shape, colour and markings. But only the Bernese has a long coat; the others are smooth-haired. At no higher than 20 inches the Entlebuch is the smallest. Up to seven inches more height makes the Great Swiss the largest, with the Appenzell in between. The two breeds are mainly used for herding, guarding and general farm work, the Great Swiss Sennenhunde being particularly adept as a draught animal because of its size.

Yet another descendant of the mastiff-type hound is found in the French Pyrenees – the Pyrenean Mountain Dog, known in America as the Great Pyrenees. It is the most spectacular, as well as the most popular, of all the Mountain Dogs.

'A dog of immense size, great majesty, keen intelligence, and kindly expression; of unsurpassed beauty and a certain elegance, all white or principally white with markings of badger, grey or varying shades of tan. In the rolling, ambling gait it shows unmistakably the purpose for which it has been bred, the strenuous work of guarding the flocks in all kinds of weather on the steep mountain slopes of the Pyrenees. The Breed Standard requires dogs to be not less than 27–30 inches, bitches 25–29 inches. The breed is heavily coated with an undercoat able to withstand the most severe weather.

After reaching the Pyrenees, probably via Spain from Asia, the breed remained virtually unrecorded for 1,000 years. It was during that time that it must have been further developed as a guard, rather than herder, of sheep. Its own physical suitability for that purpose was enhanced by the wearing of an iron collar on which were placed several rows of spikes an inch-and-a-half long, so that wolves, bears and bandits who preyed on the sheep could not get a hold of the dog's vulnerable part, the neck. Later, the breed was used as a general guard dog.

Two hundred years ago the Pyrenean's thousand years of isolation were ended when one of the breed was taken to the French court of Louis XIV by the Dauphin and Mme de Maintenon. Though much admired there, that sort of patronage did nothing to halt a decline in numbers of the breed, caused by a reduction in the population of wolves and bears, natural enemies of sheep. The Pyrenean owes much of its strength of numbers today to the importation by America and Britain between the wars of some of the best specimens to be found in France.

An adaptable dog, needing less room than its apparent bulk would suggest, it should not be forgotten when considering the Pyrenean as a companion that, because of its past, the guarding instinct is still exceptionally well developed. Managed properly, this kind of devotion to its family can be channelled sensibly, especially when there are children in the house. But care in upbringing, given both to its physical and mental needs, must be exercised if an unmanageable and therefore potentially dangerous (because of its size) animal is not to result.

Sadly, there are people who have jumped on the bandwagon of the Pyrenean's rising popularity solely in the hope of making money. Such individuals do not much care about the sort of animal they breed – including its temperament – so long as the result is financially satisfactory. So avoid these people if you wish to buy one of this breed. It really is worth the effort of seeking out a dedicated breeder – there are plenty of them – so that you may be sure of enjoying to the full all of the assets a Pyrenean has to offer and also contribute to the success of the breed.

*One of the Bernese's most attractive features is its colourful, slightly wavy coat, which is black, brilliant tan and white*

# Four breeds of working dog

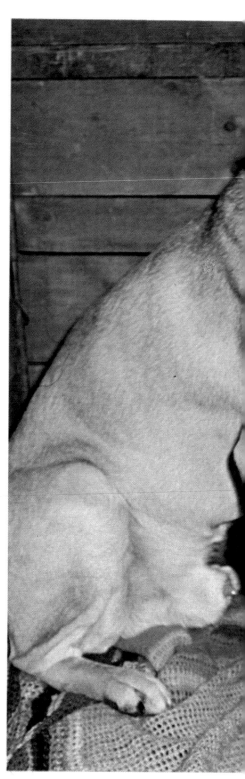

THE history of the Rottweiler goes as far back as the Roman Empire, when the breed was used by the Roman legions as a cattle driver and a guard for their supply dumps. The breed came into Germany with the invading Roman legions, who brought their dogs with them. In the days when the meat of an army travelled as live cattle, the Romans recruited numbers of the big dogs from the Italian cattle pastures to work the herds, and some of these were taken to the town of Rottweil in Würtenberg. When the Romans left, many of their dogs stayed behind, and thus the breed took its name from the ancient town. The local butchers found them ideal for guarding and herding cattle, as well as being heavy enough to serve as draught animals. During the Middle Ages and until the nineteenth century, merchants used the Rottweiler as a personal guard and to protect their money against thieves. They would hang their purses round the dog's neck before going to town.

The breed became almost extinct when laws were passed forbidding the driving of cattle. This resulted in the beasts being carried by rail, and made the services of

*Though no longer as popular as it was a hundred years ago, the Newfoundland (above) is still an impressive and handsome breed. The Anatolian Karabash dog (right) is an ancient breed still used as a working dog by Turkish shepherds in Anatolia*

the dogs unnecessary. The breed was saved from destruction when it was found that it trained well as a police dog. This dog of character is now highly thought of in Germany as a guard and companion. It has a steady following in the USA, Australasia and Britain, being introduced into the last named country in 1936.

The Rottweiler is a big and active dog with a great capacity for outdoor work. Highly suitable for farm life, the breed is a good all-round dog and a diligent, steady worker. It needs to be able to roam, and so does not adapt well to city life. It is both tender and protective towards the family it lives with. Measuring from 23 to 25 inches at the shoulder for bitches and 25 to 27 inches for dogs, the Rottweiler has a head of medium length with a well-defined stop. The muzzle is only of medium length. The body is strong with a deep chest, the back being

short and the loins strong and deep. The tail is short and placed level with the back. The coat is short, flat and coarse, a little longer on the back of the legs and on the tail. The colour is black with clearly defined markings which are tan to mahogany brown on the cheeks, muzzle, chest, legs, and over both eyes. Sturdy, alert and intelligent, the Rottweiler is an affectionate, obedient and loyal companion.

In Britain the Rottweiler has had a chequered existence. In 1936 the breed was first imported into the country by Thelma Gray, international show judge, breeder and owner of the famous Rozavel

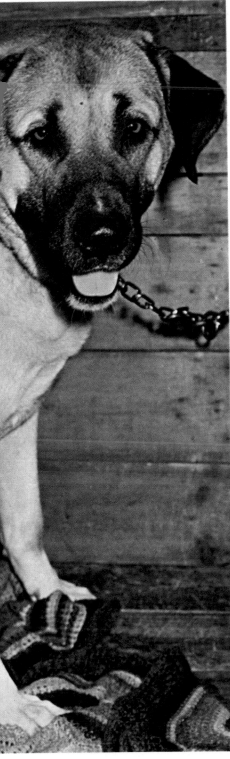

devoted to the well-being of the Rottweiler came into existence in Heidelberg in 1907, and numbers increased fairly rapidly in the years that followed. There was a setback, however, during the Second World War, and while the situation was not so desperate as it was in Britain, breed numbers were reduced.

It is to the credit of the German breeders that they set very high standards for the Rottweiler, emphasizing that first and foremost the dog's working qualities were to be given due consideration, its physical beauty being second in importance to the ability to work. The breed society exercises a very strict control over

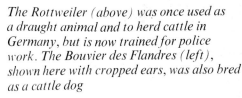

*The Rottweiler (above) was once used as a draught animal and to herd cattle in Germany, but is now trained for police work. The Bouvier des Flandres (left), shown here with cropped ears, was also bred as a cattle dog*

its members, to the extent that every district has a breed warden who inspects Rottweiler litters and decides which puppies are to be retained for breeding purposes. To ensure that the puppies are well fed, not more than six are allowed in a litter—any in excess of this number being destroyed. Furthermore, the breed society issues certificates of suitability for breeding, and without this no dog or bitch can be used for breeding.

What does the breed society look for when assessing a dog or bitch for breeding purposes? It judges the animal's temperament, and will fault it for nervousness or a lack of sufficient guarding instinct. It looks at its general appearance and in particular at its teeth. The dog being inspected must not have a faulty bite, and it must not suffer from either cryptochordism (where the testicles have not descended into the scrotum) or mono-

Kennels, and a contributor to *World of Pets*. But before the breed had time to establish itself firmly, the Second World War broke out, and throughout the war years no puppies of this breed were born. It was not until after the war, when Britain had an army of occupation in Germany, that a young veterinary surgeon brought back a Rottweiler dog and bitch, and from this pair a start was made. The breed, although only slowly, is now gaining in favour with the public on both sides of the Atlantic.

As is to be expected, the breed is well established in Germany. The first club

# Breed Standard: the Newfoundland

**CHARACTERISTICS**
A water dog, used for life-saving; should have an exceptionally gentle and docile nature.

**GENERAL APPEARANCE**
Strong and active; moving freely on his legs with the body swung loosely between them; a slight roll in gait.

**HEAD AND SKULL**
Broad and massive; the occipital bone well developed; no decided stop; the muzzle short, clean-cut and rather square in shape and covered with short, fine hair.

**EYES**
Small, dark brown; rather deeply set but not showing any haw; rather wide apart.

**EARS**
Small, set well back, square with the skull, close to the head, covered with short hair.

**MOUTH**
Soft and well covered by the lips, neither under- nor overshot but teeth level; scissor bite.

**NECK**
Should be strong, well set onto shoulders and back.

**FOREQUARTERS**
Legs should be perfectly straight, well covered with muscle. Elbows in but well let down; feathered all down.

**BODY**
Well ribbed up with broad back and strong loins. Chest deep and fairly broad; well covered with hair, but not so as to form a frill.

**HINDQUARTERS**
Very strong. The legs should have great freedom of action; feathered.

**FEET**
Large and well shaped.

**TAIL**
Of moderate length, fair thickness and well covered with hair, but not to form a flag. When standing still it should hang downwards with a slight curve at the end; but when in motion should be carried up, and when excited straight out.

**COAT**
Flat and dense, coarse and oily, water-resistant. If brushed the wrong way it falls back into place naturally.

**COLOUR**
Dull jet black, white and black, or bronze.

**WEIGHT AND SIZE**
Average height for a dog is 28 inches, weight 140-150 lbs; for a bitch 26 inches, 110-120 lbs.

**FAULTS**
Weak or hollow back, slackness of loins, splayed or turned-out feet. Kinked or curled tail.

chordism (where only one testicle has descended). Such examinations ensure that pedigree Rottweilers in Germany achieve a very high standard; even those not exhibited at shows are nevertheless a credit to the breed.

The puppies develop quickly and because of this, extra special care is needed. The diet must be absolutely first class, with supplements given to ensure that all the necessary vitamins are provided. A fine balance has to be struck so that too much exercise is not given too soon. And with this breed, early socialization is important. This trouble is repaid, however, by the strong constitution and good health of the adult dog. When fully grown the Rottweiler needs only daily grooming; it does not require trimming unless, for the sake of general tidiness, the tail hairs are trimmed with scissors. Remember to take great care when doing this.

In Britain and America the breed is chiefly regarded as a companion dog with good guarding qualities, but on the Continent its capabilities as a working dog are put to good use. In Finland it is used for pulling sledges; in Norway its hardiness and scenting ability are employed in mountain rescue work; in Denmark, Austria and Germany the breed is used for police work and in the latter by the army and the customs authorities as well.

For such a big dog–bitches weigh from 90 to 108 lb, dogs from 115 to 125 lb–the Rottweiler has a remarkable spring, its powerful hindquarters enabling it to jump a distance of up to 10 feet with one bound. Do not be deceived by its rather heavy appearance!

Greatly beloved by Victorian and Edwardian artists and writers, the Newfoundland was once a common sight as it padded its stately way through the streets. No longer a popular breed, the occasional sight of one of these large dogs still excites admiration.

The Newfoundland is named after the Canadian island of that name. Its exact origin is unknown but it is suggested that it started with a number of Pyrenean Mountain dogs which were brought to Newfoundland by Basque and French sailors in the seventeenth century, and mated with the native dogs or with Huskies. It is thought that dogs from these crosses were then taken to England, where they were carefully bred to produce the handsome dog we know today. Another theory is that the Beothuk Indians, who migrated from Canada, brought with them the large tribal dogs. There is also reason to believe that the Viking, Leif Erikson, established colonies in Newfoundland, leaving there numbers of the dogs so beloved of the Vikings and that these were the ancestors of the modern breed.

The Newfoundland is the best water dog in the world; there are many recorded instances of people being rescued from the frozen seas of Newfoundland and elsewhere. Affectionate towards humans, and children in particular, the gentle and faithful Newfoundland has a long history of service to mankind. It is strong enough to handle freight, and is an alert guard and a willing worker, so it is certain that its many admirers will not allow the breed to die out.

Weighing from 110 to 120 lb for bitches, and for dogs from 140 to 150 lb, with a height at the withers of 27 to 28 inches for dogs, and 25 to 26 inches for bitches, the Newfoundland is a very strong dog with a massive head and a muscular, powerful body. It needs at least two hours' exercise a day, preferably in the country. The coat is flat, coarse, dense, oily and highly resistant to water. The colour is a dull, jet black with sometimes a tinge of bronze or white on the chest and toes. Any colour other than black should follow the blacks in all respects except in colour, which may be almost any, black-and-white (Landseer), chocolate or bronze being especially encouraged.

The Newfoundland has a sweet disposition, is even tempered and completely stable. Not at all nervous, either of people or of other dogs (whose companionship it will often seek out), the breed is absolutely devoted to its family which it will guard with its life. Therefore, if a companion and protector for the family is wanted, the Newfoundland is the ideal dog to buy.

Like the Rottweiler, the Newfoundland has had a chequered career in Britain, due chiefly to the Second World War which reduced its numbers to about a dozen pedigree dogs in the whole of the country. It was first shown, so some experts believe, at the Birmingham Dog Show in 1860 when six of the breed were entered. They excited considerable interest and at another show two years later no less than 41 breed entries were exhibited. The Newfoundland Breed Club was established in Britain in 1886, and it drew up the Standard for the breed which was later adopted in most continental countries and in America.

Another feature shared by the Newfoundland and Rottweiler is hardiness. An owner will not be faced by a succession of bills for veterinary services. It must be stressed, however, that to keep the dog at its best its coat must be well combed: five minutes a day will be sufficient. The dog will nearly always shed its coat in the summer and this must be combed out. It is essential, too, to keep ears clean and the hair behind the ears well combed. Give the breed plenty of road work to arden its muscles, as these must be kept hard, not flabby.

The Bouvier des Flandres is an old breed which was bred by the butchers, cattlemen and farmers of southwest Flanders and the northern hills of France as a cattle dog. The word 'bouvier' means cowherd or ox driver, but the breed has also been known as the Vuilbaard, Koehond, and Toucheur de Boeuf—which roughly translated mean dirty beard, cow dog and cattle driver respectively. The early dogs were far from uniform in colour, type or size. They were big, shaggy animals with rough and tangled coats, and were intelligent working dogs but few were kept as domestic pets until breeders took steps to bring uniformity to the breed in 1910. In 1912 the Standard was adopted. Unfortunately, just as many fine specimens were being produced, the country was decimated by the outbreak of the First World War. Luckily, a few dogs survived and it is from this stock that the present day Bouviers are descended.

The Bouvier is a powerfully built dog; its back is short and straight, and its ribs are deep and well sprung. The legs are muscular with round and compact feet. The tail is set on high and docked to about four inches in length. The coat is rough and appears to be unkempt, but it is wiry and dense and capable of withstanding the worst weather. Daily grooming is necessary to prevent tangles which will be difficult to comb out if neglected.

The head is of medium length with a shallow stop, the ears sometimes cropped where the law allows (such as on the continent), and the eyes are intelligent and set fairly close together. The long hair on the muzzle and underjaw forms a beard and moustache. The Bouvier is usually a dark, nut-brown colour, 'pepper-and-salt', grey, or brindle, but black is not considered a fault in the show ring. Weight for a dog should be from 65 to 70 lb and height 23½ to 27½ inches; for a bitch 70 to 75 lb and height 22¾ to 27 inches.

The breed is very sensitive, yet spirited, being rather rough and boisterous. It is loyal, affectionate and devoted to its family and to children. It is not really suited to town life.

The Anatolian Karabash dog is considered by the Anatolian shepherds of Turkey to be the finest dog in the world. A large dog, (it can be as much as 30 inches at the shoulder) it is very swift and powerful and quite capable of fighting off any predators, animal or human, that attack the flocks. Its ears are cropped close to the head in those countries that allow it, and it wears a spiked collar to protect its throat from wolves. It weighs from 90 to 150 lb.

This very ancient breed is thought to have descended from the race of huge mastiffs known to have existed some three thousand years ago in the Middle East. Even today the dogs bear a very strong resemblance to the Babylonian bas-reliefs picturing the lion-hunting dogs trained by the Assyrian kings. A few specimens have been imported to America and Britain but have not yet won popularity, although the Anatolian Karabash Dog Club was formed in the UK in 1968.

The Anatolian Karabash dog is an impressive animal. It has a large head and a broad skull. The ears, when uncropped, are of medium size, V-shaped and pendant in carriage. The eyes are golden brown, set well apart in a broad skull, and vision is acute. The body is strong and powerful with slightly arched loins; the back is long and the chest deep. The tail is long and carried low, but carried high over the back when in action. Short and dense, the coat is weather-resistant; its colour can be cream to fawn, or striped brindle, with black mask and ears. Height is from 26 to 30 inches.

The breed is intelligent, cheerful, loyal and always ready to protect its owner or his property. Like all pastoral dogs, it needs plenty of exercise and space in which to gallop.

*The Newfoundland is of aquatic habits. The black-and-white variety is called Landseer after the painter*

# Breed Standard: the Shetland Sheepdog

**GENERAL APPEARANCE**
The Shetland Sheepdog should instantly appeal as a dog of great beauty, intelligence and alertness. Action lithe and graceful with speed and jumping power great for its size. The outline should be symmetrical so that no part appears out of proportion to the whole.

**HEAD AND SKULL**
The head should be refined and its shape when viewed from the top or side is a long blunt wedge tapering from ear to nose. The skull should be flat, moderately wide between the ears, showing no prominence of the occipital bone. Teeth should be sound and level, with an evenly spaced scissor bite.

**EARS**
Should be small and moderately wide at the base. Tips should break forward.

**NECK**
The neck should be muscular, well arched and of sufficient length to carry the head proudly.

**BODY AND QUARTERS**
The body is slightly longer from the withers to the root of the tail than the height at the withers, but most of the length is due to the proper angulation of the shoulders and hindquarters. The chest should be deep reaching to the point of the elbow. The ribs well sprung but tapering at their lower half to allow free play of the forelegs and shoulders.

**TAIL**
Set on low, tapering bone must reach at least to the hock joint, with abundant hair and slight upward sweep.

**FEET**
Oval in shape, soles well padded, toes arched.

**COAT**
Must be double, the outer coat of long hair of harsh texture and straight, the under coat soft (resembling fur) short and close. The mane and frill should be very abundant.

**COLOUR**
Tricolours should be an intense black on the body with no signs of ticking, rich tan markings on a tricolour to be preferred. Sables may be clear or shaded, any colour from gold to deep mahogany. Wolf sable and grey colours undesirable. Blue Merles, clear silvery blue is desired, splashed and marbled with black. White markings may be shown in the blaze, collar, frill, legs, stifle and tail tip.

**SIZE**
Ideal height at the withers is 14 inches for bitches, 14½ for dogs. In USA 13-16 inches.

**FAULTS**
Domed or receding skull, lack of stop, large drooping or pricked ears, over-developed cheeks, weak jaw, snipy muzzle, not full complement of teeth, crooked forelegs, cow hocks. Pink or flesh colour nose, blue eyes in any other colour than merles.

THE Shetland Sheepdog, affectionately and unofficially called the Sheltie, is an intelligent, beautiful dog, ideal as a family pet and companion. Indeed, for this smallest of all Sheepdog breeds, human companionship is absolutely essential. The Sheltie is such an individualist and responds so deeply to love and attention that it appears at its best when there is not too much outside competition, and it is kept either on its own or with, say, one other dog.

Unlike many other breeds, the Sheltie tends to be a 'one-person' rather than a 'one-family' dog. Although devoted to the entire family, it will single out its favourite member. The intelligent Sheltie is easy to train and is always happier when given a specific job than when left to its own devices. This does not mean that a Sheltie must have a herd of sheep to work–few of them have this opportunity–but the dog likes to feel it is being useful, which may involve lending a hand on the farm, being a constant companion or just being helpful about the house. It can derive much pleasure from picking up objects that have been dropped, and it is clever enough to be taught the names of specific items and to fetch them when so instructed.

The Sheltie is happy by nature, eager to please and quick to adapt to its owner's moods and habits. It will enjoy a five-mile walk should its owner be energetic, but it is not demanding. Some exercise is, of course, necessary for the good of its health, but it can get enough from a romp in the garden or from playing with the younger members of the family. The dog is usually very fond of children and will often appoint itself unofficial 'nanny', but if this happens adults must take care that the dog, especially when young, gets a fair deal. Rather than resist rough treatment from a youngster, a Sheltie might prefer to 'suffer in silence', so it does need some measure of protection from this sort of exuberance. A puppy, in particular, needs plenty of rest and sleep.

The ideal Sheltie only stands some 13 or 16 inches high at maturity and is therefore very suitable for a smallish house or even a flat, provided it is exercised daily. It is a reliable watch dog, thanks to its extreme alertness. Although at one time the breed had a reputation for being shy or nervous, this is no longer the case. The Standard describes its temperament accurately in stating that it 'should show affection and response to his owner; he may show reserve towards strangers, but never to the point of nervousness.'

Being small, the Sheltie does not eat a great deal but, like any dog, should be fed at regular intervals. If a puppy is bought from a reputable kennel a diet sheet, covering the early months, will be provided. When the dog is adult, from about nine months of age, it will require at least one meal a day, and some breeders insist upon feeding twice daily. The ideal diet is raw meat in some form, but this can be varied several days each week by substituting any of the excellent tinned foods nowadays available. For the first meal of the day the dog should have milk and cereals, occasionally with the addition of a lightly cooked egg. For the main meal it needs about half a pound of food, not a very expensive proposition. Fresh water must also be constantly available.

The coat colours of the Shetland Sheepdog are mainly sable, tricolour and blue merle, although black-and-white and black-and-tan are also recognized. The first three colours can carry white markings on the collar, legs, feet, tip of the tail and blaze. Sable is any shade from pale yellow to deep mahogany and is the most dominant of all the coat colours. A tricoloured dog is black with tan markings on the cheeks, over the eyes, inside the legs, under the tail and also has a white collar. The blue merle is possibly the most sought-after colour, and the most difficult to produce. It is a modification of black, due to a dilution factor in the genetic pattern. A perfect blue merle should be a silvery blue, dappled and splashed with black. A white collar, chest, feet, legs and tip of the tail are all permissible. The eyes may be blue and although the nose should be black as in the other colours, a slight amount of pink would not be penalized so heavily as in the other colours. The blue merle pattern cannot appear unless at least one parent is a blue merle. The best combination is to cross a tricolour with a blue merle. When merle is crossed to merle there is a danger that defective white puppies, born blind, deaf or deformed, might result. Colour breeding in Shelties is very difficult, as it is not predictable as in other breeds, owing to the various genetic changes that have taken place in the breed. The black-and-white colouration crops up from almost every possible colour combination and is totally unpredictable. The black-and-tan, although still recognized in the standard, appears to have become extinct.

The adult Sheltie carries a heavy coat, like that of a Collie, but grooming is not a great problem. Some owners like to groom daily, others consider that once a week is sufficient. Combing is not normally advisable as this risks breaking the hair. A thorough brushing is usually adequate, but when the dog is moulting it should be combed daily to get rid of the dead coat as quickly as possible and allow the new one to grow fast. Stand the dog on newspaper, to catch the loose hairs.

Because of accumulated grime, a town dog requires more frequent brushing than one living in the country. In the latter case, where there is plenty of opportunity for running and playing in long grass, much of the grooming is already done naturally. Bathing a Sheltie is seldom, if ever, necessary, except perhaps to clean its white collar, legs and front.

The origins of the Shetland Sheepdog are obscure, but the fact that it is a native of the Shetland Islands explains its diminutive size. The ponies, cattle and sheep of these islands are all much smaller than their mainland counterparts, so that in order to tend sheep of reduced size this little working Collie was evidently evolved.

In the early days it was a rather nonde-script animal, bred simply for the work in hand. Since the dog had to work in all weathers–in drenching rain and heavy snow as well as during the long, hot days of summer–it had to be extremely tough and hardy. What was required was a really weather-resistant double coat to protect it from wet and cold, in addition to keeping it cool in the heat. Selective breeding must have been carried on to establish both the working characteristics and the necessary coat, but for little else. Thus, during these early days, the little working sheepdogs tended to be unpredictable in type, varying enor-mously. It is only since it became a breed, recognized by the Kennel Club in 1914, that dedicated breeders have succeeded in producing the delightful little dog we know today.

In order to obtain the desired type of Sheltie, the Rough Collie was used as a cross in the early years, and this produced a problem of size. Careful selection then took place to reduce the size again, while retaining the other qualities. Over the years this proved successful, and although one does find oversize Shelties occasion-ally, the big one in the litter is becoming more and more rare, while type is being maintained.

Since the early 1900s various clubs have been established to look after the interests of the breed. Although some have vanished, there are now a number of Shetland Sheepdog Clubs in various parts of Britain, so that the breed is certainly in good hands.

The natural 'reserve' of the breed is one of its true characteristics and must be maintained. For this reason it may not be everyone's dog. But should you 'fall' for a Sheltie, you will never regret intro-ducing this delightful dog into your family circle.

*The Shetland Sheepdog, or 'Sheltie' as it is often called, was originally used for herding sheep. Nowadays it is more often kept as a family pet, and makes an excellent housedog*

# Chapter VII
# Non-sporting Dogs
# Toy Group

# The Chihuahua

THE owners of this diminutive dog claim that it is the smallest breed of dog in the world. The fact that adult specimens occasionally weigh between one-and-a-half and two pounds supports their view, although the majority of the best show dogs weigh between three and four-and-a-half pounds and there are one or two other Toy breeds that bear comparison with this size and weight.

The Chihuahua was named after the famous state of Chihuahua in Mexico and it was here that the breed first came to the attention of dog lovers. Travellers from America were among the first to take home with them the tiny creatures known as Chihuahua dogs. Historians interested in this ancient and fascinating breed have endeavoured to trace its development but unfortunately there is very little real evidence of its origins.

All sorts of stories have originated about them. It has been suggested that they were a race of tiny wild animals, some of which had become domesticated. If this breed was a wild animal in its original state, it must have altered greatly in recent years and must now differ entirely from the foundation stock. The modern Chihuahua, though not as fragile as it looks, is not fitted for a struggle for existence in the Mexican deserts and wild stretches of country, in a climate that varies from bitter cold to extreme heat.

Chihuahuas are also said to have been the sacred dogs of the Aztec and Toltec Indians, sometimes revered and represented by pottery figurines in tombs and pyramids, sometimes bred and fattened to be eaten. The strongest archaeological evidence of their association with the Aztec Indians was found in Colima, Mexico, where excavations revealed pottery dogs of Chihuahua type.

Some people believe that the Chihuahua was a small dog brought into Mexican territories and developed there. The most convincing explanation has been put forward by Mrs Eileen Goodchild who undertook a considerable amount of research into the origins of this breed. Mrs Goodchild's conclusions led her to believe that the breed had been developed in Malta and that when a Spanish expedition, under Hernando Cortez, set out to conquer Mexico in 1519, his soldiers and sailors took these dogs with them as pets. Certainly it is beyond dispute that very small dogs of the Chihuahua type have existed on Malta for hundreds of years.

To North American breeders must go the credit for laying the foundations of the breed. They have produced a small dog which is very different from its early ancestors, with the various colours between pure white and jet black. Black with tan markings is the favourite Mexican colour, but the USA prefers solid colours. Smooth coats are still the most popular but the long-coated variety is receiving a great deal of attention from American breeders and is gaining in popularity.

Chihuahuas were first imported into Britain in quite a small way, but numbers grew very quickly and soon the English Kennel Club recognized the breed as having sufficient numbers to qualify for registration as well as entitlement to compete for Challenge Certificates at major shows. It is by no means uncommon to see 200 Chihuahuas at an important Championship show. An entry such as this will usually be divided fairly equally between smooth-coated and long-coated Chihuahuas.

The original imports into Britain were all smooth-coated and only after some years had elapsed did the first long-coats come over from America. These were not popular at first, perhaps because they were rather different in type from the well-established smooth-coated dogs. Much to the surprise of breeders, however, even those who had bred solely from smooths found that occasionally long-coated puppies were cropping up in litters bred from smooth sires and dams. This process led to the appearance at shows of good quality long-coated Chihuahuas and the endearing appearance of these dogs helped to attract more and more people to the growing circle of Chihuahua exhibitors.

Apart from its minute size, the Breed Standard for the Chihuahua requires certain definite characteristics. There are two varieties: smooth-coated and long-coated. The former have coats that are short, very fine, glossy and in no way rough, curly or thick. The latter have long, fine hair, often slightly wavy and the best specimens are embellished with profuse feathering on ears, legs and tail, and have well-covered bodies and fluffy hair on the back legs. Apart from this distinct difference in coat, the two varieties should be exactly the same in size, type and conformation.

A good Chihuahua weighs under six pounds, the most popular weight for showing and breeding varying between three-and-a-half and four-and-a-half pounds. The head should be round. The ears are large, wide-set and flaring, and the 'stop'–the indentation between the eyes–is very steep and vertical. A skull that slopes gradually towards the muzzle

---

## Breed Standard: the Chihuahua

**CHARACTERISTICS**
An alert and swift-moving little dog with a saucy expression.

**GENERAL APPEARANCE**
Small, dainty and compact with a brisk forceful action.

**HEAD AND SKULL**
A well-rounded 'Apple Dome' skull with or without Molera, cheeks and jaws lean, nose moderately short, slightly pointed. Definite stop.

**EYES**
Full, round, set well apart, dark or ruby.

**EARS**
Large, set on at an angle of about 45 degrees.

**MOUTH**
Level, scissor bite.

**NECK**
Slightly arched, of medium length.

**FOREQUARTERS**
Shoulders should be well up, lean, sloping into a slightly broadening support above straight forelegs that are set well under, giving free play at the elbows.

**BODY**
Level back, slightly longer than the height at shoulder. Well-sprung ribs with deep brisket.

**HINDQUARTERS**
Muscular with hocks well apart, neither out nor in, well let down.

**FEET**
Small with toes well split up, but not spread, pads cushioned. Fine pasterns (neither 'Hare' nor 'Cat' foot). A dainty foot, with nails moderately long.

**TAIL**
Medium length carried up or over the back. Preferred furry, flattish in appearance, broadening slightly in the centre and tapering to a point. In long-coated dogs the tail should be long and full as a plume.

**COAT**
Shorthair: smooth, of soft texture, close and glossy. Longhair: Long, of soft texture (never coarse or harsh to the touch), either flat or slightly wavy. No tight curly coat. There should be feathering on the feet and legs, pants on the hindlegs; a large ruff on the neck is desired and preferred.

**COLOUR**
Any colour or mixture of colours.

**WEIGHT**
Up to six pounds, with two to four pounds preferable. If two dogs are equally good in type, the more diminutive preferred.

**FAULTS**
Cropped tail, brokendown ears.

is most undesirable. The muzzle is short and only slightly pointed. The eyes are large and lustrous but never prominent or 'bolting'. Many Chihuahuas have ruby eyes which shine red in certain lights and at certain angles. Eye rims, lips and noses are often black but can be light in light-coloured dogs. Such light points are perfectly correct and often greatly admired by experts, although ill-informed judges have been known to penalize them.

The head of the Chihuahua is of paramount importance but this does not mean that the rest of the dog can be discounted. A fair length of neck is required, for a dog with a short neck looks stuffy and too compact. The body is of medium length and the back perfectly straight. Early Chihuahua breeders found that humped and roached backs were prevalent but by careful breeding this ugly fault has been largely eliminated and is now very rare. The leg bone should be fine. Coarse, thick, spongy bone detracts from the required dainty appearance and spoils the look of the animal. The front legs must be perfectly straight, elbows neat and not projecting and pasterns and toes neither turning in nor out.

Feet are best described as oval. A catlike foot is not true to type, neither is a very long hare-like foot, but the ideal Chihuahua foot is certainly longer than it is round. The toes are well split up and the nails are rather long. Such nails should, however, be kept trimmed either by exercising the dog on hard surfaces or by clipping at regular intervals. The hind legs are well angulated and the hocks vertical when viewed from the rear. As in many other breeds, cow hocks are a bad fault. Some years ago the condition known as *patella luxation* greatly concerned breeders, as it caused a bad hind action and general unsoundness. This condition is by no means unknown today. Breeders are working hard to eliminate it by using sound stock for breeding.

A well-constructed Chihuahua is a smart, active mover, thrusting with its hindquarters as it reaches forward with its straight forelegs. Shoulder formation is of some importance since a straight shoulder inhibits free front movement, resulting in a jerky, strutting stride. The Chihuahua tail is a great breed characteristic. While most puppies and young dogs have rounded tails, mature Chihuahuas have very unusual, flattened tails, smooth at the root and at the tip but furry down each side. This flat tail is more typical of the Chihuahua breed than any other characteristic.

It is a curious fact that many Chihuahuas are born with a molera, which is a small opening on top of the skull similar to that known as a fontanelle in human babies. Whereas the opening on an infant's skull gradually closes, it is quite usual for a Chihuahua to keep this opening throughout its life. Particular care must always be taken to make sure that larger dogs or well-meaning children are not allowed to play roughly with Chihuahuas, since a blow on the head can have fatal consequences. At one time it was suggested that the molera was peculiar to the Chihuahua and that its presence was desirable as indicating a pure breed. This idea has recently been discounted since moleras have been noted in other small Toy dogs.

Chihuahuas come in a great variety of colours. According to ancient Mexican history, the most sought-after colours were red or clay-coloured and blue. These colours are still popular today but there are many variations, such as solid black; white with black, brown or blue patches; chocolate; chocolate and tan; chocolate and white; various shades of red, fawn, gold, cream and sable, either solid or marked or patched with white. Solid white is also seen, as is black marked with tan, fawn or gold. All colours are acceptable. This is just as well, since colour-breeding,

*Left: 1971 Cruft's winner Ch Rozavel Tarima Song; right: a long-haired black*

possible in some other breeds of dogs, is hazardous in Chihuahuas which, when mated, are totally unpredictable. Blue has always been the rare colour and the most difficult to breed. Because certain breeders have made an effort to establish blues, there are many more about today.

Because the Chihuahua breed has only been firmly established in Britain since the end of the last war, it has taken time to establish a correct type and to educate British judges to appreciate it. Only in recent years have judges given Chihuahuas top honours at the most important shows. 1971 was a milestone in the history of the breed. In February of that year a long-coated Chihuahua bitch, Champion Rozavel Tarima Song was judged to be Best Bitch in Show, and runner-up to Best in Show at Crufts where this superb specimen defeated well over 8000 of Britain's best show dogs. A few months later the same bitch was judged Best in Show at Paignton Championship Show.

In common with all small toy breeds Chihuahuas are not especially easy to breed. The smaller specimens may require expert veterinary attention at whelping time and caesarian operations are not uncommon. No Chihuahua should be left to give birth to its puppies unattended. The average number of whelps is probably three and only the larger brood bitches may produce four or five in a litter. Once born, the puppies only require warmth and quiet, and develop normally and grow into adults without further trouble.

Unquestionably this breed possesses a number of very rare and attractive characteristics, and with the increasing tendency towards life in smaller houses and flats, the Chihuahua will always have a place with those dog lovers who seek a small dog with the brains and character one expects to find in the larger breeds.

# Four Toy Breeds

ALTHOUGH, in some cases, their origins are quite ancient, the so-called Toy dogs give the impression of having been invented specifically to play a role in our modern way of life, of being 'tailor-made', as it were, for small houses and overcrowded cities. Four such breeds of dog, all modest in size, are the English Toy Terrier (formerly known as the Black and Tan), the Japanese Chin, the Maltese and the Silky Terrier.

From the beginning of its 500-year history, the small, smooth-coated English Toy Terrier has been used in Britain for killing vermin. Nowadays this dog, known in the United States as the Toy Manchester Terrier, does not have many opportunities to display its skill as a hunter, but given the chance, it will still dispatch its traditional quarry with great efficiency and courage.

The diminutive size of this breed makes it ideal for town life. Exercise is no problem for this can easily be fitted into the owner's everyday activities. Nevertheless it should be remembered that all dogs, large and small, appreciate some variety in their routine. So even if a garden is available, alternative forms of exercise should not be neglected.

Although town and country are equally acceptable, no small breed is really suited to a home in which there are very young children. A toy dog is not, as a rule, fragile and it can endure a certain amount of rough and tumble, but an enthusiastic youngster may well be tempted to pick it up and then drop it, and no small animal can survive such treatment without eventually suffering damage.

The English Toy Terrier (or Black and Tan, to give it the name by which most people still call it) is inclined to attach itself to a particular member of the family. Although ready and willing to join in all the family fun, its master or mistress takes pride of place and is rewarded with boundless affection. Such devotion to its owner and his family makes it a reliable house dog. It will give warning of a stranger's approach, but will be happy to accept anyone who is obviously welcomed by the rest of the family.

Despite being smooth-coated and finely made, this is by no means a delicate breed. The normal household temperature is sufficient to keep this terrier comfortable, although damp and draughts will cause it much discomfort. In winter or in very cold or windy weather there is no harm in allowing it to wear a coat when leaving the house, simply because of the marked contrast in temperature.

The diet of this breed in no way differs from that of a larger dog, apart from the quantity and size of meat and biscuit. The colours of the English Toy Terriers are enhanced by a shiny coat, and this can be achieved by adding corn or olive oil to its daily ration of food.

A minimum of time need be given to grooming. Frequent hand massage of the whole body will make the best of the bloom resulting from good health and that daily teaspoonful of oil.

Essentially lively, always cheerful and happy–that is the Toy dog known as the Japanese Chin. Thousands of years of living in human company have made this most picturesque of Toy breeds seemingly capable of understanding the thoughts and wishes of its owner even before any word is spoken. Chins were to the Japanese Imperial Court what Pekingese were to the ruling houses of China–companions and playthings for the female members of the dynasty. The two breeds probably originated in China.

*The English Toy Terrier (top right), and Maltese (right) make good pets as they need little exercise and are cheap to feed*

---

# Breed Standard: the Maltese Terrier

**CHARACTERISTICS**
Sweet tempered and very intelligent.

**GENERAL APPEARANCE**
Should be smart, lively and alert. The action must be free, without extended weaving.

**HEAD AND SKULL**
From stop to centre of skull (centre between fore-part of ears) and stop to tip of nose should be equally balanced. Stop should be defined. Nose should be pure black.

**EYES**
Should be dark brown, with black eye rims, set in centre of cheeks and not bulging.

**EARS**
Should be long and well feathered and hanging close to the side of the head, the hair to be mingled with the coat at the shoulders.

**MOUTH**
Level or scissor bite with even teeth.

**NECK**
Of medium length. Set on well-sloped shoulders.

**FOREQUARTERS**
Legs should be short and straight.

**BODY**
Should be in every way well balanced and essentially short and cobby, with good rib spring. The back should be straight from the tip of the shoulders to the tail.

**HINDQUARTERS**
Legs should be short and nicely angulated.

**FEET**
Should be round and the pads of the feet should be black.

**TAIL**
Should be well arched over the back and feathered.

**COAT**
Should be good length, but not impeding action, of silky texture, not in any way woolly and should be straight. It should not be crimped, and there should be no woolly undercoat.

**COLOUR**
Pure white, but slight lemon markings should not penalize.

**SIZE**
Not over 10 inches from ground to top of shoulder.

**FAULTS**
Bad mouth, over or undershot; gay tail; curly or woolly coat; brown nose; pink eye rims; unsound in any way.

**NOTE**
Male animals should have two apparently normal testicles fully descended into the scrotum.

*The Japanese Chin (above and left) is cheerful and affectionate*

The name 'Chin' means an amalgam of dog and cat, suggesting that the Japanese were originally aiming to produce a breed of dog which looked and behaved like a cat. In the United States it is known as the Japanese Spaniel, but this is a false and misleading description since it in no way possesses any spaniel characteristics.

In the West, interest was first taken in this breed towards the end of the nineteenth century when the Princess of Wales, later Queen Alexandra, became a Chin breeder. Until a few years before her death in 1925, the dog remained a fashionable pet, but as a result of two World Wars and an ever-increasing interest in the Pekingese, the popularity of the Chin gradually waned.

In appearance the Japanese Chin has something in common with its better known relation, but it stands higher from the ground, with straight, slender legs. The head is round, with a short nose (not noseless), and the coat is fine and silky but not as long as that of the Peke. White is the predominant colour but there are bright splashes of black or alternatively any shade of brown, ranging from pale lemon to darkest chestnut. The Chin has a characteristically high-stepping gait, giving it an air of superiority which is more apparent than real.

The Chin, like the Toy Black and Tan, is equally at home in town and country. Never having been bred as a sporting dog, it does not require more exercise than is possible to obtain in an ordinary garden. It is a positive pleasure to take this dog walking in the streets, for it will greet all passers-by as long lost friends. This indiscriminate affection for people makes the Chin useless as a guard dog. If it should bark (and this is rare at the best of times) when a stranger makes an appearance, it will probably be a bark of greeting.

A normal diet keeps the Chin in good shape. It is not a finicky feeder. As with the Toy Black and Tan, oil added to the food will help keep the coat in pristine condition. Nor does grooming present any problems. Always use a pure bristle brush, never nylon, because the latter will tear the hair. The long fringes need special care, but if given attention two or three times each week they will pose no problem. Neither is any particular technique of brushing required. Thorough and regular grooming will prevent moulting from being a nuisance. It is worth bearing in mind, nevertheless, that this breed does tend to lose hair, so it is not recommended for anyone who is too houseproud.

It is a pity that the singular virtues of the Chin have not been appreciated by a wider audience. For too long it has been a specialist's dog, virtually unknown, except by breeders.

Another connoisseur's item in the canine world is the most ancient of all European Toy breeds–the Maltese. Snow-white tresses of silky hair extending to the ground make this dog the last word in glamour, and it seems to be well aware of the impression it is giving. For centuries the breed has been referred to as a staunch companion, always being praised for its beauty and intelligence.

Despite its name, the Maltese has no proven connection with Malta, although it is generally believed to have originated in the Mediterranean area. It is claimed to be the oldest breed in Europe. It was a pet of the noble ladies of ancient Egypt, Greece and Rome. The breed became established in Britain during the reign of Henry VIII. They were shown in the first dog shows held in England, and the first class specifically for Maltese dogs was held at Birmingham Show in 1864. Since then their popularity has increased rapidly, and the breed has a large following in the United States.

The Silky Terrier is a pure Australian breed created from a mixture of Yorkshire Terrier, Australian Terrier and even a possible dash of Skye blood. Whatever the mixture, it is a very fascinating little dog, highly popular with Australians living in cities or in the remote corners of the outback. It was once called the Sydney Silky and it is safe to assume that it originated in that city.

It has been known as a pure breed in Australia for over 25 years; it was first exhibited in Australia in 1907. It has been exported to Britain, the USA and India. It failed to make any impact in Britain but the AKC recognized it in 1959 and it has made a modest increase in registrations ever since.

The Silky Terrier is an attractive animal of some 8–10 lb in weight. The coat is blue and tan in colour and silky in texture. The temperament is pure terrier with all the dash and fire which the name implies. It is an intelligent breed which will thrive in almost any climate and which offers no particular problems in feeding or breeding.

*The Maltese makes an excellent companion and adapts to both town or country life*

# Continental toy breeds

A miniature Spitz, the Pomeranian is closely related to the other Arctic breeds such as the Samoyed and Elkhound, and has the typical Spitz characteristics of sharp ears, full neck 'ruff', straight hind legs, and the high tail carried well over the back. Introduced to Britain from Germany, the first Pomeranians weighed about 30 lb. At first the breed had a difficult time in becoming established. British dogs at that time were mostly of the sporting type, and a foreign dog of no particular use in the field did not create much excitement. At that time, lap dogs were considered to be a waste of time and money, and were the exception rather than the rule. When Queen Victoria took an interest in the breed in 1888 on a visit to

Florence—having one as a house pet and a number in her breeding kennels—they soared in popularity. A breed club was formed in 1891. Fifty years ago the Pomeranian was the leading Toy dog in Britain, and was only displaced by the sudden upsurge in the popularity of the Pekingese.

The Pomeranian became much smaller by selective breeding from small puppies which occurred in litters from time to time. Several unusual pastel colours were produced, until today the average weight is around 4 to 6 lb and any whole colour is acceptable, including dark and light blue, orange, brown, cream and sable. A very profuse coat is only produced by judicious feeding, and needs daily grooming to bring it to perfection. Experienced breeders

damp the hair thoroughly and then brush through carefully against the growth until dry. The coat is double, soft and fluffy underneath, with a longer topcoat of straight, harsh hair. The head is foxy, with a slightly flat, large skull, a fine muzzle and is covered with short hair. The ears are set high and carried erect, giving the characteristic alert expression, enhanced by the bright dark eyes which must be of medium size and not too full or wide-set. The short back and neck and deep, well-ribbed chest make the Pomeranian a sturdy and robust little dog. The plumed tail carried over the back is an unmistakable Spitz characteristic. Its even temperament makes it a trustworthy, vivacious pet.

Created by careful breeding from normal-sized Greyhounds more than 2,000 years ago, and depicted on early Egyptian scrolls and artifacts, the Italian Greyhound is one of the most ancient of present-day breeds. The mummified body of a small Greyhound was found in the tomb of one of the Pharoahs and it is thought that the breed existed side by side with the Saluki. It has been known for centuries in Britain and has graced the palaces of many sovereigns, including that of Queen Anne whose portrait in Hampton Court Palace shows this gracious lady surrounded by several of them.

Some people have said that the Whippet was used to miniaturize the breed, but there is no evidence to prove this. Indeed it was the Italian Greyhound which was used to improve the type of the Whippet in the early days of that breed. Italian Greyhound blood was also used to improve the stock of the English Toy Terrier.

The satin-skinned Italian Greyhound was never intended for sporting purposes and is too delicate to be allowed out in inclement weather without a coat. It is an intelligent and extremely obedient house pet, easy to train and groom, and very attractive with its clean lines and unique high-stepping action.

The breed was at its most popular during Victorian times. At the turn of the century it was discovered that some breeders had been introducing Toy Terrier blood into the breed in order to reduce the size. This had resulted in destroying the true character of the Italian Greyhound. When the Italian Greyhound Club was founded in 1900 it began to take drastic steps to revive the breed. After World War One, two lovely dogs were imported from America which helped to correct the faults which had developed in British stock. World War Two had a disastrous effect on breeding and stock in Europe was nearly wiped out

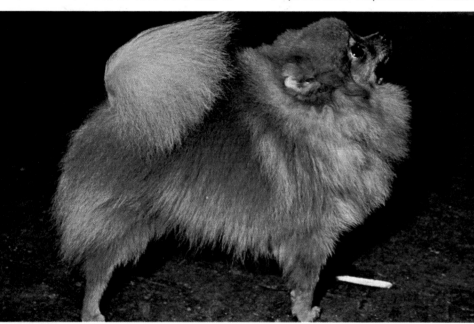

*Top left: the Pomeranian has the sharp ears, curled tail and neck 'ruff' typical of all Spitz breeds. Left: the Papillon is a toy spaniel*

By 1952 the numbers of the breed in Britain had declined so much that only five registrations were recorded by the Kennel Club that year. However, fresh blood was imported from Italy and thanks to some dedicated breeders, numbers gradually rose until by 1972 the breed was again firmly established.

The desired height of the breed is 10 inches at the shoulder and the weight should be from 6 to 8 lb. It should have a long, flat and narrow head with a fine muzzle, rose-shaped ears placed well back on the head and large, bright eyes full of expression. The long and gracefully arched neck is set into long, sloping shoulders; the chest is deep and narrow and the back curved, drooping at the quarters. The forelegs are straight, and the hind legs muscular with well let down hocks. The tail is long and fine with a low carriage. According to the Breed Standard the acceptable colours are fawn, blue, slate, black-and-fawn, cream, white and pied. The Italian Greyhound is a Toy dog with grace, symmetry and beauty.

The Papillon is a dainty breed that gets its name from the French word for 'butterfly', for these toy spaniels not only have large fringed ears closely resembling a butterfly's wings, but also a thin white blaze between the ears and bisecting the face that suggests the insect's body. The Breed Standard also allows for drop ears, and in some modern specimens the blaze is badly proportioned or absent altogether. In such instances fanciers feel that 'Papillon' is a misnomer. Indeed in some countries the two types are divided, those with drop ears being known as Phalènes.

Possibly descended from the dwarf Spaniels that have existed since the Middle Ages, dogs closely resembling the modern Papillon have been depicted in paintings through the centuries, and were especially popular in France in the early part of the eighteenth century. The breed has appeared in paintings by such famous artists as Watteau, Fragonard, Rubens and Van Dyck. Introduced to Britain at the beginning of this century, this Toy has changed little and is an elegant dog with a gay, friendly nature.

Apart from the distinctive ears and blaze, the head is small with a slightly rounded skull, the muzzle fine and pointed. The round, dark eyes are placed rather low, and the nose is dark, preferably black. The compact body with its straight back, well-developed shoulders and deep chest must not be too cobby, and the rather short, fine legs have long, elegant feet. The tail, a special feature, is long and heavily feathered

*Top right: the Italian Greyhound is a miniature version of the normal-sized Greyhound, and originated more than 2,000 years ago*

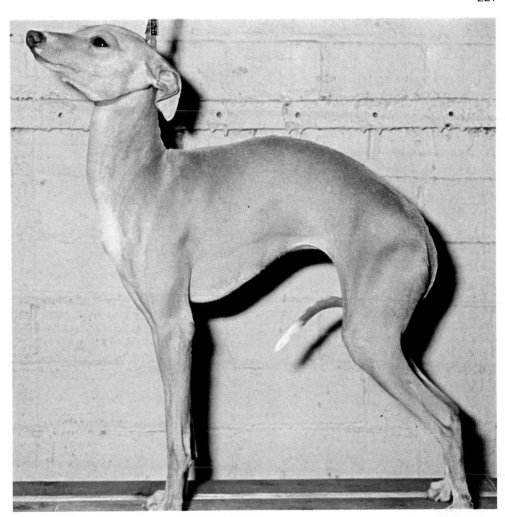

# Breed Standard: the Pomeranian

**GENERAL APPEARANCE**
The Pomeranian in build and appearance should be a compact, short-coupled dog, with great intelligence in its expression.

**HEAD AND SKULL**
The head and nose should be foxy in outline, or wedge-shaped. The skull being slightly flat, large in proportion to the muzzle, which should finish rather fine and be free from lippiness. The hair on the head and face should be smooth and shortcoated.

**EYES**
Should be medium in size, slightly oval in shape, not full, nor set too wide apart, bright and dark in colour, and showing great intelligence.

**EARS**
Should be small, not set too far apart, nor too low down, but carried perfectly erect like those of a fox.

**MOUTH**
Teeth should be level, and should on no account be undershot, or overshot.

**NECK**
Should be rather short and well set in.

**FOREQUARTERS**
The shoulders should be clean and well laid back. The legs must be well feathered and perfectly straight, of medium length and not such as would be termed 'leggy' or 'low on leg', but in length and strength in due proportion to a well-balanced frame.

**BODY**
The back must be short and the body compact, being well ribbed up and the barrel well rounded. The chest must be fairly deep and not too wide but in proportion to the size of the dog.

**HINDQUARTERS**
The legs and thighs must be well feathered down to the hocks and neither cow-hocked nor wide behind.

**FEET**
The feet should be small and compact in shape.

**TAIL**
The tail is one of the breed's characteristics, and should be turned over the back and carried flat and straight. It is covered with long harsh, spreading hair.

**COAT**
There should be an undercoat and an overcoat, the former being soft and fluffy, the latter long, perfectly straight and harsh in texture. The coat is very abundant round the neck and fore-part of the shoulders and chest, where it shall form a frill of profuse off-standing straight hair, extending over the shoulders. The hindquarters should be clad with long hair or feathering.

**COLOUR**
All whole colours are admissible, but they should be free from black or white shadings.

**WEIGHT AND SIZE**
Ideal show size is from 4–5 lb.

*The Miniature Pinscher is very popular both in Britain and America. It makes an ideal pet, especially for the dog lover with restricted free time.*

and is carried squirrel-like over the back. The Papillon stands between 8 and 11 in high and weighs between 3½ and 7 lb. Its long silky coat, according to the Breed Standard, may be white with patches of any colour except liver. The coat should be abundant, but without an undercoat. It should be long, fine and silky, falling flat on back and sides. The hair is short and close on the skull.

The Papillon is a hardy dog and can withstand extremes of hot and cold. It is active and will hunt rats and rabbits with energy. It can be trained to retrieve and follow a scent. It is an intelligent dog and

many owners have given their dog obedience training, and found that the Papillon is able to perform these tests as well as the breeds more usually associated with obedience training.

The Affenpinscher has had the greatest share in the creation of the Griffon Bruxellois, or Brussels Griffon as it is known in the USA. The Affenpinscher, or Monkey Terrier, is a German toy dog which has a quaint little face with a small beard and moustache, bushy eyebrows large dark eyes, red or grey wiry coat and docked tail.

The above portrait instantly brings to mind the Griffon who shares much of his ancestor's appearance and temperament It is claimed that the Yorkshire Terrier, the Irish Terrier and the Pug, not to mention the King Charles Spaniel, also had a hand in the development of this fascinating breed.

The cab drivers of Brussels used the plucky little dogs to guard their vehicles and keep down the vermin in the stables. Once royalty took a fancy to the breed, it became fashionable and popular. Eventually Toy Griffons were imported into Britain and the USA. In both countries their jaunty appearance, high intelligence and cheerful temperament won instant approval.

Today there are two distinct varieties, the Griffon Bruxellois which is rough-coated, and the smooth-haired variety known as the Petit Brabançon. Both may appear in the same litter. Although they are not delicate when adult, they are difficult to breed and so numbers remain fairly constant. However, in spite of this, they are well established in both Britain and America.

The coat of the Rough is harsh and wiry, while that of the Smooth is soft and close. Both varieties have identical type, with a large round head and semi-erect ears. The eyes are very large and dark with well-defined eyebrows. The black nose is very short, with large open nostrils, high set and sloping back to the skull into a deep stop between nose and skull. The muzzle should be very wide and well turned up. The chin is prominent and slightly undershot, without showing the teeth. The face is furnished with an engaging moustache and small beard. The dog is compact in build, with a short back and medium, straight legs, and the tail is carried upwards and is docked. The desired weight is between 6 and 9 lb, and colours allowed under the Breed Standard are red, black or black-and-tan. In America solid black is not allowed in the smooth variety. USA weights to be 8–10 lb. The breed is tough and long-lived and responds well to training. Although it does not require a great deal of exercise, and can adapt to town life very well, it will greatly appreciate

# Breed Standard: the Miniature Pinscher

## GENERAL APPEARANCE
The Miniature Pinscher is structurally a well balanced, sturdy, compact, elegant, short-coupled, smooth-coated toy dog. The characteristics which identify this breed from other toy dogs are its precise Hackney gait, its fearless animation, complete self-possession.

## HEAD AND SKULL
Rather more elongated than short and round with narrow inconspicuous cheeks, and in correct proportion to the body. The skull should appear flat when viewed from the front. The muzzle must be rather strong and proportionate to the skull. The nose well formed, black only with the exception of livers and blues, which may have a self-coloured nose.

## EYES
Fitting well into the face. Neither too full nor round, neither too little nor slanting. Black or nearly black.

## EARS
Must be set on high, as small as possible, erect or dropped.

## NECK
Strong yet graceful. Slightly arched. Well fitted into the shoulders. Free from throatiness.

## FOREQUARTERS
Forechest well developed and full, moderately broad shoulders clean, sloping with moderate angulation.

## BODY
To be square, back line straight, sloping slightly towards the rear. Belly moderately tucked up.

## HINDQUARTERS
Should be parallel to each other and wide enough apart to fit in with a properly built body. The hindquarters should be well developed and muscular with a good sweep of stifle and their hocks turning neither in or out.

## FEET
Legs straight, medium bone. Feet cat-like.

## TAIL
A continuation of the top-line carried a little high and docked short.

## COAT
Smooth, hard and short. Straight and lustrous. Closely adhering to and uniformly covering the body.

## COLOUR
Black, blue, chocolate with sharply defined tan markings on cheeks, lips, lower jaw, throat, twin spots above eyes and chest, lower half of fore-legs, inside of hindleg and vent region, lower portion of hocks and feet. All the above colours should have black pencilling on toes with no thumb marks. Solid red of various shades.

## HEIGHT
Should range from 10 to 12 inches at the withers.

protruding eyes, and having a longer muzzle. The result is a more clearly-defined head, wedge-shaped as desired in the Dobermann (which probably has the blood of the larger Pinschers).

Elegant and compact, this breed is ideal as a town pet, since it can exercise itself in a large enough garden, although it can take any amount of exercise. It has many sporting characteristics, such as a proud and fearless nature, a lively temperament and high intelligence. Its acute hearing means that it will make an excellent guard or watch dog.

It is now very popular in many countries of the world and well established in America, France and Britain (where it was first introduced in 1938). The Miniature Pinscher is a sturdy, game little dog, clean and easy to maintain in the peak of condition. Its smooth coat makes it an ideal pet for an owner whose time is restricted. A quick brush and wipe over with a chamois leather will keep it in peak condition. Also, the Miniature Pinscher is not a prolific moulter, so the furniture will not be covered in hairs. Despite its diminutive size, it is an excellent house dog. A characteristic of this breed is its unusual hackney gait, which is fascinating to watch. Standing at $10\frac{1}{2}$ to 12 inches at the shoulder, with the smaller size being preferred, the 'Min-Pin', as the breed is often affectionately called, has a docked tail and cropped ears which may be erect or dropped. Conforming closely to sporting and working dog standards for soundness, this breed has an extremely short, hard and smooth coat, the most popular colours being stag-red, solid red and black-and-tan, although other colours are permissible, including chocolate with rust or yellow markings. White markings of more than half an inch in length lead to disqualification under present show rules.

*Above: the Griffon Bruxellois is the rough-coated Griffon, and is of the same type as the smooth-coated, weighing something between six and nine pounds. The Petit Brabançon (right) is the smooth-haired variety of Griffon, which was imported into Britain from Belgium in the last century*

an occasional run in the country. Griffons make delightful, amusing pets.

Although the Miniature Pinscher may look like a miniature Dobermann Pinscher there is probably no direct relationship between the two; it is probable that the Miniature Pinscher was, in fact, bred in Germany from the now very rare Standard Pinscher. It was eventually given pure-bred status by the German Pinscher-Schnauzer Klub in 1895. Today's specimens differ considerably from the early members of the breed, having lost the broad skull and

King Charles
Spaniels

THE physical differences between the King Charles Spaniel and the Cavalier King Charles Spaniel have been inaccurately described over many years, and a confused idea has arisen as to which breed is which. The main variations are in size and head formation. The Cavalier, to use its everyday title, is about a third bigger than the King Charles. The breed Standards ask for weights of between 10 and 18 lb and between 6 and 12 lb respectively. But in both cases the higher figure is nearer to the normal weight of each breed today. The King Charles, or Charlie as it is often known, has a large, domed skull and ears placed comparatively low. Its nose is short, with a deep indentation between the skull and the broad, square muzzle. By comparison, the Cavalier's head is unexaggerated. The skull is flat, the ears set high, and the indentation between skull and muzzle is definite but shallow in relation to the Charlie. The muzzle, though well developed, has about 1½ inches of nose. The Charlie has a heavier body.

The most striking similarities between the two breeds concern colour and markings. They may be found in four variations: Blenheim, which is a ground colour of pearly white splashed with patches of

*Facing page: the King Charles Spaniel; right: the Cavalier King Charles Spaniel*

# Breed Standard: the Cavalier King Charles

**GENERAL APPEARANCE**
An active, graceful and well-balanced dog. Absolutely fearless and sporting in character and very gay and free in action.

**HEAD AND SKULL**
Head almost flat between the ears, without dome. Stop shallow. Length from base of stop to tip about 1½ inches. Nostrils should be well developed and the pigment black. Muzzle well tapered. Lips well covering but not hound-like. Face should be well filled out underneath the eyes. Any tendency to appear 'snipey' is undesirable.

**EYES**
Large, dark and round but not prominent.

**EARS**
Long and set high with plenty of feather.

**MOUTH**
Level; scissor-bite preferred.

**FOREQUARTERS**
Shoulders well laid back; legs moderately boned and straight.

**BODY**
Short-coupled with plenty of spring of rib. Back level. Chest moderate, leaving ample heart room.

**HINDQUARTERS**
Legs with moderate bone; well-turned stifle—no tendency to cow or sickle hocks.

**FEET**
Compact, cushioned and well-feathered.

**TAILS**
The docking of tails is optional. No more than one-third to be removed.

**COAT**
Long, silky and free from curl. A slight wave is permissible. There should be plenty of feather.

**COLOUR**
Black and Tan: raven black with tan markings above the eyes, on cheeks, inside ears, on chest, legs and underside of tail. The tan should be bright. Ruby: whole-coloured rich red. Blenheim: rich chestnut marking well broken up on a pearly white ground. The markings should be evenly divided on the head, leaving room between the ears for the much valued lozenge mark or spot (a unique characteristic of the breed). Tricolour: black and white, well spaced and broken-up, with tan markings over the eyes, on cheeks, inside ears, inside legs and on underside of tail. Black and White: permissible but not desirable.

**WEIGHT**
Twelve to eighteen pounds. A small well-balanced dog well within these weights is desirable.

**FAULTS**
Light eyes. Undershot and crooked mouths and pig jaws. White marks on whole-coloured specimens. Putty noses. Nervousness.

rich chestnut; tricolour, formerly referred to as Prince Charles, again a pearly white background but splashed with black and having tan markings; black and tan, or King Charles proper, which is self-explanatory; and ruby, or red, a rich, overall chestnut colour.

The way in which both breeds have contributed to each other's existence is probably unique in the history of dog breeding. Europe is acknowledged as the first home of Toy Spaniels. They were many and varied in size and colour, but all of clear spaniel type. For confirmation of their existence we rely on the evidence of tapestries and paintings executed for various European courts from the fifteenth century onwards. In many cases it can only be said that the dogs portrayed were Toy Spaniels; they could as well be ancestors of the Papillon as of the Cavalier. An early written reference to Toy Spaniels came in 1570 when Dr Caius, physician to Elizabeth I, describes 'Comforters or Gentle Spaniel' belonging to ladies of the Court. They came by the name 'Comforter' through being kept close to the body or feet of people for the warmth they could impart, notably on carriage journeys. At this time they were mainly red and white Italian Spaniels and black and white Holland Spaniels, the latter probably brought over originally by Anne of Cleves and later by William III. Black ones with curly coats were less common, and it is thought that the black-and-tan markings appeared later, after a cross with the webbed-footed Spaniel of that colour, the Pyrame.

By the time of Charles I and II – it was Charles II who gave his name to the breed – the dogs we now know as Cavaliers were well established in England. The Cavalier's prominence in the second half of the seventeenth century was due almost entirely to the high regard in which they were held by the King.

James II continued his brother's patronage of the breed. Thereafter they fell from royal favour. All through the eighteenth century Cavaliers were maintained on country estates where their sporting proclivities were used. One such type of sporting Spaniel, rather bigger than most of the period, was developed by the first Duke of Marlborough. They were always of the colour now referred to as Blenheim, so called because the Duke was supposed to have had one of these Spaniels with him at the Battle of Blenheim. Numbers dwindled until, in the middle of the nineteenth century, Cavaliers virtually became extinct in their previous form. They did, however, then contribute to the breed that took their place – and name – the present-day King Charles Spaniel or Charlie.

To bring about the transformation already described, several breeds may have been used to reduce size and change head shape. The Pug was probably one, and the Japanese Chin another. Charlies became immensely popular during the last half of the nineteenth century until the First World War as 'lap dogs' rather than sporting spaniels. Then the advent of the Pekingese, did much to reduce enthusiasm for the breed. But they were kept alive and in fair numbers for showing.

In 1926 an event occurred that resulted in the rebirth of Cavaliers from the breed that had supplanted them. Mr Roswell Eldridge, an American visiting England, was shocked to find no trace of the old Toy Spaniel. Determined that the breed should be resuscitated, he offered for a five-year period a prize of £25 for the best dog and bitch Blenheim Spaniels at Cruft's. Only a handful of animals competed for his early prizes and Mr Eldridge died before the fruits of his initiative were realized. But from that modest beginning, Cavalier breeders fashioned a new breed similar to those Spaniels of Charles II. Pioneers based their description (Standard) of the breed on seventeenth-century paintings. The temperament of the breed is sporting, gentle, and affectionate, with a great love of people.

The Charlie, likewise, is gentle and affectionate. But it is more a one-man or one-family dog, devoted to those it loves, if perhaps more discriminating in giving affection. Though the Charlie can be sporting, that is not its purpose in life; nor is it so well suited to such a routine.

For anyone contemplating breeding either breed but who has no previous experience, the Cavalier is the better choice. They whelp easily and care for their puppies in exemplary fashion. As with any breed that has a big head in relation to its size, the Charlie may have more difficulty in whelping than less exaggerated breeds. For this reason it is not ideal for the novice breeder who may be discouraged by problems that seem less daunting as more experience is gained.

Should you want one or the other breed as a companion, your choice must depend on the way of life such a dog will be expected to follow. Their small size ensures that both fit equally well into a small household. Both are clean and neither have such an abundance of coat as to be a nuisance. Those who want a pet which is decorative but which needs exercise and has the energy to accompany the family on hikes, the Cavalier cannot be bettered. The picturesque Charlie, on the other hand, can be happy and well pottering about the garden or park.

*Below: the King Charles Spaniel makes a devoted family pet*

# Breed Standard: the Pekingese

**GENERAL APPEARANCE**
Should be a small, well-balanced, thickset dog of great dignity and quality. He should carry himself fearlessly in the ring with an alert, intelligent expression.

**HEAD AND SKULL**
Head massive, skull broad, wide and flat between the ears, not domed; wide between eyes. Nose very short and broad, nostrils large, open, and black; muzzle wide, well wrinkled, with firm underjaw. Profile should look quite flat with nose well up between the eyes. Deep stop.

**EYES**
Large, clear, dark and lustrous. Prominent but not bolting.

**EARS**
Heart-shaped, set level with the skull and carried close to the head. Long profuse feathering on ears Leather not to come below the muzzle.

**MOUTH**
Level lips, must not show teeth or tongue.

**FOREQUARTERS**
Short, thick, heavily-boned forelegs; bones of forelegs bowed but firm at shoulder. Absolute soundness essential.

**BODY**
Short but with broad chest and good spring of rib, falling away lighter behind; lion-like with distinct waist, level back; well slung between the legs, not on top of them.

**HINDQUARTERS**
Hind legs lighter but firm and well shaped. Close behind but not cow-hocked. Absolute soundness essential.

**FEET**
Large and flat, not round. The dog should stand well up on feet, not on pasterns. Front feet turned slightly out. Absolute soundness essential.

**TAIL**
Set high, carried tightly, slightly curved over back to either side. Long feathering.

**COAT**
Long and straight with profuse mane extending beyond the shoulders forming a cape or frill round the neck; top coat rather coarse, with thick undercoat. Profuse feathering on ears, legs, thighs, tail and toes.

**COLOUR**
All colours and markings are permissible and equally good, except liver or albino. Parti-colours should be evenly broken.

**WEIGHT AND SIZE**
As a guide the ideal weight to be 7 to 11 lbs for dogs, 8 to 12 lbs for bitches. The dog should look small but be surprisingly heavy when picked up; heavy bone and a sturdy well-built body are essentials.

# The Pekingese

TO purchase a Pekingese is to become associated with ancient and romantic history. The legend regarding the origin of the breed has been told so often that the bowdlerized version becomes mundane rather than romantic. Over two thousand years ago in China there was a deity in the form of a dog named Fo, a guardian and protector whose image has been recovered by archaeologists from old tombs. Reproductions of these figures have been given the name of Kylin; they bear a great resemblance to the modern Pekingese but are no more than cousins.

History records that the Manchu dynasty was the last of a long line of Emperors, and that it possessed a type of dog very similar to our modern Pekingese. The Manchu Emperors thought so much of these dogs that they were enthroned as the Palace Lion Dog. The Emperor alone retained all rights to breed them. It is evident that certain court dignitaries and mandarins were allowed to own specimens, but heavy penalties were paid by any commoner who tried to steal a dog.

Although a variety of breeds are embodied in its make-up, the Chinese undoubtedly used the Pug and the small dog known today as the Japanese Chin in the improvement of the Imperial Pekingese. How closely our modern show Pekingese dog resembles and is related to the original dogs of the breed can best be shown by a comparison between a Standard drawn up in China and the official British Kennel Club Standard in use today. The last ruler of the Chinese empire, Dowager Empress Tzu Hai, wrote, 'Let the Lion Dog be small; let it wear the swelling cape of dignity around its neck; let it display the billowing standard of pomp above its back. Let its face be black; let its forefront be shaggy; let its forehead be straight and low, like unto the brow of an Imperial harmony boxer. Let its eyes be large and luminous; let its ears be set like the sails of a war-junk; let its nose be like that of the monkey-god of the Hindus.

'Let its forelegs be bent, so that it shall not desire to wander far, or leave the Imperial precincts. Let its feet be tufted

*The Pekingese is an ancient Chinese dog with a romantic history that goes back over 2,000 years to the time of the Manchu dynasty. It was not until after the China War of 1860 that the breed was seen in European countries*

with plentiful hair that its footfall may be soundless; and for its standard of pomp let it rival the whisk of the Tibetan Yak, which is flourished to protect the Imperial litter from the attacks of flying insects.

'Let it be lively that it may afford entertainment by its gambols; let it be timid that it may not involve itself in danger; let it be domestic in its habits that it may live in amity with the other beasts, fishes or birds that find protection in the Imperial Palace. And for its colour let it be that of the Lion —a golden sable, or the colour of a red bear, or a black or white bear, or striped like a Dragon, so that there may be dogs appropriate to every costume in the Imperial wardrobe.

'Let it comport itself with dignity; let it learn to bite the foreign devils instantly. Let it be dainty in its food that it shall be known for an Imperial dog by its fastidiousness.'

The smaller types were carried in the sleeves of the mandarins, and thus in Britain the term 'sleeve dog' came into use. Quite recently a club has been formed and registered with the British Kennel Club as the Pekingese Sleeve Dog Club.

A most complicated and exotic diet for the Pekingese was prepared, even to the extent of the inclusion of sharks' fins and curlews' livers and the breast of quails. If the dog was found to be suffering from any illness, a recommended remedy was to rub

its body with the clarified fat of the leg of a sacred leopard.

It was during the China War of 1860 that British and French troops invaded the Summer Palace in Peking. Five Pekingese —golden sables with black masks and points—were among the loot, and Admiral Lord John Hay secured a dark sable dog, referred to in the British Kennel Club Standard as a red brindle. He also took a black and white bitch, and General Dunne's part of the loot was a fawn and white part-coloured bitch. General Dunne's bitch, Looty, was given to Queen Victoria, and Landseer painted the dog. Thus was the royal association with the breed continued.

The Boxer Rebellion in China, which led to the occupation of the Forbidden City, accelerated the movement of the Pekingese in the western world, and in 1898 the British Kennel Club recognized the breed.

Americans soon recognized the merits of the breed and the Pekingese Club of America became a member of the AKC in 1909. The Dowager Empress presented several specimens to visitors and these, with the importation of English Pekes, built up dogs of a high standard.

The Pekingese is a very adaptable dog, equally suited for life in town or country. It is small enough to be kept in the house without causing any inconvenience, but it is very important to remember not to coddle it or treat it as a lap dog.

*Essentially a spaniel-type of dog, the Pekingese has bulldog characteristics in its face and jaw. Today's dogs closely resemble the original Chinese dogs, in size, length of coat and more especially in temperament*

The beautiful long coat of the Pekingese is no more difficult to look after than any other longhaired breed. Use a bristle brush and a wide-toothed metal comb. The comb should be used only on the featherings— trousers, ear fringes, tails—as it will pull out the crinkly undercoat if used on the body. The brush should be used on the body of the dog. If you are trying to achieve show condition, never handle the dog by hand more than is absolutely necessary, as this will take the bloom off the coat and give it a finger-marked appearance. Also, never, under any circumstances, stroke the coat backwards over the head as this action accentuates every bad head-point the Pekingese can possess.

It is through the regal and independent attitude of the Pekingese to its owner and towards life in general that the breed displays its Imperial ancestry, an independence which has led one lover of the breed to say 'Nine out of ten Pekingese are disobedient, and the tenth is really deaf.' Nevertheless, once a Peke has been introduced to your hearth and home you will never wish for another breed.

# The Pug:
# a dog with Chinese ancestors

PUG dogs are delightfully friendly animals; they love everyone and are gentle with children. Pugs are toy dogs, and, although they are sturdy and have a thick, fine velvety coat, they cannot live 'rough'. They need drying when they come indoors wet, some warmth in cold weather, and must not be given strenuous exercise in the heat of a summer's day as this will make them very uncomfortable.

Most Pugs are quite easy to feed. They should not be allowed to get obese, but their frame should be well covered. They are very good company and keeping this breed of dog can provide a great deal of interest. They are clean, learn quickly, and are intensely aware of things around them–birds, butterflies and even aeroplanes. They will watch television and get very excited at certain programmes.

They quickly learn each other's names. if one Pug has a ball and the owner calls out 'Rosy's got it', the other Pugs will look for her and try to take the ball away. They enjoy country walks and will career over the fields, and on sandy beaches they will search for small crabs once they have

*Pugs originated in the Far East and probably came to Europe via Portugal*

# Breed Standard: the Pug

**GENERAL APPEARANCE**
A decidedly square and cobby dog. The pug should be 'multum in parvo' (a large amount in a small space), but this condensation should be shown by compactness of form, well-knit proportions, and hardness of developed muscle.

**HEAD AND SKULL**
Head large, massive, round; not apple-headed, with no indentation of the skull. Muzzle short, blunt, square but not upfaced. Wrinkles large and very deep.

**EYES**
Dark in colour, very large, bold and prominent, globular in shape, soft and solicitous in expression, very lustrous, and when excited, full of fire.

**EARS**
Thin, small, soft, like black velvet. There are two kinds: the 'rose' and the 'button'. Preference should be given to the latter. (Button ears are close, compact ears which fold over in front.)

**FOREQUARTERS**
Legs very strong, straight, of moderate length, and well under the body.

**BODY**
Short and cobby, wide in chest and well ribbed.

**HINDQUARTERS**
Legs very strong, straight, of moderate length, and well under.

**FEET**
Neither so long as the foot of the hare, nor so round as that of the cat; well split-up toes; the nails should be black.

**TAIL**
(Twist). Curled as tightly as possible over the hip. The double curl is perfection.

**COAT**
Fine, smooth, soft, short and glossy, neither hard nor woolly.

**COLOUR**
Silver, apricot fawn or black. Each should be clearly decided, to make the contrast complete between the colour, the trace and the mask. Markings clearly defined. The muzzle or mask, ears, moles on cheeks, thumbmark or diamond on forehead. The back-trace should be as black as possible. Mask: the mask should be black, the more intense and well defined, the better. Trace: a black line extending from the occiput to the twist.

**WEIGHT AND SIZE**
Desirable weight from 14 to 18 lbs (for a dog or a bitch).

**FAULTS**
Lean, leggy. Short legs and long body.

**NOTE**
Male animals should have two apparently normal testicles fully descended into the scrotum.

been shown where to find them. They are usually very good travellers and readily enter a car, but they should be introduced to car travel while quite young.

They make good town dwellers but, of course, are happier when they have a garden, however small, in which to play. They have become more expensive to buy, but are such a joy to own that one cannot but feel it is money well spent. Their life span is approximately 12 years.

Pugs originated in the Far East and were brought to Europe probably as early as the sixteenth century, being introduced into Portugal by traders. There is a delightful portrait of a Portuguese princess with a very small Pug puppy beside her, wearing a ribbon round its neck. Her dress is of the Tudor period. Pugs have been known in England since the time of William and Mary, who brought their pets with them when they came to the throne.

Some very interesting people have owned and loved Pugs, among them the Empress Josephine, whose Pug is supposed to have bitten Napoleon on the leg when he entered her room. The artist Hogarth was also a Pug owner; his famous dog Trump appears in several pictures painted by him, notably in his self-portrait where Trump is sitting beside his master, and in the painting of Lord George Graham in his cabin, with Trump upright on a chair wearing my lord's wig! Trump was modelled in terracotta by the great Rowbiliac, and from this model the Chelsea potters made reproductions. The original terracotta model has been lost, but the Victoria and Albert Museum has a very fine early copy of it in plain white, lying on a cushion. Trump, although a Pug without any doubt, would not win in shows today.

While on the subject of pictures of Pugs, one must mention the lovely Goya painting now in the National Gallery in Washington. In this fascinating picture, a beautifully dressed lady is walking out with her parasol, preceded by her small fawn Pug with a ribbon round its neck.

Pugs were very popular with high society and royalty in the early nineteenth and late eighteenth centuries. This accounts for the many models made by Kaendler for the Meissen factory and so sought after today by all who love and collect anything to do with Pugs. Meissen models are very expensive, and matching pairs fetch enormous prices.

When you decide to buy a Pug, do not go to a pet shop or a dealer. Find a good breeder, preferably in your own area, and go to see his or her stock and talk things over before arriving at a decision.

*Friendliness is one of the major characteristics of the Pug*

A good puppy suitable for show will not be cheap to buy, but very often a puppy well bred but not up to exhibition standard can be purchased for a very reasonable price.

On purchasing your first Pug be sure to ask for a diet sheet from the breeder. Continuing with the same feeding plan is most important, especially for puppies. Puppies up to three months old should be rather fat and very active, and at this age their day needs to be regulated. The owner should play with the puppy for about 20 minutes before its first meal. It is best to play on an absolutely flat surface; getting on and off chairs, or up and down steps before the pup's bones have hardened can cause a bowed foreleg, or even a greenstick fracture (cracked bone). This is not intended to frighten the new owner, but just to warn him and ensure that he is careful when supervising the play of his Pugs.

Handling a young puppy also needs care: never lift it up by the forelegs or by a handful of loose skin. Always use both hands and hold lightly with one on the back of the dog's neck, and the other under the body. Do not ever frighten your puppy: do things gently and very deliberately. Do not forget that puppies are capable of doing sudden things and can move quickly out of your arms and so fall. This is very dangerous. Train your puppy to

come when you call and to know its name. Always praise your pet when it is good; just grumble when it is naughty. You can hit the ground with a roll of newspaper as a reprimand. This is usually quite sufficient.

House training needs patience and commonsense: always put a puppy where you want it to relieve itself as soon as it wakes from sleep. Always take it outside after meals, and any time you see it fidgeting and looking uneasy. Accompany it and say 'Good boy' when it has finished. Keep a thick layer of newspaper available which the pup can use to relieve itself if it wakes in the night, or if the weather is wet. It is quite easy to keep things clean this way. The paper can be dispensed with once the house training is successful.

Adult Pugs seem to do best on two meals a day; to be really fit they should be well covered but not fat, and the muscles should be hard. Begin the day by giving your Pug a drink of sweetened milk and a dry biscuit. At midday it should have about 3 oz of cooked meat, minced or cut fine. In the evening a little less meat and a small handful of puppy biscuit meal, prepared by soaking in stock at least one hour before using, should be given. This should not be sloppy, but soaked so that all the stock is absorbed. Puppies up to five months old still need a milky breakfast; thereafter two meat meals, like

*In appearance the Pug is a square, cobby dog with a compact, well-knit form*

the older Pugs, are sufficient. A drink of milk at tea time is also good for them.

Anyone thinking about setting up as a Pug breeder should give the matter very careful consideration. It is not only a question of making a profit or a loss; one has to weigh up the calls on one's time, for being a breeder limits personal freedom to an alarming extent. If you are not to be deterred by the certainty of hard work with little return to show, then the first point to consider is whether the stock you own is suitable as a foundation for the kennel.

If you own a champion bitch she may still be unsuitable on the grounds of age. She should not have her first litter after she is three years of age, and it is safest to plan her motherhood during her second or third 'season'. Even if she meets these requirements on the basis of age, she must also have the temperament to be the foundation of your kennel. The brood bitch needs to have a very well-made body, with a great spring of rib and firm, well-boned legs. She must conform almost to perfection to the Breed Standard. And above all, her temperament must be right for if she is over-excitable her puppies will not thrive, which would be a most severe setback to the success of the venture.

# The popular Yorkshire Terrier

THE Yorkshire Terrier may be the smallest British terrier as it is the smallest of the British toy breeds but, agile as a grasshopper, eyes sparkling with fun and intelligence, a 'Yorkie' is all terrier and ready to tackle anything on or under the ground. There is nothing it likes better than to scamper after a ball, a low-lying bird, or even a rabbit, should one be foolhardy enough to cross its path. The Yorkie is a true extrovert by nature and there is no breed that is more affectionate or loyal to its owner. Its sturdy little body loves action and it can jump astonishing heights for its size.

There are many other points to recommend this breed. The Yorkie is not a kennel dog and therefore makes an ideal pet for anyone living in a small house or

*The Yorkshire Terrier grows a long coat which can quickly become unkempt*

flat in a town; the amount of exercise it needs is minimal but it should be taken out at least once a day. The Yorkie does not have food fads so there is no need to feed it on fancy foods. Its needs are the same as the bigger breeds – good wholesome food, a well-balanced diet, plus the occasional big bone with which to keep its teeth clean and healthy.

Despite the instant appeal of this breed no one should think of acquiring a Yorkshire Terrier unless they are prepared to look after the beautiful long coat which is the principal show point of the breed. The Yorkie's coat is at once the pride and burden of the dog's owner, although it does not moult excessively. The long hair quickly develops tangles and knots which will cause the dog great discomfort if not removed at once. If knots are allowed to develop the dog will scratch and this can result in skin infections. The only ailments

to which this breed is particularly prone are dandruff and conjunctivitis, both the result of the owner's neglect of the coat. Regular brushing and bathing are therefore essential.

If the dog is to be shown, the coat must be kept long and will require constant attention involving oils, shampoos and curling papers. But even if the dog is kept merely as a family pet, the coat should be groomed at least once a day. The coat can be cut to just below the elbow and half-way up the back legs. Parted down the middle of the dog's back, it should hang evenly on either side. The top-knot can be cut short enough so that it will part down the middle and not get in the dog's eyes. A soft bristle brush, dipped in lanolin or a similar oil, brushed firmly through the coat will remove tangles and leave the coat with a glossy sheen. Most owners finish the grooming

using a wide-toothed metal comb. The dog needs to be bathed and shampooed about once a month. Use baby shampoo or a special dog shampoo obtainable from your local pet shop.

Yorkies make excellent show dogs despite their high-spirited natures. They are quick and willing to learn if the correct training is commenced while they are still young. They will respond best to short regular lessons.

If you wish to acquire an adult Yorkie the main features to be considered, besides the length, texture and colour of the coat, are a strong compact body, firm loins and a general healthy appearance.

Yorkie puppies tend to be completely black when they are first born. Few other breeds go through so many changes from puppyhood to adulthood. They should be weaned by six weeks and are very easy to feed once they have left their mother.

The history and origin of this delightful breed is somewhat of a mystery. It is relatively new, not being officially recognized by the Kennel Club until 1886. We do know that it evolved in the homes of the working classes of Yorkshire and Lancashire during the Industrial Revolution but exactly which breeds produced it, and in what order, is unknown. It was first noted at a dog show in Leeds jn 1861 where it was entered as a Scottish Terrier. It came to America in 1880.

It is known that Broken-haired Terriers were already established by Yorkshire breeders in the late eighteenth century. Probably, Scottish wool workers brought the Clydesdale, once a very popular breed, with them when they moved to the industrial wool towns of Yorkshire, and by crossing the Broken-haired Terrier with the Clydesdale produced a new type of terrier.

The first Yorkies were, of course, much larger than today's specimens. The size was reduced gradually by selective breeding and the tiny Yorkie, from its humble origins, became one of the breeds favoured by all classes of society. From deductions and speculations it would appear that the coat was made silkier and softer by crossing it with the Maltese, made darker by the Black and Tan English Terrier and made longer by the Skye Terrier. The Dandie Dinmont is also thought to be an ancestor of our present-day Yorkie by some authorities on the breed.

*The coat of a show dog requires even more grooming than a family pet*

Today, for those who are willing to care for its coat and bring it to perfection, the Yorkie is an excellent and rewarding showdog. It is equally popular as a pet and when cut short its coat needs no more than the regular grooming given to other long-haired breeds.

One thing is sure – a Yorkie in the house cannot fail to brighten the domestic scene.

# Breed Standard: the Yorkshire Terrier

**GENERAL APPEARANCE**
Should be that of a long-coated toy terrier, the coat hanging quite straight and evenly down each side, a parting extending from the nose to the end of the tail. The animal's carriage being very upright and conveying an 'important' air. The general outline should convey the impression of a vigorous and well-proportioned body.

**HEAD AND SKULL**
Head should be rather small and flat, with perfect black nose. The fall on the head to be long, of a rich golden tan, deeper in colour at the sides of the head about the ear roots, and on the muzzle where it should be very long. The tan on the head must not extend on to the neck, nor must there be any dark hair intermingled.

**EYES**
Medium, dark and sparkling, having a sharp intelligent expression and placed so as to look directly forward. They should not be prominent and the edge of the eyelids should be of a dark colour.

**EARS**
Small V-shaped, and carried erect or semi-erect covered with short hair of a deep rich tan.

**FOREQUARTERS**
Legs quite straight, well covered with hair of a rich golden tan a few shades lighter at the ends than at the roots, not extending higher on the forelegs than the elbow.

**BODY**
Very compact with good loin. Level on the top of the back.

**HINDQUARTERS**
Legs quite straight, well covered with hair of rich golden tan, few shades lighter at the ends than at the roots, not extending higher on the hind legs than the stifle.

**FEET**
As round as possible; the toe-nails black.

**TAIL**
Cut to medium length; with plenty of hair, darker blue in colour than the rest of the body, especially at the end of the tail, and carried a little higher than the level of the back.

**COAT**
The hair on the body moderately long and perfectly straight (not wavy), glossy like silk, and of a fine silky texture.

**COLOUR**
A dark steel blue, extending from the back of skull to the root of tail, and on no account mingled with fawn, bronze or dark hairs. The hair on the chest a rich bright tan. All tan hair should be darker at the roots than in the middle, shading to a still lighter tan at the tips.

**WEIGHT**
Weight up to 7lb.

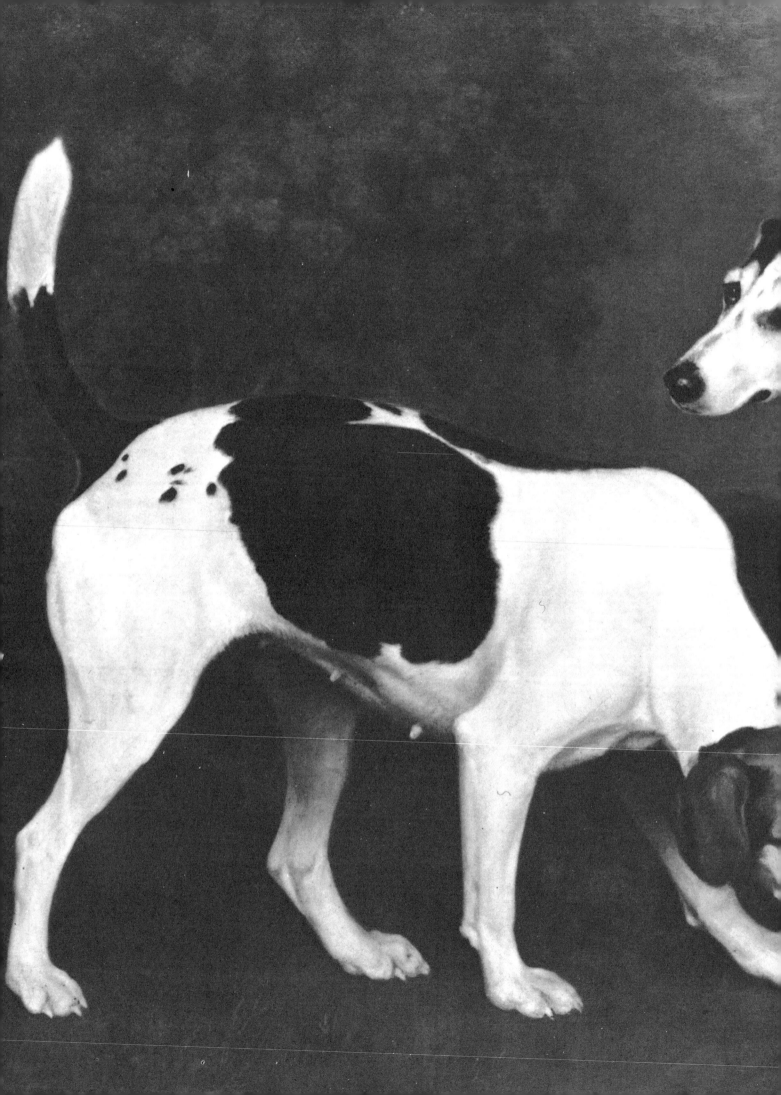